The Path to Lidice

Published by the Independent Publishing Network

Copyright © 2022 Alan Gerrard

The moral right of the author has been asserted.

All rights reserved. No part of this book may be reproduced in any form or by any electronic or mechanical means, including information storage and retrieval systems, without permission in writing from the publisher, except by reviewers, who may quote brief passages in a review.

ISBN 978-1-80068-634-2

Printed in the United Kingdom

A CIP catalogue record for this book is available from the British Library

Contact the author at alangerrard@btconnect.com
Or for updates on the project follow us @LidiceLives

For John, Sheila, May, Connie and Gladys, and absent friends xx

THE PATH TO LIDICE – CONTENTS

FOREWORD 1
INTRODUCTION 3
CZECHOSLOVAKIA 7
LIDICE 29
LIDICE SHALL LIVE 39
THE BIRTH OF THE MOVEMENT 57
LAUNCHING THE MOVEMENT 71
A NATIONAL CAMPAIGN 94
THE WRITERS' WAR BOARD 138
LIDICE – THE NAME BECOMES A SYMBOL 152
INTRODUCING THE COMMITTEE 158
LIDICE IN ART AND CULTURE 160
THE PLAYWRIGHTS' DINNER 169
LIDICE: A UNIVERSAL MEANING 170
ACROSS THE AMERICAS 175
PLANS FOR A NEW LIDICE 183
A NEW LIDICE 185
THE WINDS OF CHANGE 220
THE ROSE GARDEN 239
COLD WAR TIMES 260
DR BARNETT STROSS 266
TRIBUTES TO SIR BARNETT STROSS 290
CONCLUSION & OBSERVATIONS 293
APPENDICES 299
A SELECTION OF PROJECTS 340
TIMELINE 355
BIBLIOGRAPHY & SOURCES 361

A MESSAGE FROM LIDICE

This is a statement from the *Lidice Memory* association, founded on the 29th of July 2020:

The horrible act of the German Nazis committed in the village of Lidice in June 1942 can be evaluated as a crime against humanity. The tragic obliteration of Lidice on the 10th of June 1942 came as a shock to the whole world. It is for this reason that Lidice Memory takes care of Lidice's heritage and from the long-term perspective especially, commemorates and spreads the historical legacy of Lidice.

Only in this way can we preserve the name of Lidice as an international symbol of defiance and solidarity in the fight for freedom and democracy. To our goals belongs also the focus on revering the truth of the interpretation of the history of Lidice.

We welcome as members of our association all people who revere the commemoration of the Lidice victims. The members of Lidice Memory can be not only Lidice survivors and their offspring but also other Czech people and people from abroad.

We are also very proud of the long-term friendship and cooperation which exists between today's Lidice and Stoke-on-Trent in the UK.

Hana Pokorná
Former Mayor of Lidice
Chair Lidice Memory

Hana, Marie Šupíková and Pavel Horešovský hold an online meeting as part of the Lidice Memory organisation with international friends.

FOREWORD

I am not a native of North Staffordshire, although I love oatcakes: I am not a "Stokie," although, for various reasons, I've spent a lot of time cycling around the city. On those counts, I feel extraordinarily honoured to be asked by Alan to write this foreword to a new book about a campaign that began in North Staffordshire and spread far and wide.

I first met Alan after stopping for a breather in the open space next to the Victoria Hall, Hanley. Relatively new to the city, I took a look at a rather idiosyncratic-looking monument. It commemorated the links between Stoke-on-Trent and Czechia, formed initially through the "Lidice Shall Live" campaign.

At home, I took to the web to find out more and quickly discovered the story of a campaign that answered the actions of racist dictatorship with the values of humanity and democracy.

The names of Alan and Cheryl Gerrard kept cropping up. I contacted them and discovered the perfect example to support the old notion that if you want a job doing, ask a busy person. They told me that they wanted to rejuvenate knowledge of the campaign, using it to inspire the people of a city that had faced many hard knocks. There would be tangible benefits, too. I offered to help raise awareness by cycling to Lidice – along with ceramic artist, Mark Dally – carrying works of art by Harry Davies and Mark. It was a great trip, although the experience of visiting the memorial at Lidice is a far from joyful one – until one learns more.

The long list of atrocities to be found in the pages of the Nuremberg Trials includes pages of villages destroyed, often along with all or some of the inhabitants. Across Europe can be found the ruins of homes and memorials to those who were so brutally murdered. The Czech village of Lidice is amongst the best known. Its story is an integral part of the Czech national story, but its prominence can also be attributed to the fact that the Nazis enthusiastically hailed the murder of the men and most of the children, the transportation of all the women to Ravensbrück Concentration Camp, and the removal of their village from the face of the earth, as a great triumph to be broadcast to the world as a warning. As Adolf Hitler crowed, "Lidice Shall Die Forever!" After the war, when the hand of the Soviet Union fell heavily on what was then Czechoslovakia, Lidice was chosen as the focus for condemnation of Nazi brutality and to celebrate the brave Red Army that had liberated the Czech people. For all these reasons, the story of Lidice is amongst the best known of Second World War atrocities.

By contrast the tale of the campaign that bellowed across Europe, "Lidice Shall Live" is less well-known, even amongst the people of North Staffordshire and the City of Stoke-on-Trent - where it began. Surely, people should be shouting it from the rooftops. A campaign inspired by a local GP and Cllr, driven by the North Staffordshire Miners' Federation, without celebrity glitz, at a time of real hardship when introverted self-preservation could easily have been order of the day: how could that not be inspirational to any generation – people power, common decency, in the teeth of the tempest of war that blasted Britain's shores?

One reason must be that the Lidice Shall Live campaign is mentioned almost as an aside in current books. Alan's work goes a long way to setting that right. Sifting through disparate and complex sources, running into some dead-ends where the sources cannot be found, takes many hours. We should be grateful that we now have a volume that fills the gap in the record.

As well as focussing on the start of the campaign and the reasons why North Staffordshire provided such fertile cultural soil for it to flourish, Alan looks at the campaign as it spread to other cities, towns, villages – Coventry, Derby, Nottingham, Birmingham, Leeds, for example. International counterparts are there, too. Equally, the context of changing times is prominent: wartime solidarity turned sour as the USSR, the UK, and the USA, fell-out after defeating the common enemy. Individuals – supposedly ordinary people – are saved from obscurity. Then there is the modern context, as the Lidice Lives group attempts to establish the Lidice Shall Live campaign in a prominent position in North Staffordshire's common heritage.

Lidice was born again, in part because of the efforts of the people of North Staffordshire and a campaign that spread far and wide. Whilst it is true to say that the original atrocity grabs attention, it seems to me that we can learn from the campaign, too. Action by people in adversity, solidarity, values, vision. Whatever, it should certainly make those Potters even louder and prouder.

Stephen Dyster, October 2021

INTRODUCTION

My personal journey of friendship with Lidice began in the summer of 2010 when reading a book written by Rupert Butler in 1992 called *"An Illustrated History of The Gestapo."* Flicking through, I stumbled across the following passage:

> *"The intention of Hitler to blast the name of Lidice from the face of the earth was a conscious failure. News of the crime shocked the world, particularly in Britain, from where the assassins of Reinhard Heydrich had originally set out. The mining village of Stoke-on-Trent in the English Midlands began the British Lidice Shall Live committee and implemented plans to rebuild the village as a model mining community."*

Always keen on history, I had been aware of the Lidice tragedy from a youthful age. But this was new. Internet searches and other researching soon brought up details of the heinous crime; footage of the Lidice Shall Live campaign launch in Hanley, Stoke-on-Trent; and the activities which followed. It is undeniably true to say that it saddened and frustrated me to think of the countless children schooled in Stoke-on-Trent, including me, who were never taught the city's links to the village—as it was obvious the positive impact it could have had. Thinking why this may have been, I could only conclude that while Dr Barnett Stross and others involved in the campaign lived, the personal connections kept the links between Stoke-on-Trent and Lidice alive, despite the fall of the *Iron Curtain*. However, apart from a few exceptions, those links seemed to die, along with the doctor in 1967.

In May 2010, as a couple, my wife and I contacted the Lidice Mayoral office and Lidice Memorial. I wrote about the information discovered, the research concerning Barnett Stross, how we felt it was important to rekindle links. We asked how they felt about it! It was a wonderful moment when we received positive replies both from the Mayor of Lidice, Veronika Kellerová and the then Director of the *International Children's Exhibition of Fine Art* at the Lidice Memorial, Ivona Kasalická. Months later, in the autumn, we were planning a visit to Lidice to open a small exhibition at the Lidice Memorial around Armistice time, simply titled *Sir Barnett Stross*.

And so, the light was re-ignited.

Cheryl and I were invited to Lidice for a few days along with Stoke-on-Trent City Council's Cabinet Member for Leisure and Culture, Cllr Hazel Lyth. Our visit was recorded and documented by North Staffordshire's local newspaper, the *Sentinel*, who played a key part in raising awareness of the communities' shared links thanks to former Editor and Deputy Editor, Mike Sassi and Martin Tideswell, respectively.

And this *is* a book primarily about the Lidice Shall Live movement. Looking at the literature out there, I am sure you will find it is often overlooked by historians, sometimes treated as a peripheral, insignificant by-product of Operation Anthropoid, except for general references like *"Lidice was rebuilt with the help of British miners...."* Amongst the bookshelves and in the download sections of libraries, there is a dearth of satisfactory material dealing with how the village of Lidice came to be rebuilt; when explanations do appear in publications, still the Lidice Shall Live movement barely receives a mention, respectful but passing references only to contributions by British miners to help in the construction of a new village. I suppose this is perfectly understandable. Because the Lidice Shall Live campaign was a British movement and it is incumbent upon the British to research it thoroughly, document and present it, and in a manner which future generations can benefit. I am no historian, but that is what I have tried to go some way to achieving - for, at present, the Lidice Shall Live movement is perceived as an enigmatic symbol of brotherhood, with little in the public domain existing to give it firm foundations. Therefore, in this book, what you will discover is less emphasis on Operation Anthropoid and the subsequent reprisals for the death of Heydrich than you would normally find in many books about the Protectorate of Bohemia and Moravia.

In producing something of value for the owner of this publication, it was important to fill in some of the empty spaces which have been missing in texts up until this time. For instance, there are several significant questions which require examination, such as: Who were the significant characters in the campaign? How did the movement come about in the first place? How was it coordinated? What kept it alive post-war when the tides of political expeditiousness had turned? I have not been able to join up all the dots due to the grassroots nature of the campaign, i.e., the fact that there are just too many for one volume and some are quite parochial in nature. Another issue has been the small matter of the temporary closure of the National Archives due to the coronavirus pandemic.

I have made full use of the historical and archive sources I had at my disposal to create what I hope readers will find a sharpened image of the public and political mood of the 1930s, 1940s and 1950s and the events which precipitated both the Lidice Shall Live and the Lidice Lives movements, especially between the period 1942 and 1955, in the case of the former, when the campaign and its leading figures were at their most active. But this is a not a book which spans a mere 13 years' worth of social and industrial history in England. I argue that the kernel of spirit within campaigns such as Lidice Shall Live lie germinating for decades. The role of Chartism and Primitive Methodism I acknowledge. The book also considers the wider international reaction and the significant positive legacies spawned by building a new village of Lidice.

For example, the Lidice atrocity impacted an American society still reeling from the bombing attack on Pearl Harbour. The sense of collective moral outrage meant Lidice was an effective propaganda tool to help bolster calls for America's full entry into the European War and the fight against Nazi Germany and Japan. Britain was in a different situation: there, an affiliation comprising nationalities and classes had been actively working with a common purpose to survive the war for well over two years—motivation was not an issue. Empathy and camaraderie for those experiencing the fullest impact of Nazi tyranny led to a fundraising cause to build the village anew.

Although the majority of the contents of this volume deal with the contributions related to the Lidice Shall Live campaign, there were many other groups around Great Britain working for Czecho-Slovakia during the war who, while working to make Czech and Slovak newcomers feel welcome by raising funds for their upkeep and/or indeed raise funds for wider appeals, they did not carry out projects specifically tied to the Lidice Shall Live campaign or, if they did, not to the significant extent that it warranted a special mention in the book. In addition to the locations appearing, Czecho-Slovak - British Friendship groups and/or Lidice Shall Live Committees could be found in such diverse communities as Ashbourne, Aberdeen, Bradford, Glasgow, Cheltenham, London, Wellingborough, Leicester, Huddersfield, Hull, and Wellington.

Mindful of those qualifications, this book honours all the tens of thousands of people across Britain and beyond yet to be thoroughly acknowledged and recognised for the part they played in selflessly giving of themselves to help Lidice live again, the victims of atrocity of all sorts and at all levels everywhere. And for that reason, the book is for all of us.

I am endeavouring to add my stamp to this book by colourising it with artwork. Some people will be expecting this of me anyway, as art is my business, but it is really something which needs doing. Too many thoughts of the 1940s stir in us a dreary perception of black and whiteness, which extends past the photographs and newspaper cuttings. And while it is obviously very necessary at some key points to include them, I have tried to turn this into an art book when and wherever possible to ensure that this book remains an experience and something to treasure for all generations of people.

I am indebted to the artists Steve Shaw, Harry Davies, Lidice Calixto Moraes and the late Sid Kirkham for their kind contributions, which run alongside the powerfully dramatic anonymous works from Ivan Cigánek's publication *"Lidice."* I also thank my dear friend, poet and storyteller and fellow trustee of Lidice Lives, Alan Barrett for his powerful words and thoughts. And I really must say a massive thank you to Steve Dyster for his kind contribution of a foreword. Cycling enthusiast, teacher and author Steve pedalled all the way to Lidice with his ceramicist friend Mark and kept a fantastic diary along the way, which incidentally is now a great travel guide – available from all good book shops! Now, we are chuffed that Steve's a trustee of today's *Lidice Lives!*

There are a few individuals and organisations I would like to thank sincerely for giving me the inspiration to produce this piece of writing, without whom, quite frankly, my *Path to Lidice* would not exist; many friends in Lidice, Czechia, the rest of Europe, and the Western Hemisphere who I would like to recognise for their efforts, so here goes:

Veronika Kellerová, Ivona Kasalická, Tomáš Skála, Zdenka Kotková, Milouš Červencl, Hana Pokorná, Luba Hedlova, Antonín Nešpor, Martina Lehmannová, Martin Homola, and Petr Sejkora and the staff at Buštěhrad School; Kostas Follas, Jenny Heggvik, Edna Gómez Ruiz, Lidice Robinson, Eddy Ferreira, Kateřina Rodríguezová, Lidice Holanda, Lidice Montoya, Toni Brendel and Lidice Brooks Raymond.

Still, I would like to mention a few of those fantastic people closer to home, who've made a positive contribution towards the dissemination of this story:

Nick Archer, Jan Thompson, Marie Chatardová, Libor Sečka, Dave Proudlove, Stephen Dyster, Alan Barrett, David Amigoni, Steve Shaw, Harry Davies, Mark James, Dec Brennan, Zdeněk Valkoun-Walker, Muriel Stoddard, Judy Doherty, Bracken Moorland, Don Barnes, Steve Dunn, Maureen Hayward, Clare White, Ian Ledgar, Glenn Parkes, Edward Peacock, Tony Johnson, Alan Lear, Ray Elks, Charles Strasser, Den Siegertsz, Pete Morgan, Ian Willoughby, Jaromir Marek, Jiri Hosek, Nicky Twemlow, Danny Flynn, Martin Tideswell, Mike Sassi, Pat and Fred Phillips, Ken Hancock, Justine Cope & Fusion Dance, Natalie Bangs, Laura Stacey, Denise Powell, Michaleen Hilton, Angela Mason, Tony Walley, Nick Hancock, Cllr Ross Irving, Christine Warren, Ray Johnson, Mervyn Edwards, Dave Conway, Mick Bell, the Dorothy Clive Gardens, Cllr Abi Brown and Lord Mayor Chandra Kanneganti, Peter Coates, Tony Scholes and Stoke City. Thank you too for the inspirational support of my late friend Sid Kirkham and the late Carl Payne, Stephan McNeal, Brenda Proctor, Mick Salih, Jean Edwards, Paul Breeze, John Poole, Václav Zelenka, Marie Šupíková and Terry Crowe.

With the "enabler" on the coach to Brno, June 2017.

Most of all, thank you to my steadfast and darling wife, Cheryl, who has very much played an equal part on this journey. It would be fair to say that Cheryl is an enabler in the soundest of senses, but she is so much more than that of course; and Stoke-on-Trent's links with Lidice and the rest of the world would be *online* only if she was not around – I think all of us in Stoke-on-Trent know that. Together for the last 20 years, we hope this book means as much to the reader as it does to us in providing a narrative for future international community co-operation.

CZECHOSLOVAKIA

DEMOCRACY & DEMANDS

Czechoslovakia was officially created on the 28th of October 1918 following the collapse of the Austro-Hungarian Empire at the end of the First World War. A significant minority of the population were Germans who lived in the Sudetenland, historically rich areas which bordered on Germany and the fledgling Austrian nation.

At the beginning of 1938, Czechoslovakia was coming under pressure from Germany. Its western frontiers were surrounded by the new Greater German Reich. Here were the impressive power houses of the Czech states, the factories, the mines. Here too were the fortifications vital for the Czechs' defence capabilities. The Czechs had an efficient, well-equipped army.

Yet against the enemy within they had few defences.

The three million Germans who lived in the Sudetenland were fed propaganda sponsored by the Third Reich across the border. This was intended to increasingly agitate the feelings of dislike and contempt felt amongst Sudeten Germans towards their Czech *rulers*. In April 1938, Konrad Henlein, leader of the Nazi inspired and backed German Sudeten Party demanded self-government for the Sudetenland, in a move supported by Adolf Hitler. It was a cruel demand.

The Czechs stood to lose not just the Sudeten Germans but their industrial backbone and defensive strength as well. The Czech President, Edvard Beneš, seemed to have the choice of hanging on to the Sudetenland and risking a war with Germany or giving it up and hoping to live in peace. If he decided to NOT relinquish the Sudetenland, he could rely on the support of a highly charged Czech people, palpably angered by the Führer's demands. He would send out mobilisation papers to his army and hope to call out Henlein's and Hitler's bluff. Beneš could also appeal for help from France, Czechoslovakia's ally since 1924. But this was a prospect which alarmed the French Government, led by Édouard Daladier.

In April, Daladier flew to London to sound out the British reaction to increasing tension over the Sudetenland. He was told by Prime Minister, Neville Chamberlain to expect no help from Britain. The Maginot Line was in fact where France's military strategy stopped. The immensely strong and expensive system of fortifications the French had built along the German border had to pay for itself. This was the answer to any future threats from Germany in the west. From the Maginot Line to Daladier and Chamberlain, the Sudetenland looked an exceptionally long way away.

Hitler pressed harder.

On Sunday the 12th of September 1938, at a Nuremberg mass rally he castigated the Czechoslovakian Government as a rogue state demanding self-determination for the oppressed Sudeten Germans. He also promised to send them military assistance.

Taking encouragement from the Führer's words, Henlein encouraged the Sudeten Germans to arm themselves. The border suddenly became the scene of atrocities, as the Czech police were forbidden by the government to use weapons and could only use their fists in disputes.

Josef Josten in his book *"Oh My Country"* wrote how he was there with a colleague, Jan Drda, and witnessed the barbaric behaviour of some Nazi inspired inhabitants. In Haberspirk, near Falknov, they saw the entire gendarmerie station wiped out by villagers who ran amok after being egged on by Hitler's outburst. Near Loket a postmaster and his wife were caught in bed by a mob and beaten to death with iron bars. He reported how armed German SS troops from the Third Reich were present to encourage the Sudeten Germans into action.

The situation threatened to rapidly embroil Europe into war and Britain with it.

Neville Chamberlain, acting entirely on his own initiative decided to intervene.

He flew out to meet Hitler face to face in order to save the peace.

At the *Eagle's Nest*, the Führer's mountainous retreat overlooking the Bavarian town of Berchtesgaden, the British Prime Minister, without consulting the Cabinet, the Czechs, or the French, gave in to Hitler's demands:

he conceded self-determination for the Sudeten Germans.

This was appeasement, with a side order of entitlement, in action.

Now his peace plan had to be put to the British Parliament, the French and last but not least, the Czechs.

On the 18th of September Daladier came to Downing Street to discuss the terms; eventually he too accepted Hitler's demands. Now everything hinged on the response of the Czechs. If they decided to resist, they would have to go it alone. As Wehrmacht forces assumed positions along his nation's borders, the Czechoslovak President decided to accept the terms of the agreement. A triumphant Chamberlain set off to tell Hitler the good news. But his second visit to see Hitler on the 22nd at Bad Godesberg was humiliating. This time there was no red carpet, only fresh demands, principally that the Sudetenland must be surrendered at once, and Polish and Hungarian claims on Czech lands must be met. Chamberlain steadfastly refused to accept the ultimatum.

Suddenly war seemed imminent.

Flying back to London Chamberlain looked down at the flimsy housing estates and envisaged them laid waste by bombs. He expressed the anxiety and puzzlement of his people in an address to the nation on the 27th of September as he remarked:

"If I felt my responsibility heavy before, to read such letters has made it seem almost overwhelming. How horrible, fantastic, incredible it is that we should be digging trenches and trying on gas masks here because of a quarrel in a far-away country between people of whom we know nothing. It seems still more impossible that a quarrel which has already been settled in principle should be the subject of war."

Plans were made to move children out of the threatened capital. Hurriedly more aircraft were turned out. But Britain's air defences were still weak and thinly spread. There had to be a way out, at the least enough time to get the aircraft programme off the ground. When Mussolini suggested a four-power conference over the Czech issue Chamberlain seized the moment. Maybe it was still not too late to settle the Czech question by international agreement rather than war. Chamberlain left London's Heston airport for Munich on the morning of Thursday, September the 29th, to meet with Hitler, Mussolini, and Daladier at the Führer's Headquarters, the *"Brown House"*. As he set off for the meeting he quoted from Shakespeare's Henry IV:

"When I was a little boy, I was told if at first you don't succeed, try, try, try again. This is what I am doing. When I come back, I hope I may be able to say as Hotspur says in Henry IV: *'Out of the nettle, danger, we pluck this flower, safety.'"*

Late in the evening, Germany, France, and Great Britain came to an agreement to hand over the Sudetenland to the Third Reich. The Czechs were not consulted. They were free to resist by themselves if they wished. The Munich Agreement was eventually formalised at around 2 am on the Friday. Adolf Hitler, Neville Chamberlain, Benito Mussolini, and Édouard Daladier were the signatories of the document, which was to have tremendously significant ramifications for the people of Czechoslovakia.

The agreement was officially presented by Mussolini although in fact the Italian plan was nearly identical to the earlier Godesberg proposal: the German army was to complete the occupation of the Sudetenland by the 10th of October, and an international commission would decide the future of other disputed areas.

Sacrificial lamb. Statesmen from Germany, Italy, France, and Britain meet for the conference to decide on how to use Czechoslovakia to maintain peace. Peace in Europe was "guaranteed" by a supplementary document, hastily prepared by Chamberlain in his hotel room during the night and presented to Hitler the next day at his private apartment - the famous "piece of paper".

Chamberlain's aeroplane landed at Heston Aerodrome on the 30th of September, and he spoke to the crowds there:

"The settlement of the Czechoslovakian problem, which has now been achieved is, in my view, only the prelude to a larger settlement in which all Europe may find peace. This morning I had another talk with the German Chancellor, Herr Hitler, and here is the paper which bears his name upon it as well as mine. Some of you, perhaps, have already heard what it contains but I would just like to read it to you: *"...We regard the agreement signed last night and the Anglo-German Naval Agreement as symbolic of the desire of our two peoples never to go to war with one another again".*

Later he formally addressed the press outside 10 Downing Street, again reading from the document, and concluded:

"My good friends, for the second time in our history, a British Prime Minister has returned from Germany bringing peace with honour. I believe it is *peace for our time*. We thank you from the bottom of our hearts. Go home and get a nice quiet sleep."

With the end of the Republic in sight, President Edvard Beneš would resign as president of Czechoslovakia on October the 5th 1938, one week after the Munich Agreement ceded the Sudetenland to Nazi Germany. He fled to London. After a short time in the US, he returned to Europe to establish the Czech National Liberation Committee - the formal title for the London based Czechoslovak Government-in-exile, set up to represent a majority of political shades of opinion in pre-war Czechoslovakia; it included: *Mr. Jan Becko, Dr L. Feierabend, General S. Ingr, Mr. Jan Lichner, Mr. Jan Masaryk, Mr. Jaromir Necas, Mr. F. Nemec, Dr S. Osusky, Mr. E. Outrata, Dr H. Ripka, Dr J. Slavik, and General R. Viest.* Because of their attitude towards the war, the Communists of course were not included in the Government until the Soviets' declaration of war on Nazi Germany.

GOD HELP YOUR SOULS

In measuring the extent of the enthusiasm for the Lidice Shall Live campaign there are several matters to contemplate, not least of which is the extent of unease felt across Great Britain because of the Munich Agreement.

The *document* which sealed the fate of Czechoslovakia and its people was initially seen as a triumph of British diplomacy. The Prime Minister was perceived as the archetypal peace campaigner, evidenced by the 20,000 letters and telegrams of thanks, and all the gifts he received, including 6,000 assorted bulbs from grateful Dutch admirers and a cross from the Pope! Such was the extent of national relief that the statesman-like Chamberlain was greeted as a hero by the royal family and invited on the balcony at Buckingham Palace. All this before he had presented the agreement to the British Parliament. However, the euphoric reaction quickly soured, despite royal patronage, as unconditional relief turned to reflection on what Great Britain had done to the people of Czechoslovakia.

PARLIAMENT

There had been opposition from the start. Clement Attlee and the Labour Party opposed the agreement, as did most of the trade unions. Elements within the Conservative Party and Liberal Party made it an increasingly broad alliance against the policies of appeasement. In particular, attitudes began to change significantly following the debates in the 'Commons on the 3rd and 4th of October, which saw several Government as well as opposition politicians criticise the Prime Minister for an obvious show of obsequiousness towards Mussolini and Hitler, when he had this to say about their respective roles in drawing out a resolution to the crisis:

"After everything that has been said about the German Chancellor to-day and in the past, I do feel that the House ought to recognise the difficulty for a man in that position to take back such emphatic declarations as he had already made amidst the enthusiastic cheers of his supporters, and to recognise that in consenting, even though it were only at the last moment, to discuss with the representatives of other Powers those things which he had declared he had already decided once for all, was a real and a substantial contribution on his part. With regard to Signor Mussolini, his contribution was certainly notable and perhaps decisive. It was on his suggestion that the final stages of mobilisation were postponed for 24 hours to give us an opportunity of discussing the situation, and I wish to

say that at the Conference itself both he and the Italian Foreign Secretary, Count Ciano, were most helpful in the discussions. It was they who, very early in the proceedings, produced the Memorandum which M. Daladier, and I, were able to accept as a basis of discussion. I think that Europe and the world have reason to be grateful to the head of the Italian Government for his work in contributing to a peaceful solution."

He added:

"No one must think that because of the agreement signed by the four Powers at Munich we can relax our rearmament efforts. Disarmament on the part of this country must never be unilateral," he declared. "We must renew our determination to build up the deficiencies in our armaments and defensive precautions so that we may equip ourselves and make our diplomacy effective. I mean it."

Chamberlain announced that a British credit of £10,000,000 was to be granted immediately to the Czechs to help them overcome the chaos into which they had been flung. (The Czechs had appealed to London to help them raise a loan of £30,000,000.)

"I believe that there is sincerity and goodwill on both sides in this matter. That is why to me its significance goes far beyond its actual words."

"If there is one lesson which we should learn from the events of these last weeks' it is this: that lasting peace is not to be obtained by sitting still and waiting for it to come."

"We must renew our determination to fill up the deficiencies that yet remain in our armaments and in our defensive precautions so that we may be ready to defend ourselves and make our diplomacy effective."

"Nevertheless, I say with an equal sense of reality that I do see fresh opportunities of approaching this subject of disarmament opening up before us."

Attlee, Labour Opposition Leader, in his address stated the following:

"We all feel relief that war has not come this time. Every one of us has been passing through days of anxiety; we cannot, however, feel that peace has been established, but that we have nothing but an armistice in a state of war. We have been unable to go in for carefree rejoicing. We have felt that we are in the midst of a tragedy. We have felt humiliation. This has not been a victory for reason and humanity. It has been a victory for brute force. At every stage of the proceedings there have been time limits laid down by the owner and ruler of armed force. The terms have not been terms negotiated; they have been terms laid down as ultimata. Today we have seen a gallant, civilised and democratic people betrayed and handed over to a ruthless despotism. We have seen something more. We have seen the cause of democracy, which is, in our view, the cause of civilisation and humanity, receive a terrible defeat."

Sir Archibald Sinclair, Liberal Opposition Leader, then got up and said he would have to criticise certain aspects of the Prime Minister's policy, but that did not lessen his deep respect for the courageous way he had carried his responsibilities. He alluded to the general public's antipathy for the war, strikingly illustrated in the flood of relief which had spread over the world since the Munich Conference:

"The nightmare is over. The labourer goes peacefully to his work, and his wife to her shopping. The mother sends her child happily to school, thankful that the shadow of a great menace has been banished...My foreboding is," continued Sir Archibald, "that we shall yet live to rue the day when the Government sold the pass of freedom in Central Europe, and laid open to the march of the Dictator the people and resources of Eastern Europe, the discontented people in Germany and Italy are rallied by another dazzling triumph of dictatorship over democracy, and we have not only given Sudetenland to Germany but have restored Germany to Hitler and Italy to Mussolini...The Prime Minister's submission to Herr Hitler's demands was extorted by the threat of war."

Winston Churchill, denouncing the Agreement in the House of Commons on Wednesday the 5th declared:

"We have suffered a total and unmitigated defeat... you will find that in a period of time which may be measured by years, but may be measured by months, Czechoslovakia will be engulfed in the Nazi regime. We are in the presence of a disaster of the first magnitude... we have sustained a defeat without a war, the consequences of which will travel far with us along our road... we have passed an awful milestone in our history, when the whole equilibrium of Europe has been deranged, and that the terrible words have for the time being, been pronounced against the Western democracies: *"Thou art weighed in the balance and found wanting"*. And do not suppose that this is the end. This is only the beginning of the reckoning. This is only the first sip, the first foretaste of a bitter cup which will be proffered to us year by year unless by a supreme recovery of moral health and martial vigour, we arise again and take our stand for freedom as in the olden time."

Prior to that, as instability in Czechoslovakia took hold, in a letter to David Lloyd George, written on the 13th of August, Churchill opined:

"I think we shall have to choose in the next few weeks between war and shame, and I have very little doubt what the decision will be."

TRADE UNIONS & THE MINERS

The British Trades Union Congress and miners' unions had been growing increasingly critical of the British Government's foreign policy ever since Hitler's annexation of Austria in March. As far as they were concerned the policy of appeasement of the Fascist powers had become so supine that it was severely endangering the sovereignty of Czechoslovakia - as well as Britain's integrity. Anger mounted as Chamberlain conducted talks with Hitler over the future of the Sudetenland and when it came to the Trades Union Congress at Blackpool in the first week of September a statement was issued by the executive stating:

"Every consideration of democracy forbids the dismemberment of the Czechoslovakian State by the subjection of the Sudeten German regions to Nazi government control. British Labour emphatically repudiates the right of the British or any other government, to use diplomatic or other pressure to compel an acceptance of such a humiliation. ...The time has come for a positive and unmistakable lead for collective defence against aggression and to safeguard peace."

"The British Government must leave no doubt in the mind of the German Government that it will unite with the French and Soviet Governments to resist any attack upon Czechoslovakia."

The reaction by Britain's miners to news that Czechoslovakia had indeed been dismembered by the cabal of Hitler, Chamberlain, Daladier and Mussolini was strong and swift with the following statement issued by President of the Mineworkers' Federation of Great Britain, Joe Jones on the 4th of October:

"The Executive Committee of the Mineworkers' Federation of Great Britain, representing nearly 600,000 British miners, expresses its deep disgust with the action of the British Government in sacrificing Czechoslovakia to the insatiable appetite of the Dictators. It regards the foreign policy of the National Government during the last few years, as being that of an accomplice to the murder of the smaller democracies, and as a betrayal of all that is decent in international relations. The dangerous war situation which prevailed last week was the only possible outcome of this policy, a policy which has disorganised the peace forces and given consistent support to the Fascist war-makers.

We call upon the whole Labour Movement to organise a most vigorous struggle against the present Government and pledge the full support of the Federation in that struggle.

Further, we request that facilities shall be given to the Trades Union Movement to have its observers in the disputed areas of Czechoslovakia in order to afford some protection to the victims of aggression and to save them from the concentration camp methods of the Nazis. The Mineworkers' Federation is prepared to appoint representatives to a Commission of this nature that may be formed by the International Trade Union Movement, and also agrees to donate a sum of £1,000 to assist the miner victims in the Czechoslovakia coalfields." (October 4, 1938.)

They had reached decisions before on grave questions, though seldom worded their resolutions in such a very sharp and unequivocal way. But now, after much consideration, they were, in carefully measured language, accusing their own Government of being "an accomplice to murder of the smaller democracies" and of being a supporter of the "fascist war-makers." That this was a deliberately thought-out political standpoint was shown by their further decision on the same day:

"The Executive Committee of the Mineworkers' Federation calls upon its District Organisations to wage ceaseless educational propaganda amongst their members in order that a proper perspective of the present position arising from the crisis can be placed before them." (October 4, 1938.)

Moreover, copies of the resolutions were to be sent to the District Organisations, the Labour Party, the Trades Union Congress, Clement Attlee MP, and the Prime Minister, Neville Chamberlain MP, "urging their earnest consideration of same." It is unknown what consideration was given to it by Neville Chamberlain, who continued that autumn with his endeavours to foster closer relations with the Hitler regime on the basis of Munich.

In Germany, throughout the autumn of 1938, crimes against the Jewish population and other *undesirables* were becoming ever more commonplace and severe. A pogrom was initiated as a reprisal for the shooting of a diplomat by a Polish Jew; the punishments were vicious and completely disproportionate, impacting thousands across the Jewish community. All Jewish newspapers were suppressed, all Jewish cultural and educational societies dissolved, all Jews by decree were excluded from business, hundreds of Jews were arrested. Jewish synagogues and shops were looted, destroyed, and burned in an anti-Semitic frenzy. Meanwhile, Hermann Göring was planning a trip to England to develop good relations…

At its mid-November meeting the Mineworkers' Federation of Great Britain's Executive Committee received and endorsed a resolution from the Durham Miners' Association, as follows:

"We desire to register a strong protest against the proposed visit of General Goering to this country. We have no prejudice against German people, but we feel that to allow such a creature to come to England without any protest whatever, is to condone the most barbarous and outrageous crimes ever inflicted in the history of the world. He and his gang are seeking to convert the world into a torture chamber. Further it is to admit that the British people are prepared to tolerate the imposition of any form of torture, persecution, and injustice on liberty-loving people.

We trust that the British Government and the British people will prevent this blatant bully from polluting the free air of Britain with his objectionable presence."

(November 17, 1938.)

ABANDONMENT

The Czechoslovakian people were left feeling dismayed by the Munich settlement. They had not been invited to the conference and felt abandoned by the British and French governments. Czechoslovakian foreign minister Jan Masaryk's response on hearing the news was this:

"If you have sacrificed my nation to preserve the peace of the world, I will be the first to applaud you. But if not, gentlemen, *God help your souls*."

Soon the phrase "*Munich Betrayal*" came into common usage. With the Sudetenland ceded to Germany, Czechoslovakia lost its defensible border and its fortifications so that its independence became more nominal than real. Czechoslovakia lost 70% of its staple industries, 70% of its electrical power and 3.5 million citizens to Germany as a result of the settlement. The Sudeten Germans celebrated what they saw as their liberation.

On the 14th of March 1939, Slovakia seceded from its sister and became a puppet of the Nazi state. For the duration of the war the former Czechoslovakia would be known as Czecho-Slovakia, reflecting the dismemberment of Tomáš Masaryk's nation, but also the intention on the part of its government-in-exile to stitch it back together. The same day, the man charged with holding what was left together, new Czech President Emil Hácha travelled to Berlin and was left waiting to see Hitler. Orders to invade what was left of his country had already been given. During the meeting with Hitler, Hácha was threatened with the obliteration of Prague if he refused to order the Czech troops to lay down their arms. The news induced a heart attack from which he was revived by an injection from Hitler's doctor. Hácha felt compelled to sign the order accepting the German occupation of the rest of Bohemia and Moravia. According to the official communiqué issued in Berlin, at 3am that morning Hácha placed the fate of the Czech people and of the land "trustingly into the hands of the Führer, and the Führer accepted this, declaring that he took the Czech people under the protection of the German Reich."

In Prague there was a tense Cabinet drama as the Council of Ministers was summoned in extraordinary session. At 5am a government spokesman told the Reuter's correspondent, with tears in his eyes, that German troops were about to march in. Already, they knew that in its new form, the Czech State would be even less independent than a Protectorate; would appear on official maps within the boundaries of Greater Germany as the two locally autonomous states of Bohemia and Moravia; would have no army or diplomatic representatives of their own. Inhabitants would have German passports; the *Swastika* flag would be publicly flown; Foreign Missions in Prague would become Consulates; and Jews in Bohemia and Moravia would inevitably suffer the same fate as those in Germany.

Dr Goebbels, Nazi Germany's Minister of Propaganda, announced over the wireless at 6.07am that German troops had been ordered to march into Bohemia and Moravia. He also read the official command to the German people and told them that the Prague wireless had asked the Czech soldiers to give up their arms. He further read a special order from the Führer, declaring that:

"Units of the German Army and Air Force will enter Czech territory to assure the safety of the life and property of all inhabitants of the land uniformly. I expect from every German soldier that he behaves himself towards the inhabitants of the territory to be occupied, not as an enemy but only as the bearer of the will of the German Government to create in this territory an endurable order. Where resistance is offered to the marching in, it will be broken at once by all means. For the rest, be conscious that you tread Czech soil as representatives of Greater Germany."

Dr Goebbels' announcements were broadcast by all German stations, including Danzig, and via the short-wave station Zeesen to Asia, Africa, and America. A description of the Nazi occupation of the rest of the Czech nation was published in many British newspapers on the 16th of March:

Wednesday March 15th, 1939.

The first German soldiers entered Prague at 9.30am. An hour later they were followed by mechanised columns, which rumbled through the main streets to the great Wenceslas Square. Most of the chief administrative buildings, including the Ministry for National Defence and the General Post Office, were immediately occupied.

Crowds of both Czechs and Germans watched the Wehrmacht and SS troops drive through the streets. At some places they got out of control of the police, but there were no serious disturbances. Some hostile cries from the Czechs and at some places Czechs sang their national anthem as the armoured parade drove past.

Later that day: The whole of Bohemia and Moravia are now virtually in German hands, but the occupying forces are small, and contacts between the German troops and the Czech Army and police forces have been uniformly courteous and correct. - Reuter.

SS troops march through Wenceslas Square on March the 15th 1939, much to the consternation of the majority of the Czech population.

Depression reigns everywhere among the people of Prague, who first heard of the German occupation over the wireless this morning. They were stunned by the news but responded to wireless appeals to go quietly to work. No incidents are reported anywhere in Bohemia and Moravia, which form the new state of Czechei. Wireless appeals to the Army to remain in barracks and to surrender their arms to the Germans without resistance, and to the general public to go about their business, are being broadcast every quarter of an hour. Keep calm and await developments (says the appeal). The German must be well received. There must be no provocation to incidents.

"NO ALTERNATIVE" Listeners, who switched on their sets this morning for the usual Press Review, were astonished when they heard the brief announcements of last night's agreement. This took the place of the ordinary review. It said:

M. Chvalkovsky, the Foreign Minister, reported to the Government last night the results of the talk between Herr Hitler, Herr von Ribbentrop, President Hácha and himself.

Bohemia and Moravia will be occupied this morning by the German army. The Germans will enter with powerful mechanised forces from all directions. The Government had no alternative but to surrender,

Any resistance would only have been the loss of our nationhood. The German wireless station in Prague is inviting the German population to prepare a fitting welcome to the troops. The Prague Czech station has also started broadcasting German news. It ended with the words "Heil Hitler!"

Reuter...

Ever since its signing, the Munich Agreement had been a source of much mental discord and soul searching amongst Britons. Many wrestled with the knowledge that their sense of relief and joy at the avoidance of war had come at the dishonourable price of throwing the people of a fellow democratic nation under a bus. This was noticeable in the newspaper headlines echoing around the regions, towns and villages, and their pages filled with letters of *"thanks to the people of Czechoslovakia"* sent in by Aldermen, Lord Lieutenants, VIPs, and well-known figures. While most celebrated a return to normality at the concessions made to Herr Hitler's demands, many felt compelled to acknowledge the plight of the Czech people.

This can be seen in a couple of articles reported side by side in the Coventry Evening Telegraph on Saturday the 10th of October 1938; one article is more reflective and proposes the setting up of a fund to help the newly formed Czecho-Slovak government-in-exile, the other reports on a factory thanksgiving service. The Telegraph reported how the Bishop of Coventry, Dr Mervyn Haigh, spoke at a well-attended meeting at Coventry Cathedral the night before, and had suggested the setting up of a National Tribute Fund "to express gratitude to Czecho-Slovakia and admiration of the Prime Minister's efforts for peace should be opened at once" and said that if the idea commended itself, it might even be taken up on an imperial scale.

"Thousands and thousands of us British people and not least the young will I am sure, be feeling that they want and ought to give expression in some practical way to the profound sense of deliverance, gratitude, joy and recovery which they feel at this present time," said Dr Haigh. "It would be surely a great pity if this desire was not given immediate and adequate expression."

"I would suggest that a National Tribute Fund ought to be opened at once, that some large part of the gifts made to it should be offered to the Czecho-Slovakian Government in admiration of their self-sacrificing action and for the assistance of those thousands of refugees who will be compelled under the present agreement to leave their homes and start life again, and that the rest of the fund should be placed at the disposal of the Prime Minister as an expression of our boundless gratitude and admiration for the qualities of his leadership during the past week."

While that afternoon, four thousand employees of the G.E.C. (Coventry) Ltd had packed the company's large ballroom and its adjoining rooms and passages at the end of the working session for a Service of Thanksgiving for the Munich Peace Settlement. The Coventry Evening Telegraph wrote:

"The service, which lasted for half an hour was relayed to those who could not gain admittance to the ballroom by six loudspeakers, three in the nearby girls' canteen and three in rooms and passageways adjoining the ballroom. A crowd of nearly 2,000 were accommodated on the dance floor and on the balcony of the ballroom, and several hundred who could find no room inside the ballroom and canteen building assembled on the driveway outside, to take part in the service." ...and,

"Two hymns, "Rock of Ages" and "When I Survey the Wondrous Cross," were sung from specially printed hymn sheets to the accompaniment of the ballroom organ, played by Mr L. Wilkinson. The attendance of 4.000 represented well over half of the 7,000 employees of the Coventry works."

Soon after the occupation of Prague, Konstantin von Neurath was appointed as Reichsprotektor, serving as Hitler's personal representative in the protectorate. A wave of arrests began, mostly of refugees from Germany, Jews, and Czech public figures. By November, Jewish children had been expelled from their schools and their parents fired from their jobs. Universities and colleges were closed after demonstrations against the occupation of Czecho-Slovakia. Over 1,200 students were sent to concentration camps, and nine student leaders were executed on International Students' Day, the 17th of November.

Chamberlain felt betrayed by the Nazi seizure of Czechoslovakia. He realized that his policy of appeasement towards Hitler had failed and so took a much harder line against Nazi Germany. He immediately began to mobilize the British Empire's armed forces to a war footing, and France did the same. Although no immediate action followed, Hitler's invasion of Poland on the 1st of September 1939 ignited the Second World War.

Torture of Prague students - Géza Szóbel – from "Civilization" collection 1942

HEYDRICH, CARROTS AND STICKS

By July 1941 resistance in the Protectorate of Bohemia and Moravia had increased markedly. With occupying forces speculating about turning the vast economic potential of the Czech regions into one of the main bases of wartime Nazi production, partisans began sabotaging war production. With supplies becoming increasingly scarce, the black market was booming accompanied by soaring material costs and prices. Social conditions were deteriorating in the summer of 1941 leading to discontent and a wave of resistance centred round the state's factories. Against this background, Hitler recalled Reich Protector Konstantin von Neurath from office.

On the 27th of September 1941, Reinhard Heydrich was appointed Deputy Reich Protector of the Protectorate of Bohemia and Moravia. The day after assuming his position, Heydrich imposed martial law - whose second paragraph included a clause allowing departures from the valid laws when enforcing or restoring public security. In reality, this meant total arbitrariness. Immediately, Heydrich instigated mass arrest action or "Aktion Gitter". Security forces arrested five thousand resistance fighters in the space of a few weeks. There were arrests of Social Democrats and Communists, anti-fascists and left-wing intellectuals, German emigrants, Jews, and officers of the former Czechoslovak army. Celebrations, held on October the 28th, marking the 21st anniversary of Czechoslovakia's independence, sparked even more reprisals. Soon after, on November the 17th, the Gestapo conducted a crackdown on students, arresting them and dragging many off into concentration camps, whilst simultaneously closing all Czech universities and colleges. Even the Nazis own statistics reveal that they executed 429 persons in the period between September the 27th and November the 29th, 1941. It was a hammer blow against the Czech resistance.

In a cynical move, Heydrich balanced this terror with the reward of improved rations, working conditions and pay for blue collar workers, in order to boost Czech industrial output and get the factories humming again. For instance, employees in the armament factories received extra rations of cigarettes, clothing, food, and shoes. The ploy was successful, output went up and the resistance movement was undermined. It was a national embarrassment as far as President-in-exile Edvard Beneš was concerned. In London, the performances of resistance forces across occupied territories were regularly reviewed. Their success rate was based on the amount of damage and disruption they had inflicted on their Nazi occupiers. During the second half of 1941, due to Heydrich's measures, the Protectorate was always at the bottom of the list.

WIPING OUT THE STIGMA OF PASSIVITY

British Prime Minister, Winston Churchill had set up the Special Operations Executive, otherwise known as Churchill's Secret Army, on the 22nd of July 1940. František Moravec, head of the Czecho-Slovak intelligence services, and chief architect of Operation Anthropoid recalled the events leading up to the decision to assassinate Heydrich in his book *Master of Spies*:

"**He (Beneš) told me that in his consultations with representatives of Allied countries the subject of meaningful resistance to the enemy cropped up with humiliating insistence. The British and the Russians, hard-pressed on their own battlefields, kept pointing out to Beneš the urgent need for maximum effort from every country, including Czecho-Slovakia. But at this time, it was futile for us to send messages home asking for an increase in resistance activity. We tried it. Nothing happened.**"

"**The President of course knew that I was sending parachutists into the country to maintain communications with the underground. In late 1941 he suggested that here was our opportunity for a spectacular action against the Nazis: an assassination carried out in complete secrecy by our trained paratroop commandos. The purpose of this action would be twofold:** *First, a powerful manifestation of resistance which would wipe out the stigma of* *passivity and help Czecho-Slovakia internationally; Second, a renaissance of the resistance movement which would provide a spark activating the mass of the people."*

In discussions of the President's idea, two potential targets for assassination were discussed. One of them was the Czech quisling Emanuel Moravec, the former colonel in the Czechoslovak Army, who had been appointed to the Protectorate Cabinet by Heydrich. His continuing popularity as a Czech hero and Nazi collaborator made him a dangerous and divisive individual, and very embarrassing to the Czechoslovak Government in London. The other was Heydrich. Though only thirty-eight years old when he came to Prague he could already be classified as one of the greatest war criminals Nazi Germany had produced. Intelligent, ambitious, cunning, and cruel, he was second only to Heinrich Himmler in the Nazi police state. Clinically vicious, he had devised a *Final Solution* to a *"Jewish problem,"* which he prosecuted with a zealousness the world had never seen before. First, Heydrich had devised a system of Einsatzgruppen, or extermination squads to follow the Wehrmacht around the Eastern Front, murdering tens of thousands of Jews and those deemed useless or racially dangerous to The Reich; but in 1942 increasingly his attentions focused on the development of death camps and the use of gas as a less stressful (to Nazi forces), efficient method of wiping out hundreds of thousands of people.

Moravec continued:

"The cost of Heydrich's life would be high. I said this to Beneš, who listened carefully to my evaluation and then said that, as Supreme Military Commander, he had decided that although the action would admittedly cost lives, it was necessary for the good of the country. He ordered me to carry it out."

On October the 2nd, 1941, Reinhard Heydrich had explained the role and objectives of the Nazi Command over the Czech Lands to a confidential gathering of workers and officers of the German occupational authority at Prague's Černín Palace:

"...the Fuhrer's instruction reads:

It is my task to ensure in this region, completely and in a most radical manner, that the population, if of the Czech origin, conclude that they cannot bypass the reality of their affiliation to the Reich. The Germans must see for themselves that this portion of the Reich is its component part and that, on the one hand, a German enjoys protection and plays a leading part here but, on the other hand, that this privilege carries corresponding duties of behaving and acting as a German...

Over the past few weeks, we have been witnessing a development characterised by sabotages, terrorist groups, the burning of crops and go-slow campaigns in the factories, organised clearly by an extensive resistance organisation. Although not leading to an active uprising, this development nevertheless does prepare the ground for all that is to be used when the instant comes to spark off dangerous unrest detrimental to the Reich...

The situation over the past few weeks has indicated a clear threat to the unity of the Reich; there has been an under-the-surface turmoil of such proportions that all we can say is the time is ripe for action... However, let there be a basic guideline valid although not clearly revealed: this region must be German one day soon, with the Czech being the odd man out once and for all... The first portion of my mission here is dictated by the needs of the war. I need peace in this region so that the Czech labourer can devote his strength to

the German war efforts, so that we do not delay the building and development of the arms industries while not barring the local war-related industry.

To this effect, of course, what I have to do is give the Czech workers enough grub, if I may say so, to make them fit for their jobs... This immediate goal calls for our showing the Czech first who's the ruler here, so he should grasp the fact that what counts is the German interest, and that the Reich will always have the last say in this region. The final solution should include the following: this region must one day be completely colonised by the Germans. This region is the heart of the Reich.

A strange kind of folk, these Czechs: Some are of a good race and nurture good thoughts. So far so good - they can be Germanized. Then there's the rest, those on the opposite side: bad-race, bad-thinkers. So, these are out. There's plenty of room in the East. Then there's the middle of the road that should be tested thoroughly. This layer includes both bad-race good-thinkers and good-race bad-thinkers. My guess in the case of the good-thinkers is that they should be sent to work somewhere in the Reich or elsewhere while seeing to it that they are no longer able to have children... Bad-thinkers of good race are the most dangerous since they belong to the racially good, leading stratum. With one portion of the bad thinkers the only existing option is to try to resettle them in the Reich, in a purely German milieu. Germanize and re-educate them spiritually or, if this fails, put them up against the wall..."

OPERATION ANTHROPOID

By late 1941 the decision had been made to assassinate Heydrich, even thought it was obvious that the German reaction would be brutal. As the Special Operations Unit task force was Churchill's initiative, he sat with power of veto at the top of the chain of command, so it seems highly likely that he would have given the project the go ahead too.

The two volunteers required to do the job were selected from the Free Czech Forces training in Scotland. The men had formed a close friendship and they volunteered together. Both were former non-commissioned officers in the Czech Army, who had fled to France following the imposition of the Munich Agreement. They had fought in the Battle for France before escaping to Britain to join the Free Czech Units. Jan Kubiš was a shy and reserved man from Moravia, and a soldier before Munich. He had been decorated for heroism during the Battle for France. Jozef Gabčík from Slovakia was a career soldier. Although hot tempered he had an open and honest character and was popular with the men of his infantry company. During the fighting in France, Gabčík had earned the Czechoslovak War Cross and French Croix de Guerre. Both men were patriots and determined to reverse the shame of Munich and secure freedom for their country. It was their burning sense of mission which had driven them across frontiers and brought them to Britain to continue the fight. They symbolised the nation that Heydrich was trying to destroy. Although warned they were unlikely to survive, they volunteered for the mission without hesitation.

The final entry in Kubiš's diary read: "I have been chosen for a special mission. I will carry it out come what may."

From the start, the plan was to attack Heydrich's car on his daily journey to the office. If necessary, one of the agents was to throw himself at the vehicle with a suitcase holding 30lbs of plastic explosives. On the evening of the 28th of December 1941, Kubiš and Gabčík were loaded into a long-range Halifax bomber, flown by Squadron Leader Ron Hockey and his crew. They shared the craft with two other Czech parachute groups, codenamed Silver A and Silver B, whose task was to re-establish radio communications with London. The lone bomber flew across enemy territory, evading anti-aircraft fire and roving enemy night fighters on its perilous journey. Visibility over the Protectorate was hampered by low cloud and heavy snow. Before jumping into the winter night, Gabčík gripped the dispatcher by the arm. His last words were, **"Remember, you'll be hearing from us, we will do everything possible."** As their parachutes opened the agents did not know they had been dropped 70km off target, landing in a frozen field just outside Nehvizdy, a village outside Prague, where Gabčík injured his foot landing on the hard ground. It was an ominous beginning to a dangerous mission. The country was in the grip of a harsh winter. Despite the cold, Czechs were expected to contribute warm clothing to the German troops on the icy plains outside Moscow. The programme was promoted by the Third Reich under the title *"Winter Help."*

The Czech resistance had no knowledge of Kubiš and Gabčík being sent, but luckily the first person they met was a member of the organisation. He managed to get news of their arrival to the main resistance group in Prague led by Ladislav Vaněk, and after a few days living in the countryside it was decided to move them to the capital. They were put in the charge of Jan Zelenka, codename Hajský - a leading resistance worker, and hidden in a house belonging to Marie Moravec, one of whose sons was serving with the RAF. Hajský put them in touch with a carpenter working at Hradčany Castle, the HQ of the Nazi administration. With his information, they began monitoring Heydrich's daily routine in order to construct their plan of attack. This they did without revealing their secret orders.

Sudeten Czech, Karl Hermann Frank was left in charge while Heydrich travelled throughout occupied Europe promoting and instigating the *Final Solution*. While waiting for the right moment, Gabčík and Kubiš took time to visit ice hockey matches and an anti-Soviet propaganda exhibition; they also flirted and danced with girls in the cafes and dance halls of the city. In the spring of 1942, a wave of new parachute groups was sent from London to conduct sabotage, but none were successful. Many parachutists were killed soon after landing or lost their equipment and fled to Prague, where six of them were hidden by the resistance. As a result of this activity Heydrich called for increased Police vigilance. And there were rumours of a new round of SS terror. Some members of the Czech resistance had guessed what Gabčík and Kubiš were up to and feared terrible reprisals. Urgent radio messages were sent to London requesting the operation be called off. In an operation directed against the Silver A group, the Gestapo intercepted one of these warnings on May the 12th 1942:

"From the preparations that Ota and Zdeněk are working on and the place where it is happening, we guess, despite their silence, that they're preparing to assassinate H. This assassination would not help the Allies and would bring immense consequences upon our nation... we ask you to give an order through SILVER not to carry out the assassination. There is a danger of delay, issue the order immediately. If necessary, for international reasons, assassinate a local Quisling... the first choice would be EM."

However, there would be no response from London. As far as Czechoslovakian exiles in Britain were concerned, large scale collaboration in the Protectorate was embarrassing. It did not help that on the 20th of April puppet President Emil Hácha presented Heydrich with a complete Hospital Train for the Russian Front as a birthday gift for the Führer from *"all the citizens of the Protectorate."* It was a sycophantic gesture which the Third Reich propaganda machine promoted throughout the world. The sense of disproportion was ridiculed at home and abroad as a joke began to circulate about Hitler's health - saying how ill he must be to need an entire train! The Czechoslovak Government-in-exile could see their beloved democracy becoming a Nazi state through the carrot and stick policies being implemented by Heydrich, the servility its leaders displayed towards their Nazi occupiers and the enthusiastic acceptance of Nazism by some of its former national heroes.

Most disturbing of all was the support shown for Nazi policies by the aforementioned Emanuel Moravec, the former legionnaire and later General Staff Colonel, and a professor of war history and strategy at the University of War Studies in Prague. Prior to the signing of the Munich Agreement, Moravec was a most fervent advocate for the fight against Nazi Germany. But on January the 19th, 1942, a new Protectorate Government was formed, based on Heydrich's ideas. One of the most significant developments in its establishment was the propagandist department, *the Office for People's Enlightenment*. The entire affairs of the press, theatre, literature, art, film, and foreign tourism were subordinate to this office. And all of it was subordinate to the Minister for Education, Emanuel Moravec. A man millions of Czechs trusted prior to 1938 had become a symbol of complete collaboration. Moravec was in the perfect position for turning fellow Czechs into the Allies' enemies. This was no doubt how Edvard Beneš viewed events in early 1942.

Spring 1942, and Gabčík and Kubiš were now stalking their target. Through their contacts they knew that Heydrich travelled about twelve miles every day from his heavily guarded private residence at Panenské Břežany to Hradčany Castle, in an open top Mercedes Cabriolet, driven by SS-Oberscharführer Klein. Contemptuous of the Czechs and convinced that they were thoroughly cowardly Heydrich would travel without an escort and rarely varied his route. Perhaps he enjoyed the openness of the road and its uncrowded nature which meant he could be driven fast, which he liked. The agents decided that their mission should take place at a hair pin bend in the suburb of Libeň, at the junction of the streets Kirchmayerova třída and V Holešovičkách, below a school in Kobylisy, where Heydrich's car had to slow to a walking pace to take it safely. The corner also had a tram stop just across the road, meaning the assassins could loiter without attracting suspicion. During the spring, a third British trained agent, Josef Valčík, was parachuted in to help with the plan, and the three began to rehearse it.

A sense of urgency took hold of the agents upon hearing news that Heydrich would soon be leaving Prague for an extended period. On the 27th of May, Gabčík, Kubiš and Valčík assumed their positions at the tram stop at Libeň at 9am, ready to execute their mission. It was 10.30am before Valčík finally spotted Heydrich's Mercedes approaching. He was over an hour late. Quickly he signalled to the other two, and Gabčík and Kubiš braced themselves for the attack. 10.32 am and the Mercedes decelerated to a slow walking speed as it approached the corner. As it slowed into a crawl in order to take the bend, Gabčík jumped out onto the road and aimed his STEN-gun at Heydrich. He pressed the trigger to kill the man, but the gun would only jam. Spotting him, Heydrich stood up and fumbled for his pistol. All the time, Klein, the chauffeur, failed to accelerate away. Kubiš, taking advantage of this, stepped forward and lobbed his home-made hand grenade at the car. It exploded and Heydrich took the full force of its blast in his side.

Heydrich managed to stagger out of the car and started shouting and shooting at the agents. Followed by Klein, he started firing at Kubiš, who dropped his briefcase, grabbed his bicycle, and rode off into the city. Gabčík too abandoned his sub-machine gun and raced away. He ducked into a butcher's shop, but Klein continued after him, until Gabčík managed to shoot him down, severely wounding him. He then escaped by boarding a tram heading into the city. Once the agents had fled the scene and the adrenalin rush had subsided, Heydrich collapsed and was rushed by ambulance to hospital. He had sustained severe internal injuries from the bomb splinters and the fibres of car upholstery which had become embedded in his abdomen. Prague was at once sealed off and a curfew imposed. Heydrich was operated upon immediately but fragments from the grenade had pierced his spleen. Soon blood poisoning would set in, and he would go into a coma from which he would not recover.

REPRISALS

Immediately following the attack on Heydrich, the Nazis launched a great cry for vengeance. Hitler, in a personal telephone call to Karl Frank, State Secretary to the Reich for the Protectorate of Bohemia and Moravia demanded at once the execution of 30,000 to 40,000 Czech citizens *(this was later revised to 10,000 when Frank explained that 30,000 would seriously deplete the labour figures)*. As those arrested were to be dealt with through *"Standgericht,"* in other words, law courts in name only, Hitler's order was tantamount to condemning thousands of Czech nationals to death without trial. As early as 17:30 that very evening, Prague Radio broadcast a news item which rapidly spread worldwide:

On May 27, 1942, the Deputy Reichsprotektor, SS-Obergruppenfuhrer Heydrich was assassinated in Prague.

A reward of 10 million crowns will be paid against capturing the assassins. Anyone offering them refuge, providing assistance to them, or failing to report their whereabouts if aware of such, shall be shot together with his or her family.

As of the publishing of this announcement, a civilian state of emergency applies to the Oberlandrat District of Prague. The following are hereby introduced:

a) A curfew is imposed on all civilian population extending from 21:00 hrs on May 27, 1942, until 06:00 hrs on May 28, 1942.

b) Over the same period of time, all public houses, cinemas, theatres, and public entertainment places shall stay closed, and all public transport shall be halted.

c) Anyone appearing in the street despite this regulation and failing to obey the first appeal not to proceed any further shall be shot.

d) Additional measures are reserved and shall be announced on the radio if need be."

Senior Director of SS and Police at the Reichsprotektor of Bohemia and Moravia

Signed by: K. H. Frank

And so was launched one of the Second World War's largest police actions, with a house-to-house search instigated that very night. Over 4,500 Nazi security police went into action, together with members of the SS and three army regiments. Immediately arriving in Prague was the newly appointed Deputy Reich Protector, SS-Obergruppenfuhrer and General of the Police, Kurt Daluege. A friend of Heydrich's and his partner in the post of Director of the Nazi Security Police, Daluege was a ruthless man who had committed war crimes, both in Germany and the Netherlands.

The highest-ranking chief of the Nazi police, SS Reichsführer Heinrich Himmler, hastily undertook the formidable task of controlling the thousands of men combing through the whole of Bohemia and lent his support by personally supervising the search parties. Those involved included the Gestapo, but also the police corps, members of the Nazi Party, Wehrmacht troops, and the SS. According to official German statistics, the Nazi forces checked some 475,000 people, thoroughly searching around 500 towns and villages besides Prague. According to the lists published in newspapers, during the next few days over 3,000 Czechs were arrested of which 1,357 were executed, while 657 died during police interrogations. According to one estimate, 5,000 people were murdered in the reprisals.

On the evening of June, the 2nd 1942 the Protectorate government called a public meeting in the Old Town Square, in line with Nazi propaganda to denounce the assassination of Reinhard Heydrich and the assailants and reaffirm the Czech nation's allegiance to Hitler's Reich. Through a conflation of fear and intimidation, sixty thousand Prague residents took part in the demonstration.

CZECHOSLOVAKIA *The Path to Lidice*

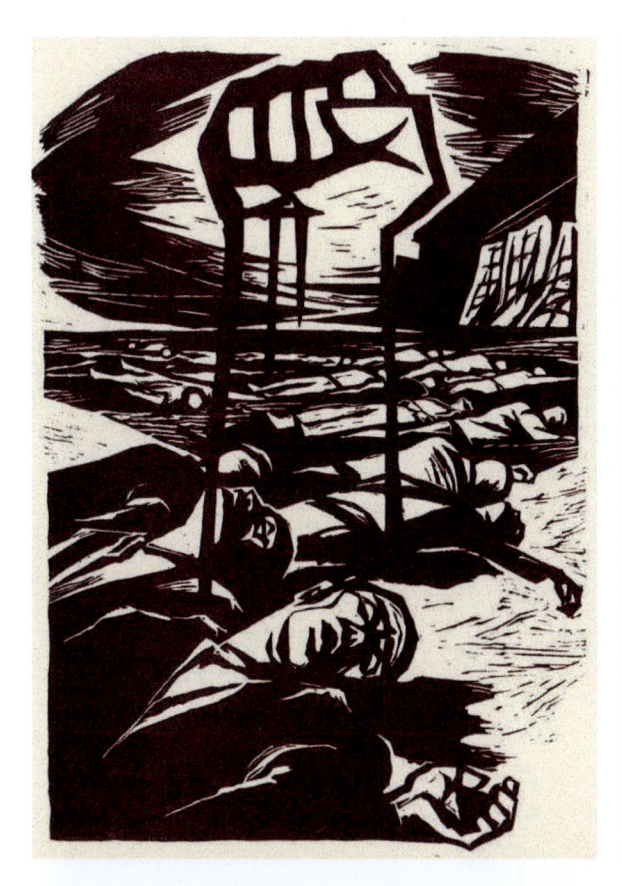

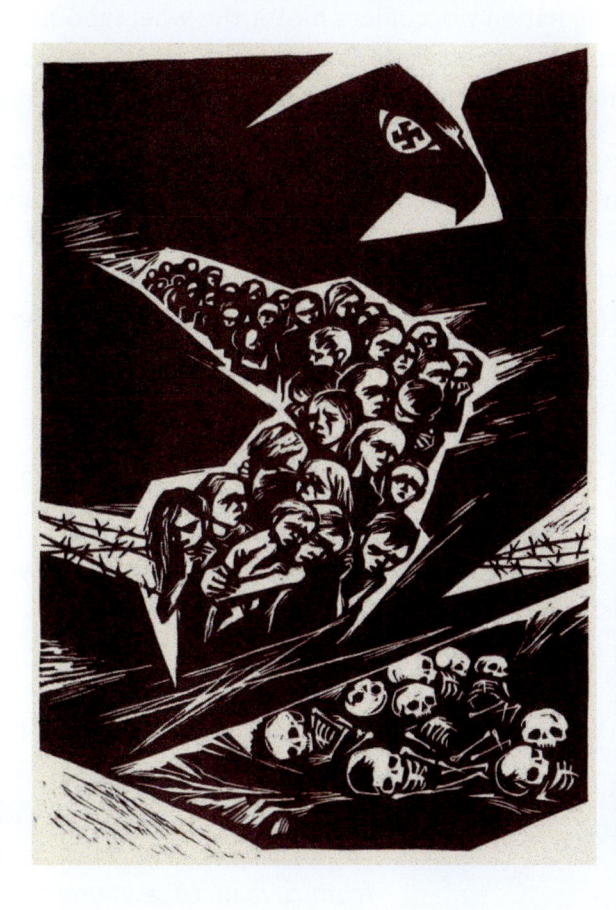

Images from the Cigánek book – Lidice – courtesy of Orbis Press, Prague 1982

LIDICE

Czech sensibilities and antipathy towards the nation's occupiers meant the whereabouts of the agents were not disclosed, though many people, especially in Prague, knew their secrets. In its brutal hunt for evidence and the agents, the Gestapo began looking for scapegoats.

An ill-conceived love letter was about to be handed to the secret Police which would have devastating consequences for the people of Czecho-Slovakia. It would give Karl Frank the excuse he needed to create a narrative, however bogus, to link the Bohemian village of Lidice with the murder of Heydrich. On the 3rd of June, the large battery making plant, the Palaba Factory in the town of Slaný, 25 miles from Prague and just outside Kladno, received an envelope in the daily mail addressed to:

Pála Factory, Ltd., at Slaný

The lower left corner of the envelope was marked with a clearly written note:

Andulka, factory number 210

The factory owner and Mayor of Slaný since 1940, Jaroslav Pála, opened the letter without authorisation and read a note from a man to a young woman, Anna Maruszáková.

Dear Anička,

Excuse me for writing so late and perhaps you will understand because you know I have much work and many worries. I did what I wanted to. On that fateful day I slept somewhere at Čabárna. I am well. See you this week and then we shall not see one another anymore.

Milan

Publicly minded Pála, sensed something was wrong. He called the local gendarme, who arrived in the shape of František Vybíral. Vybíral thought it was an ordinary love letter, but Pála as civic leader took a more studious, cautious approach. He found the nature of the letter suspicious, potentially the handiwork of one of Heydrich's attackers, and demanded further investigation. Vybíral was unable to warn Anna Maruszáková in time and the Gestapo detained her the same afternoon. Under interrogation, Anna spoke about an unidentified man with whom she had had an illicit affair without even knowing his name. He had allegedly asked her to remember him to the Horák family in Lidice; that he was well, and they were not to worry. She was unable to tell them more about him, except that he had pedalled off to the small village of Čabárna in the Slaný District.

The Gestapo had already researched the background of the Horáks. They had found out, after checking with the gendarmes at the neighbouring town of Buštěhrad, that a Horák family lived in the village of Lidice. A son, Josef, together with a young man by the name of Stříbrný, also of Lidice, had emigrated to England. Of course, the Kladno Gestapo did know of that fact, and it was no major surprise to German authorities. Nevertheless, an official of the Kladno Gestapo figured out that Anna Maruszáková did have contacts with Horák who, he felt, might have been dropped in Bohemia as a parachutist. Revelations concerning Marie Moravec's son and his possible connections within the RAF to Horák and Stříbrný would also be fresh in the mind of key agents at the Gestapo.

But there were other reasons why Lidice could have been targeted by the Nazis in reprisal for Heydrich's death:

Kladno was a natural candidate for Nazi retribution. For the occupiers, the region was a constant irritant, causing discord, disruption, and interference. The City of Kladno had a reputation for being full of troublemakers and a hotbed of resistance. Kladno grew up as an industrial powerhouse, providing the Austro-Hungarian Empire with iron and steel during the late 1800s, but received little in terms of public health, housing, and hygiene in return. Resultantly, Kladno became the centre for Trade Union activism, communist support, and anti-Nazi sentiment in the 1930s. As far as the Nazis were concerned, it was about time revenge was meted out on the place.

At dawn on June the 4th, the day of Reinhard Heydrich's death, the first search of Lidice took place. Eyewitness accounts recall the truck full of troops peeling off the main road from Prague to Kladno, racing into the village and immediately lining all the inhabitants up for identification. There was bullying and harassment but generally no one was harmed. No hard evidence was found to incriminate the villagers so perhaps out of frustration some of the contingent invaded homes, looting the residents' belongings or throwing them about the place. It became clear to the Gestapo that it was time to become creative, in the light of a lack of prima facie evidence. As for the Horák and Stříbrný families, they were arrested regardless and taken to Kladno for questioning. It was the last time several would see Lidice.

The fateful incursion came on the night of the 9th of June. It was on the initiative of SS-Standartenführer Horst Böhme, who telephoned Hitler in Berlin on the day of Heydrich's funeral to present the evidence against the village and recommend retaliation. Böhme's report relayed the reply which ran:

Subject: Lidice village, Kladno region. On 9th June at 19.45 SS-Gruppenführer Karl Frank telephoned from Berlin and instructed me verbally that, on the day, in accordance with the Fuhrer's command, the village of Lidice was to be treated in the following manner:

All adult male inhabitants are to be shot.

All females are to be sent to a concentration camp.

The children are to be collected together. If capable of Germanisation they are to be delivered to SS families in the Reich and the rest are to undergo other forms of education.

The place is to be burnt and flattened. The Fire Brigade's help is requested.

And so, on the 9th of June 1942, at 7.45 pm, precisely after the monstrous funeral of Reinhard Heydrich, and as the security machinery in the Protectorate still searched in vain for Heydrich's assassins, destruction, doom, and death came to Lidice from the direction of Kladno and the neighbouring town of Buštěhrad. Encircling the village, the Nazis then sealed it off. All were allowed in, but no one allowed out. Word of mouth passed terrible rumours of imminent horror around the community. Soon enough they became reality. A woman tried to break the cordon. As she ran, an SS man shot her in the back. A 12-year-old boy bolted to escape. He too was shot dead as he fled. With the cordon secure and all means of communication with the outer world cut off, the Gestapo acted. House to house, the Nazis banged on doors and drove people out from their homes. Dragging the residents out and making them present themselves in the village square, they stole their money, jewellery, valuables, and anything else of worth. Then, the women and children were taken and confined in the village school while the male inhabitants were shoved in the cellars, barns, and stables of the Horák farm. Again, the Gestapo searched every house, but still they found not even a scrap of incriminating evidence.

In Ivan Cigánek's book *"Lidice,"* Anna Hroníková, survivor and eyewitness, provides a haunting account of the shocking events that happened that fateful night:

"After a day's work, all tired, we were making ready for the night. Everything started just after 9 pm. Truckloads of soldiers were being rushed to the scene. We could hear the engines roar and the troops shout arrogantly. In a short while the village was alive with troops. After midnight, soldiers began collecting the people. Women and children were led into the village school. They herded men into the Horák farm. Women stood helplessly, bags in their hands, some consoling the crying and sleepy children. The question in all eyes read: What is going to happen to us? The fascists were quick in decision making. Early in the morning we were ordered to board the lorries and driven to the Kladno High School. It was hard to leave home like that. All windows remained open, with all the lights switched on despite the compulsory blackouts. All sorts of things were taken out from the houses:

sewing machines, radios, bicycles, stoves, clothes, and food displayed in the windows… Our men stood herded together in the yard of the Horák farm. That's how we saw them for the last time."

Although each man suspected he was going to die, at the Horák farm a surreal atmosphere of spiritual calm descended. Amongst the men moved their patriarchal figure, the 73-year-old Priest Sternbeck. All night he prayed for their souls as they knelt beside him. We can only hope that his work helped others find solace during those last hours.

Morning came - the morning of Wednesday, June the 10th 1942 - the last day in the life of Lidice. A firing squad, 30 strong, of Ordnungspolizei (*Order Police*) reported from Prague at 03.30 hours. Shortly after it was daybreak, and the wickedness of the order became clear.

SS Hauptsturmführer Weismann first addressed them:

"It is the will of the Führer which you are about to execute,"

They were ordered not to disclose the fate of any human being at Lidice and not to mention that they had ever heard of the village. In tens the men of the village were led out from the Horák farm to the garden behind the barn. Here, their executioners waited for them.

Careful preliminary arrangements, such as the stacking of large piles of straw and mattresses against the barn wall to prevent bullets rebounding or ricocheting had been completed. Like the victims, many of the killers were young men themselves.

The men of Lidice were not questioned and offered no blindfold. When standing trial after the war, Harald Wiesmann, the Head of the Kladno Gestapo Office had this to say on the behaviour of the Lidice men:

"The men of Lidice were relaxed, bold and upright. No scenes of personal weakness occurred. I don't know if they had chalk marks on their coats where their hearts were. Nobody read the sentence. They were shot without learning why."

And then the terrible scene unfolded. The shooting went on intermittently until 4 pm. It was a warm, serene June afternoon, completely incongruous to the events taking place. At one point, Karl Frank arrived in full uniform, just to see how smoothly his orders were being actioned.

According to the evidence given at his trial four years later, he expressed the desire that…

"Corn should grow where Lidice stood."

On Thursday the 11th of June, the next day, Jewish slave labourers from the Terezin concentration camp were brought in to bury the dead. They dug a large communal pit near the execution scene and piled in the bodies. They poured quicklime over them and finally covered the pit with boarding. Altogether this grave, designed to be unknown and unrecorded, held 173 men and boys aged 15 and upwards.

Document 379 – Harry Davies 2012

Thursday also saw the announcement of the village's destruction printed in the German occupation magazine Der Neue Tag:

Prag, 10. Juni.

Amtlich wird bekanntgegeben:

Im Zuge der Fahndungen nach den Mördern des ⚡⚡-Obergruppenführers Heydrich wurden einwandfreie Hinweise dafür gefunden, daß die Bevölkerung der Ortschaft Liditz bei Kladno dem in Frage kommenden Täterkreis Unterstützung und Hilfe leistete. Die betreffenden Beweismittel wurden trotz Befragung ohne Mithilfe der Ortseinwohner erbracht. Die damit bekundete Einstellung zum Attentat wird noch durch weitere reichsfeindliche Handlungen unterstrichen, wie Funde von staatsfeindlichen Druckschriften, Waffen- und Munitionslagern, eines illegalen Senders sowie bewirtschafteter Waren in größtem Ausmaß und durch die Tatsache, daß Ortseinwohner sich im aktiven Dienst des Feindes im Ausland befinden. Nachdem die Einwohner dieses Dorfes durch ihre Tätigkeit und durch die Unterstützung der Mörder von ⚡⚡-Obergruppenführer Heydrich gegen die erlassenen Gesetze schärfstens verstoßen haben, sind die männlichen Erwachsenen erschossen, die Frauen in ein Konzentrationslager überführt und die Kinder einer geeigneten Erziehung zugeführt worden. Die Gebäude des Ortes sind dem Erdboden gleichgemacht und der Name der Gemeinde ist ausgelöscht worden.

"In the course of the search for the murderers of SS Obergruppenführer Heydrich, impeccable evidence was found that the population of Liditz near Kladno was providing support and help to the group of perpetrators in question. Despite the questioning, the evidence in question was produced without the help of local residents. The attitudes to the assassination thus manifested are underlined by further acts hostile to the Reich, such as finds of documents hostile to the state, weapons and ammunition depots, an illegal transmitter, and managed goods to a large extent and by the fact that local residents are on active service with the enemy abroad. After the inhabitants of this village violated the enacted laws through their activities and through the support of the murderers of SS-Obergruppenführer Heydrich, the male adults were shot, the women were transferred to a concentration camp and the children were given a suitable education. The town's buildings have been razed and the name of the parish has been erased."

The Nazis destroyed every building in sight and the macabre scenes were filmed enthusiastically for international release by a professional film crew. Intended as a shock to the confidence of the United Nations and a statement of the invincibility of the Third Reich, the footage served only to strengthen the resolve of the Allies to smash the Nazis once and for all. Designed as Nazi propaganda to stamp on further resistance, the footage would be used as damning evidence against them.

The Nazis transported the Lidice women and their children to the gymnasium hall of the Kladno High School. There, on the bare floor with a handful of straw, they were to stay for two days and three nights. Suddenly a Gestapo officer announced: *"...you will now go to a labour camp for the time being...Women will go by train; children will ride a bus..."*

Then they read the names, the children had to quickly part from their mothers and were taken to another room. Lidice woman Růžena Petráková describes the pandemonium, as she recalled after the war:

"My youngest, who was only ten, did not want to become separated from me. One Gestapo official jerked him off my arms and threw him against the wall. We all started crying and Gestapo men began shooting up to the ceiling. That was a warning. The children were led away. We were counted and driven to the railway station where we boarded a train to the Ravensbrück concentration camp. That was when I last saw my children. All the time I spent in Ravensbrück I hoped and believed they were alive and that I would see them again. When I returned home after the liberation of Czecho-Slovakia, I found the grave of my husband, but not a single trace of my children."

The testimony of the children is even more upsetting. One of the 88 children was, Marie Hanfová, at the time an intelligent 12 years old with a gift for literature who tells the story of the next leg of their painful journey to - Łódź:

"The SS men told us in Kladno that we would be taken to some distant place and that our mothers would rejoin us there. We then rode in vans to a place I did not recognize as it was dark already. There we had to change the vans to a train. We were guarded by SS men and several women wearing nurses' uniforms. We travelled a very long time and were getting very little to eat: black coffee and biscuits for smaller children, a bigger cup of black coffee and bread for the older ones. The little ones cried and called for their mothers but when we started consoling them, the German women shouted us into silence. A day or two after we started our journey, the train stopped at some station. We got out and boarded several lorries that had waited outside the station. We were driven through the city into the yard of a huge camp. We were led upstairs on the second floor and were shown two rooms with no furniture at all. We had to sleep on the bare floor. We had no chairs, no table, just those naked walls and the floor. We were getting very little food, consisting of black coffee and bread and that's why the little children would cry of hunger all the time. When we tried to spare some bread for the little kids, it was taken from us by the German women who were guarding us."

To lift their spirits the Nazis encouraged the children to write postcards to their relatives. Although written in despair, they were still full of hope, gratitude, and anticipation of better times to come. All the postcards were mailed in Łódź on July the 4th 1942. A day earlier, an order had been signed to deport eighty-two Lidice children found incapable of Germanisation, to the Chełmno extermination camp - the first in occupied Poland designed expressly for the mass extermination of civilians. It is likely that the children met their fate with promises of good health, food, hot baths, and decent clothing. To assuage any fears they may have had, in all likelihood they walked along a well-lit corridor into a gas chamber reassuringly presented as a doctor's waiting room, with posters and signs on the walls, even sweeties on a table. However, once inside the converted van the door was firmly shut and the engine was started, its exhaust

Waiting – Harry Davies - 2016

outlet filling the inside of the van with lethal gas. As the cries and convulsions subsided, the van was driven to a nearby forest, some four kilometres away, to mass graves dug in advance. There the children were buried. As the tide of the war turned, the Nazis exhumed and cremated the bodies of the children, along with countless other victims of the death camps. None of the above is incontrovertible, however. The nearest relatives have to closure is the circumstantial evidence provided by the testimony of Polish gardener, Andrzej Miszak, who worked outside the Chełmno camp. As a witness at the Nuremberg Trials, he detailed an account of the "*Czech children*" arriving in lorries outside the extermination camp in the summer of 1942:

"I saw the SS men pull children out of the lorries, ranging from the youngest toddlers to maybe 14 years of age. The children were arrayed in quadruple file and led into the camp, which was surrounded with a fence about two metres high. I saw through the open gate how they led them to the mansion inside the camp... it may be that they arrived from Łódź. From the windows of my house, I saw clearly that the children [had] taken off their clothes and underwear and that they stood naked by the windows of the mansion inside the camp not far away."

For Nazi conceptions of vengeance, to kill and scatter the people was not enough: the village itself had to be erased. The Nazis placed canisters of oil and other inflammable materials in the farmhouses, shops, and homes. They lit them. Soon the whole main street was ablaze. On Hitler's orders a German film unit, commanded by Dr Franz Treml recorded each phase of the obliteration. On June the 12th, explosive charges were sunk beside the foundations of St. Martin's, the village's ancient church. Once again, the Gestapo drove in from Kladno to see their policy of annihilation in action. Under their eyes the church was shattered, public buildings and homes destroyed, a community razed to the ground, mountains of rubble replacing trees and vegetation. But still the destruction went on. Forced labour squads, possibly German undesirables, or prisoners of war from the *Todt* organisation, carted away the rubble for road making. The river was re-routed, maps with the name *"Lidice"* were destroyed, the cemetery desecrated, trespassing the land meant instant death, and gradually all signs of life were removed.

The physical deconstruction and erasure of the old village of Lidice took over two years of solid graft by an army of young apprentices, was financially costly and was paid for by the victims' bank accounts. It was not until September the 25th, 1944, that Karl Frank could finally announce with much satisfaction that the clearing work had definitively ended. And now the whole village lay mute, the village a total wasteland, a field of hidden skulls an intended symbol of repression, according to Hitler's wishes, that *"Lidice Should Die Forever."*

A fortnight following the razing of Lidice, as if the horror of that was not enough, the Nazis soon turned their attention to the small hamlet of Ležáky, where Gestapo agents had found a radio transmitter belonging to Operation Silver A down a well. In revenge, on the 24th of June 1942, 500 SS troops and policemen surrounded the village, removed all inhabitants, and razed it to the ground too. All of the village's inhabitants were rounded up and slain in a reprisal similar to that seen at Lidice; but this time all 33 adults, men, and women, were shot; of the 13 children of the village only sisters Jarmila and Marie Šťulík escaped death by gassing at Chełmno extermination camp, by being selected for *Germanisation* instead. Fortunately, both were found and returned to their families after the war. Unlike Lidice, Ležáky was not rebuilt after the war; only memorials remain today.

Tears – Steve Shaw - 2015

LIDICE SHALL LIVE

NATURAL REACTIONS

Prague Radio broadcast on the evening of Wednesday the 10th of June 1942 that:

"...all men in the village of Lidice, a Czech coal-mining centre, have been shot on suspicion of harbouring the murderers of Heydrich, the women have been deported to a concentration camp and the children sent to "educational centres"."

Initial reactions upon hearing the horrors which took place there were a mix of despair, anger, and bewilderment. Naturally, the instant suggestions for responses involved giving the Nazis a taste of their own medicine. Captain Alan Graham, MP for the Wirral, proposed that at the end of the war "**the Germans should receive similar treatment to that which they are now meting out to Poles**". Graham submitted to the Prime Minister that in view of the fact that Polish professors from Lvov, arrested in July 1941 had completely disappeared, he should now inform the German Government that, "**...after the war all Nazi professors will receive long terms of imprisonment, and compulsory labour service will be introduced for all Germans aged 18 to 60 years.**"

The Manchester Evening News reported how on Thursday the 11th, MP for the Isle of Wight, Captain Peter McDonald immediately contacted the Minister of Information, Brendan Bracken, a key member of the War Cabinet, close friend and Parliamentary Private Secretary to the Prime Minister Winston Churchill requesting the British Government,

"...publicise the brutality of the Germans in obliterating the Czech village of Lidice and to commemorate for all time the martyrs of that place."

Having brought it up in Parliament on the 16th June, the Parliamentary Secretary to the Minister of Information, Mr Ernest Thurtle MP explained to him that the Czechoslovak Government-in-exile was already taking action along the lines of his suggestion, and that the Ministry of Information would give it all possible assistance.

On Wednesday the 17th of June, the Czechoslovak Government in London pledged in a resolution broadcast to Czecho-Slovakia through the BBC that those responsible for the crime of Lidice and the 382 Heydrich executions would be brought to justice wherever they fled. "**The blood shed by them is redding the sunset of their power and the dawn of our victory,**" added the resolution.

Dr Beneš announced that they would:

"...take the necessary steps which it may regard as desirable to secure retribution for these atrocities and will relax no efforts to bring to account all those who committed these crimes or who were in any way responsible for them."

The state of indignation was echoed in the USA and Canada where debates sparked as to the best way of dealing with the Nazis. The Quebec Gazette wrote on the 12th of June how the day before Canadian Senators in Ottawa had backed American campaigner and journalist Dorothy Thompson's *'Eye for an Eye'* Proposal. In it she wrote:

"At present the Nazis feel self-pity is no path to repentance. It is escape from repentance. When every hostage killed brings swift reprisals upon themselves, upon their own villages, the German people, who share the neurosis but in lesser degree than their sicker overlords, will turn their aggression against the Nazis themselves. Until then, the sufferings of other peoples will make not the slightest impression on them."

The proposition was that Allied air power be used to demolish a German village for each community in occupied Europe demolished by Nazi forces. Senator Adrian Knatchbull-Hugessen drew the Senate's attention to the incoming news, pointing out what an "obscene crime" it was. He suggested that the plan recommended by Dorothy Thompson should be followed: that a widespread warning be given out on radio that a German village in an area *to be named* was to be destroyed; this village should then be wiped out by air action and the news of its obliteration given wide radio publicity - with the warning that similar Allied reprisals would continue should actions like those perpetrated on Lidice be meted out on other communities.

"These people are our Allies," Senator Hugessen said of the Czechs. "We count on them now and we will count on them more when we invade Europe. They have a right to count on us." Senator James Calder expressed "thorough sympathy" with the proposal. "This horror that is taking place is worse than gas," he said. "We don't like the idea of revenge but how is it going to be stopped unless these people are taught a lesson. It will go from bad to worse; it has already."

Back in Britain, and Prime Minister Winston Churchill reacted with fury upon hearing the news. In all probability, he had read Dorothy Thompson's words; perhaps he had received a message from Peter McDonald MP via Brendan Bracken. At some point, Thursday the 11th or Friday the 12th he had spoken with President Beneš to discuss the Czecho-Slovak situation, along with immediate options - including retaliatory attacks.

At the next secret meeting of the War Cabinet on the 15th of June, Churchill was insistent that the Royal Air Force should wipe out three German villages in retaliation for the destruction of Lidice. According to Bomber Command, to do this the attacks would require bright moonlit skies, around 100 bombers, low level flying and the use of incendiary bombs to inflict maximum damage.

Looking through the minutes of the meeting, kept by Deputy Cabinet Secretary Sir Norman Brook, which show that it took place underground in the War Rooms during late afternoon from 5.30pm, we form an extremely vivid account of what went on. Clearly several members were genuinely taken aback at the Prime Minister's suggestion, in what must have been an extremely intense, smoky, and claustrophobic atmosphere. Although Foreign Secretary Anthony Eden MP at first agreed, there were serious objections raised. Secretary of State for the Air Force, Archibald Sinclair disliked the idea and asked the Prime Minister to consider the diversion of effort from the military objective as well as the risk to aircraft and crews. Deputy Prime Minister, Clement Attlee MP doubted if it was useful to enter into a competition in "frightfulness" with Germans. Herbert Morrison MP at the Home Office asked Churchill to consider the possibility of "tit for tat" reprisals on British villages. Australian High Commissioner Stanley Bruce warned against the possibility of even greater atrocities against the Czecho-Slovak people, should it go ahead.

Winston Churchill's Coalition War Cabinet in May 1940: Clockwise: Sir Stafford Cripps, Ernest Bevin, Lord Beaverbrook, Herbert Morrison, Anthony Eden, Clement Attlee, Winston Churchill, Sir John Anderson.

While there was broad support for the sentiment, with Ernest Bevin from the Ministry of Labour stating that the **"Nazis respond to brute force and nothing else"**; Sir John Anderson, Lord President of the Council, made the point that **"the danger is that it costs us something and them nothing."** Lord Privy Seal, Stafford Cripps, rounded off by summing up that the operational argument against the plan was very strong. For once, Churchill acquiesced: he backed down with the line - *"I submit (unwillingly) to the view of the cabinet."*

It may be that the plan of retaliation rejected by the Cabinet was a joint scheme designed by Churchill and Beneš and that the British Government's failure to act had left him feeling frustrated. President Beneš had acknowledged the likelihood of reprisals when discussing the pros and cons of Anthropoid with Colonel Moravec the previous autumn; and must have expected some backlash following the death of Heydrich. Nevertheless, even he seemed genuinely shocked at the savagery of the Nazi response. When he made a public statement about Lidice to the nation on the 29th of June through the Movietone newsreel Beneš's sense of hurt and moral outrage were unmistakable as he expressed a natural reaction which struck a chord with many:

"I have seen the eyes of Czecho-Slovak soldiers and airmen blaze with anger because of the massacre of Lidice. Some of those airmen took part in the fierce raids over Cologne and Essen. They will take part in many other raids before the war is ended. The whole Czecho-Slovak nation is determined to exact stern retribution for Lidice. That Justice, believe me, will come. The Nazis may have destroyed every single building in the village of Lidice and even obliterated the name of Lidice from their records. But in our own records and in the records of humanity, the name of Lidice will loom large and live forever."

As the days passed it seemed to more people that the only effective answer was to focus energies on the fundamental task of destroying Nazi power. It was important that the Allies set the agenda instead of falling into the trap set for them – that of mimicking Nazi acts of depravity. A creative response, in order to exact not vengeance but justice was what was needed; a constructive approach that could lead to a real, positive outcome.

The Nottingham Journal was on the right track on the 13th of June when it commented –

"It is impossible to bring to life again the French hostages and Polish prisoners and Russian and Czech civilians whom the Germans have slaughtered by killing any number of Germans. But we can compel Germany to rebuild Lidice and Rotterdam, to restore or make good the booty stolen from France, to re-establish and re-endow the wrecked Polish universities. We can do this and we ought to do it."

TREATIES & NEW HOPE

Across the free world, shock at the news of Lidice was tempered with the announcement by Moscow Radio on Thursday, June the 11th of the highly significant news of the signing of an Anglo-Soviet Mutual Assistance agreement - which would see the two nations support each other in real terms for the next twenty years.

The Treaty had been signed in London on May the 26th by Vyacheslav Mikhailovich Molotov, the Soviet Union's People's Commissar for Foreign Affairs and Anthony Eden, British Foreign Secretary.

As Molotov flew out to the United States, news of the agreement was kept secret in the hope that an accord could be secured between the two super-powers in Washington. It could. The implications for the Allies meant a consolidation of efforts and the opening up of a second front with a subsequent commitment from the Americans to enter the European theatre of war.

The buoyancy people felt at the news of the Anglo-Soviet Alliance led to national celebrations taking place over the weekend of the 19th to the 21st of June. Parades, flag days, fetes and demonstrations with Anglo-Soviet themes were organised at remarkably short notice at the prospect of a return to some semblance of normality. The atmosphere amongst the population was one of joy and togetherness, an admiration for Britain's Soviet allies, commemoration of the heroes of Moscow and Leningrad, and reverence for the work of the partisans who continued to undermine the Nazis on a daily basis.

This sense of camaraderie gave new hope, renewed strength, and resilience to millions of British people. At the thought of some light at the end of a dark, arduous road many towns and cities revelled in the summer sun of 1942. The overall effect on communities across Great Britain was a much-needed boost to morale. This was felt most readily by Britain's Czecho-Slovak and Polish population in particular, who for the first time could see some hope for liberation on the horizon.

Staffordshire's Evening Sentinel reported on an event which took place in Hanley Park, Stoke-on-Trent on Sunday the 21st of June:

"**Stoke-on-Trent made a worthy and notable contribution to the nationwide celebrations, which have taken place this weekend, to commemorate the anniversary of the British - Soviet Alliance, and to mark the new Treaty of Alliance between the two countries. The event also served to celebrate the first anniversary of the German attack on Russia on June 22nd. Through the media of a mile-and-a-half long procession in Hanley yesterday afternoon, decorated tableaux, la mass meeting in Hanley Park, and messages of friendship and good will sent to the Prime Minister and to Mr Maisky, Soviet Ambassador to Great Britain, North Staffordshire gave an inspiring demonstration of its admiration of the heroic Soviet resistance to German aggression and reaffirmed deep and lasting friendship with the Russian peoples."**

According to reports, the event was organised by Stoke-on-Trent's Anglo-Soviet Friendship Committee and featured representations from all sections of the city's political spectrum, trade unions and wartime services of the district, in addition to many thousand members of the general public. Symbolic of the unity of Britain and the Soviet Union were tableaux depicting the two countries marching hand-in-hand to victory under the banners of the Union Jack and the Red Flag.

The procession was devised and arranged by Mr Gordon Forsyth, Superintendent of Art Instruction for Stoke-on-Trent, and formed in the square before Hanley Town Hall before proceeding to Hanley Park via the market-place, Stoke Road, and Park Avenue. A solid wall of spectators lined the route of the procession, which was marshalled by the Deputy Chief Constable and was headed by a symbolic tableau depicting the partnership of Britain and Russia. Standards of St George, Britain and Russia were held aloft by respected members of the community, while local women wearing traditional costume represented the figures of Britannia and Russia.

Workers from a local factory provided an effective wartime tableau, showing the production of aeroplane armament, while 25 pupils of *Podmore's School of Dancing*, Burslem, dressed in traditional costume presented a tableau dealing with the contribution to civilisation which has been made by famous men of the arts and sciences of Britain and Russia. Inspired by Lidice and the other reprisals taking place in Czecho-Slovakia was a tableau created by Czech adult refugees - which depicted a Nazi SS man, with revolver drawn, standing against a background of a large Swastika to which was pinioned a blind-folded woman. Another effective tableau was that of the *Burslem School of Art* depicting the four Pillars of Freedom: Peace, Justice, Security, and Stability. Other refugee children provided a *"Fight for Freedom"* tableau, with a strong patriotic appeal.

Dr Barnett Stross, GP and Cllr for the Stoke-on-Trent district of Shelton, made an appeal for funds to supply from North Staffordshire a mobile X-ray unit for the Red Army. Mr Karl Kreibich, a member of the Czecho-Slovak States Council, said that the Anglo-Soviet Alliance gave great and new hope to the oppressed countries of Europe. He believed that, without such a union Nazi Germany would never be defeated. Hitler on the other hand, could never defeat the new alliance.

A WORLD AGAINST OPPRESSION AND TYRANNY

In Britain, the first seeds of a national public response to the tragedy which befell Lidice were sown a mere three days following the atrocity, at an exhibition of artworks organised by the North Staffordshire Branch of the Czecho-Slovak - British Friendship Club at the old *Hanley Museum, Pall Mall, Stoke-on-Trent (see below)* - on the afternoon of Saturday the 13th of June. The display contained photographs, photomontages, and posters illustrative of seven years of Soviet - Czecho-Slovak friendship. Here, to a delegation of dignitaries from Czecho-Slovakia and the Soviet Union, a hint that the Lord Mayor should make an appeal for funds to rebuild the village as a *"permanent memorial to the victory of the free peoples of the world against oppression and tyranny"* was made by Dr Barnett Stross.

PALL MALL, FREE LIBRARY & SCHOOL OF ART, HANLEY.

The chief speakers were Mr Alexej Shiborin, Secretary of the Soviet Embassy in London, and Mr Václav Majer, a member of the Czecho-Slovak States Council. The Deputy Lord Mayor of Stoke-on-Trent Cllr Arthur Hewitt presided, accompanied by the Mayor of Newcastle, Mr Ronald Milne Ford; Mr Shiborin; Mr Majer; the Rev. Treacher, Rector of Hanley; and Dr Barnett Stross. In his opening address, the Deputy Lord Mayor stated that the exhibition was to celebrate seven years' friendship between the Soviet Union and Czecho-Slovakia, countries which had much in common. He added that in North Staffordshire the community had been fortunate in being able to offer hospitality to **"friends from Czecho-Slovakia,"** who, in turn had been **"taken into the hearts"** of the people of Stoke-on-Trent.

Václav Majer, who spoke in Czech, said that Czecho-Slovak - Soviet friendship and collaboration, symbolised by the exhibition were not founded only on political considerations, but had their source in the sincere and true mutual sympathies of the two peoples. Majer spoke of Nazi terrorism and persecution in Czecho-Slovakia, and said their sorrow was only mitigated by a sense of pride that the nation remained firm and unbroken. Their people never hesitated or wavered and would persevere until full victory was gained, whatever the cost. Referring to the death of Heydrich, Mr Majer said:

"We are proud that this blow was struck from the streets of Prague, although we know that it has to be paid for heavily by our people."

Mr Shiborin said he was very pleased to be able to express the greetings of his country at the opening of the exhibition - it would soon be the anniversary of the treacherous attack by the Germans on the Soviet Union, but instead of the quick victory which the Nazis expected, millions of Nazi soldiers had lost their lives. With feverish haste, Hitler was gathering bandits from all over Europe to send to the Eastern Front, and, at the same time foreign workers were being forced into the German factories – **"More than 2,000,000 of them were already working there now"** he said. But the German Army was no longer the same as that which instigated the European *"blitzes."* Of the new alliance between Great Britain and the Soviet Union, Mr Shiborin stated that it was certainly of great political importance, not only for the two countries, but for all the Allied nations at war with Germany:

"The words of this treaty sound like the death sentence to Nazi Germany," he added, **"Germany today is living under the shadow of two fronts in 1942."**

A vote of thanks to the speakers was proposed by Ronald Milne Ford, the Mayor of Newcastle, who referred to the suffering of the Czechs and said that they had given us a "splendid example."

Seconding, Dr Stross said that when the USSR was first attacked, Britain and the Soviet Union very quickly - thanks to the integrity, honesty and vision of Mr Churchill and Mr Stalin - came to an understanding for the sake of their mutual protection. Now they had mutual confidence in each other. There had been many struggles against oppressors in past history, but he thought that the destruction of the Nazi Fascists by the free nations would stand as the greatest achievement of all.

Dr Stross added that if he were Lord Mayor, he would make a great appeal for funds to rebuild, after the war, the village of Lidice - *"destroyed in vengeance by the Germans - as a permanent monument to the victory of the free peoples against aggressors, and a sign that oppression and tyranny could not endure for ever".*

Dr Barnett Stross, a campaigner, influencer, and social conduit, connecting together pressure groups and organisations within and outside the region would be having meetings in the near future to ensure that the British people had a significant part to play in the building of a new Lidice. Like all calls to arms, the need for a powerful, resonant battle cry to stir the troops into action against the foe was vital. The Führer was unequivocal when he demanded that *"Lidice Should Die Forever."* Between them - Stross, the miners of North Staffordshire and the 'Friendship Club came up with the most potent weapon they could in their fight against the Nazi's actions at Lidice – ***"Lidice Shall Live"*!**

MIDLAND MINERS' FEDERATION
SISTER DORA WALSALL
CANNOCK & RUGELEY
This is to Certify that
UNITED WE STAND
DIVIDED WE FALL

THE NORTH STAFFORDSHIRE MINERS

In 1942 the British coal industry was in the hands of a multitude of colliery owners grouped into employers' associations of assorted sizes, from the North Staffordshire Colliery Owners' Association to the Monmouthshire and South Wales Coal Owners' Association, from the South Yorkshire Coal Owners' Association to the Durham Coal Owners' Association. Each separately conducted industrial relations within its coalfield. These employer associations were linked up nationally in the Mining Associations of Great Britain - which had little to do with industrial relations.

Miners and related workers were largely members of trade unions, across some 60 county or district associations or specialised unions, such as the North Staffordshire Miners' Federation, and they linked up under the banner of the Mineworkers' Federation of Great Britain.

During the 1930s, at a time of rapid, sweeping political changes worldwide, like their comrades overseas, miners in Britain were charged with the cause of social justice. Suitably, the North Staffordshire Miners' Federation grew from *Chartist* roots in the north of the county in the latter part of the 19th century. Informally the federation had at its heart the religious and institutional principles of *Methodism* as its guide. As a trade union it worked for improvements in pay, working conditions and living standards for its members and their families, with a wider political remit which aligned itself to the national Mineworkers' Federation of Great Britain. In the 1930s and early 1940s the North Staffordshire Miners' Federation was a division of the Midland Counties Miners' Federation, which took in the South Staffordshire, Leicestershire, and Warwickshire coalfields.

The 'Federation gained a 100% boost in membership from 1917-20 such that in 1921, of the 35,000 men employed in the local coal industry, 29,000 were members of the 'Federation, and its accumulated funds were £67,000. The painful national coal dispute of 1921 resulted in the utilisation of those funds, creating a deficit of £85,000, a sum owed to the Burslem Co-operative Society for food supplied to the miners and their families on a credit coupon basis. With a reduced membership, the 'Federation struggled to meet that liability. By 1934 the deficit had been reduced to a sum of £45,000, but it remained a millstone round the neck of the organisation. Eventually, through the good will of the Co-operative Society a debt settlement for £10.000 was arrived at. There was difficulty in raising even that amount, but an application to borrow that sum from the Co-op was successful and by 1935 the 'Federation, having met its obligations in full was debt free.

Since that time, the 'Federation had never looked back. At the start of 1942 there were roughly 21,000 workers in the North Staffordshire mining industry, 16,000 were members of the organisation, and funds stood at £45,000. Most other workers belonged to other trade unions connected with the coal industry. Thus, the swing of the pendulum had taken place, and the 'Federation now faced a successful future.

The hope was often expressed by the trustees that there must be a sincere respect for the point of view of the coal owners, but that the organisation could not be a puppet body in its dealings with them.

THE EXECUTIVE

At the start of the 1940s the 'Federation was run by the prolific and articulate executive of Hugh Leese, Arthur Baddeley and Fred Hancock. These men not only ensured the union contributed to the national war effort, such as donating £5,000 to Stoke-on-Trent's *Weapons' Week*; they also petitioned colliery owners, as well as local and national politicians for improvements to members' working conditions and facilities as necessary; or brought to its members' attention deserving causes wherever they may be. The executive often succeeded in securing change, receiving significant support and donations for their campaigns. Some causes were extensions of those already agreed at the annual conference of the Mineworkers' Federation of Great Britain in Blackpool, and would be in line with national federation policy, such as the campaign for British miners to send *Aid to Russia* in 1941. Others were local, instigated by the executive themselves.

Activism was in the blood of Leese, Baddeley and Hancock thanks to their grounding in Primitive Methodism and their Chartist roots. These men sprang from the Kidsgrove and Talke area of North Staffordshire - a hotbed of Methodism that saw John Wesley preach to miners in 1739 and Hugh Bourne and William Clowes continue the tradition - starting with a large open-air service at Mow Cop on the 31st of May 1807. For several years during the 1930s and 1940s Leese, Baddeley and Hancock would live as neighbours at *The Rookery* (nr Kidsgrove) and during his time as President of the 'Federation, Leese and Baddeley were next door neighbours at the Miners' Hall, Moorland Road, Burslem. The executive were also inspired by some of the finest 19th century trade unionists and Chartists, local men such as Joseph Capper, John Richards, and from more recent times Enoch Edwards - the Talke born son of a pitman, who worked as a boy in a coal-mine and rose to become President of the Miners' Federation of Great Britain in 1904; but also, nationally prominent Chartists like the early 19th century reformer William Lovett, a man who fought for universal suffrage and equality through the powers of creativity and vision.

Like other contemporaries in the British mining federations executives Hugh Leese, Fred Hancock and Arthur Baddeley were also committed Methodists and lay preachers, and could be found at the heart of ideas, schemes and projects aimed at improving industry and wider society for the benefit of future generations. In the era of privately owned collieries, successful industrial reform tended to spring from the minds of individuals such as Leese, who was a social campaigner working to a higher agenda. Leese, Baddeley and Hancock were successful in their application of William Lovett's concept of *moral force*. Several articles appearing in the local press across the 1930s show the progress the 'Federation was making in improving the lot for local miners and their families by stoically leading by example; encouraging employers to see the wisdom of their vision in order to increase productivity and standards for both owners and workers the support of owners:

For example, on Saturday the 24th of September 1932, the Staffordshire Advertiser reported on the newly opened pithead baths at Norton Colliery. In addition to Leese, the event was presided on by James Cadman, Managing Director of Norton, and Biddulph Collieries, Ltd. Supporting him were his brother and nationally renowned industrialist, Sir John Cadman; the Lord Mayor of Stoke-on-Trent, Alderman Miss F. A. Farmer; Mr T. C. Maynard, Manager of the Colliery, and a Trustee of the new baths; and Mr W. H. Ruston and Mr Edwin Dutton (trustees):

On the 17th of September 1932, another step towards the time when coal-dusted miners will no longer be seen outside the premises of the collieries where they are employed was taken when pithead baths were opened at Norton Colliery by Sir John Cadman, the distinguished industrialist, and Mr Hugh Leese, President of the North Staffordshire Miners' Federation. Both made insightful speeches, importantly emphasising the value of co-operation between employers and miners in obtaining better conditions in the industry. The new baths were provided out of the Miners' Welfare Fund and were erected on a site given by the owners. The opening ceremony was performed in the presence of a large gathering, representing many sections of local industrial and civic activity:

On behalf of the industry, in his speech, Sir John Cadman recalled that, 90 years ago, a committee appointed to inquire into certain aspects of mining conditions made a comparison between the "puny, pallid, starveling little weaver" and the "broad, stalwart frame of the swarthy collier as he stalks home all grime and muscle."

Steve Shaw – Kings of The Underworld - 2020

"The sight of a grimy miner may have been thought pleasant by the people of 90 years ago. Grime to them meant work, expanding trade, more prosperity to the country in general. In those days, our forefathers were delighted with the palls of smoke that permanently obscured the sun from all manufacturing areas. To-day we think differently. We try to abolish smoke, because we recognise it as an undesirable impurity and evidence of waste. And, when we see a grimy miner, we are less inclined to think of his work than of his wife, and the quite unnecessary trouble which his griminess causes at home. The baths which Mr Hugh Leese and I are having the pleasure of opening today are an indication of the change which has taken place in our view on such matters..."

"A pithead bath is more than a concession to faddiness. Indeed, its significance is even more important in its general aspects than in those relating to individuals; and it is not making too great a claim to say that every new pithead bath is a step forward in the social progress of the nation as a whole..."

"...work in the mines, if you set back the clock by 90 years, would be performed by men, women and children, and you might see youngsters of five or six sitting underground all day working a ventilator, while their older brothers drew heavy trucks of coal from seam to shaft. Away from the mine also, life would be very different and I think, very much worse. At home you would have no drainage, no running water and certainly no bath. If you were free of fever of one sort or another throughout the year, you would consider yourself fortunate, and if you lived to be 39 years then you would have done very well. If you were unemployed, you would probably starve, your children would not be educated; and if you wanted to amuse yourselves in your spare time you would have no cinemas, no football, no horse racing; of course, the public houses would be open all day and most of the night."

Hugh Leese in his speech pointed out that 67 pithead baths were opened in the country in 1931, while there were approximately 50 under construction. They would readily see, therefore, that North Staffordshire was not the only part of the country which was having the benefit of these facilities. He paid tribute to the excellent co-operation between the members and concluded that there was no greater *welfare* in the Miners' Welfare Fund than that provided by pithead baths. There was no greater boon to the men, from a health point of view. There was no greater boon to the women in the home, and to their families. Mr Leese, referencing his Methodist roots, proceeded to describe the home conditions of a miner at the time that he himself worked underground.

He stressed the great inconvenience to which the miners, their wives, and families were subjected:

"I am certain that we are getting away from conditions like that. It has taken us a long time to do it. At the Methodist uniting conference this week, someone reminded those present that 54 years ago he had suggested Methodist union - and that they had laughed at him. At Birchenwood Colliery, 2 years ago, we were saying that we would have pithead baths. Some of the men said, *"Don't be silly. You can't maintain them, if you do get pithead baths, and if you do maintain them, the men won't use them."* Yet now, like Methodist union pithead baths are an accomplished fact. It was a step in the right direction. It gives you a better chance of raising the standard of your life."

"There ought to be no squabbling, or anything that tends to pull down the conditions, or which will make it worse for industry and especially the miner. It is bad enough in these days. The Welfare Fund shows what can be done by the workers and the owners."

"Times are sufficiently bad, without making the position any worse, and I am one of those who believe this: That the owners and miners have all along not felt sufficiently proud of their occupation. They have not respected their own occupation sufficiently in the past. You are one of the greatest planks in the nation, as owners and miners. We have people saying that we ought to make it easy to produce coal at as low a price as possible, but there should never be any question of producing or selling coal at such a price that there is not sufficient return for the outlay of the owners, and a decent wage and decent conditions for the miners. We should pursue that policy and should not at any time lose a chance of co-operating, as workers and owners; not to exploit the public, but to see that our people get a fair chance and a reasonable return for what they have to do."

A second example of cooperation between colliery owners and the North Staffordshire Miners' Federation involved the use of the Miners' Welfare Fund to secure the donation of land with the opening of a sports facility at the Mossfield Colliery, betwixt Longton and Fenton, reported in the Staffordshire Advertiser on Saturday the 24th of August 1940:

Here, a new spacious sports and recreation ground was provided by the joint contributions of the directors of the Mossfield Colliery, Longton, and the North Staffordshire Committee of the Miners' Welfare Fund for the benefit of the employees of the colliery company. Opened on Saturday the 17th of August, the ceremony was performed by Hugh Leese, then President of the North Staffordshire Miners' Federation, who was introduced by Tom Yates, Managing Director of Mossfield Colliery. In opening the main gates with a key handed to him by Mr H. Atkinson, Regional Organiser of the Miners' Welfare Commission, Leese expressed the hope that it would prove of great benefit to the miners in their leisure hours. Sir Francis Joseph K.B.E., Chairman of the company, added his tribute, saying that one of the most welcome changes in the coal-mining industry was the increasing recognition of employers and workers - that they were partners, not only in the prosperity of the industry, but also in making the world a better place to live in. According to the Advertiser, **"the land for the recreation field adjoined the colliery and was given by the company, and the cost of levelling and equipping it, amounting to £3.000, was met by grants from the Welfare Fund."**

LOCAL CONTEXT & THE SNEYD PIT DISASTER

Stoke-on-Trent is the city that enjoys notoriety for being a city that is not a city. It is a complete aberration for city planners. It is a construct composed predominantly by the owners of 19th century pottery factories and collieries who were looking to benefit from the same economies of scale as other entrepreneurs and philanthropists in traditionally laid out urban sprawls. I say *traditionally laid out* because Stoke-on-Trent is not a traditional radial city at all, but a series of six erstwhile industrial towns glued together, practically linearly, for a distance of 7 miles, from north to south: Tunstall, Burslem, Hanley, Stoke, *(not overlooking)* Fenton, and Longton.

Stoke-on-Trent developed through the industrial revolution as the centre for pottery manufacture in the United Kingdom. This culminated in a frenzy of activity between the years 1870 and 1910, where around 1890 you would encounter the zenith of innovation and productivity. In fact, the backstamps that you see on turning over old pieces of North Staffordshire manufactured pottery may often show a bee or beehive - meant to portray the busyness *(and the nepotism)* of the ceramic industry at the time - with ware being shipped to all corners of the British Empire, as well as the United States and Europe. Thenceforth, in line with much of the rest of British industry, for one reason or another, Stoke-on-Trent has been subject to an incremental but inexorable decline. Recognised by millions as the international epicentre for the creation of durable and delightful pieces of porcelain and earthenware, problematically for Stoke-on-Trent and its workers, its principal industry was not an essential one. You would rarely see the members of the potters' union, the *National Society of Pottery Workers*, successfully coming out on strike. That also meant that pay in the Potteries rarely kept up with colliers, steelworkers, shipbuilders, and those of others employed in the staple industries. Hence, North Staffordshire tended to be a relatively impoverished area with silicosis taking men and women at an early age because of the absence of adequate health and safety regulations on potbanks, and in the mines.

Harry Davies – White Damp - 2009

The 1940s was a time of deep austerity for many in Britain, and that meant extreme deprivation for some in places like Stoke-on-Trent. There, babies would go to sleep in bedroom drawers, the elderly could expect to be buried in paupers' graves, and many working families would rely on the charity of others for food and basic essentials—understandable then that apart from the impositions of wartime restrictions like blackouts, rationing offered security to those on the lowest rung of the societal ladder. Nonetheless, many people were looking for scapegoats to make them feel better about their station in life and Stoke-on-Trent offered a significant extremist support base to both communists and fascists, with a branch of the Fascist League open to those willing to listen in each of the six towns.

As the people of Czecho-Slovakia struggled to accept twelve more months of subjugation under the weight of Reinhard Heydrich, so would the community of Stoke-on-Trent be severely affected by a catastrophic mining disaster. This medium-sized, industrial sprawl, completely alien to the vast majority of continental Czecho-Slovaks, suffered a tragedy on New Year's Day 1942, which shook its people to the core and brought much of the city to a standstill. With time, it fuelled the empathy that drove the Lidice Shall Live campaign forward in Stoke-on-Trent, bringing residents together around a common cause.

An old superstition that said the cutting of coal on New Year's Day was ill-starred meant that miners traditionally did not work that day, but because of the war effort, the men of Sneyd turned out to work a normal day. Sneyd Colliery was one of the region's most productive pits and by 1940, the mine was being worked by 2,000 men and boys. The mine, like many others, had suffered deaths before, such as in 1904, when a fire broke out and killed three workers. But on that calamitous day, 295 men were working when at 7:50am an explosion caused by sparks from wagons igniting coal dust occurred half a mile down, its force powerful enough to blow men off their feet.

News of the explosion soon spread through the community, and wives and relatives ran to the pit-head to wait for news of their loved ones. The bodies of 16 men were recovered on the first day, when rescue operations had to be abandoned because of the presence of afterdamp. It was announced at that time that there was no hope of finding anyone else alive. The Sneyd Mines Rescue Team was the first to enter the mine, but other teams were quickly drafted in from other collieries across North Staffordshire.

The Lord Mayor Harry McBrine opened a fund for the relief of the dependents of those who lost their lives. The Directors of Sneyd Collieries Ltd headed the fund with a donation of £5,000 and also agreed to pay the funeral costs of the unfortunate victims.

Said the Mayor, in a letter published in The Evening Sentinel on the 2nd of January:

"The whole of North Staffordshire is shocked at the terrible calamity which occurred on New Year's Day at the Sneyd Colliery, Burslem, in which, it is feared, very heavy loss of life has been involved, and our heart-felt sympathies go out to the relatives of the miners trapped in the pit. It is well known that miners have a superstitious dislike of working on New Year's Day, yet in response to the Government's call for the maintenance of the output of coal, in order that the war shall be maintained, these men descended the pit to do their duty, and in doing so many have lost their lives. I am sure it will be the desire of everyone that a fund should be opened to help the dependents of these brave men and to see that their loved ones are cared for. The proprietors of the colliery have authorised me to say that the company will head the appeal with a donation of £5000 and also pay the funeral expenses of the unfortunate victims."

On the 19th of January, the fund stood at £14,757 9s 8d with significant donations coming in from the Theatre Royal, Stoke City FC, local banks, members' clubs, pubs, and private individuals. The final death toll of 57 also resulted in 32 widows; 35 children were left without fathers; and the 24 men who were unmarried left 8 mothers who were also widows and 13 had grieving mothers and fathers.

At an emergency meeting of the North Staffordshire Miners' Federation held at the Miners' Hall, Burslem on the 6th of January members expressed profound regret and sorrow at the passing of fellow members and sincere sympathy with the relatives and friends at such a sad happening. The executive resolved to send a letter to each bereaved family tendering the 'Federation's sincere sympathy and assuring them of every provision being made for their compensation where there was dependency. Moreover, the union made a commitment to send £250 to the Lord Mayor's benevolent fund, and it declared that those prevented from working at Sneyd Colliery because of the disaster would receive payment under the *Essential Work Order* in accordance with the procedure of that order. Finally, there was an agreement that a letter would be sent to the Sneyd Branch of officials and members thanking them for their help and assistance in all matters, and especially for their help with the challenging task of dealing with the bodies of the deceased.

President Arthur Baddeley commented:

"They stood to their task, at great risk, very nobly; also, the members of the rescue teams and other workers who took part in the recovery work, we owe them our best thanks and appreciation, right from the pit top to the coal face area..."

A copy of the letter is reproduced below:

To Mr Isaac Hart: January 7th, 1942, SNEYD BRANCH:

Dear Mr Hart,

I am requested by our District Executive to convey our sincere appreciation to yourself, your President, Committee, and all other members who worked so heroically in the recent sad disaster at the Sneyd Colliery.

As you will know I, along with our President, Mr Baddeley, visited the Colliery every day for long periods and we were able to see some of the work that was done and considering the very trying conditions of recovery by the Rescue Men and others underground, together with those who had to deal with the bodies of the victims when they reached the surface, and how efficiently they rose to the occasion without perhaps having first-hand knowledge of such work makes us feel very proud of such patient and valuable men. From the Pit Top to the affected area at the Coal Face not one ever shirked or halted in doing his best to recover his fallen comrades, and we extend to you all on behalf of this Federation our best thanks and good wishes and sincerely hope, although fatigued, none will suffer physically, and their health will not be impaired by their valuable and noble work.

We all say, thank you.

Yours faithfully,

H. LEESE, Secretary.

As one of the most deprived cities in the United Kingdom reeling from a mining disaster during the darkest days of the war, passive onlookers might have viewed the situation in Stoke-on-Trent with concern. Would the collective mindset pervading Stoke-on-Trent during the first months of 1942 been that of a community approaching the brink of psychological collapse with the potential for low morale, social paralysis and antipathy for the war effort?

Reassuringly, for more discerning observers, the miners, miners' executive in North Staffordshire, city council and industry leaders, and the public were already presenting a clear sign of the city's innate resolve. This was not a community that was about to cave in. Rather, in part because of Sneyd, the city of Stoke-on-Trent would rise up decisively and courageously to support a fellow community facing massive losses *deliberately inflicted*, a thousand miles away.

Drawn to the Light – Sid Kirkham - 2017

Steve Shaw – Sneyd 57 - 2014

THE BIRTH OF THE MOVEMENT

THE FEDERATION BACK DR STROSS

There was a symbiotic relationship between Dr Stross and the executive of the 'Federation. They shared similar sensibilities. Both fought for nationalisation and the social democratic cause. For Leese, Baddeley and Hancock, they had experienced mining's dreadful working conditions for themselves; it was the grounding they had received in Methodism, its undeniable connections to Chartism and the rights of man that drove them to fight to improve pay, terms, and conditions for the next generation. Since 1926, Dr Stross had been the 'Federation's chief medical advisor. A cultural young man of 27 was bound to be affected once confronted by the *"old"* youthful men of Stoke-on-Trent overwhelmed by lung disease, with its chronic cough and sputum, and the crippled former colliers now dependent on their wives and children for support. Stross's determination to see a free *National Health Service* would surely have been reinforced by the sight of this. The North Staffordshire Miners' Federation reciprocated the expert advice Dr Stross gave the 'Federation, and the free health care he proffered its poorest members by offering support for Stross's political campaigns. This increased in line with the popularity of fascism locally, Hitler's ascendancy, the British government's policy of appeasement and the bullying of China by Japan. This was a watertight relationship.

In March 1938, the North Staffordshire Miners' Federation protested vehemently against Chamberlain's appeasement to Hitler's aggressive annexation of the Sudetenland. It had the vision to set up a political fund, as noted in the minutes logged in its 1938 Yearbook. The same meeting saw an acknowledgement of a campaign by Dr Stross, who was campaigning to boycott the sale of Japanese goods in response to the *Manchurian Incident*, and how the executive approved of the pro Spanish Republican Government meetings being held in this District sponsored by Dr Stross and others—in fact the 'Federation contributed towards the printing and exhibiting costs for these meetings. Stross would have been the conduit too for the 'Federation making one-off payments, as well as an annual grant, to the fund which contributed towards the upkeep of Czech refugees who had been coming to North Staffordshire since 1936. The adults and children settled in the area with the help of the Czecho-Slovak – British Friendship Club. Upon arrival, they were basically destitute and needed complete support at first. The miners' contributions helped them to establish themselves.

But the Miners' Federation did not support everything. The Fund for *Help in Blitzed Areas* did was unsuccessful, *"We claim the right of considering and deciding if we shall make a grant, and what the amount is to be to this or any other fund."* Neither was The Spitfire Fund: *"it was agreed that we do not make any grant from our Federation Funds, but workers are at liberty to contribute at the pits if they so desire."* The North Staffordshire miners did support Lord Mayor, Austin Brook's campaign for a Youth Centre in Hanley in commemoration of Reginald Mitchell. And they did support other international campaigns such as *Aid for Spain, Aid to Russia,* and *Aid for China*. In the case of Russia, the funds were to buy urgent medical supplies. In accordance with the national executive, branches and their officials ran collections at pit-heads. Money was totalled up at the Miners' Hall, Burslem, prior to passing on to the national headquarters of 50, Russell Square, London.

Victoria Hall, Hanley

MASS RALLY

SUNDAY, Jan. 29th
7-30 p.m.

CHAIRMAN:
Coun. Dr. B. STROSS

COME AND HEAR THE TRUTH ABOUT

SPAIN

FROM —

CLIVE BRANSON
(Hon. Secretary British Battalion of International Brigade)

Col. J. C. WEDGWOOD, M.P.
Ald. A. HOLLINS, M.P.
Rev. T. HORWOOD

SPAIN'S CONQUEST MEANS BRITAIN'S PERIL

We Demand in the name of Justice
FOOD FOR ITS PEOPLE
ARMS FOR ITS SOLDIERS

Doors Open 6.30 p.m.   Come Early to avoid Disappointment
COMMUNITY SINGING
Balcony and Orchestra 6d. Pay at Door
Stewards from all quarters meet at 6 p.m.   ENTRANCE BY POLICE YARD

THE FALL OF BARCELONA IS NOT THE FINALE OF REPUBLICAN SPAIN'S STRUGGLE

Dr Barnett Stross, who presided, said that *"if the foreign invasion of Spain were successful and the Spanish people were defeated, it would also be Britain's defeat. That the Spanish Government had not been allowed to buy arms, as they were entitled to under international law, was the fault of the British Government. From 1931 up to that present time the National Government had a record which could not be surpassed for folly, stupidity, and reaction. Manchuria, Abyssinia and now Czecho-Slovakia had been betrayed and that betrayal destroyed the greatest bulwark of Europe - a bulwark set up by the blood of young men in the last war to prevent the very calamity they now saw before them."* About 2,000 people were present and a collection taken for the purpose of sending food to the Spanish people amounting to more than £112, exclusive of promises of foodstuffs valued at more than £50.

WE SAY THIS VILLAGE SHALL BE RE-MODELLED AND RE-BUILT

At a meeting of the District Council Executive on July the 13th, 1942 at the Miners' Hall, Burslem, the North Staffordshire Miners' Federation came out formally to support Dr Barnett Stross's proposal to rebuild Lidice. It is not clear from the Miners' Year Book who it is written by as the quote is uncredited, but it most probably came from then Secretary, Arthur Baddeley or President, Hugh Leese, as both were to play active roles in the movement to rebuild Lidice; Leese, in particular, had a history of campaigning. Whoever it is, there is a clear agenda to make the campaign international by gaining the support of the Mineworkers' Federation of Great Britain.

"... we support the proposal for the re-building of the mining village of Lidice in every possible way, and that we submit this proposal to the Midland Miners and, if approved, on to the National Federation and, if possible, make it an international question and let it be made known to the world. Though it has been totally destroyed, and our brother miners have been murdered, and the women and children battered and brutally treated by the Nazis, we say this village shall be re-modelled and re-built and the people shall rise and live again in a new spirit of fellowship and brotherhood. And to show our practical appreciation, Branches are requested to say if they would be willing for this Federation to make a grant not to exceed £100 towards this proposal and decided at the next District Council Meeting."

In calling for nationalisation, the North Staffordshire Miners' Federation called for the amalgamation of all the district organisations into one national body to stand for all the mineworkers of Great Britain. Talk between the federations at the Blackpool annual national conference had been ongoing since 1938. The Lidice Shall Live campaign was another clarion call for the nation's miners to come together as one and was sympathetic to the cause of public ownership.

The scheme envisioned by Dr Barnett Stross and the North Staffordshire Miners' Federation gained clear support from the Midlands Miners' Federation. George Jones, the Midlands Miners' Secretary from the Warwickshire branch put the proposal forward as a suggestion on behalf of his members on the 20th of July 1942, the opening day of the Mineworkers' Federation of Great Britain's Annual Conference at the Winter Gardens, Blackpool. The President, Will Lawther, was an eloquent speaker and a respected trade unionist. Proud Northumbrian with industrial roots, he became a collier on leaving school and soon became actively involved in the Northumberland Miners' Association. He at once empathised with the plight of the Czech mining community and saw the renewal of Lidice as a statement of defiance against Nazi tyranny.

With the sense of moral outrage still raw, Lawther's endorsement saw over 200 delegates representing 7,000,000 miners stand in silent tribute to their fallen comrades in Lidice as Alderman Jones referred to the:

"... wiping out of the Czecho-Slovak mining village in revenge for the death of Heydrich." Jones suggested that *"the miners of this country should join with the miners of the world in providing sufficient money to lay the foundations of a new Lidice - not in America, but on the ashes of the original village."*

When it was time for Will Lawther's address, it seemed the President of the Mineworkers' Federation of Great Britain had already decided:

"Especially do we refer to that mining village of Lidice in Czecho-Slovakia, where for the death of a human fiend named Heydrich, nigh every human soul has been wiped out; For that foul carnage of Lidice, for the butchery of Russian workers, for the suffering and toil that Fascism has imposed, we not merely bow our heads in silence, but renew our pledge to wipe out the slayers. Those assassins of liberty must pay the penalty."

Then, rounding off his speech with subliminal references to future undertakings, he said,

"There from the battle front, there from the Fatherland of Socialism comes the grim warning, and if I know my countrymen, my fellow miners, the response will be that the mark of the Fascist Beast shall be obliterated. All we have, all we can give, shall be freely given in order that freedom of the common people, liberty of the common man shall not perish but shall live for evermore to exalt and enrich all mankind."

As a final reference to Lawther's speech, it is a matter of conjecture how much the death of one of the 'Federation's most respected delegates the evening before the conference affected Lawther. Chief Clerk of the Miners' Federation, Mr Joseph Elliott, died at Blackpool's Victoria Hospital prior to the opening of the miners' conference. Mr Elliott had been in the Durham Miners' Association for 24 years and joined the 'Federation staff in 1937. Elliott was a great friend of Lawther's. He had fought in the First World War and had tried to enlist in the Second. It is exactly the Winter Garden event which could have stirred emotions in the President of the 'Federation - who paid a warm tribute to Joe in his opening address before requesting a minute's silence.

The Lidice Shall Live campaign turned out to be one of two solemn pledges carried within the conference's first hour, the other being a pledge to produce the coal Britain needed for victory. The speed of the campaign accelerated following the ratification. There was an immediate publication of a piece in Staffordshire's Evening Sentinel on the 21st of July describing the ambitious plans for the rebuilding of Lidice, the movement, and its national character. The article listed the chief drivers of the campaign as Dr Barnett Stross, the North Staffordshire Miners' Federation, and the Czecho-Slovak – British Friendship Club. Importantly, the aim was not revenge, but a creative solution to generate something of pioneering value from darkness. It announced the news of a launch and the likelihood of President Beneš attending. If Beneš had received a letter of invitation, so too had the Prime Minister and the Foreign Secretary. With millions taking an interest in the fate of Lidice, the pressure was intensifying for Anthony Eden MP to annul publicly the Munich Agreement.

At a later meeting of the North Staffordshire Miners' Federation, at the Miners' Hall, on the 10th of August, Dr Stross presented fresh news to the union executive - with a view to securing a greater depth of commitment from Britain's coal-mining communities:

"Some few weeks ago there was an Exhibition in the Hanley Art Gallery under the auspices of the Czecho-Slovak - British Friendship Club to commemorate Seven Years of Czecho-Slovak - Soviet Friendship. It was my privilege to thank the speakers which included the Lord Mayor of Stoke, Mr Shiborin, second Secretary to the Soviet Embassy, and Mr Mayer representative of the Czech Government, and to mention the destruction of the mining village of Lidice."

"I reminded the audience that the Nazis had put to death all the men, that the women were herded into concentration camps, and that the children had been taken away to be educated so as to learn to support the Nazis. The Ghost of the murderer Heydrich needed appeasement and the name of this village must be completely forgotten and no relic of it left standing. I declared at that Meeting what the Nazis had planned should never come to pass, and I would call other Civic Leaders of other Towns and Cities to support this, and I was sure that the Miners of Great Britain would act in this matter as they acted in the past and would declare their intention to help the innocent victims of this abominable outrage. The Miners would say to the world at large and to the Nazis in particular, that their comrades of Lidice would never be forgotten, and that the widows and orphans would be rescued, and that the village itself would be rebuilt as a lasting monument that this crime against humanity should never succeed."

"A report of this appeared in the Local Press and a discussion occurred among the members of the Czechoslovak State Council in London. *Dr Beneš himself is very anxious to see the next step and would gladly come to Stoke-on-Trent and speak on this subject.* He considers that such action would be of practical assistance to the Free Nations in their struggle against the Axis powers. Repeated broadcasts would give encouragement to the Czech people and to all who live under the Nazi heel."

"It must never be forgotten that centres of resistance exist everywhere in Europe and that the men who struggle in the underground movement need all the help we can give them. Such a pronouncement as this will give this help and men who are prepared to die will know that we shall never forsake their wives and children."

"There are other reasons why the Miners of Great Britain should take this step. The history of their opposition to fascism and oppression needs no advertisement but compels them to be in the van when a fresh blow is struck against the foe. By their action, the miners declare their International solidarity to all their comrades and to all men who are prepared to fight for freedom. The Miners' lamp dispels the shadows on the coal face. It can also send a ray of light across Europe to those who struggle in darkness."

"It is therefore proposed that the Miners of North Staffordshire, and through them the Miners of Great Britain, shall take the lead in establishing a fund earmarked for:

The rebuilding of Lidice.

The rescue of the widows and orphans of those who were murdered.

A committee of Architects and other experts shall be created to draw the plans of a village which shall be a model to the world at large of what a mining village should be. These plans will be available to all and should leave their mark not only on rebuilt Lidice but everywhere else."

Later, Dr Stross informed the Executive Board that a rally had been fixed for September the 6th, at the Victoria Hall, Hanley, and confirmed the attendance of Dr Edvard Beneš and other Czech Ministers, together with the Mineworkers' Federation of Great Britain's President and Secretary, Messrs Will Lawther and Ebby Edwards, respectively.

Dr Stross's moving appeal for the rebuilding of Lidice captured the hearts and minds of the miners and the other attendees. He praised and encouraged the miners, saying how the appeal, the first in the country, was being taken up by all sections of society. Considering events, he requested the miners emulate their earlier efforts to Spain and Russia. When he had finished, the executive warmly thanked Dr Stross for his address and decided that his suggestions be recommended to the area branches.

From the kernel of their Chartist roots, the fundamental principles of all trade unions were the struggles for social justice; particularly relevant for the miners, given the working conditions they endured and the ever-present threat of mortal wounding or even sudden death.

The early 20th century executive of the North Staffordshire Miners' Federation followed a creative "moral force" manifesto for its members which saw the provision of new cottages for its members, social clubs, sports grounds and facilities for workers, aid to international causes, aid for national causes, local charitable causes; as well as funds to support dependent families following pit disasters, and the hosting of events relevant to the local, regional, and national 'Federation. Much of the aforementioned was achieved in the spirit of moral force, through leading by example and successfully inviting colliery owners to contribute.

It was a strategy which would be employed in the creation and prosecution of the Lidice Shall Live campaign.

At the Miners' Hall, Burslem on Friday, September the 4th, the executive of the North Staffordshire Miners' Federation declared:

5. *That our District Secretary, along with the Trustees, pay over to the "Lidice shall Live" fund, the sum of £1,250 out of the funds of our Federation.*

6. "MINERS' GUARD OF HONOUR."—

That we approve and appreciate the efforts made by the Committee and Members of the Deep Pits Branch to provide a Guard of Honour for the meeting at Hanley, on September 6th, and:

7. That we thank the Management of the Shelton Deep Pits for the provision of Helmets and Cap Lamps for the occasion, and that we arrange for a number of our present delegates to make up the number for the Guard of Honour.

It seemed all was in order.

THE CZECHO-SLOVAK BRITISH FRIENDSHIP CLUB

Ann Swingler was an important figure in the resettlement of Czech refugees. She left school at 14 and took a secretarial course with the Workers' Education Association (WEA) which led to a job at the Labour Research Department. Like Dr Stross, she was enthusiastic about adult education, and became a part-time lecturer in *Community Responsibility*. An active supporter of trade unions, she joined the front line of the 1930s hunger marches and was present during several London strikes and campaigns to defeat the *British Union of Fascists* and its leader Oswald Mosley. In 1935, at 20 years of age, Ann travelled alone through Nazi Germany, returning with accounts of antisemitism and the one-party threat to Europe's democracies. It was whilst working for the Research Department that she met Oxford student Stephen Swingler. They came together through their political affiliations and married within months. Though communist leaning in their affiliations, Stephen admitted that to achieve any influence it would be necessary to join the Labour Party. This he did in 1937 and the young couple came to live in North Staffordshire where they both tutored for the WEA. Like the Mosleys, the Swinglers' choice of the Stoke-on-Trent district as political home inevitably involved a significant slice of missionary resolve to implement *"God's work,"* arguably *de haut en bas,* tied to a fascination with the Mosleys' relationship with the people of the area.

The two activists befriended a Jewish, Czech immigrant named Hans (Jan) Strasser and a German Jewish immigrant named Franz (Frank) Hampl. The four of them met in the interests of mutual aid to help the resettlement of Czech refugees; and Strasser introduced his friends to Dr Stross, the Shelton GP; and to a supportive Stoke-on-Trent City Cllr, Austin Brook, accountant, future Lord Mayor, and neighbour to Strasser on Waterloo Road in Cobridge. The Swinglers, Strasser, Hampl, Stross and others combined to create a new national branch of the Czecho-Slovak – British Friendship Club - an organisation whose primary aim was the successful relocation of increasing numbers of refugees fleeing the subterfuge of Nazism. Dr Barnett Stross, with his creativity, connections, and supporters both abroad and within the local community, became an important and valued partner.

The general feeling of repugnance across society at the sheer duplicity and level of pandering which came attached to the Munich Agreement was discernible. The club was to receive significant support from much of the community, including the unions, the council, and the public, all of whom sought a tangible way of making it up to the Czecho-Slovak people for their former Prime Minister's actions. Not only had the British Government been embarrassed because of the efforts to placate Herr Hitler through the policy of appeasement, but the black stain of dishonour had also cast a shadow over the entire population; something completely unjustified when one considered the very active work done by many in Britain to combat fascism on a daily basis.

The inauguration of the North Staffordshire Branch of the Czecho-Slovak - British Friendship Club was announced on the evening of Saturday the 1st of November 1938 by its Chairman, Jan Strasser, in front of an audience at Wellington Road Senior School, Hanley. An audience had come to see a range of drama pieces to celebrate Czech Independence Day – the 28th of October. Strasser, who had escaped Jewish persecution by fleeing his own town of Teplice in Nazi occupied Sudetenland earlier in the year, explained his optimism for the project. Many leading personalities in the area had already agreed to be patrons.

He said their aim was for a *"complete understanding between the Czech and British peoples."*

Meetings and entertainments would be arranged and prominent British and Czechs would address the members.

Hitherto, Frank Hampl is undoubtedly the least known character in proportion to his contribution to the movement. Hampl's determination and dedication to the cause as Secretary of the Lidice Shall Live Committee in Stoke-on-Trent and then later in London ensured the campaign disseminated itself to all parts of the nation and eventually found an international voice. On March the 16th, 1939 Hampl turned up at a youth hostel at Ravenstor, near Buxton, with about 30 or 40 fellow refugees fleeing antisemitic persecution. He knew practically no English but gradually picked it up and was reunited with his wife and two children. They lived on London Road, Stoke. Both found employment with a local dental surgeon and Cllr for Stoke-on-Trent City Council, Mr A. A. Wain, an associate of Dr Stross. Later, it was Stross who called upon Wain to ask if he would release Mr Hampl for a few weeks in order that he could help organise the Lidice Shall Live campaign.

According to Wain: "I readily agreed to this because I was only finding him employment out of a desire to help him. He did not return to me after that but continued to organise this work throughout the country."

The Stross family too had left Poland at the turn of the century to escape a flare up of antisemitism moving in from the East. But this time the accession of Hitler and his National Socialists in 1933 had brought antisemitism and the threat of another war to the West. Germany's Third Reich was looking for scapegoats for its defeat in the First World War. Activities against Europe's populations were ominously drawing war closer to home. Stross was someone already involved in the resettlement of betrayed Czecho-Slovakian nationals and was helping Jewish refugees. However, he understood the effects persistent austerity can inflict on communities and the division it can cause. He had seen it in the Stoke constituency in 1931 with the near political success of Oswald Mosley and the increasingly totalitarian voice of the *New Party*. For Barnett Stross, it was necessary to provide a moral, creative good during these dangerous, transformative times.

Stross, along with the other Jewish immigrants and other members of the Club would have been severely affected by harrowing reports about the maltreatment of Jews in his ancestral home of Pabianice. Fed through the national and local newspapers with increasing frequency, news of the Nazi horrors became more brazen and terrible. Indeed, as early as the 27th of January 1940, Stross and his fellow campaigners in the Czecho-Slovak - British Friendship Club, and the North Staffordshire Miners' Federation, would have read in the Evening Sentinel, how the Nazi paper *Das Schwarze Korps*, the organ of Heinrich Himmler, described how the Nazis intended to treat the Poles:

"No German comrade can be expected to breathe the same air as a Pole...A complete physical and cultural separation between Germans and Poles is inevitable."

Then on June the 30th, 1942, a mere 20 days following the tragedy in Lidice, the British national popular newspaper, The Daily Herald broke the news:

"400,000 Died in Nazi Gas Chambers"..."GAS-CHAMBER executions by the Nazis were described in London yesterday to the British section of the World Jewish Congress. Dr I. Schwarzbart, a member of the National Council of Poland:"

"Between November 1941 and March 1942 about 5,000 Jews from the towns of Koło, Dąb, Bugaj and Izbica, and about 35,000 from the ghetto of Łódź were taken to the town of Chełmno, in the Kolski district. There a new method of slaughtering was applied to them...They were herded into mobile gas chambers and were gassed to death. Their bodies were buried in the Lubarski Forest."

"Compiled from secret sources by the Governments of Poland, Czecho-Slovakia and Russia, reports given to the Congress tell of barbarism unequalled in history. They told how Jews deported from Holland, Germany and Czecho-Slovakia are being shot in Central Poland at the rate of a thousand a day. Case after case was given in which the entire Jewish populations of towns were wiped out."

The press conference in London reported that one million Jewish people had already been killed. The figures reported in the media were treated sceptically by many British and Allied politicians. At the time it was politically and emotionally pragmatic to do so. However, in the numbness encapsulated by the shocking figures there still lingered in the minds of millions the growing realisation that a malevolent force was wreaking havoc across Europe because the free world had chosen the path of least resistance in response.

Though a humanitarian, campaigning for those in Manchuria, Spain, Russia on the international stage, and the pottery, steel and coal workers on his doorstep, Dr Stross's impassioned disapproval of the Munich Agreement is noteworthy in the minutes recorded at meetings of the local Czecho-Slovak - British Friendship Club. One such example is a speech given by Barnett Stross on the evening of Thursday the 22nd of January 1942 at Hanley Town Hall, where he spoke about the bond between Great Britain and Czecho-Slovakia.

Jan Strasser, who presided kicked things off by recalling that Stoke-on-Trent was one of the first places in the country to hold a mass meeting of protest in 1938 against the Munich Pact. Dr Stross then proceeded to trace the gradual worsening of the international situation from 1931 onwards and said that from that time, when the Japanese invaded Manchuria, many of them feared that Britain was

"...gaining the reputation of truckling to the strong, of having sympathy with the Nazis and Fascists and antipathy towards the righteous demands of the democratic states, including the most democratic of all Czecho-Slovakia."

Discussing the Munich crisis of 1938, Dr Stross described the attitude adopted by the then Prime Minister, Mr Chamberlain as one of an exceptionalist who spoke of *"a dispute in a far-off country between two peoples of whom we knew nothing"*. Contrastingly, Mr Churchill, spoke of a model democratic state having been *"devoured"* by a betrayal. Stross described how the Munich Pact meant the loss to the democratic powers of the Skoda works, the best armament works in the world and its great mass of war equipment and of the labour of 15 million people who were now being forced to work for a Nazi state. Shortly after Munich, Soviet Russia proposed a final effort for collective security by the remaining democratic states, but Mr Chamberlain dismissed the proposal as *"premature"*. As a result, Russia signed a non-aggression pact with Germany, being driven into the kind of isolation hitherto practised in this country. Nevertheless, after the Russians had invaded the parts of Poland which formerly were theirs, captured Polish and Czech pilots began to arrive in this country, having come by sea via Turkey and the Cape. They were sent here by Russia to play their part in saving Britain from falling.

Of the Battle of Britain, Dr Stross said this proved that despite all the mistakes of the old men, the youth of this country saved the world. Had Britain fallen, the weight of the whole of Europe would have been thrown against Russia. Was it not possible that for some hundreds of years the world might have fallen back into barbarism under Nazi and Fascist rule? Dr Stross said British experts prophesied that Russia could not stand up against the German Army; that her aeroplanes were held together with string; that her tanks would not "go;" that the Russians were not a mechanical race and could not repair their weaponry. Hitler himself believed that he could beat the Russians, not in six weeks, but in three. Now, the Germans had been thrown back from the very gates of Moscow. There had been no Russian quislings. The tide had turned, Britain's strength was rising, and with the unlimited resources of America coming into play, he believed the time to victory was short. To the Czechs he would say this:

"The British people, as a people, did not betray you, but would have gone to war on your behalf. It is not likely that the people of these islands will ever again allow any men, old or young, to say that what happens in a far-off country to a free people is no concern of theirs."

A clue as to the interconnectivity between the Friendship Club and the North Staffordshire Miners' Federation, with Dr Stross as conduit, is provided by the contents of this article which appeared in Stoke-on-Trent's Evening Sentinel on the 26th of February 1942 for two appeals involving Czech artists performing to raise funds for the Sneyd Pit Disaster Fund at the Spode Works in Stoke:

"...Two interesting ceremonies were performed at the lunch hour concert at the Spode Works before a large audience, when owing to the unavoidable absence of Madam Liza Fuchsová, the famous Czech pianist, Dr Percy Young deputised at short notice and kept the audience highly entertained and amused with guessing games and community singing:

A collection by the employees during the week resulted in Mr Hans Strasser *(Secretary of the Czecho-Slovak - British Friendship Club)* **receiving from Mr J. A. Harvey two cheques to the value of £6 6s to add to the amount raised at the recent concert given by Madam Fuchsová in aid of the Sneyd Relief Fund and Czech Children's Homes."**

On Tuesday, the 8th of June 1943, in the Staffordshire Evening Sentinel, it was reported how Hugh Leese, Secretary of the North Staffordshire Miners' Federation, would be addressing the Czecho-Slovak - British Friendship Club, 15 High Street, Hanley the following evening on *Lidice and Britain*. It is a matter of conjecture as to what Mr Leese's address would have included but loosely it can be assumed that the North Staffordshire Miners' Federation had taken on a responsibility of approaching other mining federations and through Hugh Leese and its President Arthur Baddeley its moral role was to keep other campaigners informed. It is around this time Hugh Leese, as representative of the Lidice Shall Live committee, would be reporting on the positive reactions across the Midlands and other areas, including Birmingham, Derby, Coventry, and Nottingham.

There would be an exchange of information, with Jan Strasser, Frank Hampl and/or Barnett Stross, updating the group on other national and international contributions and developments. News of developments in the USA might also be broached at these meetings. We can also assume that they would have talked about future fundraising ideas and collaborations and how to increase the spread of the Lidice Shall Live movement

A GATHERING STORM AND A FRANK EXCHANGE

Formal negotiations on the renouncement of the Munich Agreement began at the end of January 1942. At a luncheon given by Anthony Eden on January the 21st and attended by Dr Beneš; Ambassador to Czecho-Slovakia, Philip Nichols; and Hubert Ripka, Czechoslovak Secretary of State for Foreign Affairs, Beneš was asked by Eden to prepare a proposal addressing the consequences of the Munich Conference - which would be acceptable to the British Government. Beneš's paper was titled *Principles for the agreement between the Czechoslovak and British Governments.* Inside, the President-in-exile argued that any decisions made regarding Czechoslovakia since September 1938 were not valid in international law because they were imposed on Czechoslovakia under duress or by violation of international treaties and Czechoslovak laws; and also, that the pre-Munich legal status of Czechoslovakia should be restored and confirmed by the victorious Allied countries during any negotiations concerning post-war re-organisation.

In response, the British Government took a cautious stance. It was prepared to annul Munich and recognize the Czechoslovak Government-in-exile's jurisdiction in British territory over all nationals from the former Czechoslovak Republic on the condition that adequate Sudeten representation was given in the State Council. This condition was expressly stated by Philip Nichols on February the 5th, 1942, during his conversation with Hubert Ripka, which was again confirmed by Nichols on February the 28th. This was flatly opposed by the Czechoslovak Government-in-exile and negotiations were deadlocked until May.

Things changed dramatically following the assassination of Heydrich, as reports hit Britain of the savage Nazi reprisals meted out against Czech civilians. Edvard Beneš sent Anthony Eden another compromise proposal on the 4th of June asking that the British Government recognize the legal continuity of the Czechoslovak Republic.

Developments took a further turn with the news of Lidice and the growing reaction to it throughout the mining communities of Britain.

On Tuesday, July the 7th, 1942 Dr Beneš, Jan Masaryk and Hubert Ripka met Eden and Nichols once more and reached an Agreement which was approved the same day by the British War Cabinet. In this solution the British would renounce the Munich Agreement provided that their legal view concerning the validity of the Agreement during the period up to March the 15th, 1939 was not challenged. The question of the participation of the Sudeten Germans in the Czechoslovak State Council was postponed until a future convenient time, which in fact never came about. The same applied also in respect to the recognition of the Czechoslovak theory of legal continuity of the Czechoslovak Republic. The British still maintained their reservations concerning the final resolution of the question of the Czechoslovak German minority.

What followed was a month-long hiatus with no public announcement or press release; and yet Government ministers and the Foreign Secretary Eden would undoubtedly be aware of the groundswell of support for the growing calls to build Lidice anew amongst Britain's mining communities – and especially since the miners had overwhelmingly ratified the Lidice Shall Live campaign at their national conference at Blackpool on the 20th of July. On Tuesday the 4th of August, North Staffordshire's newspaper the *Evening Sentinel* confirmed the news that Dr Beneš had already accepted an invitation sent to him by the Lord Mayor of Stoke-on-Trent Alderman Harry McBrine, to visit the Potteries officially to launch the Lidice Shall Live scheme - and it was hoped that a cabinet minister, possibly Sir Stafford Cripps or Anthony Eden, would also be present. The civic heads of the Midlands cities along with national miners' President Will Lawther had also been invited to attend.

For the matter of *"Munich"* to be left unresolved at a time when the output of coal was such a crucial factor in the nation's fortunes and when the miners had sent out such a clear message of their intent in support of the Czecho-Slovak people was reckless and irresponsible. Eden turned a potentially embarrassing situation into an opportunity:

On Wednesday the 5th of August 1942, Foreign Secretary Eden announced in the House of Commons that he had exchanged notes with the Czecho-Slovak Foreign Minister, Jan Masaryk, in which he stated that the policy of the British Government in regard to Czecho-Slovakia was guided by the formal act of recognition of the Czecho-Slovak Government in July 1941, and by the Prime Minister's statement in September 1940, that the Munich agreement *"had been destroyed by the Germans"*. The notes show a British Government attempting to abrogate itself from any sense of moral responsibility for the consequences of the Munich Agreement. Mr. Eden's note dated August the 5th stated: "*...in order to avoid any possible misunderstanding,* **I desire to declare on behalf of His Majesty's Government in the United Kingdom that as Germany has deliberately destroyed the arrangements concerning Czechoslovakia reached in 1938, in which His Majesty's Government in the United Kingdom participated, his Majesty's Government regard themselves as free from any engagements in this respect. At the final settlement of the Czechoslovak frontiers to be reached at the end of the war, they will not be influenced by any changes effected in and since 1938.**"

Mr Masaryk's reply expressed "warm thanks" on behalf of his government and himself, "**as well as in the name of the whole Czecho-Slovak people, who are at present suffering so terribly under the Nazi yoke.**" His government accepted Mr. Eden's note as a practical solution of the questions and difficulties of vital importance for Czecho-Slovakia which emerged as the consequence of the Munich agreement and considered it as a "**highly significant act of justice towards Czecho-Slovakia.**" In closure, Masaryk went on to "*assure you of our real satisfaction and of our profound gratitude to your great country and nation. Between our two countries the Munich Agreement can now be considered as dead.*"

In the House of Commons, during his response to Jan Masaryk's acceptance, Mr Eden added: "**I should not like to let this occasion pass without paying tribute on behalf of the British Government to the tenacious and courageous stand which the Czecho-Slovak people are making against their ruthless German oppressors.** *Acts such as the destruction of Lidice have stirred the conscience of the civilized world and will not be forgotten when the time comes to settle accounts with their perpetrators.*"

Later that day in a broadcast to the people of Czecho-Slovakia, Masaryk was less reserved in his views about the British Government's actions:

"The pre-Munich Republic of Czechoslovakia will take its seat at the peace conference, ready to come to agreement but irrevocably determined to defend all its sovereign rights and prerogatives. I know only the frontiers of the republic as they existed before "Munich". I have represented this point of view ever since the day when I gave up the London Legation after the Munich agreement had been signed, and today I and all of us received full satisfaction. Foreign Secretary Eden, in his speech (in the Commons), thanked you for your manly and courageous resistance to the Hun scum, and he officially promised that they will have to pay the reckoning. Retribution for Lidice will be our concern."

"I can assure Foreign Secretary Eden in your name that that is also your and our position - no pardon, no mercy, no forgiveness...*The Czechoslovak Republic of the summer of 1938 lives and will live for ages.*"

There was a fitting closure to the renouncement process which took place just four days before the launch of the movement in Hanley. It was an informal exchange of letters between Edvard Beneš and Churchill. In his letter of September, the 2nd 1942 Churchill wrote:

"You already know my attitude toward the Munich Agreement. Two years ago, I said publicly that it had been destroyed by the Germans. It therefore gives me particular satisfaction that our two Governments have formally placed on record their agreement that Munich can now be considered as dead between them. The exchange of letters of August 5th is a further proof to the whole world that the days of compromise with aggression and tyranny are now long past. My hope is that it may also prove a source of inspiration and encouragement to your compatriots at home who are suffering so terribly under the German yoke."

The British Government however *did not agree* with the Czechoslovak Government-in-exile's stance regarding Munich. Basically, unlike Charles de Gaulle who denounced the Munich Diktat completely, the British Government stood by Chamberlain's actions in considering that surrendering the Sudetenland to Hitler was a potentially reasonable solution to the European crisis - and for the Czechoslovak people at the time; if only Nazi Germany had kept its word and not followed up its gains with a full occupation of the Czech nation on the 15th of March 1939...

THE BIRTH OF THE MOVEMENT											The Path to Lidice

Clockwise: Anthony Eden, British Foreign Secretary; Dr Edvard Beneš, Czechoslovak President-in-exile; Jan Masaryk, Czechoslovak Foreign Minister; Sir Stafford Cripps, Leader of the House / Lord of the Privy Seal; Sir Philip Nichols, British Ambassador to Czechoslovakia; Hubert Ripka, Czechoslovak Secretary of State for Foreign Affairs. During the late summer of 1942, as the launch date for the Lidice Shall Live campaign appeared on the horizon, pressures to publicly revoke the Munich Agreement intensified.

LAUNCHING THE MOVEMENT

CLARIFYING THE OBJECTIVES

On Saturday the 8th of August, the Evening Sentinel reported on a meeting which took place the day before at Stoke Town Hall. A committee of activists, all heavily involved in the Lidice Shall Live project and led by Dr Barnett Stross – met to discuss arrangements for the launch at the Victoria Hall on the 6th of September. Although it mentions no other names, we can assume members of Stoke-on-Trent City Council were present, along with the executive of the North Staffordshire Miners' Federation and North Staffordshire Branch of the Czecho-Slovak - British Friendship Club. Although it does not expressly say so, it sounds like the press received a resume from Dr Stross listing the campaign's objectives:

"The object of the fund is to rebuild Lidice - the martyred Czecho-Slovakian village destroyed by the Germans - as a model mining village.

The idea has been enthusiastically adopted by North Staffordshire miners, who have already agreed to a voluntary levy on all members of the North Stafford Miners' Federation as heavy as any levy they have ever had for a similar cause.

Midland miners are following the lead of North Staffs wholeheartedly, and, as soon as the scheme has been officially launched.

It is expected that the campaign will become nation-wide and will spread to America."

Dr Barnett Stross c 1945 in relaxed mood

Stross made the point that as the idea was born in Stoke-on-Trent, it was right that the campaign should be officially launched in the city. He announced that many of the Czechoslovakian ministers, in addition to Dr Beneš, had expressed their desire to be present because they saw in it **not merely a material help to their country after the war, but an immediate act intended to cement the friendship of the two countries.** The point was made that **"ways and means"** would be found to keep the world informed of the progress of the scheme and therefore give hope to people in all occupied countries. In so doing the movement would be symbolic of the new order of friendship between nations to which the Allies have pledged themselves.

The committee made it clear that Leader of the House,' Sir Stafford Cripps would be unable to attend; but they expected to receive either Anthony Eden, the Foreign Secretary, or Mr Brendan Bracken, the Minister of Information on the Government's behalf. They further announced that Mr Will Lawther and Mr Ebby Edwards would be the miners' chief representatives. And already many of the civic heads of Midland cities and towns had promised to take part in the proceedings. Dr Stross added that after the launching of the scheme, local committees would be set up in all parts of the country, working under the umbrella of a central National Committee, but that the Stoke-on-Trent Committee would be making all arrangements until then, and any donations in the meantime should be sent to Mr J. T. Garratt, Lord Mayor's Secretary, Stoke-on-Trent.

The response to the assassination of Heydrich and to the destruction at Lidice and the smaller village of Ležáky had been huge. Now the Lidice Shall Live movement was about to burst into life all over the free world, and soon the word *Lidice* would become synonymous with Nazi oppression. With the gravity of public support on his side, Beneš and his Foreign Secretary, Jan Masaryk, convinced the British Government to ditch its Munich obligations once and for all. Radio joined the campaign as the news was fully celebrated on BBC broadcasts and on newsreel, with President Beneš reading a special address on the revoking of the Munich Pact on the 8th of August.

THE SPIRIT OF 1842

The spirit of Chartism revisited North Staffordshire during the weekend of Friday the 28th to Sunday the 30th of August 1942, when a series of three mass meetings were held across the City of Stoke-on-Trent. The rallies were organised by Albert Bennett, a key figure in the local trade union movement and someone with Chartist sensibilities, to create an atmosphere of excitement in The Potteries the week before the launch of the Lidice Shall Live campaign at the Victoria Hall.

According to news reports the meetings were held at Fenton, Smallthorne and in the open air of Hanley's Market Square. All were well attended. Bennett, who was to play a significant role in the future economic development of Stoke-on-Trent, was joined by guest speakers Dr Barnett Stross and the former collier, now MP for Llanelli Mr Jim Griffiths. The future Secretary of State for Wales was in Stoke-on-Trent to resurrect the spirits of inspirational local 19th century Chartist leaders such as John Richards, Joseph Capper, and Thomas Cooper. Griffiths, Stross, and Bennett roused the good men and women of Stoke-on-Trent with talk of social and industrial lineage, the dignity of labour, *moral force* and, of course the need to beat Hitler.

It was a mere fortnight since the centenary of the Chartist riots across the Potteries, which had seen miners, pottery workers and their families unleash a torrent of violence and abuse at the British Government, its local agents and beneficiaries on the 15th and 16th August 1842. The trouble was reported nationally as the most violent, belligerent display of class conflict yet seen in Great Britain. There were severe ramifications for the perpetrators, but also the innocent too, as many people legitimately protesting for their rights that weekend were severely punished, flogged, or even transported to Australia. While today the riots may seem in the distant past for some, in 1942 - in a world without a National Health Service, decent social housing and welfare state, the story of the Chartists was not too far in the dim and distant past; and the cause seemed as relevant as ever.

The first meeting, held at Fenton Town Hall saw Jim Griffiths deal with various aspects of the war situation. Churchill had recently visited the Soviet Union and Griffiths emphasised the significance of this action. He explained:

"...when they spoke of aid for Russia, they really meant aid for us." Mr Griffiths also expressed the view that Britain's propaganda was not convincing people of the seriousness of the situation, in that

"...its people realised what they were fighting against but did not really know what they were fighting for."

In his opinion, this was a missed opportunity for although this was admittedly **"a great war"**, it was inevitably creating a great revolution in ideas and concepts. Therefore, he appealed to the miners to do their utmost to ensure that the nation had the coal it needed to produce weapons of war, and for other essential purposes. The miners were playing a great and important part in the war effort, and all engaged in the mining industry should feel that they had an individual responsibility to the nation.

This was most forcefully reiterated during an inspirational address in Hanley's Market Square. Mr Griffiths described to his audience how one hundred years ago their forefathers had gathered at the same place under the Chartists' banner to press their claims upon the government of the day.

"That night, he said, they claimed the right to present their views on the policies now being pursued by the Government. In exercising that right, however, they must remember that it carried obligations. They must be prepared and anxious to put every ounce of strength into their job so that, first of all, victory, full and complete, over Hitler might be obtained."

STOKE-ON-TRENT LIVE

The meeting which launched the Lidice Shall Live movement was preceded by a colourful pageant organised by Barnett Stross, which assembled outside Hanley Town Hall in the morning.

"Our most memorable occasion was to be part of a large parade in support of the victims of the Lidice massacre organised by our local MP Dr Barnett Stross. The parade gathered outside Hanley Town Hall, down Cheapside and along Bagnall Street and consisted of Army, Navy and Air Force cadets, the A.R.P, W.V.S., Salvation Army and the British Legion and us."

The parade was to leave the square and go down Albion Street to end at Hanley Park for a rally. There were several bands set to play at various times. Marching bands led the way as the procession made its way down through Piccadilly, on to Stoke Road and along Park Avenue.

"…our turn came quite early halfway down Broad Street. We were so anxious to make the biggest possible noise ever that in our enthusiasm we lost the sound of the big drum and our tempo. Consequently, as we got louder, we got faster, and Peter broke a drumstick; but quickly reached behind and took one off a boy playing a kettle drum. Confusion reigned for a while and the parade behind us nearly broke into a trot. We were eventually stopped but nevertheless we were satisfied that the Tinkersclough Lads Brigade had given a good account of themselves."

Don Barnes, a Shelton lad.

Accompanied by Madame Beneš and members of the Czechoslovak Government-in-exile, Dr Beneš was met on his arrival in Stoke-on-Trent by the Earl of Harrowby, the Lord Lieutenant of Staffordshire. Following a short lunch with him, the party was welcomed in Hanley by Dr Stross and leaders of the new Lidice Shall Live committee before enjoying an enthusiastic reception comprising representatives from business, trade, and industry; the trade unions; the wider civic community; the church; and the general public from across the region. After the playing of the Czechoslovak National anthem, Beneš inspected a guard of honour, including members of the Home Guard, Cadet Corps, personnel of the Civil Defence Services, and a large contingent of North Staffordshire miners – the ardent backers of Dr Stross's proposal to rebuild Lidice - wearing their pit helmets.

Dr Edvard Beneš, the Czech President-in-exile, officially launched the Lidice Shall Live campaign at the Victoria Hall, Hanley, at 3pm on Sunday the 6th of September 1942:

Beneš, his Ministers and the rest of the Czecho-Slovak attendees saw in the faces of the people they met, not merely a material effort to help their country after the war, but a Statement of Disassociation with any aspect of the Munich Agreement. Although it had been recently annulled by Foreign Secretary Anthony Eden MP, in the face of massive growing support for greater Anglo-Czech relations, *interestingly only four weeks before this rally*, the vast majority of workers in Stoke-on-Trent had never agreed with it. And they were about to make it clear to Beneš and his party, outside and within the Victoria Hall. It was a message of encouragement and reassurance for all Czechs that most people, at least in the industrial Midlands, Wales, and the North, had felt empathy for the Czech cause all along.

Reporting on the event on the 7th of September, the Evening Sentinel wrote:

The Victoria Hall has been the scene of many noteworthy gatherings and many famous people have spoken from its platform. But never has the hall held an assembly so remarkable in its significance...

...Following a reception by the President in the Lord Mayor's Parlour there was an impressive procession to the Victoria Hall, led by members of the City Navy League and Army and Air Force Cadet Corps, carrying the flags of the 29 United Nations. They formed a guard of honour down the centre aisle of the Victoria Hall as the President walked to the rostrum, followed by Madame Beneš, the Deputy Lord Mayor of Stoke-on-Trent (Mr A.E. Hewitt), Lord Dudley (Midland Regional Commissioner), the Earl of Harrowby and the Bishop of Stafford (the Right Rev. L. D. Hammond). The representative of His Majesty's Government, Mr Philip B. B. Nichols, Envoy Extraordinary and Minister Plenipotentiary

to the Czecho-Slovak government was accompanied by M. Vecaslav Vilder, Envoy Extraordinary and Minister Plenipotentiary to the Czecho-Slovak government, representing the Prime Minister of Jugo-Slavia, and M. A. Bogomoloff, Envoy Extraordinary and Minister Plenipotentiary to the Czecho-Slovak government of the Union of Soviet Socialist Republics.

Ministers and representatives of the Czecho-Slovak government were General Ingr (Minister of Defence), Dr H. Ripka (Minister of State), Mr Prokop Maxa (Chairman, State Council), Mr David, M. Uhlir, Mr Majer, Mr Furth, and Mr Nosek (members of the State Council), Dr Drtina (Private Secretary to the President), Captain Veselý (Captain of the President's Guard), Captain Barták (Adjutant of the Minister of Defence), Professor Nugrin and Dr Tuchacek (Defence Ministry), along with Dr Peres, Mr Pollak, Mr Lobl and Mrs Glasner (Czech-British Friendship Club), and Frank Hampl (Secretary of the Lidice Shall Live movement).

Mr Ellis Smith MP and Sir Joseph Lamb MP were followed by Sir Francis Joseph Bart, Sir Ernest Johnson, Dr Barnett Stross, Mr Will Lawther (President of the Mineworkers' Federation of Great Britain), Mr E. N. Scott, the Chief Constable of Stoke-on-Trent (Mr F.L. Bunn), Colonel W. Greene, Captain T. Lockett, the Deputy Town Clerk of Stoke-on-Trent (Mr H. Taylor), Alderman C. A. Brook, Alderman G. J. Timmis, Alderman J. Barker, Alderman the Rev. T. Horwood, Alderman J. A. Dale, Mr Hugh Leese and Mr George Jones (Midland Miners' Federation), Mr G. H. Meir, Miss J. Kimpster and Mr J. T. Garratt. Concluding the procession, the Town Clerk of Stoke-on-Trent (Mr E. B. Sharpley) was accompanied by the Mayors of Rowley Regis, Congleton, Hereford, Rugby, Macclesfield, Oswestry, Buxton, Bilston, Stafford, and Crewe.

After the flags of the United Nations had been grouped around the organ, at which Dr S. Weale (City Organist) had given a recital of Czechoslovak music, the meeting started with the singing of "*All Hail the Power*" and a song by the Czechoslovak Army Choir. Introducing Lord Dudley, the Deputy Lord Mayor, Mr Hewitt, referred to the strong link which already existed between Czechoslovakia and North Staffordshire by reason of the pottery industry, and expressed the hope that the inauguration of the Lidice Shall Live movement would set alight a flame that would unite the two countries for time immemorial and not just for a few years after the war.

Lord Dudley, welcoming Dr Beneš, said the meeting was likely to prove historic. The outrage of Lidice had profoundly shocked the people of Great Britain, but it had had the effect of cementing the love and friendship which existed between the two nations. It had stimulated the British Empire that nothing should prevent us from obtaining the earliest possible victory so that Czecho-Slovakia and other occupied countries could be returned to their own peoples forever. The Deputy Lord Mayor then read messages of greeting from the American Ambassador, the Chinese Ambassador, the Prime Ministers of Poland, Norway, Belgium and Greece, the High Commissioner of New Zealand to Great Britain, the Archbishop of Canterbury, the Free Church Federal Council, and the Czechoslovakian Miners Committee in Great Britain. Similar messages were delivered by M. Vilder for Yugoslavia and by M. Alexander Bogomolov for the USSR.

Mr Philip Nichols said that the Leader of the House of Commons, Mr Anthony Eden had authorised him to tell of the British Government's greatest measure of moral support for the movement. Mr Eden had sent a message in which he said North Staffordshire had found a *practical way* of expressing the horror we all felt at German barbarities, and that,

"... the faith and confidence which inspired the movement was the right answer to Nazi tyranny and destruction and would encourage all the suffering populations of Europe." He said that the British Government had already made it their policy to ensure retribution for these crimes against humanity and they intended that Britain should play its full part in restoring the decencies of civilised life in the territories now overrun by the enemy.

Next, the Bishop of Stafford expressed the hope that many parishes in the diocese would give practical help to the movement.

Will Lawther, President of the Mineworkers' Federation of Great Britain, then approached the podium on the spacious stage of the capacity filled Victorian amphitheatre. He pledged the determination of all Britain's miners:

"...to rebuild Lidice and renew that faith and determination, and to see the struggle through to the bitter end. To the goal we have set ourselves with the rest of the United Nations, namely victory for liberty, freedom and democracy and death to Nazism and Fascism."

Lawther said that when they committed mass murder and arson at Lidice, the Nazis never realised that they had put a match to a fire which would not be put out until those who applied the match were destroyed. Peace would not come to a stricken world until that day arrived. On behalf of British miners, he could give the assurance that in every conceivable way they would do their share to sabotage the Nazi machine...

"Today," he said, **"it is essential to realise in this country that we are saved from the horrors of Lidice and the grim tragedy of the Donbas coalfield by the fact that we can keep on producing the weapons of war. Nothing is more vital than coal for the guns, tanks, and planes to avenge Lidice. It is no use giving our money if tomorrow we withhold, by any action of ours, from those men who are bombing Germany, from those who are "strafing" the foulest system, and most wicked of human scum, the weapons they need in their job."**

There was a great silence around the auditorium as Will Lawther told quietly a personal account, of a sacred pledge given him by one who gave his life against fascism. He was speaking of his younger brother, Clifford, who went out to fight in the Spanish Civil War with the International Brigade:

"...Father and mother had passed away and so my younger brother would write to me. This is one of the things he wrote: *"Will, wherever you can, give all your influence all your support, anything, to get men roused to fight this menace of Fascism, the greatest evil that mankind has ever faced. I am going up the line to give my life if necessary, so do what you can.""*

"To me," stated Lawther, **"that was a sacred trust which I cannot and will not betray."**

It was proving to be an emotional afternoon as the Czechoslovak Army Choir sang *Kde Domov Můj (Where My Home Is)* - the Czech national anthem, heralding the exiled Czech President, Dr Edvard Beneš to take to the rostrum. After expressing his appreciation and gratitude on behalf of the Czechoslovak Government-in-exile for the inauguration of the Lidice Shall Live movement, there was a pause before he took the microphone.

Then, in an emotional speech he emphasised that Lidice was only one of many victims of Nazi Germany's cruelty and oppression. He said:

"In the matter of fact there have undoubtedly been a number of similar crimes committed by the agents of the Herronvolk throughout occupied Europe. Villages have been exterminated in Norway, Poland, in Yugoslavia, in Russia and in other countries under German rule. But in all these other cases the Germans tried to conceal their barbarous action from the outside world. In the case of Lidice, on the other side, the crime was coldly premeditated in all details in the German press with evident joy and satisfaction."

"Lidice," he said, "has become a symbol of the terrible suffering of the Czecho-Slovak people in a particularly significant way. It has shown to the whole world the true meaning of the German New Order. It has revealed to civilised mankind the real character of the relationship between the master race and the despised inferior races who they have taken under their protection. I wish to say a few frank words about the justice which we hope to achieve after the war. To ask those who have suffered innocently as the victims of Lidice to forget and forgive, to ask their fellow countrymen to ignore it, it is not human, is not reasonable and is perhaps madness.

We want to see, we must see, this war through victoriously, whatever sacrifices it may cost us, in order to see a legal order reconstituted and all inhuman acts of the Germans, wherever committed, really punished. This is, in my opinion, the only way of reckoning with the Fascist tyrants wherever they appear. Only a hard lesson, not of revenge but of retributive justice, will teach the Germans that it does not pay to attack other nations.

I repeat I am not for revenge: I am for real justice; it is more than revenge. Only in this way will the German nation be convinced that they must not start a third world war within two generations."

Dr Beneš spoke of the grand alliance of the United Nations and forecast that it would swing from the defensive to a powerful offensive:

"Czecho-Slovakia," he said, "fights on and stands firmly on the side of the British Empire and of the United Nations. The evident manifestation of this active resistance to German domination is our Army and our Air Force, both here in Great Britain, in the Middle East and in Soviet Russia. They are fighting with their comrades, as in the last war, on all battle fronts. But the whole people of Czecho-Slovakia are engaged in this war of liberation. Our people at home are until now primarily concentrating on acts of sabotage which slow down the military machine of Nazi Germany. The day will come when the whole Czecho-Slovak nation will rise up to burst the bonds of tyranny."

He ended in addressing the people of Stoke-on-Trent by echoing the rallying cry of Dr Barnett Stross:

"With your generous help and our collaboration, Lidice, God willing, shall really live again. And we must all stand together in order to prepare, after victory has been achieved, a peace in Europe of which we could already have today solemnly declare that all we are passing through, now, today, in this war, will never happen again."

The audience of 3,000 men and women heard Dr Beneš's concluding remarks:

"This meeting has made it clear that Lidice has not died: it lives on in the hearts of the people of Stoke-on-Trent at least. From now on, Stoke-on-Trent will live forever in the heart of every Czech citizen."

At the conclusion of his address, Dr Beneš was presented with a buttonhole and Mrs Beneš with a bouquet, both handmade by Czechoslovak refugee children. The proceedings were fully recorded for broadcasting purposes. Before the meeting closed a vote of thanks was proposed by Dr Stross to Dr Beneš and those who had taken part. Finally, the President recorded a message in his own language to his countrymen serving with the Allied Forces or enslaved in Czecho-Slovakia.

A PROMISE AND A THREAT

A sign of the success of the launch was the quantity of national press and the extent to which the Movietone footage circulated. It would inspire sponsors and more authorities to set up their own committees. For the nation, the launch brought a sense of levity and creativity in the midst of the daily drudgery of wartime life - for despite new alliances nothing much had changed at ground zero. The launch also punched another hole in the shredded veil of integrity attached to the Munich Agreement – bringing together the British and Czechoslovak people. The fact that the campaign involved an international cross section of society, including ordinary working miners from Stoke-on-Trent as well as Czech, German, and Jewish refugees, and with a Polish, Jewish GP at the helm, was even better as far as Britain's leaders were concerned. The miners and trade unions were presenting a face of the nation that was ideal to the Coalition Government. *Where Nazi Germany was the model intolerant state so Britain was a model of accommodation.*

For Stoke-on-Trent, the meeting gave the city a huge lift following a dreadful first six months, following the disaster at the Sneyd Pit on the 1st of January. Not only was there a resoluteness about the people but the launch of the Lidice Shall Live campaign had brought them and their lives and industry to the attention of the world. The impact Beneš's presence had on the psyche of the Potteries' community can be gleaned from the report published in the Daily Herald, at the time Britain's favourite national newspaper the next day - Monday the 7th:

" "LIDICE SHALL LIVE!" - In these words, lies a promise and a threat. They mean that what Hitler has destroyed shall be recreated. They mean, too, that what Hitler has created shall be destroyed.

...at one of the most moving demonstrations I have ever known, it seemed almost possible to glimpse the new Lidice beginning to rise out of the blood-stained wreckage of old.

Dr Beneš, accompanied by some of his Ministers, took this part of Staffordshire by storm. People gathered in the streets to welcome him. There was a guard of honour of Home Guards, men and women of the Civil Defence Services, and miners with their steel hats and their lamps."

Encouraged by the success of the launch, Will Lawther at once authorised the making of a government-sponsored propaganda film telling the story of a *"Lidice"* played out in Britain. Directed by the young and innovative Humphrey Jennings it was produced by the British propagandist Crown Film Unit. It is called *The Silent Village* and its sublime use of community combined with the deadly narrative still emotionally impacts today *(see appendix)*.

On the following Wednesday, the 9th of September, the Evening Sentinel reported a press release from the Lord Mayor's Parlour at the Council Chambers in Stoke, that a fund for re-building Lidice had been opened by the Lord Mayor of Stoke-on-Trent, Cllr Harry McBrine, with a donation of £100, and that the North Staffordshire Miners' Federation had contributed £1,250, a result of a levy which the men made themselves of 2/6s or half a crown.

The article was accompanied by a statement from the Lord Mayor which read:

"**Lidice Shall Live was born in this city, and I hope that everyone who can, will assist. Mr Eden, the Minister for Foreign Affairs, told us through His Majesty's Ambassador to Czecho-Slovakia, that we had hard heads and warm hearts. This is our opportunity of proving that his estimate of us is justified. The will to give life to Lidice will become a great national movement, and I naturally would have Stoke-on-Trent ever to the fore..." Donations should be made payable to Stoke-on-Trent "Lidice Shall Live" Fund and should be addressed to The Lord Mayor, Town Hall, Stoke-on-Trent - Yours sincerely, H. W. McBrine, Lord Mayor. Lord Mayor's Parlour. Stoke-on-Trent, September 9th, 1942.**

The Deputy Lord Mayor of Stoke-on-Trent, Cllr Arthur Hewitt, received the following letter from Mr Prokop Maxa, President of the Czechoslovak State Council:

"**Having returned to London, I consider it my foremost and pleasant duty to thank you and all the members of the Stoke-on-Trent "Lidice Shall Live" Committee as well as all the speakers at Sunday's meeting and all those who have contributed to its splendid success, on behalf of the Czechoslovak State Council for the great reception you have bestowed upon us and for the glorious way in which you have honoured our country in general and the victims of Lidice in particular.**

We shall never forget this grand token of your friendship, which we trust will continue to strengthen and develop, and also enable us to repay you your generous hospitality, at least to some extent in our liberated homeland. I am sure that I am expressing a fervent common wish if I hope that the time of liberation is not too far off. Will you please kindly convey my message of gratitude also to the Right Honourable, the Earl of Dudley; His Worship the Lord Mayor; Dr Barnett Stross; and to all other committee members, speakers and functionaries who have assisted in arranging this memorable meeting."

Prokop Maxa

A few weeks later the Secretary of the North Staffordshire Miners' Federation, Hugh Leese received the following correspondence from Lieutenant Tomcik, of the Czechoslovak Forces in England:

Dear Sir,

As member of Czechoslovak Army Choir, I was present on last Sunday in Stoke-on-Trent at meeting in Victoria Hall, where the fund "Lidice Shall Live," was raised and inaugurated. Being schoolmaster in my country and active in Labour movement in Moravia, now Lieutenant of Czechoslovak Army in England, I do appreciate the human spirit and deep sympathy of English people; let me say of English working class, I have seen on Sunday last in Victoria Hall, towards my unhappy country and people of Lidice. The meeting was so impressive, at once I saw and felt the real spirit of English people, of miners, which in past years was so often different from that one in Downing Street. It was most impressive moment for me, after staying in this country more than 2 years. I wished only, the women and children of Lidice could see it too.

Due to my bad English, I can't express everything I felt at that moment and what I still do feel. I want to tell you only, that I am so grateful to you for everything you have done for "Lidice Shall Live" Committee. So, I would express my deepest gratitude to Staffordshire's Miners and working people, who raised this idea and are carrying it out. Please excuse my mistakes. Wishing you all the best.

I remain yours very sincerely, Mr H. Leese

J. TOMCIK.

Another example letter, received by Leese on the 17th of September and shared in the North Staffordshire Miners' Federation Year Book came from Hubert Ripka, former correspondent of the Czech newspaper Lidové Noviny, adviser to President Beneš and Czecho-Slovak Minister of State, who had this to say about the launch:

Dear Mr Leese,

I am writing to say how deeply moved I was by the Lidice Demonstration on September 6th. I should like to take this opportunity of expressing to you my heartfelt thanks for the support you have given to this scheme and to say how greatly we all appreciated your efforts on our behalf.

Yours sincerely,

HUBERT RIPKA.

The inaugural Lidice Shall Live Committee was formally constituted in Stoke-on-Trent in early October 1942 and comprised a mix of elected representatives, members of the North Staffordshire Czecho-Slovak - British Friendship Club, miners' delegates, Rotary Club members, members of the North Staffordshire Architectural Society and concerned, influential members of the public. The full list of members of first Lidice Shall Live committee is as follows:

Executive Committee:

Dr Barnett Stross (Chairman), Mr H. Booth (Vice Chairman), Mr Frank Hampl (Secretary), Mr Hugh Leese (Treasurer), Alderman Austin Brook, Mr J. B. Adams (Vice President North Staffordshire Architectural Society), Mr W. Emmott (Secretary Burslem Co-operative Society), Alderman G. Timmis, Mr George Meir, Mr Hubert Dudley, Mr Arthur Baddeley, Mr B. Berman and Miss Joyce Kimpster.

The Financial Sub-Committee:

Mr W. Emmott (Chairman), Mr F. W. Langley (President, Stoke-on-Trent Rotary Club), Mr H. Dudley, Mr A. Simcock, The Rev. A. Perry, Mr Arthur Baddeley, Mrs F. Hutchinson, Mr T. Garratt, Dr Barnett Stross and Mr Frank Hampl.

In mid-October 1942 Dr Beneš responded to an appeal sent by Mr Frank Hampl, Secretary of the Fund; accepting an invitation to become a patron and contributing personally £500. In the course of his letter to Hampl, Beneš stated:

"I was deeply impressed with the genuine sympathy and understanding for the suffering of our people. As to the kind suggestion that I should become a Patron of the movement, I will certainly do so. I feel that the steps you have taken in commemorating the name of Lidice in this fashion will have great moral significance and is a very sympathetic gesture to my afflicted country."

The success of the launch of the Lidice Shall Live movement was reflected in a flood of grassroots donations. This was picked up by the national press. Expectations were suitably high as the efforts of the fledgling committee were recognised in newspapers throughout autumn and into winter 1942. The Evening Sentinel carried the following headline on December the 7th:

The Lidice Fund: SUPPORT FROM MANY AREAS!

Since the first Lidice Shall Live Committee was organised and the mass meeting of September 6th was held, other areas and cities have adopted the movement. The Durham miners have subscribed £15,000, with £100,000 as their objective. The miners of the Midlands have also offered a levy of 2s.6d. per head, and the districts of Yorkshire, Lancashire and other areas are following suit. It is expected that contributions from miners alone will reach a large sum-between fifty and eighty thousand pounds.

Some articles contained a fair amount of promotional hyperbole and, in retrospect, fantastic claims in order to stir passions, raise national awareness and apply soft pressure for support on the Coalition Government. At this stage of the campaign, based on a keen reaction the fund's target ranged from £100,000 to £1 million. This could have been down to indecisiveness about the popularity or aims of the appeal. Quotes of £1 million could have been based on early plans to fund entirely the creation of a new Lidice, while smaller targets were accounting for a re-installed Czechoslovak Government funding the project with smaller contributions from Allies.

In the absence of any Lidice Shall Live committee minutes, the promotional strategy for the movement remains a matter of conjecture. It would be usual procedure for the secretary of a committee to send press releases out. In this instance, that would be Frank Hampl. But whether Frank wrote them in reality is another matter. The newspaper went on to report the list of donations. It provides a picture of a campaign with broad, grassroots appeal, reflecting the general sense of empathy for the Czech nation which existed at the time:

"A mass meeting has been arranged for February at Birmingham, where the Lord Mayor has signified that he will adopt the scheme. Following the lead of the Birmingham Trades Council, many organisations are in favour. During this month, a committee is being

formed at Leeds, and the Lord Provost of Edinburgh has signified his interest. Other cities, including Leicester, are expected to follow suit."

"The efforts in Stoke-on-Trent are meeting with considerable success and it is expected that the £10,000 mark will be reached by next autumn. The district is not rich, as some other cities are, or so populous, but the committee fully expect exceptional support in Stoke-on-Trent, where the idea originated. Two things are needed if Lidice is to be rebuilt on its ashes. One is the site and the other the money. For the former we need victory. Both factors are now attainable."

STOKE-ON-TRENT FUND – *as reported on the 7th of December 1942*

Second List of Donations:

	£	s	d
Amounts previously acknowledged	1,721	10	3
His Excellency Dr Edvard Beneš	500	0	0
Burslem and District Industrial Co-operative Society	100	0	0
Collections at Exhibition of Czech Art, Leamington Spa	100	0	0
Hanley Hospital Supply Depot and Sub-Depots	70	0	0
Mr J. C. Holdcroft, Dance, King's Hall, Stoke	69	0	0
National Society of Pottery Workers	20	0	0
Staff and Workers, Messrs Beaton and Son	16	5	0
North Staffordshire Teachers' Association	10	10	0
Hanley Housewives	10	2	4
C. E. Girls' Club, Cheadle	10	0	0

North Staffordshire Branch, Cinematograph Exhibitors' Association, £5 5s; Durham County Colliery Association Crookgate Branch, £5; Medical Services Cauldon Depot £13 13s; Hanley Section, Burslem Co-operative Society, £3 6s 3d; South Wales Miners' Association, Area 4, Park and Dare Lodge, £3 3s; Mr Raymond Edwards, Wolverhampton, £2 10s; Mrs L Wright and friends, Harriseahead £2 3s 6d; British Red Cross, Burslem Branch Staffs, 86 V.A.D. £2 2s; National Association of Head Teachers, Stoke-on-Trent Branch, £2 2s; Durham County Colliery

Enginemen's Boiler Menders and Firemen's Association, Chopwell Branch, £2 2s; Durham County Colliers' Association, Thornley Branch, £2 2s; Trent Women's Co-operative Guild, £2; Mr G. Smith, £1 5s; Mr W. J. Fitzgerald, Middlesex, £1 1s; North Staffordshire Inner Wheel, £1 1s; Pantyffynnon Lodge No. 57, South Wales Miners' Federation £1 1s; South Wales Miners' Association, Area 5, Tower Lodge £1 1s; Wolstanton Co-operative Women's Guild, £1; Durham Colliery Mechanics' Association, Harton Lodge, £1; Lanarkshire Mineworkers' Union, Ponfeigh Branch, No. 29, £1; Miscellaneous, £1 14s 3d.

Total to date £2,672 19s, 7d.

On Saturday the 22nd of August, all proceeds from a special Stoke City's public practice match at the Victoria Ground were given over to the "Lidice Shall Live" Fund. The match commenced at 3.15pm and included some legendary names such as Neil Franklin, Frankie Soo, and Frankie Bowyer; with the blue and whites taking on the red and whites. The sum of £15 16s was raised.

Not everyone was happy with the city's efforts to rebuild Lidice. An article, written anonymously under the pseudonym *"The Calcutta Statesman"* and published in the Evening Sentinel on Wednesday October the 21st 1942, was keen to point out Britain's lack of obligation towards the Czech people and the terrible burden of sacrifice helping those in need would bring to a desperate city like Arnold Bennett's Stoke-on-Trent. This was how this contributor saw the *Five Towns* and the miners' decision to help rebuild Lidice:

"Hanley is the least dingy of that industrial region of Britain popularised by Arnold Bennett as the Five Towns. But nobody would regard it as the best home for shining ideals- nobody that is to say, who does not share the intense local loyalty of the people of the Five Towns or Potteries, for to them anything in the Potteries is better than everything elsewhere. We have it on his own authority that in 1931 a Parliamentary candidate for Hanley said in an election address: "You see that glorious blue sky above you." He paused, then added: "It should be covered with smoke". He was elected.

The people of the Potteries are proud of their smoke: anywhere else, smoke abatement would be practised: "Mugs" and "Potters" believe smoke is healthy. There was not much smoke in 1931 because of the depression. The depression in the pottery trade was attributed to imports from abroad. This imported pottery, equivalent to two years' production of Stoke-on-Trent according to one estimate was believed to be dumped and some of it undoubtedly came from Czecho-Slovakia. The Potteries, as a whole, therefore, have no special call to love Czecho-Slovakia or the Czechs Rebuilding Lidice.

Housing conditions in the Potteries are poor, although improving in an uninspired fashion. Most of the working classes of the Potteries still live amid surroundings and in conditions which would make fastidious Czechs shudder. Up to a few years ago, at any rate, the typical Potteries man was pasty-faced a very different type from the Czech Sokol and, if he was a coal miner, when he left the pits, his face was black as a nigger minstrel's.

He was interested in football and football pools, and maybe in dog-racing. Yet the Hanley miners have undertaken to rebuild Lidice, the Czech village destroyed by the Germans as a reprisal for the shooting of Heydrich, and Dr Beneš has accepted their offer. The faces which should now be blackened are those of Hitler and Himmler. From the clay and the coal and the steel and the smoke of the Potteries emerges the spirit of human brotherhood."

It has been difficult to trace the inward-looking author of the letter. It seems likely that they could have been a former disciple of Oswald Mosley's British Union of Fascists, disgruntled at the fact that his hero was now doing time in Holloway; or just a member of the public fearful of antagonising the Third Reich at a time when the outcome of the war was still uncertain.

Notwithstanding the odd letter of complaint, Dr Barnett Stross, the Czecho-Slovak - British Friendship Club and the North Staffordshire Miners' Federation - in particular Hugh Leese, Fred Hancock, George Jones, Arthur Baddeley, Frank Hampl, Jan Strasser and other campaigners (some experienced, some less so), had turned relations on their head by creating a tangible expression of Britons' solidarity with other nations. The Czechoslovak Government-in-exile was solidly behind it and had an office in London to help coordinate national events. The movement was gaining in momentum and expanding in terms of coverage.

A couple of weeks after the launch, a tribute to the **"hard heads and soft hearts"** of the North Staffordshire miners was paid in an article about the Lidice Shall Live movement in the *Central European Observer*. The article also described Barnett Stross as the **"spiritual father of the movement"**. The legend was much deserved, for Stross took on a personal responsibility for driving forward the momentum of the campaign for the rest of the war and beyond. Broadcasting the Lidice Shall Live fund as the "*Week's Good Cause*" on the BBC's Home Service on Sunday evenings was just one way he led by example in ensuring the movement was a success.

The warmth between the peoples of Czecho-Slovakia and Stoke-on-Trent was clear at a schedule of events to celebrate Czech Independence Day at Wellington Road Senior School in Hanley, on the evening of Saturday the 14th of November. There, the Lord Mayor and Lady Mayoress of Stoke-on-Trent, Alderman and Mrs Charles Austin Brook, attended what was a very successful and well attended presentation put on by the North Staffordshire Branch of the Czecho-Slovak - British Friendship Club, the Czech Children's Committee and Young Czecho-Slovakia. The Evening Sentinel reported:

> **"The Lord Mayor expressed his pleasure at being able to attend the celebration of the 24th anniversary of the formation of the Czechoslovak Republic. He said that about four and a half years ago he had the privilege of visiting the beautiful city of Prague and was delighted to find a people who loved freedom - a people as democratic and liberty-loving as the best of Englishmen."**

Dr Joseph Winternitz, from the Czech headquarters in London, said Stoke-on-Trent had a splendid record of friendship with the Czechoslovakian people, shown not in words alone, but in deeds. Winternitz spoke of the history of Czechoslovakia, its struggle for freedom, and the birth of the Republic, which he said was not an artificial design of the victorious powers of that time but was the result of many years' striving by the Czech and Slovak people. He added that as long as Russia and Great Britain - the two most powerful nations in Europe - stood together, it would assure future peace and freedom for the continent.

Mr Edwin Dutton, Chairman of the Stoke-on-Trent Czech Children's Committee outlined the formation and work of the committee. On behalf of the committee, he expressed thanks to all those people and organisations which had helped.

Two films were shown - *Eternal Prague*, showing the beautiful city before the occupation, and *Czech Army Marches* with humorous commentary by the motorcycle racer Eric Oliver. The programme also included a poem, *Lidice* spoken by child refugee Ruben Auerbach and Mrs Mautner; a dramatic play depicting how the Germans are haunted by the victims of their atrocities; a song written by Dr Stross called *Lidice Shall Live Again* sung by Czech children from the Penkhull Homes; a song recital by Miss F. Hewson; and a Czech poem, *October 28th*, spoken by Mr F. Kisch. Finally, a **"colourful and pleasing display"** of the *Beseda*, the traditional Czechoslovak national dance, concluded the entertainment.

As the first anniversary of that fateful day approached, on June the 7th 1943, Staffordshire's Evening Sentinel reported how the Lord Mayor of Stoke-on-Trent had been presented with a cheque for £2,748 towards the Lidice Shall Live Fund from Mr Ebby Edwards, General Secretary of the Mineworkers' Federation of Great Britain as a contribution from the Midland Miners' Federation.

Indicative of the type of fundraising activity taking place in Stoke-on-Trent for the duration of the war, were flag days and fetes. Quite often, at these events would be hundreds of handmade toys, dolls, games, needlework, cards, and other articles for sale – as well as traditional Czechoslovak and British cakes and savouries. Jan Strasser and other members of the Czecho-Slovak - British Friendship Club took an active part in raising funds across all six towns of the Potteries, working with the 'Miners' Federation - as in the case of the Flag Day illustrated below, helping the message of the campaign disperse into every nook and cranny of the city. In another case the event was a Christmas bazaar in aid of Lidice held at the Kings Hall in Stoke on Saturday the 18th of December 1943 – with the full support of Lord Mayor Charles Austin Brook:

The successful event was attended by the Lord Mayor and Lady Mayoress, Dr Barnett Stross, Chairman of the Lidice Shall Committee, and Mrs Olive Stross; Mrs A L Barker; Mrs Leason, organiser of the Women's Voluntary Service; Mrs A. Williams, and Mr A Riley MP. Many of the gifts had been made by Czecho-Slovak, Austrian and German refugees in the city; and others by students of the Thistley Hough School for Girls, and the Wolstanton County Grammar School. More than 600 visitors paid a visit to the sale during the afternoon, and the sum of £137 12s. 5d. was raised – the equivalent of £6,300 in today's money (2022). Speeches commending the aims and work of the Czecho-Slovak - British friendship movement were made by the Lord Mayor and Lady Mayoress - and by Dr Barnett Stross.

Jan Strasser, Chairman of the North Staffordshire Czecho-Slovak - British Friendship Club was also one of the keenest fundraisers for the Lidice Shall Live campaign, working well with the general public and miners of the area. Strasser worked in the pottery industry and was responsible for the Strasser Cup Handling Machine - something to which the author can attest as still being used in the mid-1980s in the factories of Stoke-on-Trent.

Fenton Town Hall c1960. Built in 1888 and scene of many political rally, including one of the mass meetings given by Jim Griffiths, Dr Barnett Stross, and Alfred Bennett on the weekend of the 28th – 30th of August 1942, to promote the launch of the Lidice Shall Live movement.

Top: Ann and Stephen Swingler, members of the Czecho-Slovak - British Friendship Club; former miner, Jim Griffiths MP for Llanelli, main speaker at mass rallies a week prior to the launch of the Lidice Shall Live campaign in Stoke-on-Trent – at Fenton, Smallthorne and at... Bottom: The Market Square in Hanley - scene of the final and largest rally, and site of Chartist gatherings 100 years earlier.

LAUNCHING THE MOVEMENT *The Path to Lidice*

Clockwise: Fred Hancock was born in 1873 in Talke and attended Butt Lane National School, Stoke-on-Trent. Hancock was connected for the greater part of his working life with the coal industry; Arthur Baddeley, of the Chatterley Whitfield Collieries, is closely linked to the Lidice Shall Live campaign having been President of the Federation at its inception; Mr Leese, who had been brought up in a Methodist household became one of the best-known miners' leaders in the Midlands in the first half of the 20th century. Leese entered the mining industry as a boy of 12 and became Registration Officer of the North Staffordshire Miners' Federation in 1918, and was subsequently Treasurer, Secretary and President; George Jones, was a British trade unionist and politician. He began working as a pit-boy and became active in the Cannock Chase Miners' Association becoming general secretary and agent for the North Warwickshire Miners' Association in 1914 - and was made general secretary and agent for the larger Warwickshire Miners' Association in 1919.

Clockwise: Will Lawther, President of the Mineworkers' Federation of Great Britain; Frank Hampl, Secretary of the Lidice Shall Live Campaign; Alderman Arthur Hewitt, Deputy Lord Mayor of Stoke-on-Trent; Alderman Harry McBrine, Lord Mayor of Stoke-on-Trent.

LIDICE DESTROYED BY THE NAZIS—

Ticket for the Arena or Gallery

to the

Inaugural **MEETING**

OF THE

"Lidice Shall Live" Campaign

on SUNDAY, SEPTEMBER 6th, 1942, at 3 p.m.

at the **VICTORIA HALL, Hanley.**

LIDICE SHALL LIVE AGAIN.

"LIDICE SHALL LIVE" COMMITTEE — STOKE-ON-TRENT
President ... Alderman H. W. McBRINE, Lord Mayor

Mass Meeting—Victoria Hall
HANLEY

SUNDAY, SEPTEMBER 6th
at 3 p.m.   Doors Open 2.0 p.m.
Chairman ... EARL OF DUDLEY, Regional Commissioner
Speakers—Dr. EDUARD BENES, President of Czecho-Slovakia
Mr. P. B. B. NICHOLS, C.M.G., M.C. H.M. Ambassador to the Czech Government
Mr. WILL LAWTHER, President M.E.G.B
Right Rev. L. D. HAMMOND, Bishop of Stafford
Dr. BARNETT STROSS.
Messages of Greetings from Allied Governments read by the Deputy Lord Mayor
SELECTION by the Famous CZECH ARMY CHOIR — 45 Men
Tickets from—Miss Joyce Kimpster, Federation House, Stoke.
Mr. George Meir, 45, John-street, Tunstall.

THEATRES	TO-DAY'S CINEMAS
THEATRE ROYAL, HANLEY Phone 5251.	GAUMONT BRITISH THEATRES

Top: President Beneš is greeted outside Hanley Town Hall by miners of the North Staffordshire Coalfield prior to the launch of the Lidice Shall Live campaign at 3pm on the 6th of September 1942; Bottom: With many hundreds unable to gain access, the hall was packed inside as members of the City Navy League and Army and Air Force Cadet Corps, carrying the flags of the 29 United Nations formed a guard of honour down the centre aisle of the Victoria Hall as the President walked to the rostrum.

*Top - Old colliery houses - Hartford Colliery estate Northumberland; bottom - new housing - Slipstone Colliery estate, Nottinghamshire. The miners' executive sought to provide the **"model mining village"** with the most up to date facilities for the future colliers of Lidice and their families. The Lidice Shall Live movement provided the miners with an opportunity of playing out the vision of what many hoped a British nationalised coal industry would provide for millions of working people.*

An Ode to Lidice Shall Live

Lidice Lives!

I went to Lidice this Summer, attended the commemoration

75 years since Hitler declared his aberration,

and I wept my silent tears, with anger in my heart

but walking round the rose garden, I realised the part

that my home city – Stoke-on-Trent – had played in a revival

so that Lidice would not die, but be part of the survival

not just of a simple village, hundreds of miles away

but of the human spirit, that still shines bright today.

That destructive retribution, was met with creative force

and Barnett Stross led the call, and history took a different course

when the miners of our city answered his rallying call

that Lidice Shall Live, not simply be another village to fall.

The money raised in war time was not the greatest gift

but the love for complete strangers that gave my heart a lift

and now the tears that flowed, were tears of civic pride

that our city played its part, and Lidice never died.

We must not forget the massacre, born of vengeance and of hate,

but we must also remember a more important date

that 70 years ago saw a brighter, better dawn

and the foundation stone was laid, and Lidice was reborn.

We're famous for so many things, our heritage and history

world renowned sons and daughters, and our incredible pottery,

but generous is our nature, evidence down the years

Lidice lives, because Stokie hearts reached across frontiers.

Alan Barrett - 26th of August 2017

A NATIONAL CAMPAIGN

A London Office of the Lidice Shall Live movement had already been set up at 18 Garway Road, Bayswater. It was administered principally by members of the Czechoslovak Government-in-exile, in partnership with the Stoke-on-Trent Lidice Shall Live committee. As well as his duties in North Staffordshire, Secretary Frank Hampl increasingly took on a national role.

It was the London Office who would arrange for key Czechoslovak ministers and representatives, as well as other Allied dignitaries, to attend and speak at national events, mass rallies and inaugurations in support of the increasing number of regional Lidice Shall Live committees.

The London branch was managed by a mix of representatives and staff from the Czechoslovak Government-in-exile and other activists sympathetic to the cause.

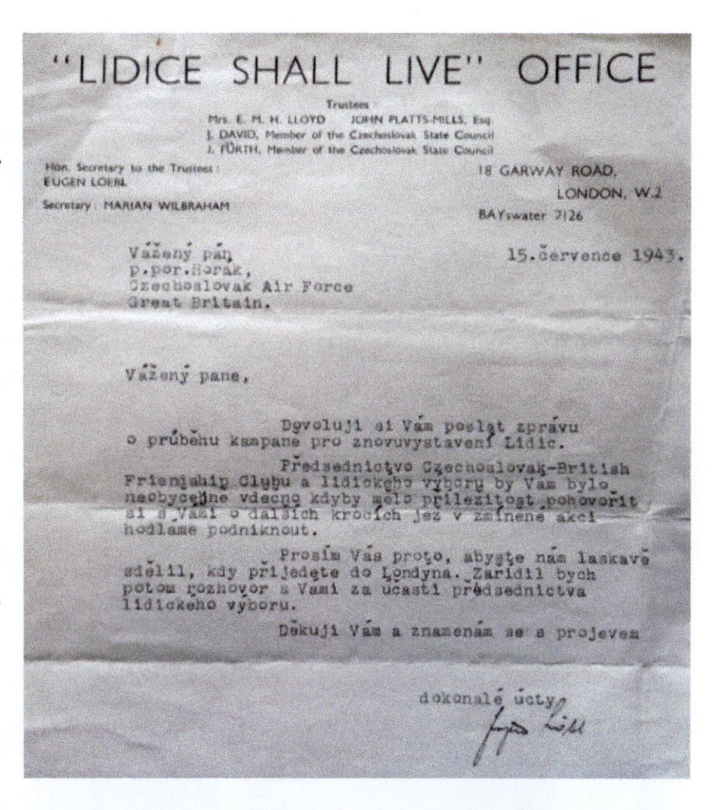

A letter written on the 15th of July 1943, addressed to Flt Lt Josef Horák requests he receive an update on the progress of the Lidice Shall Live campaign the next time he is in London, and offers to set up appearances for him at campaign launches and events across the country.

Honorary Secretary of the group was the economist and politician Evžen Loebl. As the first Secretary of the Czecho-Slovak British Friendship Club he lent considerable gravitas to the role. Loebl provided economic consultancy to the Ministry of Trade and a conduit to Jan Masaryk, the internationally popular Foreign Minister of the Czechoslovak Government-in-Exile. Beneš connection with the campaign came via Josef David, future Chair of the Czechoslovak National Assembly, and like Beneš a National Socialist and globalist. Finally, we speculate that Julius Firt, a former director of the Borový and Lidové Noviny publishing houses, had a more promotional role. Firt had escaped Czechoslovakia to Britain in 1936, where he worked for the Czechoslovak government-in-exile as a journalist and publisher. Later, from 1945 to 1948, he served as a deputy in Parliament and was in charge of the Melantrich publishing house – again connected to the Czech National Socialist Party.

Like Dr Barnett Stross, New Zealand born John Platts-Mills QC was an MP who earned his seat in the 1945 General Election. Platts-Mills served as a founding member and chair of Justice International and took part in anti-fascist activities from 1936, including the establishment of the *British-Soviet Friendship Societies*, and the *Societies for Cultural Relations with the USSR*, around Britain from 1941. The connecting link between John Platts-Mills, Frank Hampl and Dr Barnett Stross may well have been Cllr A. A. Wain. As a local Stoke-on-Trent councillor Stross had dealings with Wain on a frequent basis. There, at the Civic Chambers on Glebe Street, they would have shared similar views regarding economics and politics, appeasement and the European situation, and refugees. It is certainly clear that they collaborated on projects as Wain was an associate of the Stoke-on-Trent Branch of the Czecho-Slovak - British Friendship Club and would help find employment for new arrivals. Indeed, he found jobs for both Mr and Mrs Frank Hampl at his dental surgery. But Wain was an activist who knew Platts-Mills through his extra-curricular work, taking on the significant wartime responsibility of directing the numerous Stoke-on-Trent branches of the British-Soviet Friendship Society, and the North Staffordshire branch of the Society for Cultural Relations with the USSR. Mills-Platts was a member of both these societies. Wain too headed the Aid for Russia campaign in Stoke-on-Trent, which would have tapped into support from Platts-Mills and the national office of the Anglo-Soviet Friendship Society. It is likely that it was through this coming together: Wain, Stross, Platts-Mills, Hampl, along with their trustees from the Czechoslovak Government-in-exile, David and Firt, with their direct connections to Masaryk and Beneš, that the London Office of the Lidice Shall Live arose.

During the war John Platts-Mills volunteered to become a miner, and this he followed through, working for 18 months down a North Yorkshire pit. He made Queen's Counsel in 1964 and pursued an illustrious legal career, defending the Kray twins and the Great Train Robbers. He was president of the Haldane Society, the Society for Cultural Relations with the USSR and the National Council of Civil Liberties; In 1943, as a 30-year-old Secretary of the London Office of the Lidice Shall Live campaign, Marian Wilbraham/Šlingova was completely devoted to her husband, baby son and the wider wartime cause. Through her work helping to settle refugees, she had met a Czecho-Slovak Jewish exile, Secretary of Young Czechoslovakia (a Communist organization for the émigrés in London) and fellow communist, Otto Šling. Their marriage in 1941 would eventually cost her British citizenship. The couple had two children: Jan was born in 1943, and Karel in 1945. After the war they returned to the newly restored Czechoslovakia, where Otto became the Communist Party of Czechoslovakia's regional secretary, known as the "Gauleiter of Moravia," the most powerful person in the Brno region. In 1952, Šling was sentenced to death as part of the Slánský trial and executed along with Vladimir Clementis and 10 others; Evžen Loebl received a life sentence.

DURHAM

Since the first Lidice Shall Live meeting was held other cities had adopted the movement. And by late 1942 most of Britain's mining Federations were beginning to commit to support the cause, having received an official appeal from George Jones of the Midlands Miners' Federation, stamped and syndicated through the national Federation's network. It invited their members to follow North Staffordshire's lead and for miners to pay a levy of half a crown (or 2s 6d) each towards the fund. A show of disinterest could have severe consequences for the appeal.

Most symbolic would be the response from the Durham Miners' Association – the largest trade union in England. With the spirited backing of the Association's President, former collier and Methodist preacher, Jas Gilliland; and former Durham son, politician, and President of the Mineworkers' Federation of Great Britain, Will Lawther; the Durham Miners' Association enthusiastically led the way for others to follow. And so, on October the 28th it was reported in the *Sunderland Echo* that miners' lodges in the Durham coalfield had been unanimously recommended by the Executive of the Durham Miners' Association to agree to a grant from the General Funds equal to 2s 6d per member *for the Mineworkers' Federation scheme to rebuild the Czech village of Lidice.*

Dr Beneš, visited Durham on Sunday the 22nd of November 1942, at the invitation of the Durham Miners' Association. On his way to Durham, the well-liked Dr Beneš made several stops, first calling at the Chester Moor and South Pelaw Aged Miners' Homes, where men straight from the pit had gathered to receive him. After meeting the occupants of the homes, the committee presented the President with a leather wallet. Beneš also visited Durham Cathedral, where the Dean, Dr C. A. Alington, functioned as guide. Later the President called at the Town Hall, where he met the Mayor, Cllr F. A Howard, and the Town Clerk, Mr G. D. Rowland. Later still, Dr Beneš received the honorary degree of Doctor of Civil Law of the University of Durham at a special audience in one of the lecture rooms.

Harton Colliery Band signalled the President Beneš's entry into the crowded Miners' Hall, with a fanfare, followed by the Czech national anthem. Although reportedly an unemotional man, the Czech President-in-exile was visibly touched by the warmth of his welcome. The men of Durham had pledged themselves to help to build a new Lidice in Czechoslovakia after the war and Will Lawther, who presided said,

"Nothing is more vital than coal for the guns, the tanks and the planes to avenge Lidice." Declaring that they had noted with horror the crime committed at Lidice, Lawther said:

"We shall express that horror, that indignation in a practical manner. We shall do it in such a way that future generations will enter Lidice as a holy place consecrated by humble sons and daughters of toil who lived there until their destruction on the 10th June 1942."

Remarking that he was among friends to whom the Czecho-Slovak people owed a special debt of gratitude, Dr Beneš said, **"In this war the will of the workers is decisive. Behind the superb defence of Stalingrad, you see not merely the "Red" soldiers but the will of the Russian workers, which is breaking the German war machine. This is no less true of the British worker. He, too, has played his part both in the brilliant victory in Egypt and Libya and in the Allied occupation of French North Africa."**

"Personally, I have never doubted that by the late autumn of this year the main issue of the war would be decided." said Dr Beneš. **"It has been decided. And the mask is now torn from Vichy. We have reached the stage when Frenchmen can at last discern their true patriots from the false, and I rejoice to see Frenchmen once more taking an active part in driving the Germans back to their own homeland...The Russians, too, will harry them very soon, as they try, perhaps in vain, to occupy new defensive positions, and the German vitality will be lower. Today the Allied pincers are already doing deadly work."**

After referring to the persistent quarrels among the Nazi generals, Beneš said that the reports his government received told a great deal about the bribery and corruption rampant from one end of Occupied Europe to the other. **"I do not want to under-estimate the great strength of the German war machine even at the present moment: but the Nazi leaders at the top are anything but supermen. Their jealousies and rivalries, their fury, blindness, and terrible fear of the inevitable catastrophe play havoc with their judgment, and they have now made mistake after mistake which they cannot hope to retrieve. I believe that the end when it comes will be speedy."**

Emphasising the need for achieving victory as quickly as possible, Beneš said speed was worth many risks. It did not depend upon military actions alone. It still depended very largely upon the workers of Great Britain and upon the workers' front throughout the world. The British people had done much and the people of Occupied Europe still depended upon them:

"The time for them to strike out on their own account has not yet come. German difficulties of transport which have hampered them so gravely upon the Eastern Front owe a great deal to the truculence of their slave workers throughout Occupied Europe. But final victory depends upon you."

Beneš paid tribute to the North East for the role it played in defeating the Nazis. The coalfields of Durham and the industries of Tyneside were some of the most vital sinews of war. He thanked the miners of Durham and Great Britain for their camaraderie in supporting the people of Czecho-Slovakia during their darkest days:

"You have shown by your adoption of Lidice how closely you associate your own war work with the rescue of the people of Czecho-Slovakia, and I regard every extra ton of coal brought to the surface as a token that this rescue will come quickly."

The meeting was also addressed by Mr Jan Becko, Minister of Social Welfare in the Czechoslovak Government-in-exile; and an unexpected guest was Senior Lieutenant Vladimir Pchelintsev of the Soviet Red Army - a sniper who, speaking in his own language described how, in the defence of Leningrad, reputedly killed 152 Germans with 154 bullets - such was the normalisation of the macabre at the time.

1942 was also a year plagued with tragedy in the Durham coalfield, as a total of 100 accidents led to 115 deaths, the worst being the Murton Colliery Disaster on the 26th of June where 13 lives were lost because of a pit explosion. The executive of Sam Watson, Financial Secretary; Jas Gilliland, President; and John Swan, General Secretary, were preoccupied with the safety of its members and the financial security of the victims' dependents. These were the daily battles the executive committees of industrial trade unions were fighting to keep Britain's war effort against the Nazis on an even keel.

Subsequently, it was reported on the 12th of December 1942 that the Durham miners' contribution towards the Lidice Shall Live campaign would be in the region of £15,000. And on the 12th of January 1943 the Yorkshire Evening Post reported news that Will Lawther had recently received offers of collaboration from the miners of Australia and America, and that the Mineworkers' Federation of Great Britain's executive committee had now formerly appealed to its district organisations to support the Lidice Shall Live fund. It was formally announced that the Durham miners had agreed to subscribe half a crown per person to the fund. The lead taken by the North Staffordshire Miners and their associates within the Lidice Shall Live campaign had drawn in the largest trade union in Britain excepting the South Wales miners.

The involvement of Durham gave impetus to other coalfields and were soon followed by the Midland Miners' Federation with a promise to levy the 2s 6d. George Jones, the Midlands' General Secretary, remarked that **"there is no doubt that the miners of Yorkshire, Nottinghamshire and South Wales and elsewhere will co-operate."** These combining factors fuelled very optimistic predictions for the results of the campaign at the start of 1943 that the donations from the miners alone would achieve in the region of £50 - 80,000.

On the 31st of January 1945 it was reported by the Newcastle Journal and North Mail that the sum of £150,569 had been donated by Durham miners to various organisations since the outbreak of the war:

"...principal figures being £83,040 for the Red Cross: £21,637 Aid to Russia; *and* £13,869 to the Lidice Fund. Two Spitfires and six ambulances have been donated to the war effort and assistance provided for China, the Indian Famine Relief Fund, shipwrecked men, prisoners of war, and Greece. In workmen's compensation approximately £1,285,959 was paid in 1944, more than double the total of 1943."

LEAMINGTON SPA

LEAMINGTON TOWN HALL MARCH 15TH 1942

At 3 o'clock, on Sunday afternoon, March the 15th 1942, at Leamington Town Hall, a joint meeting of the general public and of members of the Czech Forces was convened under the auspices of the Czechoslovak State Council in remembrance of the third anniversary of the invasion of Czecho-Slovakia. The object also was to inaugurate a new branch of the Czecho-Slovak - British Friendship Club.

The Free Czechoslovak Army had made Leamington its home during the Second World War following the invasion of Czecho-Slovakia by Nazi Germany. As a spa location the town felt reassuringly familiar to many of the soldiers, reminding them of pleasurable times had at destinations such as Karlovy Vary, Marianské Lazně and others.

Thanking the promoters for asking him to be the first President of the Leamington branch of the newly formed Czecho-Slovak - British Friendship Club, the Mayor, Alderman Martin Moore, said he had pleasure in accepting, as the aims and ideals of the Club were so very English, that it would further help to cement the wonderful feeling of goodwill that already existed, and thus create a lasting friendship when the war was over. Alderman Moore added:

"It has been my good fortune since you arrived in the Midlands to meet not only your higher command, but also your private soldiers, and I can truthfully say I hold the highest possible opinion of them," said the mayor. "They have rendered me services on many occasions which I very much appreciate. I can understand that sometimes your thoughts must wander to your homeland. Having made your acquaintance in England it will be my fervent hope to meet you in your own country. I am longing to see Prague, and with a victorious finish to this conflict I can assure you we intend to visit you." *(Applause.)*

Mrs Mallett, organiser of the event, gave a summary of the occupation of Prague on March the 15th, 1939, and since that momentous day; while Václav Majer, member of the Czechoslovak Government-in-exile, and future Prime Minister of Czechoslovakia for two periods, from 1945–1950 and 1958–1961, gave a patriotic speech in Czech - which was translated by Mrs J. Gurney, County Council Welfare Officer. Rounding off, the meeting unanimously decided to send a telegram to Dr Beneš expressing the consensus and ending with the words: *"United we move forward to victory."* Songs were sung by two members of the Prague Opera, Madame Riedová and Mr J. Gutmann.

The following telegram was received by the Mayor from Mr Hubert Ripka, acting Czechoslovak Minister of Foreign Affairs: -

"Please convey to your audience my message of thanks for your presence at meeting to demonstrate the struggle of the Czecho-Slovak people against Pan Germanism - since March 15th, 1939. The arrival of the German troops at Prague was the signal for our people to start an underground war against Germany and thus assist the Allied effort before war actually began. Today's meeting is a manifestation that we shall not relax utmost exertions until final victory over the aggressive imperialism of Germany and Japan."

Shortly thereafter, the fledgling Club began raising funds for a variety of causes, including the Red Cross and the Lidice Shall Live fund as well as putting on exhibitions and events promoting Czecho-Slovak - British friendship within Leamington, and creating awareness of Czechoslovakian culture and the current war effort.

THE POLKA DOT CAFÉ – NOVEMBER 1ST 1942

A meeting of the Czecho-Slovak - British Friendship Club marked the closing of a week-long exhibition of Czech Art at the Polka Dot Café on the afternoon of Sunday the 1st of November 1942. Held in aid of the Lidice Shall Live fund, £100 had been raised through the week.

The Leamington Spa Courier reported how

"... many hundreds of Leamington people have associated themselves in this expression of love for the Czechs," and how the organisers requested that one street in the new Lidice be named *"Leamington Street"* as a constant reminder to the Czechs that somewhere in the Midlands of England the Czech soldiers had captured the hearts of the people. Sokol girls attended the exhibition one evening and people who came to view the exhibits were keenly interested in what they were told of the Sokol movement. Photographs of Sokol displays were greatly admired.

Much of the literature that had been sent to the exhibition from the Czech Ministry of Propaganda - that dealing with Heydrich's reign of terror was eagerly bought by patrons. Many people learned for the first time of the fighting and experiences of the Czech Army in France, and of the hazards which many personnel had to endure on their way to Britain.

Like other Czecho-Slovak - British Friendship groups the Leamington Branch celebrated Czechoslovakia's Independence Day – *the 28th of October* – and whilst doing so principal speakers Mesdames Raik and Mallett supplied interesting interplay as both gave their views on the roles of guest and host in 1940s English society. Mrs Raik, in the course of her speech, expressed sincere gratitude to the English people, and particularly to the people of Leamington Spa, for their grand hospitality. She said:

"To-day could only be for the Czechs a symbolical celebration, which could have no meaning in a material sense. Their waiting now is a part of their task, and surely most difficult one. They have long forgotten the happiness of life without a dictator." She went on to say: "We have now a dictator - *Our Nerves*. It is here that the most difficult task of the refugee begins.".

Mrs Mallett spoke of frustration: not merely on behalf of Czechs-in-exile, but also for those who remained behind - to have to see their beautiful country possessed and despoiled by an oppressor each day. For them *Independence Day* could only be a matter of the spirit. Mrs Mallett thought that the outstanding characteristics of Czech people were courage and resistance; not so much the courage that leads to heroic deeds, as the dogged day-today kind that refuses to know when it is beaten. She said:

"Here in Leamington, we have had unique opportunities of learning about a people, who came not empty-handed, but rich in ideas on such subjects as painting, politics. music, education, and the conduct of daily life."

Mrs Raik advised that "Czechs in England must always bear in mind that they are ambassadors for their race." While Mrs Mallett posed the question: "Have you ever thought what a day of judgment is coming for England?" Nothing to do with the wrath of God or a big black book, but one day, she hoped not far distant, in hundreds of Czech homes little voices would say:

"Tell us about England, Daddy."

"In that moment we shall be judged, because from his answers Czechoslovakia will learn what kind of hosts, we have been and what are the ideals we stand for as a people."

Referring to the request that a street in the new Lidice should be named "*Leamington Street*" the Czechoslovak Ministry of Foreign Affairs assured the organisers that something would be done to "perpetuate a link between this small Bohemian village and the very attractive town of Leamington Spa."

BEAUCHAMP HALL – MAY 17TH 1943

The light-heartedness injected into meetings could be witnessed at the second gathering of the 'Club. Held at Beauchamp Hall, on Sunday afternoon, May the 17th, it took the form of a garden-party, which was thoroughly enjoyed by everyone present—according to the press:

"At the outset, English and Czechs were well mixed up by an ingenious and amusing game of finding partners—which effectively broke down all barriers of shyness, for who could be stiff and dignified when "mustard" was searching for "cress" and "King Arthur" was uncertain whether "Guinevere" or "The Round Table" was the object of his quest?"

The Mayor and Mayoress Moore were present at the party, and Alderman Moore spoke in high praise of General Miroslav and other members of the *Independent Czech Army*, adding that when, after the war, it was possible to travel abroad again, his first expedition would be to Prague. Other attendees included Eugen Löbl, Secretary of the Union for Czecho-Slovak – British Friendship; Mrs Gurney, Vice-Chairman of the Leamington Club, who presided in the unavoidable absence of Dr Morava; and Mrs Raik and Mrs Mallett—honorary secretaries.

In her succinct speech, Mrs Mallett outlined the aims of the 'Club, stating that some people might think that its use had ceased with the departure of most of the Independent Czech Army: but that actually, the small number of Czechoslovaks remaining would need more than ever the friendship of Leamington people, and the opportunity the 'Club afforded to pursue individual and collective interests. It was essential to keep alive an understanding between British and Czech people, for the two nations must co-operate to produce the peace together. Mrs Mallett appealed for more members of the 'Club, saying that Mr Eden had signified his approval and sympathy by becoming a Patron. Thanks were expressed to Miss Sweet, to the Committee for providing tea, and to the members of the Leamington International Refugee Club for the entertainment, which was of a high standard, and to which two Britishers, Mrs Barton and Mr Toulmin, contributed.

In late December 1943, at the Polka Dot Café, a fortnight long display of Czech craftsmanship, artwork and paintings, photographs, and needlework - in aid of the *"Lidice Shall Live Again"* fund raised £150. The goods were all given, with the exception of a few art treasures loaned, and made chiefly by the Czech Army and the Czech School of Art. Unsurprisingly, there were some wonderful paintings of Leamington beauty spots produced by artists in the Czech Army whilst stationed in the town, including a particularly lovely view of Jephson Gardens, and a portion of Newbold Terrace, as seen by the Czech Army artist from the window of their room - a snow scene with the Parish Church and spire in the distance. Other items featured included a fine painting of the River Leam with the Parish Church and Pump Room in the distance, as well as items of pâte-sur-pâte on finest porcelain and glassware. The new Mayor and Mayoress, Cllr and Mrs Ashton, visited the exhibition, along with Alderman and Mrs Moore. Tea was provided, and a draw made for one of the painted dishes, which was won by Miss Keeling.

Today, in Jephson Gardens, you will find the Czechoslovak Memorial Fountain. Originally erected in 1968 by Czechoslovak veterans in remembrance of fellow soldiers, airmen and patriots who lost their lives in World War II. In 2018 the fountain underwent restoration thanks to funding from the Friends of the Czechoslovak Memorial Fountain, The Czech Ministry of Defence, Warwick District Council, Leamington Town Council, Czechoslovak House in London, Reading Help (a Czech Charity) as well as a substantial donation from one of the last living veterans in the Leamington area. Sculpted by John French, who designed the fountain in the shape of a parachute to honour the brave soldiers who took part in Operation Anthropoid, it also commemorates all Czechoslovak soldiers who lost their lives in the Second World War. The fountain was awarded Grade II listed status by English Heritage, recognising it as a monument of historic interest.

The 50th anniversary of the fountain coincided with the centenary of the formation of Czechoslovakia as a sovereign state. Representatives from Leamington Town Council, Warwick District Council, the Friends of the Czechoslovak Fountain, and MP Matt Western gathered at the site to lay a rose. Children from the Czech and Slovak Club in Birmingham sang a traditional Czechoslovakian song, and Warwick District Council's Green Spaces team planted red roses from Lidice adjacent to the fountain.

BIRMINGHAM

Birmingham, the largest city within the Warwickshire Miners' Federation Coalfield, was the first to accept the invitation to join the national Lidice Shall Live campaign. Its citizens demonstrated complete empathy for the struggle of the Czech people as they inaugurated the second Lidice Shall Live committee by having a *Lidice Week*. It was a popular formula which was to be adopted by other Midlands cities. The Lord Mayor, Cllr Walter Lewis, took on the mantle of Chairman of Birmingham's Lidice Committee, while Cllr Charles G. Spragg, Secretary of the Birmingham Trades Council, took on Honorary Secretary to the Committee; Mr Frank Packwood JP, accepted the job of Honorary Treasurer; and Mr Frank Webster, a member of the Trades Council Executive, volunteered to act as Steward-in-Chief at the launch event.

BIRMINGHAM TOWN HALL – MAY 30TH 1943

The launch at Birmingham Town Hall on Sunday the 30th of May 1943 attracted more numbers than the Hanley event. It was organised and orchestrated primarily by George Jones of the Warwickshire Miners' Federation. Jones, as a Lidice Shall Live committee member, was the link between the North Staffordshire Miners' Federation and Dr Barnett Stross on the one hand, and Birmingham City Council and the Warwickshire miners on the other. As the delegate who secured nationwide support for the Lidice Shall Live movement at the national mining conference the previous July, he was leading by example. This was his mass meeting. It was intended to be a beacon for other areas across the British Coalfield to put on similar events, to ensure the breadth and scope of the campaign. He, therefore, felt a deep personal interest in the event's progress.

Birmingham's Lidice week opened with a march past of Czechoslovakian troops. Accompanying them were Lord Mayor Lewis and Jan Masaryk, son of the founder of Czechoslovakia (Tomáš Masaryk) and the Czechoslovak Foreign Minister - who had made a tremendous success of being a member of the BBC Brains Trust, a national radio programme popular during the 1940s on which a panel of experts tried to answer questions sent in by the audience. Masaryk was the principal speaker at a pageant and demonstration arranged by the Birmingham Lidice Shall Live Committee in the Town Hall. The Birmingham Post takes on the report:

> "The Lord Mayor, Cllr W. Lewis, presided and other speakers included Mr P. J. Noel-Baker, MP Parliamentary Secretary to the Ministry of War Transport; Alderman George Jones, J.P. of the Midlands Miners' Federation who was chiefly responsible for organising the event and representative of the Lidice Shall Live committee; and Canon Guy Rogers, Rector of Birmingham. Also, present were Counsellor of the Soviet Embassy Mr Vasily Valkov; and Colonel Alex Sizon, Military Attaché to the Soviet Embassy; General Fuffrin (from Fighting French headquarters); as well as the following Czech Ministers: for Czecho-Slovak Social Welfare, Mr Jan Becko; State, Dr Hubert Ripka; Industry and Commerce, Dr J. Slavik; and Mr P. Maxa, chairman of the Czechoslovak State Council. Powerful testimony came in the form of the two young men from Lidice who were serving as RAF Flight Lieutenants, X and Y."

Following their warm reception, the meeting observed a minute's silence for the oppressed people of Europe. Then, between them, the two airmen *(X and Y)*, in actuality, Flight Lieutenants Josef Horák and Josef Stříbrný, read out a pledge to the Czech nation, as follows:

"We the people of Birmingham, the industrial heart of Britain, call to you our friends and brothers on the Continent,

We call to the glorious partisans, gallant fighters for freedom, and heroic underground workers in all occupied countries.

We call to all those of you who lead, in spite of terror, execution squad, atrocities and quislings, an incessant epic struggle against the Nazi monster.

We people of Birmingham who are producing the tanks, planes, guns, and ammunition to smash Hitler.

We, who serve in the armed forces, are united in one desire, to work, fight and prepare even harder in the future: in order to bring to you the help you need so urgently.

We want you to know that we have not forgotten, nor shall we ever forget, your sacrifices, and your suffering.

Lidice, the execution of countless patriots, the extermination of millions of Jews, and the martyrdom of all those living under the Gestapo terror are reminders we shall never forget.

We people of Britain, knowing the degree of your suffering, want you to know we are with you in your ordeal. The spectacular defeats of the German and Axis armies on the Eastern Front and in North Africa are undeniable signs of the fast-approaching doom of Nazi Germany.

We know that you are waiting for us to set foot on your soil, to help you to free your home and country. But we are also sure that when we come, and come we shall, you will be ready to join us in the final battle.

Knowing therefore that, unless your country is free, there can be no free Europe, we recognise that any victory of ours must be also a victory for you.

Together we fight in a world at war. Together, let us build a world of freedom and peace."

The speech was not overlooked by the Birmingham Post, which wrote:

"Last night those two, wearing the uniform of the RAF, spoke at Birmingham Town Hall, a message of hope from the people of Birmingham to their own people and to all people in the occupied countries. Outside the crowded hall, people in the streets of Birmingham heard it over loud speakers.

A record of it went out over the air to the people of Europe, across as one speaker put it, 'the Atlantic wall of Hitler's guns and Goebbels' lies.' The message was that *Lidice* should live."

Prior to the meeting in the Town Hall, there was a parade and march past of units of the British Armed Forces, Civil Defence, Auxiliary Territorial Service and Youth Organisations and the band of the Grenadier Guards played in Victoria Square from 4.15 to 6 p.m. Separately, but in support of the campaign, a garden party and concert was being held at Dame Elizabeth Cadbury's Manor Farm, at Northfield. The Birmingham Post continued:

"**The Town Hall was filled for the meeting at which the Lord Mayor, who was accompanied by the Lady Mayoress, presided. Flags of the Allies were carried in procession to the platform. After prayers for all sufferers from Nazi aggression, Czech songs were sung by members of the Czechoslovakian Army Choir. The Lord Mayor said the citizens of Birmingham were proud to pay tribute to their gallant Allies - the Czechoslovak Republic. He hoped that soon they would be restored to their former greatness in Europe. He suggested that the estimated cost of rebuilding Lidice was £1,000,000 and that Lidice would be rebuilt as a model mining village. But, he said, it was more than a question of Lidice. It was a symbol of hope for all the oppressed people of the world:** *"Oppressed Europe is calling for our aid, and Birmingham now answers that we shall help,"* **he said."**

Mr Noel-Baker hailed the re-building of a new Lidice as '**a spiritual guarantee to other oppressed men and women.**' He explained that the Allies did not intend simply to smash the Nazis, nor restore British power, but to revive the Christian civilisation Hitler had tried to destroy. Words would be redeemed by deeds. The criminals who slaughtered Lidice would be punished; but the wish was to seek justice, not revenge. "**When we build Europe and the world again,**" he concluded, "**I hope we shall wipe away the weaknesses, corruption and folly which in our countries in the West brought down Czecho-Slovakia down in 1938, a world where for all men in all countries the things that made life bitter for us shall be done away with.**"

Jan Masaryk, Deputy Prime Minister of Czechoslovakia, said: "**I am grateful to this great city for doing this noble thing for us.**" He said that Lidice was not a little village but a symbol and that when he spoke of Lidice he thought of hundreds of places in China, Poland, and other countries. There was unity among the Allied nations at the moment, and that unity must remain after the war and especially with the Russian people. Alderman George Jones said that when the town was rebuilt, he hoped it would be possible to accept the invitation already given to hold the first international miners conference there. Mr Philip Nichols, HM Ambassador to the Czechoslovak Government-in-exile in London, commented: "**The cause you have at heart is a noble one. It will help others and promote friendship between peoples.**" In the evening, there was a parade of members of the military, nursing, and Civil Defence Forces, including a contingent of the Czech Army. The salute was taken in Victoria Square by the Lord Mayor, who was accompanied by Jan Masaryk.

Birmingham's marketing slogan became *"Birmingham Will Answer!"—"The Nazis Destroyed Lidice - Help to Destroy the Nazis!"*

Following the committee's launch, a significant driving force behind Birmingham's campaign became Cllr Spragg. Adverts inviting donations to the Birmingham branch of the Lidice Shall Live Fund were a common site in the Birmingham Post during the summer and autumn of 1943—space sponsored by the brewery, Mitchells and Butlers.

Birmingham's Czecho-Slovak - British Friendship Club, near New Street Station opened in the autumn of 1944, and staged an attractive programme of lectures and parties. According to the press, "its canteen possesses that rare jewel, a cook who loves cooking, and Birmingham people who enjoy continental dishes should persuade a member to invite them to sample her Czech specialities, such as "vepřová pečeně," "Wiener Schnitzel," or "knedlíky," which can be more than warmly recommended." The exhibition was designed to show the part being played by the Czechoslovak Army in the war. Opened by the Lord Mayor of Birmingham it consisted of photographs and displays from the time of Munich, including Czech soldiers in Britain, France, and North Africa, while another told of the constant "fight against the invader that has gone on inside the Republic since 1939". Displayed above was the Czechoslovak coat of arms, together with its motto, "Pravda vítězí" (Truth prevails). Lieutenant Colonel, Josef Kalla, who was at the launch of the exhibition said, "When I was a young man in Czechoslovakia, I was always taught that the word "Englishman" was synonymous with gentleman...Nothing that I have seen or heard since coming here many years ago has caused me to change that view. British and Czech troops are fighting side by side in many parts of the world, and these troops will prove to the world that "Truth will prevail." The exhibition was organised in conjunction with the Czechoslovak Ministry of Information.

DERBY

Early March 1943, and the Czechoslovakian Minister of State, Dr Hubert Ripka opened a new branch of the Czecho-Slovak – British Friendship Club. Later that day, speaking of his aspirations for the new Derby committee,

"I wish the club much success in the coming year; I do this because I am fully aware that this will mean success contributed to the common Czecho-Slovak and Allied cause."

The Derby Telegraph reported:

"Perhaps you were not aware of the existence in Britain of such an organisation. A proposal is afoot to start a branch of the club in Derby and a woman Doctor of Law from Czecho-Slovakia (she came here when Hitler marched into Prague) is one of those responsible for the arrangements for a public meeting to be held in the Merchant Hall on Sunday. She tells me she has obtained permission to hold a flag day in Derby similar to one held at Stoke. *The "flag" is a round disc of cardboard with the words (in red) "God calls us," and an inset "We are coming."* I did not know, until she informed me, that Mexico has a small township re-named Lidice, although I did understand that another has arisen in America."

The mystery lady revealed that the speakers at the meeting would be Alderman Arthur Neal and Karl Kreibich, Czechoslovak MP and representative of the State Council. The flag day was set for the 17th of July by the Derby Czecho-Slovak – British Friendship Club. It was a fine effort, with the fledgling Derby Lidice Shall Live Committee raising £326, equivalent to approximately £15,000 in 2022 prices. The committee got down to work and on the 22nd of July, the Derby Telegraph reported how a Lidice Shall Live Week was to be held in the city from August the 23rd to the 29th:

"...This was decided at a meeting held in the Guildhall last night when the Mayor Alderman Hind presided and about 100 representatives from various organisations attended...The Mayor said that Derby's aim was to assist in the raising of £1,000,000 towards the rebuilding of the village of Lidice. Already, a sum of £326 had been raised as a result of a flag day held in Derby last Saturday. He mentioned that the programme would include parades of Service personnel, demonstrations and talks in schools."

Dr Barnett Stross, speaking on the practical aspects of the campaign said that the village would not only be rebuilt in memory of all suppressed nations, but that a scientific research station would be erected there to study health and safety issues in mines and bring improvements to the lives of miners throughout the world.

On the 21st of July 1943, the following officials were elected to Derby's Lidice Shall Live Committee: Chairman, the Mayor, Alderman Herbert A. Hind; Deputy Chairman, Alderman Arthur T. Neal; and Secretary, Mr E. G. Partridge.

At a session of the Derby office of the Lidice Shall Live committee on August the 9th, it was decided to reschedule Lidice Shall Live Week for September the 5th to the 12th, and not as previously arranged from August the 23rd to the 29th. This decision was made when it was pointed out by Mr Partridge that the executive felt the new dates would give the relevant organisers and committees more time to prepare plans. The programme of events for Derby's Lidice Week, held at various cultural locations within the city, was promoted in the Derby Evening Telegraph as to *"assist in raising £1,000,000 towards the rebuilding of the village of Lidice"*.

DERBY'S LIDICE WEEK

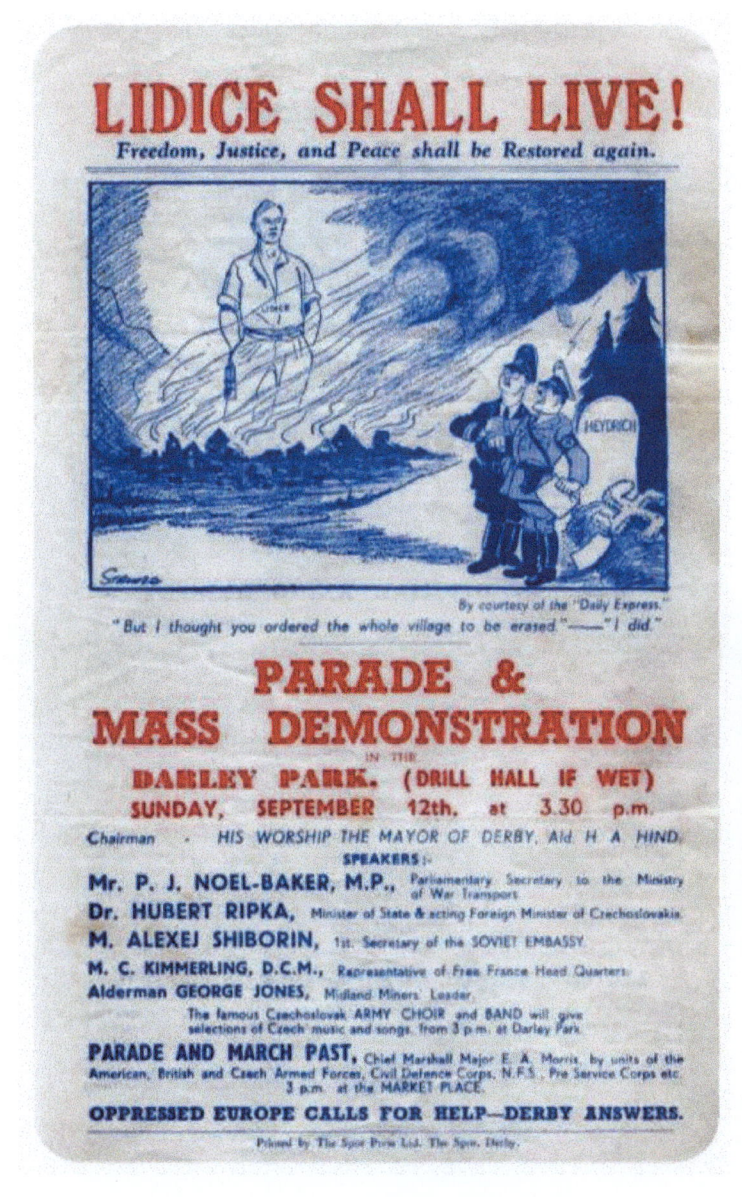

Many events took take place throughout the week. Proceedings began at 3pm on Sunday the 5th of September with a service in the City's cathedral when Lidice's victims were remembered.

On Monday, another prominent Czech, Mrs E. G. Gansová of the *Council of Czechoslovak Women in Great Britain*, was the principal speaker at a women's meeting at the Guildhall.

On Tuesday evening, the famous Czech pianist, Madame Liza Fuchsová, gave a recital at the Art Gallery and on Thursday there was a non-stop fund-raising dance at the Plaza Ballroom. A European Brains Trust took place in the Guildhall on Friday. The subject was *"Post-war Europe"* with the question-master Mr T. A. Lewis and presided over by the Mayor, Alderman Hind.

The Czech Army Choir and Army Band performed a concert and dance which took place at the Drill Hall on Saturday evening.

The Lidice inspired Humphrey Jennings film, *The Silent Village* had been released and was now showing at the Coliseum Cinema throughout the week with a *"Collection in aid of the Lidice Fund"* taken in the auditorium by Czech girls in national costume; the Lidice Gift Shop in the market-place was open from Monday to Saturday and sold a range of traditional Czech foods and gifts. There were talks at works in the town, for which the Ministry of Information organised films and guest speakers. The arrangements were made by representatives from the executive board.

There were heart-warming stories of international fellowship too. From the secretary of the Derby Lidice Shall Live Committee, Mr Partridge, came the news that an Austrian refugee living in Derby was raising quite a lot of money by selling a Viennese cake made by her mother; and a special parade in support of the Lidice Shall Live fund during the interval of the *Derby County v West Bromwich Albion* football match at the Baseball Ground on Saturday the 4th of September realised a total of £32 10s.

Derby *Lidice Week* received prominent Czech citizens, including Minister of State and Acting Foreign Minister, Dr Hubert Ripka as well as units of the Czech Armed Forces. Many events had been arranged, but the principal one and finale was a mass rally in Darley Park on Sunday the 12th, to be preceded by a parade and march-past in the market-place by British, American, and Czech soldiers, Civil Defence Corps, National Fire Service, and pre-Service organisations.

Speakers in the park included dignitaries of the Allied nations and representatives of the Lidice Shall Live campaign: Dr Barnett Stross; Dr Ripka; Mr P. J. Noel-Baker MP, Parliamentary Secretary to the Ministry of War Transport; M. Alexej Shiborin, First Secretary of the Soviet Embassy; M. C. Burnay, representative of the Fighting French Headquarters; and Alderman George Jones, Secretary of the Midland Miners. Again, the meeting was supported by Flight Lieutenants Josef Horák and Josef Stříbrný. The demonstration began at 3.30pm with the Czech Army Choir and Band performing traditional music from 3pm.

DERBY "LIDICE SHALL LIVE" CAMPAIGN

LIDICE WEEK, 5th. - 12th, SEPTEMBER, 1943

Week's Programme :-

SUNDAY, SEPT. 5th. at 3 p.m. Service at the Cathedral, in Memory of the dead of LIDICE and on behalf of the oppressed and persecuted peoples of Europe.

MONDAY, SEPT. 6th, at 6.45 p.m. Ladies' Meeting in the Guildhall.
  Chairman : Mrs. Councillor LOCHRANE.
  Speakers : Mrs. E. G. GANSOVA, Council of Czechoslovak Women in G.B.
  Ald. H. A. HIND, Mayor of Derby.
  Selection of Czech Folk Songs.

TUESDAY, SEPT. 7th. 7 p.m. at the Art Gallery, Piano Recital, by the well-known Czech Star Pianist—MADAME LIZA FUCHSOVA.
  Tickets available from Messrs. FOULDS, IRONGATE.

THURSDAY, SEPT. 9th, 7.30 - midnight, Plaza Ballroom, GRAND Non-Stop Dance, Arranged by the Derby C.P.
Lew Stone and his Radio Band and Bram Martin's Swingtet. Tickets 5/- Forces 3/6.

FRIDAY, SEPT. 10th. at 7 p.m. in the Guildhall,
  EUROPEAN BRAINS TRUST. Subject, "Post War Europe."
  Chairman : His Worship the Mayor (Ald. H. A. Hind).
  Question-Master : Mr. T. A. LEWIS, of the M.O.I.

SATURDAY, SEPT. 11th, 7.30 - 11.30 p.m. in the Drill Hall,
  Grand Dance Concert,
  by the famous CZECHOSLOVAK ARMY CHOIR AND ARMY BAND.
  Conducted by Lieut. Obruca and Taussig.

SUNDAY, SEPT. 12th, at 3.30 p.m. Darley Park, (Drill Hall if wet,) Parade and Mass Demonstration.

MONDAY, SEPT. 6-11th, at the Coliseum Theatre, "The Silent Village." The Story of Lidice.
  With kind permission of Mr. Semple, a collection by Czech Girls in National Costume, in aid of the Lidice Fund, will be taken during the intervals.

MONDAY, SEPT. 6-11th, at 20, Market Place, "Lidice Gift Shop." Exhibition of Czech Handicraft work.
  Come and buy to aid the Lidice Fund. Gifts and donations gratefully accepted.

People of Derby give generously and support this worthy cause.
All donations should be sent to the
  Hon. Treasurer, Mr. D. L. Copeman, Borough Treasurer's Dept., Babington Lane.

H. A. HIND, Mayor.   Derby "Lidice Shall Live" Committee.

Published by the Derby L.S.L. Committee. Hon. Sec. Eustace Partridge, 3, The Pingle, Allestree.

THE STORY OF LIDICE

Lidice, a peaceful mining village—until the NAZIS came.

On June 10th, 1942, the village of Lidice, about 18 miles from Prague, was wiped out by detachments of the Gestapo. Lidice is a small picturesque place in hilly countryside near Kladno. It was not really a town, but a village of about 120 houses, with a population of between 1,200 and 1,500. Most of the inhabitants were miners, organised in their Trade Union. They went every day to work in the Duby coal mine near Kladno, while others were iron workers employed at the Poldi Iron Works in the same town. There were also some masons and carpenters, while the rest were farmers.

GERMAN OFFICIAL ANNOUNCEMENT

"In the course of the search for the murderers of S.S. Obergruppenführer Heydrich, incontestable proof was found that the population of Lidice, near Kladno, gave support and assistance to the perpetrators of the crime. The relevant evidence, in spite of interrogations, was collected without the co-operation of the inhabitants. The attitude to the whole truth—hereby is still further emphasised by other activities hostile to the Reich, by stores of seditious printed matter, dumps of weapons and munitions, an illegal radio transmitter, and also of manufactured goods in great quantity, and by the fact that the inhabitants of the village are in active service of the enemy abroad. Since the inhabitants of this village have in the most uncompromising manner opposed the published laws through their activities and support to the murder of Heydrich, the male adults have been shot, the women sent to concentration camps and the children placed in suitable educational institutions. The buildings have been razed to the ground and the name of the place has been erased from the records."

THE TRUTH

The Nazis boasted of this inhuman crime, hoping to strike fear and horror into the hearts of all freedom-loving peoples. But they did not dare to disclose the whole truth—how they "erased" a peaceful village and the entire population. Children and old people, women and men alike were murdered. From statements by German Officers and N.C.O.'s now prisoners of war in Russia and from other reports from Czechoslovakia, we now know what really happened. At dawn of June 10th, 1942, Lidice was surrounded by German tanks. German planes bombed the small village to ruins. Those few still alive, trying to escape this undescribable horror, were mown down by the guns of the waiting tanks.

LIDICE—SYMBOL of Hitler's "New Order."

Since then there have been hundreds of other Lidices all over Europe. For this very reason this Czechoslovak village, the fate of which was openly announced by the Nazis as a threat to the Czech people, has to-day become the banner and symbol for all the devastated and stricken places in Hitler's "space of living," to us known as Europe. Lidice has become a symbol of the fearless resistance and of the suffering peoples of oppressed Europe in a particularly significant way. It has shown to the whole world the true meaning of the German "New Order." It has revealed to civilised mankind the real character of relationship between the "master race" and the despised inferior races whom they have taken under their "protection."

THE PEOPLE OF GREAT BRITAIN ANSWER.

The heroism of the inhabitants of Lidice has fired the whole world. The free peoples under the impact of this abominable crime closed their ranks more closely with the oppressed nations of occupied Europe. To-day, all Lidices, each new crime—no matter whether or not Goebbels tries to accuse his enemies with atrocities ordered by his master Hitler with the object of splitting the unity of the Allied nations—must be turned into an effective spiritual weapon against the evil of mankind—Hitlerite Germany.

A few days after the news of the destruction of Lidice, the idea of rebuilding Lidice on its ashes in Czechoslovakia was born. It was taken up with enthusiasm by the North Staffs. Miners. Mr. G. H. Jones, J.P., Midland Miners' Federation, brought the suggestion to the annual conference of the M.F.G.B., from which an urgent call for help goes out to the world.

On September 6th, 1942, the inaugural meeting of the "LIDICE SHALL LIVE" campaign took place in Stoke-on-Trent, and the first "LIDICE SHALL LIVE" Committee under the Patronage of the Lord Mayor of Stoke-on-Trent, Ald. McBrine, was formed. More than 3,000 citizens heard the messages of Dr. E. Beneš, Mr. Anthony Eden, Mr. Will Lawther, and other speakers at a solemn ceremony. Dr. Beneš and the Rt. Hon. Anthony Eden, P.C., M.P., are the chief patrons of the Lidice campaign which spreads now throughout the country.

Since then, in the following cities, "LIDICE SHALL LIVE" Committees have been formed or are being formed: Birmingham, Nottingham, Leeds, Cardiff, Coventry, Edinburgh, Glasgow, Aberdeen, and last but not least London. Under the patronage of the Lord Mayors and Lord Provosts of these cities arrangements for the Lidice campaign will be made with the aim of rebuilding Lidice on its ashes as a MODEL MINING VILLAGE, a perpetual reminder of the solidarity of the people of Great Britain with the oppressed peoples of the continent; and a proof of sympathy and help with suffering nations during their darkest hours, in their bitter struggle against the Nazi monster.

The destruction of Lidice and other places, the extermination of millions of Jews in Poland, the starvation and torture of Russian prisoners of war, the mass execution of anti-Fascist patriots all over oppressed Europe—all these sinister crimes express the meaning of the mad and ruthless Nazi regime.

In the U.S.A., in Mexico and in South Africa, villages were renamed "Lidice," and a National Committee with outstanding American writers, scientists, politicians, etc., has been formed with the object of similarly renaming villages in each country of the United Nations.

In Derby, the initiative for forming a "LIDICE SHALL LIVE" COMMITTEE was taken up by the Mayor, Ald. H. A. Hind. On July 21st, at a Conference at the Guild Hall, with the Mayor in the Chair, the "Derby 'LIDICE SHALL LIVE' Committee," with Ald. H. A. Hind as Chairman, was formed. At this very representative meeting the decision was taken to arrange a "LIDICE WEEK" from 5th–12th September. All sections of the County Borough's social, industrial, religious and political life are giving their wholehearted support.

To-day, the peoples of FRANCE, CZECHOSLOVAKIA, YUGOSLAVIA, POLAND, GREECE, NORWAY, HOLLAND, BELGIUM, and of the occupied districts of the U.S.S.R. call for help; help which must come soon, or it may be too late. The Lidice campaign has and will have still more significance as a means of moral encouragement to the heroic peoples who in spite of terror and executions are daily raising their resistance to new heights and who will soon rise up and burst the bonds of tyranny.

Lidice, the people of Czechoslovakia and the peoples of Europe call—

Derby—known for its solidarity and generosity—will give the answer:

"LIDICE SHALL LIVE,"

Freedom, Justice and Peace shall be restored again.

THE RALLY AT DARLEY PARK

On the evening of Monday the 13th of September, the Derby Telegraph reported on Sunday's rally:

"British American, Czech, and the Free French armies were represented on the platform at a mass meeting in Darley Park, under the auspices of the Derby *"Lidice Shall Live"* Committee. Speakers included representatives of the Czecho-Slovak Government and of the Soviet Embassy, Mr P. J. Noel-Baker (Parliamentary Secretary to the Ministry of War Transport), and Dr B. Stross. In addition, one of the only two men of Lidice believed to be alive told an audience of several thousand people yesterday afternoon that when the little Czecho-Slovakian mining village comes to be rebuilt, he hopes that Derby will be represented at the laying of the foundation stone."

It was a large crowd that thronged Derby market-place as the Mayor of Derby, Alderman Hind, took the salute at a march past by units of the British, American and Czech Forces, Home Guard and Civil Defence crews, and pre-Service organisations. According to press reports, the parade included about 1,000 participants. Hundreds of people followed the procession to Darley Park, where the Czechoslovak Army band played. The mayor, as chairman of the city's Lidice Shall Live board, greeted the speakers and opened the event. First of all, Parliamentary Secretary to the Ministry of War Transport, Mr Noel-Baker recounted the story of Lidice, before adding: **"We are here to swear that the name of Lidice shall live forever and be famous in every continent as the happiest village in the freest republic in the world. The** aim of this meeting is to fulfil the splendid conception of Dr Stross and raise a fund by which Lidice shall be rebuilt to become one of the finest mining villages in the world. Stone by stone the church shall be rebuilt, children shall forget what is now being taught to them, and there shall be erected an institute of mining research in saving miners' lives at the rate of 100 for everyone that Hitler took from Lidice a year ago. We shall punish the criminals who slaughtered Lidice and shall wipe away the weakness, corruption, and blind folly that brought the Czech nation down at Munich in 1938; we shall destroy aggression and build a world in which so great a people as the Czechs can live in peace and safety."

Mr Alexej Shiborin, representing the Soviet Embassy, said that the recent successes in Russia and in Italy would give greater morale to the conquered countries. In summing up, he said, "Much had been done to achieve final victory, but the enemy still possessed great strength with which to delay the hour of his final collapse. It was necessary to open a second front in Europe, which would compel the Germans to withdraw 60 or 80 divisions from the Eastern front, and thus help to restore independence to the oppressed people of the continent."

Dr Stross then spoke. He appealed to people to distinguish between Nazis and Germans. He argued that while it was natural to feel that the whole German nation was at fault for the horrors of the war, the Allies' philosophy should be more along the lines of "If the pupil commits murder, hang the schoolmaster... "We were going to hang the schoolmaster soon!" he said.

The next speaker was the Lidice survivor, referred to as *Flt/Lt.* "X" in the press, but in all likelihood, this was Josef Horák, who was now serving as a flight lieutenant in the 311th Czechoslovak Bomber Squadron of the Royal Air Force. In fairly good English, "*Flt/Lt.* "X"' 'thanked the Derby Lidice Shall Live Committee for its effort and assured it that his people would be happy to know that they had such valuable friends in Britain. Referring to the RAF, he stated how glad he was to be able to serve in one of the finest services in the world, which gave him and his friends of the Czechoslovakian Air Force an opportunity of helping to defeat *the Huns*. "We like it," he went on, "and when the bombs go down you can always hear us say, 'For my parents, my sister, my country, and all who suffer.' We are all waiting for the day when Germany will get heavy toll for all she has done, not only to the small village of Lidice, but to thousands of others."

In the absence of Dr Hubert Ripka (Minister of State), Mr J. Kraus, a fellow minister representing the Czech Government-in-exile, expressed thanks to the people of Derby on behalf of his people. Speaking of the future, Mr Kraus said that Germany as a whole could not be exonerated. This did not mean that it should be destroyed or excluded from human society, but it did suggest that the German nation must bear the consequences of its guilt and give an effective and tangible expression of its will to renounce Nazism forever.

The final meeting of the Derby Lidice Shall Live committee took place on Friday, the 8th of October. It announced a total of £1,466 raised by the Lidice Week and associated activities. Expenses amounting to £202 left a net sum of £1,264, and it was decided to send £1,000 to the Czech Office in London at once, with the balance remaining in the hands of the treasurer until all the donations were received. The account was to be closed as soon after October the 31st as possible.

BRISTOL

Although a Lidice Shall Live committee had not been created in Bristol, such was the furore surrounding the fate of Lidice in 1943, that a significant part of the city's *Four Nations Appeal* would be devoted to the National Lidice Shall Live Fund.

As for the Four Nations, it was an international celebration of youth which was to bring many thousands of people to the City of Bristol during the week of October the 16th to the 23rd, 1943. The aim of the programme of cultural events was to give a platform to the young people of the occupied states of Yugoslavia, Czecho-Slovakia, Greece, and Poland, allowing them to explore, debate, fashion and creatively present the culture and heritage of their respective homelands to British audiences.

The idea for the Appeal came about at a meeting at Bristol's Council House on the 26th of May 1943. The Lord Mayor, Harry Wall, said that the four countries deserved support in every feasible way: **"We all know how they have suffered"** he said, **"and if we can launch this fund and get it well supported, we are doing a sound job."** Other key supporters of the project included the city's *great and good,* including the Sheriff, Mr H. M.C. Hosegood; the Duke of Beaufort; the Dean, the Very Rev H.W. Blackbourne; and many others. The following resolution was moved by the Lord Mayor and carried:

"Recognising the enormous task of sustenance and rehabilitation which lies before the countries of Czecho-Slovakia, Poland, Greece and Yugoslavia, and moved by the knowledge of the present sufferings of the peoples of the countries and their heroic struggles against the common enemy, this gathering of representative Bristol citizens pledges itself to do all in its power to promote an appeal for funds and to assist in any other way, and to the utmost of its ability, this endeavour to relieve the cruel burden which has fallen on these four European peoples."

The following officers were elected: - Hon treasurer, Mr E. J. Taylor; hon secretary, Mr H. V. Hindle; Exhibition Committee chairman, Mr A. H. Addison; Meetings' Committee chairman, Mr C. M. MacInnes; Flag Day Committee organiser, Mr W. L. Derrick; Music Committee chairman, Miss Madge Thomas; Events Committee chairman, Miss Helen Strimer; Publicity Committee, Mrs Britton, Mr Bryan Pearce and Mr Hindle.

A civic build-up of several months saw most of the city well invested in the project and excited about October's programme of events. A week before commencement, the Lord Mayor of Bristol, Henry Wall, wrote in the local press:

"During next week, many distinguished visitors will be visiting Bristol in connection with the Four Nations Appeal, October 16-23, 1943, and I sincerely hope that as many as possible of the citizens will display flags and bunting, especially Union Jacks and flags of the four nations concerned - Czecho-Slovakia, Greece, Poland, and Yugo-Slavia - should they be available. I am sure that this will serve to draw attention to the effort which we are making for these gallant nations and shall be grateful to those who will help to mark the Week in this way."

A special Four Nations art exhibition was opened by the Duchess of Kent at the Victoria Rooms on Monday the 18th of October, in the afternoon. According to the Bristol Mirror:

"The ceremony was performed in the presence of the Ambassadors of Czecho-Slovakia and Poland, as well as the Lord and Lady Mayoress and many notable Bristolians." The display was free to enter each day from 10.30am to 5pm. Notable personalities who visited included, **"the Greek Ambassador on Tuesday, Count Balinski Jundzill of Poland on Wednesday, and Princess Romanovsky-Pavlosky of Yugoslavia on Thursday!"**

Through art, the organisers of the exhibition had assembled 4,000 years' worth of culture in the hall, presenting representative samples ranging from ancient Greece sculptures of c2000BC to contemporary paintings by Czech artists of 1943AD. Many of the artisans were refugees, and their work had a grim, stark, powerful reality about it that sprang from a creative sensibility sharpened yet tempered by war:

Notice the frightening indictment of Karel Molnar's "Lidice," and the same artist's "Wounded Earth" and "Mourning Women;" the bitter commentary on Munich, "A Fateful Dinner Party" by Oskar Kokoschka; the forceful economy of line of Matousek's "Bren Gun Carrier" and "Reconnaissance Party."... reported The Bristol Mirror.

On Thursday the 21st, the art exhibition received a second opening ceremony when Dr Ladislav Karel Feierabend, economist and Minister of Finance to the Czechoslovak Government-in-exile visited the Victoria Rooms.

In his speech, Dr Feierabend declared: **"I firmly believe that the war in Europe will end next year. Then Czechoslovakia will live again."** With reference to Lidice, the doctor explained, **"As far as possible, the women of the village, now in concentration camps, will be returned there, but many of them must have died in Germany already. We intend to make Lidice a symbol of the resistance in our country, and we want to honour those who died there for Czechoslovakia."**

Presiding was the Lord Mayor, who gave thanks to Dr Feierabend for his support and attendance. It was then that it was announced that *all the money collected for Czecho-Slovakia as a result of the "Four Nations Appeal" would be used for the restoration of the village of Lidice.*

Events took take place daily. The programme included broadcast concerts by famous continental stars and film shows provided by the Ministry of Information. On Monday the 18th, celebrated conductor Dr Malcolm Sargent led a memorable concert by the Liverpool Philharmonic Orchestra and Ilona Kabos, the Hungarian pianist, at the Colston Hall; a Four Nations Ball organised by Miss Helen Strimer and held at the Victoria Rooms, Clifton, on the evening of Friday, the 22nd raised a sum of £163 8s 6d; and at the Museum Lecture Theatre, a special talk with piano illustrations was given by Geoffrey Higgins. Concerts were performed on Wednesday the 20th by the *Czech Trio* of Lisa Marketta (piano), Jan Sedivika (violin), and Ranel Horitza (cello). According to reports, **"...the trio of capable artists played with native Czechoslovakian charm, works by Dvořák and Smetana."** On Friday, the well-known pianist, Maria Donska, gave piano recitals at one o'clock in the Museum / Lecture Theatre, and then later at 5.30pm at the Victoria Rooms. The admission at all the events was free, though there were collections for the Four Nations.

FOUR NATIONS RALLY - COLSTON HALL - 23ᴿᴰ OCTOBER 1943

Audiences witnessed the climax of the programme on Saturday the 23rd with the Four Nations Flag Day followed by the Four Nations Rally - which took place at Colston Hall, starting at 2.30pm. The Bristol Mirror depicted the events:

"Saturday was a great day for Bristol youth. Something like 2,500 boys and girls, representing almost every young people's organisation in the country, thronged the Colston Hall. The gathering was held in connection with Bristol's Four Nations Appeal to give the young people an opportunity of playing their part in it. Members of the girls' organisations sat on the platform in the traditional garb of the Four Nations."

After representatives of the leading national youth movements had paraded, the flags of Czechoslovakia, Poland, Greece, and Yugoslavia were carried across the stage to a position behind the chairs of the Lord Mayor of Bristol the Lady Mayoress, and speakers of the Four Nations, to the accompaniment of their national anthems. The Lord Mayor thanked the youth of Bristol for supporting the appeal in such a grand way, and addresses were given by the young representatives of the countries.

"The speakers were Miss L Keppichova, of Czecho-Slovakia, Miss Susan Westarkis, of Greece, and Mr H. Klemenchich of Yugo-Slavia. A Polish airman spoke of the great gratitude his country felt for the assistance Britain was rendering her and thanked the women of Bristol heartily for aiding the Four Nations Appeal."

"After folk dancing by the girls' clubs and a physical training display by the boys, the Lady Mayoress received gifts from representatives of the world organisations. A boy and a girl, representatives of the youth of Bristol, proposed a vote of thanks to the Lord Mayor and Lady Mayoress."

COVENTRY

It was announced in late 1943 that Coventry was to join the Lidice Shall Live movement. The decision was made at a meeting at the Council House on Wednesday the 1st of December, attended by representatives of the churches, Civil Defence force, social and other organisations. The meeting was called at the invitation of the City's Lord Mayor, Cllr Alec Turner, to discuss the organisation of a series of events to raise funds to help rebuild the village and was addressed by Dr Barnett Stross and Mr Frank Hampl, Chairman and Secretary, respectively, of the Stoke-on-Trent Lidice Shall Live committee.

In his address, Dr Stross said the movement was formed to give the only answer which could be given to the Nazi method of trying to instil fear through brutality. He explained that plans were to be prepared for a *"model miners' village"* including an *"international research institute for the investigation of safety measures in mines."* Frank Hampl, who was now organising secretary of the movement, explained what had been done in other places to organise special efforts for a week: the special services and parades, with their entertainments in which prominent Czech musicians, vocalists and speakers took part; special film shows at cinemas; specialist gift shops and stalls; meetings at factories and other places.

Together it was decided to go ahead with the scheme and February 1944 was originally suggested as the most convenient month for high officials of the free Czechoslovakian Government-in-exile to take part, *though this was later put back to mid-March*. A fund total of £1,000,000 was the target to be raised at the time. Cllr Ben Mason, Chairman of the Coventry Czecho-Slovak - British Friendship Club, told the meeting that campaigners had organised events with success in Stoke-on-Trent, Birmingham, Sheffield, Derby, and other places. Dr Stross further outlined the possibility of holding events such as church services, special film shows, meetings in factories, the visit of a Czech leading statesman, the concert of Czech music by one of the best-known Czech orchestras. A parade of Civil Defence personnel, a visit to Coventry by the Czech Army Band and Choir, and a Sunday theatre concert were also suggested. After a lengthy discussion, the meeting appointed the following committee with the power to co-opt, to discuss details and decide on a date:

Ben Mason (Chairman), the Rev G. W. Clitheroe (Vicar of the Holy Trinity), the Rev W. H. Cookson (Minister of the Central Hall), Monsignor Laurence Emery, Captain N. T. Thurston (or his deputy), Mr J. A. Harrison (Editor "Evening Telegraph"), Mr F. H. Harrod (Director of Education), Dr A. H. Marshall (Deputy City Treasurer), Mr James Taylor (City Development Officer), Mrs W. F. Strickland, Mrs Fretton, Mrs Bendall, and A. D. Perry (Secretary Coventry Czecho-Slovak - British Friendship Club)

On Tuesday, March the 14th 1944, President Edvard Beneš presented a cheque for £1,000 to the Lord Mayor as a personal gift to Coventry and Warwickshire Hospital. For two years the city had stood up to particularly heavy attacks because of the number of ordnance firms, engineering factories and motor companies running in the immediate area. The attack which occurred on the evening of the 14th of November 1940 and continued into the morning of the 15th wreaked terrible trauma upon the city. Dr Beneš gift was emblematic of the empathy and fraternity the Czech people felt for the people of Coventry and their resilience in the face of

Luftwaffe bombing. It was the start of a reciprocal arrangement built around the widening of cultural understanding and international peace and friendship which would thrive to this day.

Beneš was in Coventry for the launch of its *Lidice Week*. There had now been several Lidice campaigns in support of the National Lidice Fund, but Coventry's was regarded as one of special significance, not only for Britain but for the people of Czecho-Slovakia: for these industrious provincial people had faced the same weight of TNT as the residents of Warsaw, Stalingrad, and London, yet were still prepared to support a fellow community 1,000 miles away. The week of dedicated events organised by the newly formed Coventry sub-committee, set out to raise a £2,000 contribution towards the construction of a new Lidice. It was launched on the afternoon of Sunday the 12th of March with a memorial service, symbolically held at the City's bombed out Cathedral. The Coventry Evening Telegraph reported the occasion of the launch:

The event was conducted by the Provost, Richard Howard and was attended by the President of Czecho-Slovakia, Dr Edvard Beneš; and Czech leaders, including M. Nemez, Minister of Commerce and Industry; M. Pecko, Minister of Social Welfare; Mr. Maxa, President of the State Council: and General Rudolph Viest, Minister of State. The Soviet Union was represented by the Minister-Plenipotentiary, Mr Vasily Valkov, and the Russian Military Attaché, Colonel Zizov. The Mayor of Coventry, Cllr Alec Turner, and the Mayoress accompanied the visitors together with the Mayor of Leamington, Captain W. F. Strickland, MP, Dr B. Stross, Chairman of the Lidice Committee, aldermen, Cllrs, and Corporation officials.

The congregation which attended the service at Coventry Cathedral was so large that it overflowed the cleared portion of the ruined building. The lesson was read by Squadron Leader L. Vit, Minister of the Protestant Church of Czechoslovakia, and a hymn, "*Through all the changing scenes of life*", sung by the Czechoslovak Army Choir, who also sang their national anthem, "*Kde Domov Můj.*" The flags of the United Kingdom and Czechoslovakia were then ceremoniously and sombrely laid upon the altar. There then followed the Hussite Choral including the hymn "*Loving Shepherd of Thy Sheep*" sung by a child, before the congregation prayed silently for the surviving children from Lidice and for all the children of Czecho-Slovakia. Prayers for the United Nations by the Provost preceded the service's conclusion with the hymn, "*Fight the Good Fight,*" and the national anthems of the United Kingdom and Czechoslovakia.

As the nation looked tentatively towards a different future, with the growing domination of the Allied nations working together in defeat of Nazi Germany and Japan, there was a feeling that the week had a wider significance. Perhaps offering more cause for reflection than other *Lidice Weeks*, this one offered the citizens of Coventry and Great Britain more space to consider what the world should be like after the war. It felt as though the Lidice Shall Live campaign in its current form was at a zenith - as it suggested the need for collaboration in friendship and construction with the people of Czechoslovakia, as much in the peace to come as in the present war.

"Immediately following the service, the salute was taken by Dr Beneš at a march past. The parade was led by the City of Coventry Band, and consisted of contingents of Royal Naval Ratings, W.R.N.S., Units of the British Army, USA. Troops and Band, Czecho-Slovakian Troops, the Standard Pipe Band, The Home Guard, the Sea Cadet Corps, Army Cadet Force, Air Training Corps and their respective bands; the Girls' Training Corps,

the N.F.S., the W.V.S., Police Messengers, C.D. Messenger Service Band, C.D. General Services, Fire Guard Service, Public Utility Services, British Red Cross Society, St. John Ambulance Brigade, St. John Cadets, The British Legion, the Women's Land Army, the Church Lads' Brigade and Band, the Boys' Brigade, Sea Rangers, and Girl Guides."

In true Chartist style, the parade marched to gather at Pool Meadow, a historic location used for fairs, rallying and open-air meetings; and from there representative detachments made a parade entry into the Hippodrome Theatre, preceded by Civil Defence personnel bearing flags of the United Nations, where they were enthusiastically greeted by a large assembly. Here, the Mayor of Coventry introduced the visitors to the meeting, and said the event was unique in the history of the city. He mentioned Coventry's age-old connection with Czechoslovakia referencing King John and *"The Winter Queen"* of Bohemia - Princess Elizabeth, who spent some time in the city.

In his speech, Dr Barnett Stross outlined the progress of the movement, and compared Coventry's experiences with those of Czech towns:

"Your voice is all the more loud and significant." He expressed strong hopes for the immediate future and said, *"We hope to wipe from the pages of history the shameful passages written in 1938...The Czech Day of Liberation is at hand, and soon our friend will be a free and independent nation."*

Dr Stross reminded the assembly that the British people accepted liberty as naturally as they did fresh air, and he compared this with Czecho-Slovakia's fight against the stranglehold of Nazi oppression. Jan Masaryk, Czechoslovak Deputy Prime Minister, was unable to attend. Cllr Ben Mason read a message from him in which he said: *"I am convinced that the friendships that are being formed today will be permanent."*

According to the Coventry Evening Telegraph, Soviet representative Vasily Valkov received thunderous applause when he rose to greet the meeting on behalf of the USSR. He referred to the continual defeat of the German Forces on the Eastern front, and to the part played by units of the Czechoslovakian Army fighting with the Red Army.

In his address, Dr Beneš reminded the audience that March the 15th marked the fifth anniversary of the German invasion of Czechoslovakia, and although his people had been oppressed for five years they would continue to resist until Germany's unconditional surrender. He expressed the gratitude of his countrymen for what Great Britain had done under the leadership of Mr Churchill. He paid tribute to the Fighting Services and the Merchant Navy. If the Germans had invaded Great Britain, the President believed that the Royal Navy would never have allowed sufficient supplies to reach them. He came from a country without a Navy, but after his stay here he would return with unforgettable memories of Britain's *"sea power."*

Beneš spoke of how Czech troops in Warwickshire had always been taken into the home life of the people, and of the opportunity they had had of becoming acquainted with Shakespeare's country, and with characters similar to those immortalised by that great woman whom Coventry loved to honour, *"George Eliot."* The President said it was his first speech outside London since his return from Russia, and he described his visit to Stalingrad, which, together with Lidice and Coventry, was a great symbol of the sufferings of all three countries.

Later, the Deputy Mayor, Alderman George. E. Hodgkinson, proposed a vote of thanks to Dr Beneš, and revealed that during his visit the President had presented the mayor, on behalf of the Czechoslovakian Government-in-exile, with a cheque for £1,000 towards Coventry's new voluntary hospital. A selection of Czech music and songs was given by the Czech Army Band and Choir, who were especially appreciated for their rendering of a Russian folk song, for which an encore was demanded.

The Lord Mayor, Cllr Alec Turner, then handed President Beneš a sheet of the crested notepaper which the council used for its official communications. He said there was something on the crest which he would recognise. Feathers at the back of the shield were those of King John, the famous *Blind King of Bohemia*, who gave his life at the Battle of Crécy in 1346. The victor, Edward Woodstock, *he said*, had taken the dead King's body to his tent and adopted his crest and his motto, *"Ich Dien,"* as his own and as the inspiration for his life.

Also known as the *Black Prince*, Edward had been invested as the first Prince of Wales by his father, King Edward III in 1343 and for generations to come, until the mid-16th century Coventry would now become the property of the Princes of Wales. The Lord Mayor observed that for the last 785 years the *"vulture crest"* of old Bohemia had graced the City's coat of arms. The Lord Mayor also spoke of the Czech *Winter Queen*:

"Some years before she became Queen she was in danger and the citizens formed a bodyguard to keep watch and ward over the house until the danger had passed. Hence, we in Coventry had special reasons to remember Bohemia...Princess Elizabeth was known as "the Winter Queen" because she only remained in Prague for one winter. Upon leaving Bohemia Elizabeth settled down at Coombe Abbey, where a collection of Bohemian glass is still preserved. Our present Queen is a direct descendant of a Bohemian King through the House of Hanover."

The week of events held a range of exciting cultural, social, and artistic happenings designed to attract those from all social spheres and backgrounds to Czech heritage and culture:

On Monday the 13th of March, a concert of traditional Czech music was given in the Central Hall by the London Philharmonic Orchestra, led by Vilém Tauský, the prominent conductor and composer who at the time was serving for the Czech Army. Tuesday the 14th saw an adaptation of Louis MacNeice's radio play, "*A Town Without a Name*," performed by a selected company of Coventry amateurs at the Sports and Social Centre – this was repeated on Thursday. The Czech Army Choir gave a selection of songs, and a gymnastic display was given by the Czech Army Sokol Team on Wednesday the 15th. A Women's Rally was held in the Central Hall on Thursday the 16th - among the speakers was Mrs Kathie Beckmann, of the National Council of Czechoslovak Women in Great Britain; the Mayoress, Mrs Alec Turner presided, and Madame Lisa Fuchsová, the well-known Czech pianist, gave a recital. Every day during the week, lunch hour concerts and meetings were given at various factories and hostels by the Czech Army Band, Choir, Sokol Team, and prominent Czech speakers.

On the 9th of May, the Coventry Evening Telegraph reported how Coventry's Lidice Shall Live Campaign held in March **"to raise funds for the rebuilding of the Czech village destroyed by the Germans"**, had resulted in their £2,000 target being exceeded. **The final figure was £2,078 9s. 11d. all of which had been handed over to the national account for the campaign**. The total included £386 from the flag day, £348 in donations and £222 17s. 2d. from a gift shop which sold Czech goods. The dance, play and concert produced £76 17s. 1d. The rest was made up of collections taken at Coventry Cathedral, Coventry Hippodrome, churches, hostels, schools, works, at the London Philharmonic Orchestra's concert, and the women's rally, Central Hall. The works collection was £579 12s. 2d.

"The flags of the United Kingdom and Czecho-Slovakia were then ceremoniously and sombrely laid upon the altar. There then followed the Hussite Choral including the hymn "Loving Shepherd of Thy Sheep" sung by a child, before the congregation prayed silently for the surviving children from Lidice and for all the children of Czecho-Slovakia."

"...the parade marched to gather at Pool Meadow, a historic location used for fairs, rallying and open-air meetings; and from there representative detachments made a parade entry into the Hippodrome, preceded by Civil Defence personnel bearing flags of the United Nations, where they were enthusiastically greeted by a large assembly." **The BBC made a recording of the Hippodrome ceremony but no trace of this has been found thus far.**

In his formal address the Provost, the Very Rev. R. T. Howard, said: *"The sufferings of Lidice have drawn forth from the people of England a generous desire to serve them by helping to rebuild Lidice. Coventry should lead the rest of England in this service...These stones of Coventry Cathedral are not going to remain dead forever. They will rise again into the structure of a new building - new, living, and more glorious than ever before.* ***And so, Lidice shall live.****"*

NOTTINGHAM

On the 4th of April 1943, the Nottingham Evening Post reported:

The Lord Mayor of Nottingham, Alderman Ernest Braddock, has called a meeting at the Council House for April 8th in support of "The Lidice Shall Live movement" to be addressed by Dr Stross, of Stoke-on-Trent. In his letter inviting attendance at the meeting the Lord Mayor refers to the Nazi murders of the inhabitants of Lidice, and continues:

"Our miners and citizens feel that such an act of barbarism must have filled with horror not only this country, but all the freedom loving peoples of the world, and that a gesture of repudiation of such acts must be made to which all may have an opportunity of associating themselves."

A fund is to be raised for the purposes of rebuilding Lidice (in Czecho-Slovakia) after the war.

At the meeting, which received the full support of Nottingham City Council, under the sponsorship of the Lord Mayor, Alderman Ernest Braddock, Dr Stross explained that the fund was started by North Staffordshire miners, who agreed to a levy of 2s. 6d. (half a crown) per head and miners as a whole had promised support to the extent of over £50,000. It was an opportune moment for another attendee, Mr Val Coleman, Secretary of the Nottinghamshire Miners' Federated Union to announce his association's support and contribution of £1,000 towards the Lidice fund.

A certified locomotive driver and a gifted poet, Colonel David Bourner was a prominent local figure around Nottingham, who played key roles in the Home Guard and the British Legion as well as other areas of public service. His work on behalf of the Czechoslovak refugees began at the time of the annexation of the Sudetenland when he served as adjutant to the British Legion Volunteer Police Force - which was to have monitored proceedings during the handover of power and the subsequent plebiscite in Czecho-Slovakia. It was this keen interest in the welfare of the Czechoslovak state and its people, which prompted him to become Chairman of the Nottingham "Lidice Shall Live" committee.

Once established, the Nottingham committee swiftly got down to planning a Lidice fundraising campaign for autumn 1943. A programme for a *Lidice Week* was drafted, with a launch set for the 20th of September, to be attended by a host of dignitaries including the new Lord Mayor, Cllr Fred Mitchell and Dr Lobkowicz, the Czech Ambassador. This was to be followed by a series of activities and events, which were to include: a parade to St. Mary's Church involving local organisations and the military; a meeting in the Shire Hall, presided over by the Lord Mayor; a concert to be held at the Albert Hall involving wounded soldiers from the City and General Hospitals; as well as numerous dances, a Czech gift shop and exhibitions across the city.

However, on the 19th of August at a meeting held at 47 Park Row, the Nottingham Lidice Shall Live committee decided to defer its Lidice Week until the following Easter. Presiding at a meeting of the board, when the matter arose Colonel Bourner said he agreed with the recommendation and spoke of the necessity to educate public opinion as to the real objects of the scheme. He said,

"It was not merely question of raising money to replace a destroyed village, necessary as that was. More important, the fundamental principle behind it was to erect something that would be a lasting memorial and show the Nazi world that this sort of thing could not happen, that nothing could be destroyed simply by savagely tearing it down."

It was suggested, instead, that local churches should be approached with an appeal to support the effort for raising funds, and that designated organisations and factories should receive forms to start collections as soon as possible. Other suggestions were that local cinemas might co-operate by showing the two Lidice films and have collections in Czech national costume, and that Nottingham ladies might arrange teas and small *"whist drives"* in their own homes to supplement the fund.

On Monday the 3rd of January 1944, the Nottingham Journal reported how the Nottingham Lidice Lives Committee was targeting £5,000 for its *"Lidice effort"*, now planned for Easter week. Chairman of the committee, Col. Bourner mentioned to reporters that Derby's effort for Lidice the previous year had raised between £1,500 and £2,000, and that being the case, Nottingham ought to aim for £5,000 as a minimum.

A meeting, chaired by Colonel Bourner with Mr. D. W. Rattee as secretary, was to be held to complete the arrangements, which had received the full backing of the Lord Mayor. It was hoped that it would be possible to secure Dr Beneš as one of the speakers at a big public meeting during the week. Colonel Bourner told the 'Journal that **"...the taking of factory collections for the fund has been suggested, and the city churches will be invited to support the effort with indoor and outdoor events. It is also intended to apply for permission to hold a flag day. Concerts by the Lidice String Quartet, composed of Czechs, are among the features being planned for the week."**

We can only surmise as to the more complex *or simple* reasons there could have been for the indefinite postponement of Nottingham's Lidice Appeal. Judging by Colonel Bourner's impressive life story, he was a competitive man. Perhaps a smaller total raised following a successful resolution of the war and with the onset of geopolitical uncertainty would be easier to explain away. But Easter 1944 came and went and the Nottingham Lidice Shall Live committee went into a hiatus until the war in Europe ended.

On the 30th of May 1945, at the invitation of the City's new Lord Mayor, Cllr Frank Carney, representatives of various interests in the city and county met in the Council House to consider launching a fresh appeal for funds for the rebuilding of Lidice. This time the meeting was addressed by Frank Hampl of the Lidice Shall Live Committee, who spoke of the need to rebuild Lidice and thus strengthen the ties of friendship between Britain and Czechoslovakia. He explained how the whole scheme was being run in the closest collaboration with the new government of Czechoslovakia and how it was proposed that when the village was rebuilt, foundation stones would be laid by representatives of the cities and counties which had supported the movement. Hampl revealed that about £60,000 had been raised and that *the movement* was looking forward to Nottingham playing a vital role in the continuing appeal. He also defined the movement, how it was not organised jointly by the Allies but was a British symbol of interest in Czechoslovakia. However, according to him, though the idea for the rebuilding of Lidice on modern lines came from Britain, there had been promises of support from America and other countries.

Hampl re-energised the Nottingham Lidice Shall Live movement, so much so that it began planning a Nottingham Week for September. In the meantime, an exhibition called "*Our Czechoslovakian Ally*" was held at the Public Library at Sherwood Street from June the 3rd to the 23rd. Working in conjunction with the Czecho-Slovak - British Friendship Club the committee put on a well-attended dance held at the Victoria Ballroom on the 24th of June. In commemoration of the Lidice tragedy, special programmes were given at the News Theatre on the afternoon and evening of the 10th of June, with all proceeds donated to the Lidice Fund.

NOTTINGHAM'S LIDICE APPEAL

Charity ballroom dancing and concert performances.

Two examples of charitable events which preceded Nottingham's main event on the 30th of September.

Others were to include a concert to be held at the Albert Hall involving wounded soldiers from the City and General Hospitals, as well as numerous dances, a Czech gift shop and art exhibitions across the city.

Images are advertisements from the Nottingham Evening Post on the 3rd (above) and 6th (below) of September 1945, respectively.

Nottingham's Appeal Week was opened on the 30th of September 1945. It reflected a sequence of events planned in 1943 and followed a format proved successful by other cities. Many Czech dignitaries, members of the Lidice Shall Live committee and local elected representatives attended the launch. Interestingly, there were no international dignitaries acting on behalf of the British Government and the Soviet Union present; nor were there any delegates from the miners' union in attendance. According to the Nottingham press, the guests included:

Dr J. Cisar, Plenipotentiary and Counsellor to the Czecho-Slovak Embassy (who was deputising for the Czecho-Slovak Ambassador, Dr Lobkowicz); Gen. J. Boby (head of the Czecho-Slovak Mission to Great Britain) and his aide-decamp Lt. Hohnberg; Col. J. Kalla, O.B.E. (the Czecho-Slovak Military and Air Attaché to Great Britain); Frank Hampl (General Secretary of Czecho-Slovak H.Q.); Dr Fischl (Press Attaché), Mr Julius Guttman (Prague National Opera House); Mr K. Kirschnek; and Dr B. Stross, M.P (National President of the Lidice Appeal); The Lord Mayor and Lady Mayoress; Sheriff of Nottingham (Dr W. B. Blandy) and Mrs Blandy; the Town Clerk (Mr J. E. Richards); Ald. R. Shaw, J.P; and Colonel Bourner (Chairman of the Nottingham Lidice Committee).

The day's proceedings opened with a luncheon at the Council House, given by the Lord Mayor to meet Dr Cisar. This was followed by a military parade, at which the Lord Mayor took the salute outside the Council House, a service at St Mary's Church and a public meeting in the Shire Hall. The Lord Mayor, proposing the toast of *"The Lidice Shall Live movement,"* expressed the hope that not only Lidice but also the whole of Czechoslovakia would be restored to its old prosperity. In and around Nottingham was a mining population whose hearts and affections flowed out to the people of Lidice, whose town was razed by flame and its homes, reduced to ashes; he prayed to God that in the days to come, Lidice would rise again in greater glory.

Dr Cisar explained that if Lidice had been destroyed by a tornado, or an earthquake, or some such cataclysm of nature he would have had some hesitation in accepting Nottingham's help, for it was not good to one's pride to feel that one's country or one's hometown had become an object of charity. But Lidice was one of many dozens, if not many hundreds, of villages in occupied Europe violated,

"… according to plan by deliberate acts of cruelty, its men executed on the spot, its women dragged away to Germany, the elderly to serve in labour camps and the younger to serve the lust of Nazi sub-humans, and children dragged away to German institutions to be made typical Führer-adoring sub-humans. Lidice had become not only the memorial of the great sacrifice of peace-loving and a freedom-loving people in the struggles of freedom against darkness and slavery, but it had become the one great symbol of the universal solidarity of all men of goodwill without which, and without the ultimate victory of which, this war would have been fought in vain."

The subsequent church parade service at St. Mary's was conducted by a Free Church minister, the Rev. R. K Ross, with Dr Cisar reading the lesson and Mr Julius Guttman singing two anthems by Czech composers. The Rev. Canon R. H. Hawkins, Vicar of St. Mary's, in his sermon described the visit to St. Mary's of the Plenipotentiary of Czechoslovakia as being a unique occasion in the history of St. Mary's Church. On behalf of the church wardens and people of St. Mary's, Canon Hawkins offered a hearty welcome to Dr Cisar and his companions.

After expressing his pleasure at the fact that in Britain the Government of Czechoslovakia had found a home and the nationals of his country a haven, while the Czechoslovak and British troops served together, side by side, he dealt in detail with the fate of the inhabitants of Lidice on the 10th of June 1942 and observed:

"It was difficult to find words to express the horror we felt in the presence of such a foul act. On that very day when the exponents of the Nazi creed appeared to be and felt themselves to be so completely triumphant, they actually brought about their own defeat through the death, sufferings, and tears of the gallant people of Lidice. If this was so, those gallant men had not died in vain, or their womenfolk suffered in vain."

The service concluded with the singing of the Czechoslovak and the British national anthems, and a collection was taken for the building of a village church at Lidice. Later, at a meeting at the Shire Hall, the Lord Mayor read letters from Mr Will Lawther, President of the National Union of Mineworkers, and Mr F. G. James, on behalf of the Nottingham Trades Council, together with communications from Mr G. deFreitas, MP for Central Nottingham, and Mr James Harrison, MP for East Nottingham; all parties urged support for the rebuilding of Lidice. In response, Dr Cisar said that:

"Lidice, by its destruction, became a symbol: it belonged not only to Czechoslovakia but to all nations. It should become for us a memento and a pledge never to allow the conditions to arise that would make an occurrence of this type possible again."

The closing week of Nottingham's Lidice appeal saw several other fairs, events and activities take place including: a lunch hour concert at Boots Factory, Beeston on the 3rd of October, a cinema show at the Futurist Cinema, Basford, on Sunday the 7th of October, and a dance at the Victoria Ballroom in aid of the fund on Friday the 12th.

On Saturday, the 7th of December 1946, in a final report, the Nottingham Lidice Shall Live board wrote that:

"This country has raised £100,000 especially for the Miners' Welfare Institute, wherein research will be carried on in miners' diseases and today the Lord Mayor handed over a cheque for £1,542 13s 9d to Dr Barnett Stross, MP for Hanley and Chairman of the "Lidice Shall Live" committee. The Chairman of the Nottingham committee was Col. D. Bourner, and Treasurer, Mr E. W. Smith." A special tribute was paid to the Nottinghamshire miners for their contribution of £1,000.

CREWE

Crewe's *Czecho-Slovak Week* ran from October the 9th to the 14th, 1944.

The campaign's creation is owed, in large part, to the local Trades Council who accepted a proposal from the Lidice Shall Live committee to found a series of events in the local area. On Thursday the 18th of May 1944, at a meeting of the Crewe Trades Council, the Secretary, Mr G. E. Hodgkinson, reported an appeal from the Stoke-on-Trent Lord Mayor's Committee for support in aid of the National Lidice Fund. It was agreed to invite the organising secretary, Frank Hampl, to give an address at the next meeting.

On the evening of the 15th of June, Hampl explained the intentions of the campaign to the council's members—to build a new Lidice and to create a mining research institute. Having found the scheme sufficiently inspiring and realistic, members started talks with Crewe Borough Council in order to stage a series of fundraising events. Subsequently, on the 19th of August, the Crewe Chronicle reported that the town's Mayor, Mrs Mossford Powell, had agreed to support an appeal for the National Lidice Fund. There would be flag days on October the 6th and 7th.

Once more, the Stoke-on-Trent Secretary, Frank Hampl, was instrumental in setting things up and promised to contribute by bringing a cultural exhibition on a Czech theme. The Trades Council agreed to back the appeal and asked for flag sellers.

The campaign was realised when *The Exhibition of Czecho-Slovakian Friendship* opened at the Prudential Buildings on Monday the 9th of October 1944 by a Czechoslovak Army Captain, in the presence of Dr Victor Fischl, the Czech Minister of Foreign Affairs, and a company of Czech infantry from nearby Cholmondeley Castle. The exhibition, which remained open for the week and was free to enter, was arranged locally by a committee formed by the new Mayor, Mrs F. E. White, in co-operation with Crewe Trades Council. According to the Crewe Chronicle on the 14th of October:

"The exhibition shows our Czech ally in a vivid and unique way and brings a momentous message of friendship and goodwill to the people of Crewe. It tells the story of those who escaped from German oppression to fight, and of the armies in the Middle East, Russia, and Great Britain, which they joined. It shows the exploits of the airmen in the Battle of Britain - men who now fly over France; the Czech war effort in Britain and of how the German war is sabotaged in Czecho-Slovakia: illustrations of German plunder and terror."

Mrs White, who presided at the opening ceremony, expressed the pride that Britons felt in their Czech allies, who by their courage and fortitude had written a chapter in the history of the present war which would live forever. She expressed her view that the villagers' sacrifices had not been made in vain, for Lidice would live again and right would triumph over might.

In the name of Crewe, the Mayor welcomed the Czech visitors and wished their country prosperity and peace in the future. In response, the Czech Army representative gratefully acknowledged the kind and hospitable treatment provided to Czechoslovaks during the past four years and commented on the immediate predicament:

"The Czechs, he said, *lost their freedom for centuries, but it was restored in 1918, and for 20 years they had had a happy and progressive democratic country; they remained true to their democratic ideals, although their neighbours succumbed to fascism and the Nazi influence. Czech soldiers were now fighting on both the western and eastern fronts. Lidice had become a symbol for freedom-loving people, and they were determined to fight for that freedom."*

In declaring the exhibition open, the officer expressed the thanks of the Czech people for the interest manifested in the Lidice Shall Live appeal and wished the local committee success in their effort. Mr Emmett, of the inaugural Stoke-on-Trent Lidice Shall Live committee, explained that the national committee had set themselves the task of raising £1,000,000 for the purpose of resurrecting Lidice and they had been encouraged by the assistance given by various towns.

Other events which took place were flag days on Friday and Saturday, October the 13th and 14th. Presentations were given in schools to children of eleven years and over, prizes offered for the best essay on the talks and the exhibition received from each school. On Sunday the 15th, a concert was put on at the Kino Cinema by Czech performers. In November, in a breakdown of the mayor's charitable work, it showed that £163 had been raised towards the Lidice Shall Live fund through the events taken place in Crewe.

FELTHAM

During the Second World War, General Aircraft Limited (GAL) became an important designer and manufacturer of gliders. It was part of the Civilian Repair Organisation, to repair Supermarine Spitfires and modify Hawker Hurricanes to enable catapult-launching from convoy escort ships. The work was done in Hanworth, near Feltham. As a result of the operations conducted there, the town experienced particularly heavy bombing even though it was 15 miles outside Central London. Understandably, staff at GAL may well have felt a special kinship towards members of the overseas crew fighting for the RAF, including the many Czech pilots, and especially the two former Lidice residents, Josef Horák and Josef Stříbrný—But also, the fate of Lidice had a harmonising effect on the workers and managers alike; Lidice Shall Live was a cause to coalesce around in order to ensure a successful prosecution of the war.

On Saturday the 3rd of July 1943, the Middlesex Chronicle reported that working in conjunction with the national Lidice Shall Live campaign, a Feltham based Lidice Shall Live Committee based within the General Aircraft Ltd Works had arranged a series of events for the coming week:

"...in support of the fund for the rebuilding of the Czech mining village, which the Nazis destroyed a year ago after a massacre of its people."

A programme gave details of the scheduled activities, which were to conclude with a demonstration on Feltham Green on Sunday, July the 11th. Sponsored by General Aircraft Limited Works Committee, who met all expenses, these social activities and competitions were to support the national Lidice Shall Live fund and took place in and around Feltham from the week beginning Sunday the 4th of July. In addition to a snooker handicap, darts and table tennis challenges, the events included a dance in the GAL Clubhouse on Wednesday under the direction of Mr A. Russell, with music by *Wynne and Her Boys*; a variety show in the Parish Hall on Thursday with addresses on the object of the effort; another dance for GAL employees on the Friday evening; and a charity cricket match on Saturday the 10th at Sunbury.

An example of the sponsorship allocated by GLA was the £100 awarded to the winners of the Lidice Shall Live Darts Tournament—Reporting on the 25th of September, the Middlesex Chronicle declared:

Cup goes to "Horse & Groom...

The "Lidice shall live" darts semi-finals and final were played on Saturday at the G.A.L. Social and Sports Clubroom, Feltham before a large number of spectators:

The first semi-final was between Kenure "B" and "Horse and Groom," the latter winning very easily to everyone's surprise, in two straight games. Finishing doubles were thrown by Jordon and Manning. In the second semi-final Genair "A" beat Automotive after two very close games, the two winning shots being scored by Stan Garnier. In one leg Llewellyn started the game with 140, and in the second leg G. Frost registered 111.

With the stage all set for a grand finale, the first leg was won quite easily by Genair, Bedford finishing on double 3. The second was a neck and neck affair until after the last check when "Horse and Groom" went right away, and Watson finished on 28. In the second leg, as in the first, up came Watson, needing 46. He threw single eight and double 19 to finish the game and take the cup to the "Horse and Groom," where it will stay for the next 12 months...

The cup and prizes were presented by Cllr P. C. McNally, who informed the audience that a cheque for £100 had been handed to the Lidice Rebuilding Fund," with more to follow. The cup was donated by the shop stewards of General Aircraft Ltd. Feltham

FELTHAM RALLY – JULY 11TH 1943

The climactic rally at Feltham Green, whose slogan read *"Lidice reborn means the defeat of Fascism"* went ahead as planned. It began at 3pm on the afternoon of Sunday the 11th and it drew a large crowd. In attendance were the Czechoslovak Minister of State, Dr Hubert Ripka; Mr Ebby Edwards, Secretary of the Mineworkers' Federation of Great Britain; Mr Jack Tanner of the Amalgamated Engineering Union; Commandant G. Tilge, representing the Free French; Mr Vasily Valkov, for the Soviet Embassy; the London office of the Lidice Shall Live committee arranged for the *"Two Czech pilots"* to be in attendance once more—Flight Lieutenants Josef Horák and Josef Stříbrný; and there were several more members of the Czechoslovak Government-in-exile present.

Music was provided by a Home Guard Band and a Czechoslovakian Army Choir. It was successfully arranged that the BBC and Movietone be present to record and broadcast the event, including a message from the residents of Feltham to the people of occupied territories. *However, thus far, research has failed to unearth the material.*

Having developed a relationship with the London Office, a deputation visited the Czechoslovak Embassy on Thursday the 22nd of July to hand over the proceeds of the Feltham Committee's efforts, all of whom were General Aircraft Limited employees. The party consisted of P. C. McNally, works convenor of shop stewards and head of the deputation; W. H. Chamberlain, secretary of the organising committee; A. H. Bone, publicity secretary; and A. Burgess. Addressing Dr Hubert Ripka, Czech Minister of State, Mr McNally said he had much pleasure in presenting a cheque for £100, to which - 4,000 aircraft workers had subscribed. He also read the following message:

"We, the workers of General Aircraft, Feltham, sad because of the terrible sufferings of our comrades everywhere under Fascist domination, but inspired by their example, pledge ourselves to redouble our efforts towards an early invasion of Europe, bringing relief to our enslaved comrades, so that Lidice and all it represents shall rise from the ashes of oppression at the earliest possible moment."

Dr Ripka, acknowledging the gift, expressed appreciation of the enthusiasm shown by the British people in the Lidice Shall Live campaign, coupled with the hope that the friendship between the two nations would be everlasting.

A new round of pub fundraisers and other events extended the appeal into late summer and autumn, including the men and women's *Lidice Shall Live* Darts Tournament. However, it seems that Feltham's campaign quietened as 1944 approached, based on the lack of press coverage.

NEWCASTLE UPON TYNE

On the 12th of July 1942, a service of Intercession for Czecho-Slovakia was held at Newcastle Cathedral in memory of the victims of Lidice and Ležáky, and led by Dr F. M. Hnik, Secretary of the Czechoslovak Church. Hnik expressed gratitude on behalf of the Anglo – Czecho-Slovak Christian Fellowship for the support his countrymen and women were receiving in Britain and was hopeful that similar services could be held throughout the country, before offering prayers for Czecho-Slovakia, the members of its government and for her allies. He asked those present to remember all victims with deep gratitude.

Addressing all Czechs in his native language, Dr Hnik recalled President Beneš's conviction that such acts of savagery were part of a *spiritual war* for the soul and foundations of Christian civilization, the dignity of human beings and equality before God as members of the Christian Church. He concluded with a reminder to his compatriots that it was not for them to enjoy their comparative security without helping by every possible means to restore the liberties of Czechoslovakia.

The Newcastle Journal and North Mail reported how Lieutenant Colonel Josef Kalla, Czech flier, and Air Attaché to the British Government, was guest speaker at a special matinee concert at Newcastle City Hall on Sunday the 1st of November. The programme was presented by the Newcastle Czecho-Slovak – British Friendship Club and the British Council to raise funds for the Lidice Shall Live fund and featured several artists drawn from the Czech Army, including the Czecho-Slovak Army Choir & Orchestra, Captain Válek *(tenor)* and the eminent pianist,

Vilém Tauský - one of a significant group of émigré composers and musicians who had settled in Great Britain after the war.

This was the latest of many varied cultural presentations organised by the Newcastle Branch of the 'Friendship Club, led by the executive of President J. Mlejnek, and Secretary Jan Jalůvka, whose creative energies were described **"as comprehensive as they are useful"** by the regional press. The club grew to a significant membership during the war and provided at its headquarters in Gosforth facilities for recreation, social gathering and sleeping, with a special department to help the refugee children keep up with their Czech language skills whilst attending English school.

Through its connections with some of the largest Czechoslovak industrialists on Tyneside, for instance, pump manufacturer Miroslav Sigmund *(later, the creator of the Green Goddess fire engine)* and J. Martinasek, the group secured goodwill from many within the Czech Government-in-exile, as well as the local authority. A dinner celebrating Czech independence held on October the 27th 1941, received an audience of 400 grandees and dignitaries from across the region.

BERMONDSEY

The citizens of Bermondsey, the most bombed out part of London during *The Blitz*, certainly made a brave showing for their memorial service to the martyred village, which was held on the early evening of Friday the 11th of June 1943.

Appropriately enough, the service took place amongst the wreckage caused by recent Luftwaffe bombing. In this statement of solidarity, the devastated site chosen for the ceremony at Spa Road was adorned with bunting, and in each of the corners of the rostrum had been hoisted flags of the United Nations.

According to the press, **"Behind the rostrum were uninhabited houses, from the glassless windows of which looked out a number of small boys and girls, a grim reminder of other times."**

Owing to difficulty with the loudspeakers the proceedings began late, but according to reports a Czechoslovak Army choir, **"singing with fervour and delighting in their vivid contrast of loud and soft tone, and particularly in an admirable staccato,"** gained the admiration of a large audience.

Of the speakers, Jan Masaryk, Czech Foreign Minister, was the most notable: **"His style, and his remarkable fluency in the English idiom, went straight to the hearts of the crowd."**

Following his description of Bermondsey's sufferings, he declared that **"we could now say to Mussolini, that mouldy, moth-eaten Black shirt. Pantellaria to you;"** and we should shortly be saying to Hitler, **"A couple of Berlins to you."** On the platform also were representatives of the Soviet and American Embassies.

The Nottingham Journal 11th June 1943

Lidice Shall Live – Sid Kirkham - 2010

LEEDS FLAG DAY

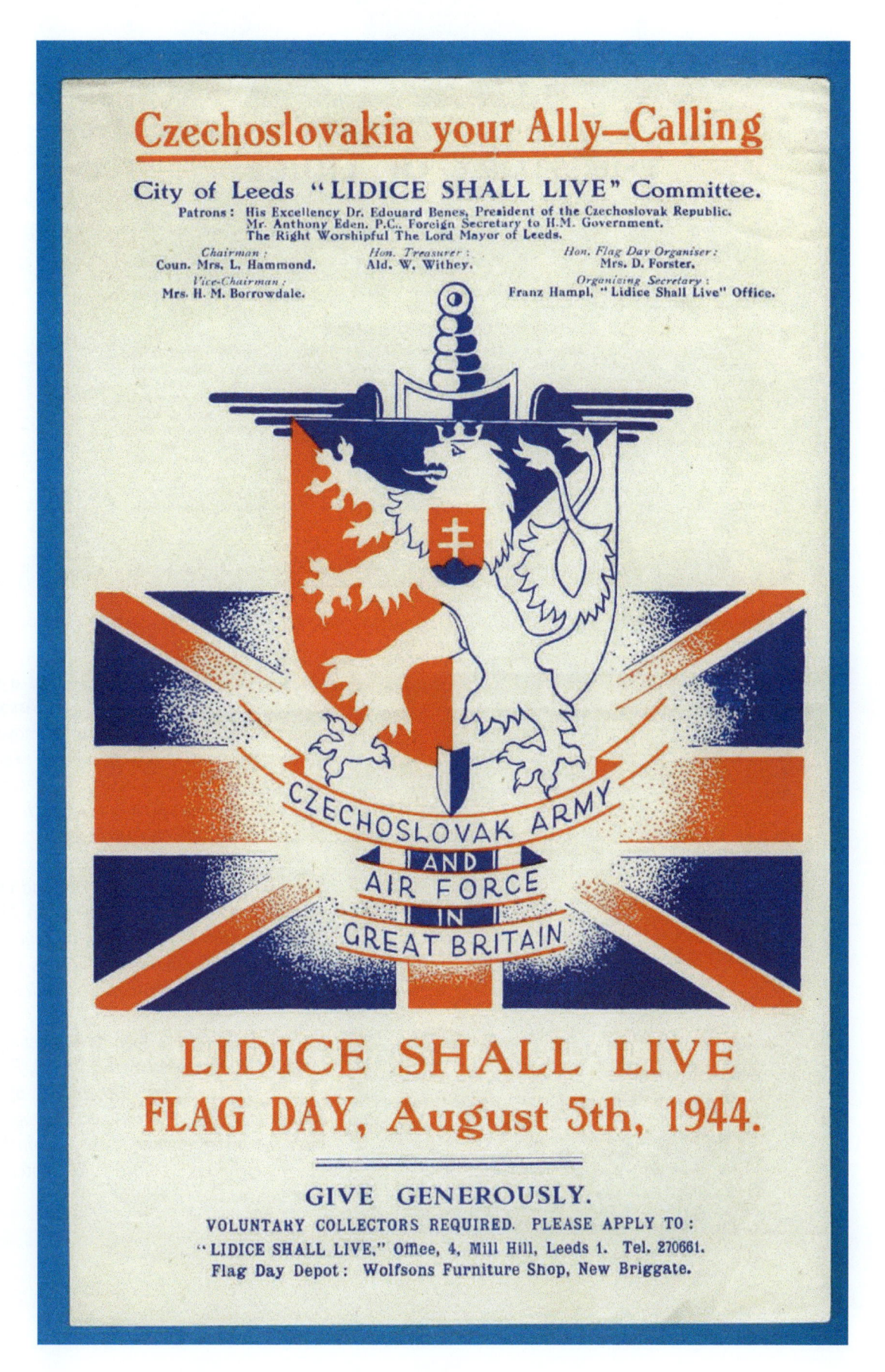

Czechoslovakia your Ally—Calling

City of Leeds "LIDICE SHALL LIVE" Committee.

Patrons: His Excellency Dr. Edouard Benes, President of the Czechoslovak Republic.
Mr. Anthony Eden, P.C., Foreign Secretary to H.M. Government.
The Right Worshipful The Lord Mayor of Leeds.

Chairman: Coun. Mrs. L. Hammond.
Hon. Treasurer: Ald. W. Withey.
Hon. Flag Day Organiser: Mrs. D. Forster.
Vice-Chairman: Mrs. H. M. Borrowdale.
Organising Secretary: Franz Hampl, "Lidice Shall Live" Office.

CZECHOSLOVAK ARMY AND AIR FORCE IN GREAT BRITAIN

LIDICE SHALL LIVE
FLAG DAY, August 5th, 1944.

GIVE GENEROUSLY.

VOLUNTARY COLLECTORS REQUIRED. PLEASE APPLY TO:
"LIDICE SHALL LIVE," Office, 4, Mill Hill, Leeds 1. Tel. 270661.
Flag Day Depot: Wolfsons Furniture Shop, New Briggate.

On Saturday May the 1st 1943, at a special conference of the Durham Miners' Association - Sam Watson, Financial Secretary moved that a message to the Czech miners expressing *"admiration of the underground struggles and unbreakable spirit of the Czech people"* be sent. It was unanimously passed.

The conference hall was packed and included several special guests, including Jan Masaryk who said that "...nothing had touched the people of his country so much as what the British miners had done after Lidice".

Jan Masaryk (left) is seen here meeting Hugh Dalton MP and Will Lawther (right), President of the Mineworkers' Federation of Great Britain, Durham Miners' Association agent, and later the first President of the National Union of Mineworkers, before they entered the conference.

Josef Horák
24th June 1915 - 18th January 1949

Josef Stříbrný
28th July 1915 - 12th November 1976

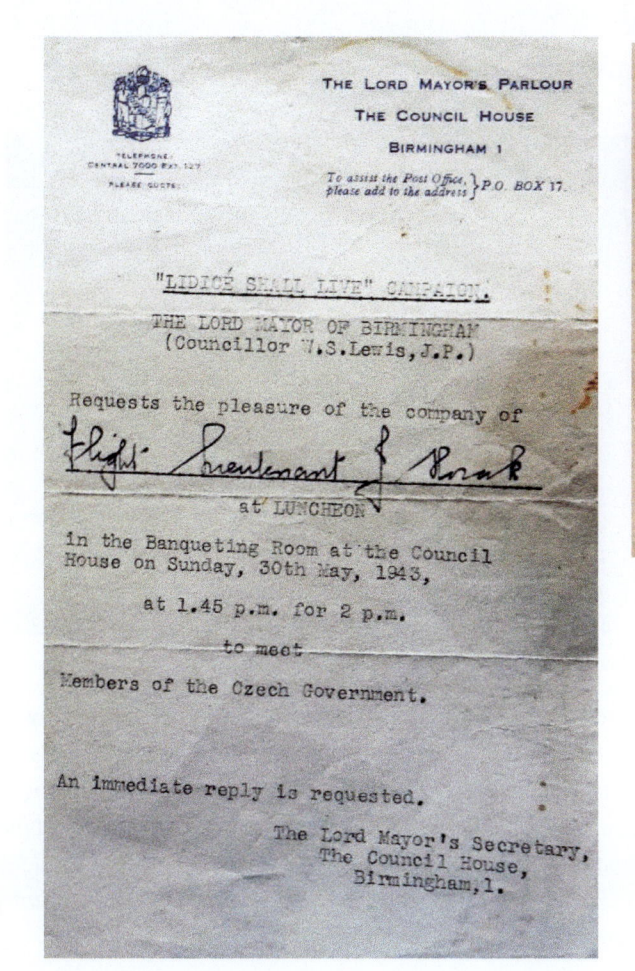

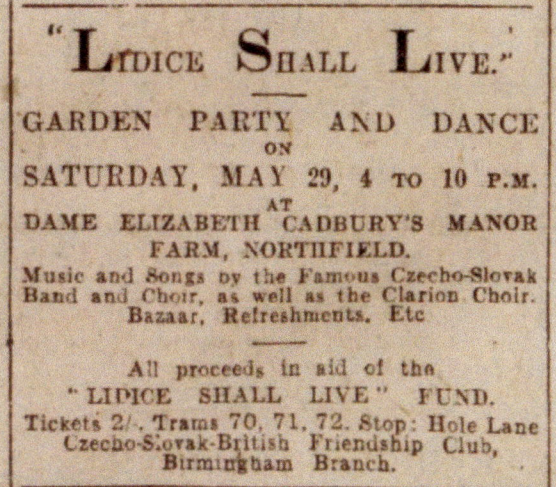

Josef Horák and Josef Stříbrný, known simply as "Czech army personnel" or "soldiers X and Y" to their audiences for security purposes.

They soon became significant members of the national Lidice Shall Live movement because of the popularity of their message and the empathy they imbued.

Colonel David Bourner was a regular soldier from the age of 17, and by the outbreak of the First World War was a sergeant in the East Yorkshire regiment.

Bourner saw service in Gallipoli, Egypt, and France, was mentioned in dispatches, and twice wounded. He was commissioned with the King's Own Yorkshire Light Infantry in 1916 and finally he retired in 1921.

Colonel Bourner would be invested with the Order of the White Lion by Jan Masaryk during his visit to Czechoslovakia - for the inauguration of Lidice in June 1947.

Representatives from Birmingham and Midland towns were among the delegates who left London by air on Friday June the 13th, 1947 to Czechoslovakia for a week of commemorative and cultural events and to attend the laying of the Foundation Stone official ceremony at Lidice. Taken before flying out, from left to right: Mr Harry Baker, Secretary Birmingham Trades Council; Cllr Charles G. Spragg JP, President of the National Federation of Building Trades Operatives Midlands Area; Cllr George Briggs - Mayor of Coventry; Alderman George Hodgkinson - Secretary Coventry Labour Party; and Mr Charles Barratt - Town Clerk of Coventry. All delegates were to be invested with the Order of the White Lion by Jan Masaryk during their visit.

LIDICE AND THE AMERICAS

Prior to the Second World War, the USA's viewpoint on *News* dissemination was one of neutrality—that the nation should operate a *strategy of truth*, with no intent to propagandise for or against a given agenda or country. On the 11th of December 1941, that changed when Japan and Germany became official enemies of the American people, following the Japanese shock attack on Pearl Harbour days before, and the policy of impartiality within the press was officially dead and buried.

THE WRITERS' WAR BOARD

The idea for a production line of professional writers, who would create high-quality propaganda to ensure America's war effort remained resilient during the years of conflict ahead was initially proposed by Secretary of the Treasury, Henry Morgenthau Jr., who agreed to an initiative to seek civilian writers to help promote the war effort of the United States to its citizens.

The task was delegated to Julian Street Jr., head of the writing staff for the US Treasury Department. On the 9th of December, Street set up the legal structure to represent the authors and spoke with playwright Howard Lindsay about organising a group of prominent writers to promote the sale of war bonds and raise public morale. Lindsay spoke with his writing partner and dramatist Russel Crouse, and they approached Authors' League President Rex Stout, known for his novels about the character Detective Nero Wolfe, who they felt should lead the group.

On January the 6th 1942, Stout met with Crouse, author Pearl Buck, broadcaster and philosopher Clifton Fadiman, radio commentator Elmer Davis, lyricist Oscar Hammerstein and author John P. Marquand; and the Writers' War Committee was formed. The organisation soon outgrew its modest founding mission as thousands of writers from around the country all agreed to help the government by writing anything from poems to novels to songs, emotive material that would promote the causes of the Government of the United States in its prosecution of the war. The committee, whose writers were headed by a group of 20 authors primarily from New York City, was re-named the Writers' War Board (WWB).

For the duration of the war, the 'Board was an independent organisation that was never officially under government control and never censored. However, the WWB would be partially funded by the government, with subsidies from the Office of War Information (OWI). It was they who provided the board with a nine-employee *"liaison office"* as well as office rental and stenographic support. Due to 'Board members' popularity, the WWB exerted a disproportionate influence over the entire range of media: from Broadway, to magazines, to newsreels, and to radio. This allowed their message to reach millions of people nationwide. One official from the OWI, which was organised by the government shortly after the formation of the WWB, said:

"With the Writers' War Board, we have the services of almost 5000 writers; we reach thousands of newspapers; more than 600 radio stations; and have a vast army of writers ready to co-operate in the government's war work."

Because they were not censored in any way by the United States Government, the 'Board had total freedom in the organisations and topics it wanted to promote. But the 'Board tended to follow government policies exactly. It strictly supported President Franklin Roosevelt's handling of the war. And the criticism it did encounter was insignificant compared to that it would have received if functioning as part of the government. For example, the mass distribution of its columns and stories would have been frowned upon if coming from state departments—there would have been accusations of inefficient use of public resources and the material would have been treated with a level of cynicism by some. Instead, functioning as it did, the WWB did not face much opposition at all - and the State had conceived a highly efficient propaganda machine.

THE GERMAN AMERICAN BUND

Many of the authors, journalists and poets involved in this New York centric Writers' War Board would remember the days of the German American Bund. For several years, across the United States, it preached a doctrine and propagated itself in an analogous way to the Nazis of the Third Reich. Anti-Semitic and Anti-Communist. The 'Bund persuaded increasing numbers of ordinary American citizens to sympathise with the National Socialist cause by brandishing Jews, blacks and outsiders as law breakers, frauds, deviants, and traitors. The ultimate test of their power came on the 20th of February 1939, with Hitler a mere fortnight away from the complete takeover of Czechoslovakia.

Despite calls for the pro-Nazi gathering to be banned prominent US attorney and politician, and Mayor of New York City, Fiorello La Guardia granted leader of the 'Bund, Fritz Kuhn, permission to hold a mass rally at Madison Square Gardens' Hall in the name of "free speech".

The self-styled *American Führer* brought 20,000 followers to New York from across the USA; he spoke prophetically of a nation for the Americans before a backdrop of a 30ft high George Washington and conflated Swastikas with Star-Spangled banners. La Guardia forecast that the public would be repulsed by the distastefulness of Kuhn's manifesto. He was correct. The occasion was filmed and shows 26-year-old activist Isadore Greenbaum rushing the stage to attack Kuhn out of a sense of repulsion, as he in turn demonises non-Anglo-Saxons. Kuhn hoped that the high-profile event would attract the attention of the world and boost the popularity of his cult but, in fact, it had the reverse effect. With racial disturbances lasting late into the night, the rally shocked many New Yorkers. La Guardia would later become a fervent advocate for the building of a new Lidice and would visit the site as the Director General of UNRRA, helping war-torn nations such as Czechoslovakia help themselves.

Although Kuhn and his devotees were incarcerated at the outset of the conflict, it was clear that variances in viewpoints persisted across the States. It was a mere *three years* since the rally in New York. Millions of Americans still harboured misconceptions about Nazi Germany, if not Imperial Japan. Clearly, the message contained in the Lidice tragedy was one that some needed to hear louder and clearer than others.

GETTING THE MESSAGE OUT

The Writers' War Board had many different distribution methods to ensure that the views and causes of the government should easily be known and creatively promoted throughout the media. They did this through their own productions and through external sources. In its second year of existence, the WWB had sufficiently organised itself to be able to send out many written publications to help its cause. The main one was the WWB Monthly Report. This report was sent to more than 4,000 professional writers across the United States. Each report carried approximately five projects that the 'Board had been working on and which now needed publicity. Suggestions were made and facts, deemed important, included in the 'Report to further provide an outline of themes and events the authors should write about in their books, stories, or plays for that particular month.

Another propaganda method the WWB used to influence the American public was its editorial service. This sent out four to eight articles to approximately 1,600 newspapers nationwide to be published anonymously. The effect of this was to make the public invested in the same beliefs and causes as those promoted by the 'Board. By using opinion pieces, it caused the public to believe a majority of citizens shared positive views about the war. Since people, whether consciously or subconsciously, tend to go along with what their peers believe and are thinking, the editorial system was extremely effective in influencing public opinion.

The Writers' War Board also circulated *"Brief Items"* each month. These contained an assortment of slogans, poetry, cartoons, and articles pertaining to current campaigns. They gave different versions to newspapers, in-house newsletters of approximately 2,600 industries, and to 1,100 army camp news-sheets. Another circulation was the *"War Script of the Month."* These were dramas meant for performance on radio shows. At certain times during the War, these scripts were sent to 825 radio stations, schools, and colleges that broadcast on the wireless. Along with these transmissions, 800 prepared speeches on war related topics were sent out each month.

REACTIONS FROM LEADING STATESMEN

JAN MASARYK'S REACTION

News of the terrible happenings in Lidice provoked a wave of moral indignation across the United States. Czechoslovak Foreign Minister and Vice President-in-exile, Jan Masaryk, was the first statesman to speak out publicly about the devastation which had taken place, when he spoke from his home in Washington on Friday, June the 12th to the United Press. Masaryk proclaimed that Nazi Germany's wiping out of Lidice would serve only to harden the resolve of Czechoslovakia and the other United Nations to smash the Nazi leaders who had led the "German people down the black road towards destruction." Masaryk made articulate the sentiments of the rest of the civilized world as he ridiculed Hitler's boast that the village would *"Die Forever,"* for in determining to see Lidice wiped out, he had secured its longevity. He said:

"In their cruel and inhuman way, the Nazi marauders have immortalized the name of Lidice and the names of each and every one of its heroes who now lie silenced. Wherever and whenever freemen continue to fight, they will remember the name and learn to say: 'Leed-eat-say.' Lidice stands today not as a symbol of the power and the might of the German terror but as a flaming sword around which all fighters for freedom will rally."

"The Czech people will never forget Lidice nor forgive what has taken place there. Fighting in the darkness of night from one end of their country to the other, the Czech people will not permit this outrage to discourage them. As long as there is one Czech left on earth, he will carry on his lips and in his heart the word 'Lidice'."

As in Britain, there had been initial calls for vengeance from the Canadians and celebrated writer Dorothy Thompson. There were also suggestions that all American towns with Germanic names should be re-christened, though Clifton Fadiman of the WWB realised it would be silly to change German names on a map or a menu merely because the US was at war with the Third Reich. He thought, **"that would smack of churlishness and emotional immaturity."** Besides, he said, **"… some great German people are having towns or streets named after them in the US, kindliness and friendliness are in some of the fine old German words on the bill of fare."** Instead, a suggestion was that they should look over the map of the United States and find towns or streets bearing German-sounding names with neutral or unpalatable associations. Then, as an answer to the Nazis' brag that they had **"extinguished"** the name of Lidice, the offending name should be supplanted by the name of the martyred village.

The suggestion that some German-named town in the USA should be re-named *"Lidice"* was publicly endorsed on the 13th of June by Masaryk, who was in Boston to attend a United Nations benefit rally at Boston Garden the following day. Referring to the New York editorial which had produced the proposal, Masaryk said, **"I think it is a good idea."** He added that Boston or some other town might want to sponsor the reconstruction of Lidice, for he recalled that in the First World War, a number of United States communities sponsored the restoration of war-torn Belgian towns.

FRANK KNOX'S REACTION

In terms of a full-scale public response from the US, it was the Minister of the Navy, William F. Knox, who was the first to make his views unequivocally known. Like Dr Stross, who had spoken in less auspicious surroundings across the Atlantic the day before, Secretary Knox gave the pledge that the Allies would fight until "**the Nazi butchers**" were swept from the face of the earth "even as they obliterated Lidice.":

Knox was speaking as President Roosevelt's representative to 15,000 persons at the same United Nations rally at the old Boston Garden Arena. It was Sunday, the 14th of June. In the presence of Jan Masaryk, he declared that the Czecho-Slovakian mining town, which the Germans razed, would rise again and that Nazi ideas of degradation and enslavement would be crushed. He stressed that, although force of arms would crush the Nazi system, the German people, for the sake of their consciences and their skins, owed it to themselves to repudiate the Nazis:

"**Before mankind takes them back into the family of nations,**" he added, "**it is their job to convince the world that the whole polluted system is abhorrent to them and will never rise again on their soil. Then, and only then, can the German people take their rightful place in the post-war world erected by the nations united to defeat bandits.**"

"**If future generations ask us what we fought for this war, we will tell them a story about Lidice… And here is our answer to the Nazis. You did not exterminate Lidice - you gave them an eternally lasting life. You have given them a name that will live forever in the hearts and minds of free people everywhere. You have made them a symbol of the struggle for freedom - the war call of millions who value freedom more than their lives. We will not stop this struggle unless these butchers are exterminated from the face of the earth, just as the Nazis exterminated Lidice. But there is a difference. Lidice is alive and rising again. Nazi ideas of degradation and enslavement of the human soul will be crushed.** "

While the news from Czecho-Slovakia had led to a deluge of visceral reaction from an animated and morally incensed public, it did include this "letter to the editor" which offered a more creative solution - published on June the 16th in the New York Times:

TO THE EDITOR OF THE NEW YORK TIMES:

"**Man does not live by bread alone, nor is a war won by bullets alone. Your editorial in the June 12 issue of THE NEW YORK TIMES, which so effectively describes 'Lidice the Immortal', inspired me to make a suggestion which, if carried out, would truly establish Lidice as an immortal village throughout history.**

I realize that our efforts are being strained to lend financial assistance to the war effort in many ways. The War Savings Bonds, War Savings Stamps, the USO, Red Cross and others are worthy of our complete support. These funds furnish the 'bread and bullets of the war efforts, but the plan which occurred to me would furnish that 'something more' which would crystallize the ideal of this democracy and of all peace-loving people in one act.

Fuelled by enthusiasm, the magazine, acting upon the inspiration of the Writers' War Board, carried an appeal to the American people to help resurrect the ill-fated village. Many leading newspapers and magazines accepted the idea. Under the stewardship of Marshall Field III, the Chicago Sun started offering coupons for those wishing to contribute to the fund. It was an overwhelming success: railways, public services, coach transport companies, community leaders and ordinary citizens were working hard to make the event worthwhile.

Sunday July the 12th, 1942, saw the re-naming ceremony of Stern Park Gardens to Lidice draw in a crowd of some 50,000, according to some reports. The promotion that followed had a significant impact across the USA and worldwide and included: a national radio hook-up set up to broadcast the ceremonies coast to coast, which was also sent overseas by short-wave and translated into several languages including Spanish and Portuguese; full international newsreel coverage to be seen in cinemas around the world in order to embolden the Allies in Britain, especially, and full photographic, news magazine and front-page newspaper coverage.

Many of those dedicating the town, which started as a simple federal housing project, were of Czechoslovak descent, and one 80-year-old woman, Mrs Barbara Brazava, was presented on the platform, according to reports, because she was born in the original Lidice, while others told of their visits to St. Martin's Church. The Most Reverend Abbot Procopius Neuzil conducted a quasi-pontifical outdoor mass as a part of the ceremony. The Czechoslovak Ambassador to the United States, Colonel Vladimir Hurban lit an eternal flame on a granite shaft monument dedicated to the victims of the massacre.

At the podium, Republican Presidential candidate and principal speaker, Mr Wendell Willkie, described the assassination of Heydrich. He detailed the act of vengeance which transpired, as he quoted the official German Press announcement of the destruction of the village, before asserting,

"Let us here highly resolve that the memory of this little village of Bohemia, now resurrected by the people of a little village in Illinois, will fire us, now and until the battle is over, with the iron resolution that the madness of tyrants must perish from the earth, so that the earth may return to the people to whom it belongs, and be their village, their home, forever."

Mr Willkie continued with this declaration:

"But these great objectives cannot be accomplished unless every citizen of this country learns to think in terms of attack," he warned. "...For we must carry the battle to the enemy. We must fight him on his own ground. We must teach a lesson for all time to barbarians who seek in their arrogance to restore the rule of the torture chamber and the whip. We must win a total victory." In his aspirations for the future, Wendell Willkie warned: **"I look about me here, and I can see in the distance the black smoke of steel factories, swarming with American workers of all bloods and races. No contrast could be greater than the peaceful Lidice the Nazis thought they had destroyed, and this Illinois country, alive with factories in which the arms of victory are being forged. But I tell you that the two are related. For while such deeds as Lidice are done in another country, we cannot rest until we are sure that they will never be done in our own."**

Chicago Tribune 13th July 1942

Besides Willkie's, there were speeches by Clifton Fadiman, who took on the role of master of ceremonies for the day; Colonel Vladimir Hurban; as well as Marshall Field III, founder of the Chicago Times. Messages were received from Dr Edvard Beneš, US Vice-President, Henry A. Wallace, and President Roosevelt.

In a message to the inauguration from President Roosevelt, Fadiman read:

"On June 10, the Nazi Government announced the murder of a word-Lidice. That little village in Czecho-Slovakia not only was destroyed but its men were murdered. Its women and children were scattered, imprisoned and killed."

"The name of Lidice was to be erased from time, blotted out of history, forever forgotten."

"We know what happened despite the arrogant efforts of the Nazis to destroy Lidice. By inspired action, the citizens of a small community in the United States have adopted the word Lidice. Instead of being killed as the Nazis would have it, Lidice has been given new life."

"In the great valley of the Lakes and Mississippi, the name and town of Lidice has now become an everlasting reminder to us that the Nazi force could not destroy either the love of human freedom or the courage to maintain it."

Colonel Vladimir Hurban told the gathering that the rebirth of Lidice in America was **"... proof of the complete solidarity of the United Nations. One of the member nations cannot be injured without pain being felt by all the United Nations,"** he said.

Dr Edvard Beneš, Czechoslovakia's President-in-exile, radioed from London his **"deep appreciation of the magnificent gesture of the American people in founding a new Lidice near Chicago."** While the Czech Foreign Minister-in-exile, Jan Masaryk, said that **"Pearl Harbour and Lidice - two symbols of determination and freedom are daily reminders to all of us."** A message expressing **"deep sympathy with your movement"** was delivered from Vice President Wallace.

During his second stay in the USA in May and June 1943, Dr Beneš did not forget to mention Lidice in a memorable speech in front of both chambers of Congress on May 13th, when he said: **"The undying memory of the martyrdom village of Lidice obliges us to never stop fighting the world led against the forces of evil and darkness."** On May the 23rd, he bowed at the monument to the Lidice tragedy in Lidice - Stern Park Gardens.

The United States Government planned to release a 3-cent purple stamp commemorating Lidice on the 14th of August, with the former Stern Park as the site for first day sale of the stamp. Through the Office of War Information, the Office of Facts and Figures had commissioned Paul F. Berdanier, Secretary of the Collectors' Club and director of a volunteer group of artists, who had been working on sketches for proposed war stamps, to prepare a design for a Lidice 3-cent. It was contemplated that the vignette would be of symbolical character or present a view of the village and carry the inscription *"Lidice - We Won't Forget"* and a black mourning band. The group offered assorted designs which would appropriately symbolise Lidice. One was that the town be portrayed as having been crucified. Another idea was that an adaptation might be made of the monument at Illinois' Lidice, the perpetual flame

"to symbolise the Light of Liberty which America is determined to preserve." The Czechoslovakian Consulate General in New York supplied the group with a panoramic view of Bohemia's Lidice, and this was sent to the artists. The Office of Facts and Figures said it would pay $30 for each design presented to President Roosevelt for consideration and $300 for a finished sketch of the work selected for illustrating the Lidice 3c. There was talk of an exhibition of accepted designs traversing the land.

Regrettably, no one had told the Post Office of the plans, who, when contacted by the New York Times on the 2nd of August, announced that they had no plans for the release of a Lidice commemorative stamp.

Czechoslovak President-in-exile, Edvard Beneš lays a wreath at the Lidice, Illinois perpetual-flame memorial in the afternoon, on Saturday the 22nd of May 1943. It was part of a four day stop in Chicago which saw him speak at a mass rally on the Sunday at the Chicago stadium, where Beneš asked "What Are We Fighting For?"

The New York parade of Saturday the 13th of June was just one of many events taking place across the United States on United Nations Day - a special designation given by Franklin D Roosevelt. Los Angeles re-named its West Lake Park in honour of General MacArthur; in Boston legionnaires from the revolutionary city of Lexington met with shipyard workers and publicly vowed to avenge the sinking in the Coral Sea of the aircraft carrier Lexington; in Philadelphia, the Flag Day Association sponsored a ceremonial parade to hallowed Independence Square before proceeding to the home of Betsy Ross - the maker of the very first Stars and Stripes US flag - and wreaths were placed on her grave; in Baltimore at the birthplace of the Star Spangled Banner was planned a combination observance of MacArthur Day and Flag Day Sunday; whilst a corresponding parade in Chicago on Sunday the 14th reputedly involved 700,000 participants, over 1,000 floats and continued well into the night.

*Top: A float declaring that **"CZECHOSLOVAKIA FIGHTS ON"** designed by Czech artists Antonín Pelc and Adolf Hoffmeister added to the sense of patriotism and defiance.*

*Bottom: Though many Americans were still unaware of the news concerning Lidice, the village received pride of place near the head of the parade, as a funeral carriage was hastily adorned with a poster stating, **"THE CRIME OF LIDICE - WE WILL NEVER FORGET - AMERICA MOURNS FOR THEM"**.*

Clockwise: Clifton Fadiman, Chairman of Lidice Lives Committee; Rex Stout, Chairman of the Writers' War Board; Early arrivals stroll down the main street of the Stern Park Garden unincorporated housing community on the morning of the 12th of July 1942 before the start of the ceremonies which gave the estate the name of Lidice.

Clockwise: A promotional photograph taken the day after the Stern Park re-christening event on the 12th of July (Miss Ellen Sollar (left) of Berwyn Illinois and Mrs Adeline Vana of Chicago stand beside the memorial shaft at Lidice - Miss Sollar was Miss Czechoslovakia of the Chicago area in 1940); Marshall Field III, owner of the Chicago Sun-Times; promo pic showing the headquarters - the newspaper was instrumental in setting up the re-christening event which the Writers' War Board then promoted worldwide; Krank Knox, Secretary for the US Navy and the first prominent US politician to publicly speak out about the Lidice atrocity.

LIDICE – THE NAME BECOMES A SYMBOL

Emboldened by the successful outcome of the *Stern Park Gardens - Lidice* transformation and resulting promotion there were concerted efforts to see the front *Lidice Lives* Committee formally established. Attempts by Fadiman's Lidice board to find more potential locations, towns especially, which could be re-named Lidice intensified, as its members continued trawling maps and travelling extensively in an effort to arrange other Lidice remembrance projects.

MEXICO - SAN JERONIMO

After considerable frustration and difficulty, a second ceremony was organised, this time in Mexico. The Editor-in-Chief of the Mexican magazine El Popular, Alejandro Carillo, launched a broadly based campaign in conjunction with Fadiman's Committee to find a community to help perpetuate the name of Lidice. The project idea soon gained a weight of support from other Mexican papers. In the event, they chose a tranquil village named San Jerónimo-Aculco to be re-christened San Jerónimo-Lidice. This old town of San Jerónimo, eleven miles outside Mexico City centre, at that time was best known for its fruits and flowers, and was home to 1,200 mostly textile workers, descendants of the ancient Aztecs and Mayos. Sincere, hardworking, and tightknit, the community of San Jerónimo presented a noble choice of resident for Mexico's Lidice, a kind offering to support the empathetic reaction to the narrative created thus far by Fadiman and his team.

Thus, on August the 30th, 1942, the farm village of San Jerónimo changed its name to Lidice. Once again, a nationwide broadcast was made, this time on the NBC network. Interior Minister Miguel Aleman, member of the Mexican Cabinet, and chief speaker at the event, declared:

"The flames which burned Lidice lifted it from quietness to become a symbol of that for which the democracies are fighting under oath, never to lay down their arms until the merciless haughtiness of obscene power is brought down."

Deputy Rojo Gomez performed the official change of the village's name. He had this to say:

"In keeping with the executive powers bestowed upon me by Mexican laws, I hereby declare that the community of San Jerónimo-Aculco is called, as of today, San Jerónimo-Lidice, which means in the Czech language *the House of the People*."

Hortensia Roja, a resident of the town, addressed the rally. She called out in friendship to the Lidice women across the ocean:

"Women from remote Lidice, widows from concentration camps who know not where their children are, our home is your home, too. We shall never forget you."

Those words resonated amongst the women of Czechoslovakia and especially those of Lidice. Mutual contacts were set up as soon as the war ended. The Lidice of Czechoslovakia sent gifts to the children of the Lidice of Mexico, together with a complete library. The correspondence and cooperation between the two communities continues to this day. Edna

Gómez, who has led the Lidice Choir in San Jerónimo for 36 years, says symbols of this solidarity appeared in the heart of the neighbourhood decades apart. In 1975, for example, the mayor commissioned a sculpture for the Lídice plaza, the site of an annual commemoration. In 2002, on the 60th anniversary of the tragedy, a mural called Fields of Light and Death *(Campos de Luz y Muerte)* was unveiled. Its creator, Ariosto Otero, says it reflects a mixture of the Mexican and Czechoslovak cultures:

"Lidice is a memory that will never fade. Even with the passage of time, the suffering of a people struck down not because of a pandemic but because of human brutality still remains."

US Vice President Henry Wallace impressed the assembled crowd by addressing them in both English and Spanish, saying that **"as symbols of the unbreakable spirit of the common man, Lidice in Mexico and Lidice in the United States are immortal."** Once again, there was full photographic, newsreel, and newspaper coverage. The amount of attention given to the ceremony in the Mexican and South American press was, in the Writers' War Board's opinion, *"astonishing."*

The WWB attempted to arrange a similar ceremony for Canada. The premier of Quebec province, Adélard Godbout was a Lidice Lives Committee sponsor. With his aid, the authorities of the region agreed that the town of Frelighsburg, near to the American State of Vermont, should be used for the name change. So, the Lidice Committee went about arranging a three-cornered broadcast involving President Roosevelt; Prime Minister of Canada, Mr Mackenzie King; and President Beneš and General de Gaulle. It was lined up to be aired from the White House, Canada, and London on the 25th of October. Fadiman duly made the announcement in Washington, and the committee began to prepare for yet another well publicised service. Of course, willingness on the part of the residents of Frelighsburg was a crucial ingredient when it came to the re-christening process going ahead, and this had not been assured:

QUEBEC, Sept. 23 (U.P)—Frelighsburg will remain plain Frelighsburg and not Lidice as far as its most prominent resident, Premier Adelard Godbout of Quebec, is concerned. Premier Godbout said today there was nothing to be done but to respect the wishes of the village's inhabitants and leave Frelighsburg. Mr Fadiman, chairman of the "Lidice Lives" Committee, formed to commemorate the Czecho-Slovak town the Nazis razed, had announced in Washington that Frelighsburg would change its name to Lidice on Oct. 25. As of Sept 23, Mayor E. M. Sheppard of Frelighsburg was saying nobody had asked his permission and it would not be done. The village council, hearing rumors of the proposal, turned it down flatly. Premier Godbout's refusal to intervene made it appear unanimous. Mr Fadiman said yesterday that the mix-up apparently was due to failure of Quebec provincial authorities to seek Frelighsburg's permission. The matter was handled through the provincial authorities, he said.

The provincial jurisdictions and the Writers' War Board committee had no choice but to back down. Eventually, to save face, arrangements were made to name a lake near Québec after the Czech village.

Above: The Mexican Minister of the Interior, Miguel Aleman (centre, dark suit) was present at the re-christening ceremony arranged by the Writers' War Board's Lidice Committee on the 30th of August 1942.

On his left is Senor Javier Rojo Gomez, Mayor of the new Lidice. The Vice President of the USA, Henry Wallace sent a message in which he said, " San Jerónimo is raising the flag of human freedom by changing her name to Lidice."

Above: the famous Mexican band of Lerdo De Tejeda play the Mexican national anthem at the opening ceremony; Left: children of San Jerónimo at the opening of the inauguration.

THE CZECHOSLOVAK COMMUNITY

PITTSBURGH

According to Toni Brendel's book, *"Lidice: Remembered Around the World,"* in Pittsburgh, Pennsylvania, there was a great response. It was no wonder, for here, in 1918, Czech and Slovak statesmen gathered to sign the *Pittsburgh Agreement* that led to the creation of Czechoslovakia. When news of the atrocity came through, a general call to action inspired many local women with Czechoslovakian ancestry to raise funds to buy the *"Spirit of Lidice"* Ambulance Plane. In addition, the ladies sold more than $225,000 in war bonds through their dedicated "Lidice Booth."

Already there was a *Spirit of Lidice*. It could symbolise an act of defiance in the face of tyranny; the victory of good over evil; the renewal of life after death; the ascendancy of purpose over procrastination and apathy. It could mean more. The Austin American Statesman reported on the 1st of July 1942 how the funds raised in response to the Lidice tragedy were to serve a different purpose. Little over a fortnight since the destruction of the village, out of a sense of moral outrage, Czechs across McLennan County, Texas were buying war bonds to help pay for a four-motored bomber called *"Spirit of Lidice"* to **"keep alive the memory of the Czech village wiped out by the Germans."** *It was reported that a total of $556,000 was sought by midnight on July the 3rd to buy two bombers, and that half the fund had been collected.*

TABOR

At an impressive ceremony held on Saturday the 29th of August 1942, Tabor in South Dakota formally dedicated its main street to the memory of Lidice, reported the Rapid City Journal newspaper the following Monday. Most of Tabor's citizens, who are of Czech ancestry, had voted at an earlier meeting of the Town Board to change officially the name of the high street from Cechnie to Lidice. The Journal noted:

> **The day's ceremonies opened with a field high mass in Sokol park at which the Most Rev. William O. Brady, D.D. Bishop of Sioux Falls, preached a memorial sermon. He was assisted at the mass by eight other prelates. The formal dedication of the street took place during the afternoon parade, in which allegorical floats depicted periods of Czech history, and this was followed by a memorial programme in Sokol Park. The speakers were Dr Arnest Zizka, the President of the American Slav Congress, and Professor Julius Kuchynka of Loyola University.**

PHILLIPS

Similarly, for the people of Phillips, Wisconsin, the news of Lidice felt particularly painful. Many locals would have remembered the village of Lidice from the days of their youth or as the home of some friend or relative. The residents decided they would like to erect a memorial to the citizens who were sacrificed **"on the altar of freedom."** A community led door-to-door fundraiser grew to an amount sufficient to build the handsome monument still standing on a Sokol property in Phillips.

Toni Brendel, in her book, *Lidice Remembered Around the World* describes: **"In Phillips, when news of Lidice was heard on the radio, friends met on the streets, in stores, and at Sokol Hall. Theirs was a very personal pain. They were sickened to hear about the indescribably inhumane events. Many surnames of the victims were identical to their own... With a sense of anger, helplessness, and despair, once heads began to clear, they made a plan to memorialize Lidice in their own village. Knowing that the intended symbolic memorial would take time to build, they created a temporary monument that was viewed for the first time in July 1943."**

Construction started on the permanent memorial on June 21st, 1944. All workers and committee members gave their time voluntarily without need of payment, a sign of the community's devotion to the project. Václav Hajny, a Czech immigrant who was a professional commercial artist, designed both monuments. His father had been a coal miner and once lived in Lidice. Another Czech, Karel Novy, was the mason who sculpted the work. Members of the Sokol organisation and the Czech language newspaper, ZCBJ helped with manpower. Joe Skomaroske, a local blacksmith, forged the letters *"LIDICE"* in bronze and iron, which were placed across the top of the memorial stones.

"A large silo-like pillar symbolises the United Nations. Three rods fused into the pillar portray the Czech, Slovak, and Moravian people leaning on the U.N. for support. A large evergreen spray on the face of the monument portrays everlasting life for the brave people of Lidice. A moulded stone circle symbolises the rising sun—to indicate that the people of Lidice and Czecho-Slovakia will rise again."

The dedication of Phillips' Lidice memorial occurred on Sunday, August the 27th 1944, in two parts: an afternoon and an evening programme. Despite rainy weather, the afternoon programme was held outside at the newly constructed monument. The event began with the Phillips High School Band playing the *"Star Spangled Banner."* Then, a Czech music group called *"The Internationals"* played the Czechoslovakian anthem while the memorial was unveiled. Following the unveiling, Phillips' Mayor, Fred R. Struble welcomed district members and guests to the ceremony. The crowd then watched a brief sketch, written by Václav Hajny, the memorial's designer, and performed by community members in traditional dress. Otto Jakoubek then gave a brief history of the events that occurred in Lidice before the Phillips High School Band played a few more selections.

The headline speaker for the ceremony was Vincent Vrdsky, the Secretary of the Czech American National Alliance CANA in Chicago. Vrdsky complimented the local community on its efforts to commemorate Lidice and emphasised the importance of voting in elections. Vrdsky continued by suggesting that Lidice would live eternally.

"It lives again 45,000 miles from the original village—in Lidice, Ill., and here in Phillips in the memorial erected, and in many other places in the world. Lidice stands as a symbol of sacrifice and as an unfaltering flame of liberty for all future generations."

Several Czech members of the Phillips neighbourhood, as well as visitors for the dedication, addressed the crowd at the evening dedication programme, which took place inside Sokol Hall. All congratulated the Phillips community for its work. The key speaker was John Panek, a member of the Wisconsin CANA from Milwaukee. Panek opined that the commemoration was a fitting tribute to the lives lost at Lidice and suggested that it could well be the first Lidice memorial to be erected by *"citizens of Czechoslovak origin"* anywhere in the world. He was right.

Over the years, the Phillips community has become synonymous with Lidice commemoration. **The Lidice Monument appears on both the Wisconsin and US National Registers of Historic Places. Thanks to the work of Toni and her friends and family, Phillips is a crucial cog in the network of international communities who annually celebrate peace and fellowship through the rebirth of Lidice. AG.**

A PRAYER FOR LIDICE 1945

In June 1945, Governors of nine States joined with members of Congress in calling for the commemoration on the third anniversary of the destruction of the village. Governor Thomas E. Dewey of New York described Lidice as **"a symbol of the inhumanity of the totalitarian mind"** and reminded its citizens that **"it is well that the obliteration of that village should be commemorated *lest we forget*."** He added that **"the anniversary will stand as a token that mankind's fight for liberty must be perpetual and unceasing."**

Formal proclamations were also issued by the Governors of Ohio, Indiana and Kentucky, and statements made by the Governors of Massachusetts, Florida, South Dakota, Idaho, and the Acting Governor of New Jersey.

Governor Maurice J. Tobin of Massachusetts asserted that **"the anniversary of Lidice is a day sacred to the memory of all freedom's martyrs and its observance will be an infinite contribution to the cause of peace."** He called upon the citizens of Massachusetts to **"offer solemn prayer in reverent homage to the people of Lidice and all the peoples of the world who died in freedom's cause."**

Acting Governor Frank S. Farley of New Jersey urged the citizens of his state to pause for a moment **"in solemn observance of this symbol to mankind's fight for liberty."** He reminded them that **"now that the fighting in Europe has ended, we must not forget the wiping out of Lidice and its inhabitants has become a memorial to the savagery and inhumanity to warfare which we must do all in our power to prevent ever recurring again."**

New York Times, June the 10th, 1945

INTRODUCING THE COMMITTEE

Meanwhile, the quest for more champions of the Lidice Committee moved ahead at a pace. Joseph E. Davies, a well-known lawyer, politician, former ambassador to the USSR and, since Pearl Harbour and America's entry in the war, chairman of the *War Relief Council*, was persuaded to accept the chairmanship of the WWB group. In fact, the Board obtained an extensive list of sponsors, attracting such diverse individuals as physicist Albert Einstein, motion picture magnate Samuel Goldwyn, Russian Ambassador Maxim Litvinov, Czech President-in-exile Dr Beneš, comedy legend Charlie Chaplin and much-admired actors Raymond Massey and Madeleine Carroll. There was the odd exception, but the sense of repulsion felt towards the Nazis following the Lidice atrocity was conducive to membership, and there was little problem obtaining the consent of those whose services the 'Committee looked to employ. When the formation of the committee was formally announced on September the 21st, 1942 in Washington D.C., the Lidice Lives Committee declared its ambition to create **"a village named Lidice in each Allied country, reaching a number of 30 to 36 Lidices all over the world by the end of the war."** Some 110 individuals were listed as part of an informal *"Lidice Lives"* committee, including:

Agent General for India; Tallulah Bankhead; Edvard Beneš, President, Czecho-Slovak Republic; Justice Hugo L. Black; Roark Bradford; Louis Bromfield; Van Wyck Brooks; Sidney Buchman; Justice James F. Byrnes; Juliar R. Caceres, Minister from Honduras; Henry Seidel Canby; Carl Carmer; Charles Chaplin; Mary Ellen Chase; J. Circhanowski, Ambassador from Poland; Aurelio F. Concheso, Ambassador from Cuba; Marc Connelly; Norman Corwin; Russel Crouse; Frank Crowninshield; Count Ferdinand Czernin; Jo Davidson; Leon DeBayle; Justice William Douglas; Walter D. Edmonds; Albert Einstein; Major George Fielding Eliot; Edna Ferber; Don Luis Fernandez, Minister from Costa Rica; Lion Feuchtwanger; Marshall Field III; Dorothy Canfield Fisher; Dr Harry Emerson Fosdick; Constantin Fotitch, Minister from Yugoslavia; Rose Franklin; Paul Gallico; Lewis Gannett; Adelard Godbout, Premier of Quebec; Samuel Goldwyn; Jack Goodman; Ernesto Jaen Guardia, Ambassador from Panama; John Gunther; Lord Halifax, British Ambassador to the USA; Madeleine Carroll Hayden; Professor Aleš Hrdlička; Joseph L. Hromadka; Langston Hughes; Col. Vladimir S. Hurban, Ambassador from Czecho-Slovakia; Hu Shih; Robert M. Hutchins; William Koska; Fiorella LaGuardia; Robert J. Landry; Albert D. Lasker; Frank J. Lausche; Margaret Leech; Hugues Le Gallais, Minister from Luxembourg; Herbert J. Lehman; Howard Lindsay; Lin Yutang; Walter Lippmann; Maxim Litvinov, Ambassador from USS.R.; Alexander Loudon, Ambassador from the Netherlands; William Kingsland Macy: Thomas Mann; Bishop William T. Manning; John P. Marquand; Jan Masaryk; Raymond Massey; Andre Maurois; Leighton McCarthy, Minister from Canada; Edna St. Vincent Millay: Mrs Harold v. Milligan; Robert A. Milligan; Wilhelm Morgenstierne, Ambassador from Norway; Dr Walter Nash, Minister from New Zealand; Robert Nathan; Adrian Recinos, Minister from Guatemala; Fritz Reiner; Quentin Reynolds; Elmer Rice; Mary Robert Rinehart; Angelo J. Rossi; Carl Sandberg; Prince and Princess Saphieha; Count and Countess Carlo Sforza; Robert Emmet Sherwood; William L. Shirer; Krishnalal Shridharani; Luise Milleni; Robert Gordon Sproul; Rex Stout; Frank Sullivan; Arthur Hays Suizierger; Booth Tarkington; Deems Taylor; Alexandra L. Tolstoy; J. M. Troncoso, Minister from the Dominican Republic; Sigrid Undset; Count Robert van der Straten Ponthoz, Ambassador from Belgium; Carl Van Doren; Mark Van Doren; Hendrik William Van Loon; Wei-Tao-Ming, Ambassador from China; and Franz Werfel.

Prominent members of the Lidice Lives "front" committee. Clockwise: Scientist Albert Einstein and film star and comic Charlie Chaplin; US based British film star, Madeleine Carroll; Film producer Samuel Goldwyn, best known for founding several motion picture studios in Hollywood; and renowned American film actor Raymond Massey.

LIDICE IN ART AND CULTURE

Terror - Géza Szóbel – from "Civilization" collection 1942

LEST WE FORGET

The Lidice Committee commissioned memorials to Lidice in several art forms. A statute titled *"Lest We Forget"* showing a Lidice man and family facing their Nazi executioners was created by sculptor Jo Davidson and donated to the Lidice Lives Committee, represented by British actress Madeleine Carroll, at the American Associated Art (AAA) Galleries in New York, in a ceremony on October the 12th, 1942. Following the exhibition, the sculpture toured the United States at locations which, according to Fadiman: **"will do the most good."**

Colonel Vladimir Hurban, Czechoslovak Minister to the United States, in a brief address at the presentation commented: **"Everyone who sees it on tour must join the ranks of men and women who will see to it that no such deeds will ever be possible again,"**

Illustrations by various artists, including the famous painter-cartoonist William Gropper, were created, and given wide promotion. These, together with a model of the monument that had been dedicated at Stern Park Gardens—Lidice, Illinois, were initially displayed in an exhibition at the Colonial Bank and Trust Company in the Rockefeller Center, with the usual publicity, and later sent on tour throughout the country.

MURDER OF LIDICE

Among the many eulogies written to Lidice by the members and associates of the Writers' War Board, the pathos in poems transmitted the tragic events of Lidice with most effect. Poetry and verse was often radio broadcast at prime time, simultaneously across the entirety of the nation's networks. For extra effect, it would be dramatised. News of its broadcast would be published separately a week prior to airing to ensure the maximum numbers of listeners. Many pieces were created and delivered, but two achieved greatest impact. The first by poet and novelist Robert Nathan was titled simply *"Lidice"* and read at several events and ceremonies, published with a full page spread in the Sunday supplement magazine *"This Week"* and issued as part of a "Nathan" anthology of poems. However, for some on the Board of the WWB, it did not go far enough...

In direct alignment with the 'Board's propaganda objectives was Edna St. Vincent Millay's dramatic poem, *"The Murder of Lidice."* As a controversial, avant-garde author, Millay had never written poetry to order before, but when the specific request came from the WWB it was so persuasive that, according to the poet herself, **"I knew I should not be able to draw one contented breath unless I tried to do the job."**

The poem, which was to draw more public attention to the Lidice atrocity than any other single project of the Lidice committee, was aired nationwide over the National Broadcasting Company network at 10:30pm on Monday, October the 19th, 1942. The dramatised production was lavish. Poet and critic Alexander Woollcott made the introduction as master of ceremonies, and the narrator was the distinguished actor Paul Muni, who headed the cast of nine. Frank Black, who conducted the orchestra, composed a special musical script. Presented before an overflow crowd, the programme was simultaneously short waved to Hawaii, Alaska, Australia, and New Zealand, and a Spanish translation was sent to most of South America. The next day, delayed broadcasts were sent to the British Isles and the Middle East and, in Portuguese, to Brazil. A pamphlet form of the poem was published by Harper and Brothers. There were later re-broadcasts in November and well into 1943; and transcriptions were sent to independent radio stations.

VICTORY THEATRE

Likewise, the Writers' War Board, the United States Office of War Information (OWI) sponsored and provided the concept for the highly popular Victory Theater with the help of CBS and legendary film-maker Cecil B. DeMille. From June the 7th, 1942, with the aid of national names from the world of stage and screen, it fostered a national spirit of wartime determination and camaraderie through a series called *Victory Parade*. A little over a month after the horror which befell the village, Hollywood actors appeared on the first episode of Victory Radio Theater on July the 20th. While the bulk of the presentation was a stage adaptation of the hit 1940 movie, *"The Philadelphia Story"*, at the end of the show the main cast of James Stewart, Cary Grant and Katharine Hepburn made patriotic comments to promote the war effort. Hepburn referred to Lidice in her address and warned an audience of millions that towns across the USA could face a similar fate if the American people did not take the Nazi threat seriously. In deliberate, unemotional fashion, she spoke:

"I think I would like to ask every mother if she's heard of the crime of Lidice."

"That's the village in Czecho-Slovakia where every man was killed by the Nazis. I would ask her to imagine a knock at her door tonight — a knock and a door crashing in. A father and his son dragged out to be shot. The girl and the mother scattered in cruel concentration camps, never to see each other again.

I would say to that mother, if our side doesn't win this war, you can cross out the name of Lidice and write in the name of Middletown, USA.

When the Gestapo issued the first order to seize Lidice, when the firing squad gunned down the first of the Lidice men, when the arsonists set ablaze the first house of Lidice, when the first child of Lidice was snatched from the arms of its mother - the fascists then failed to realise that the most brutal force would be countered by a force far more powerful:

the force of humanism, human solidarity, love of life…"

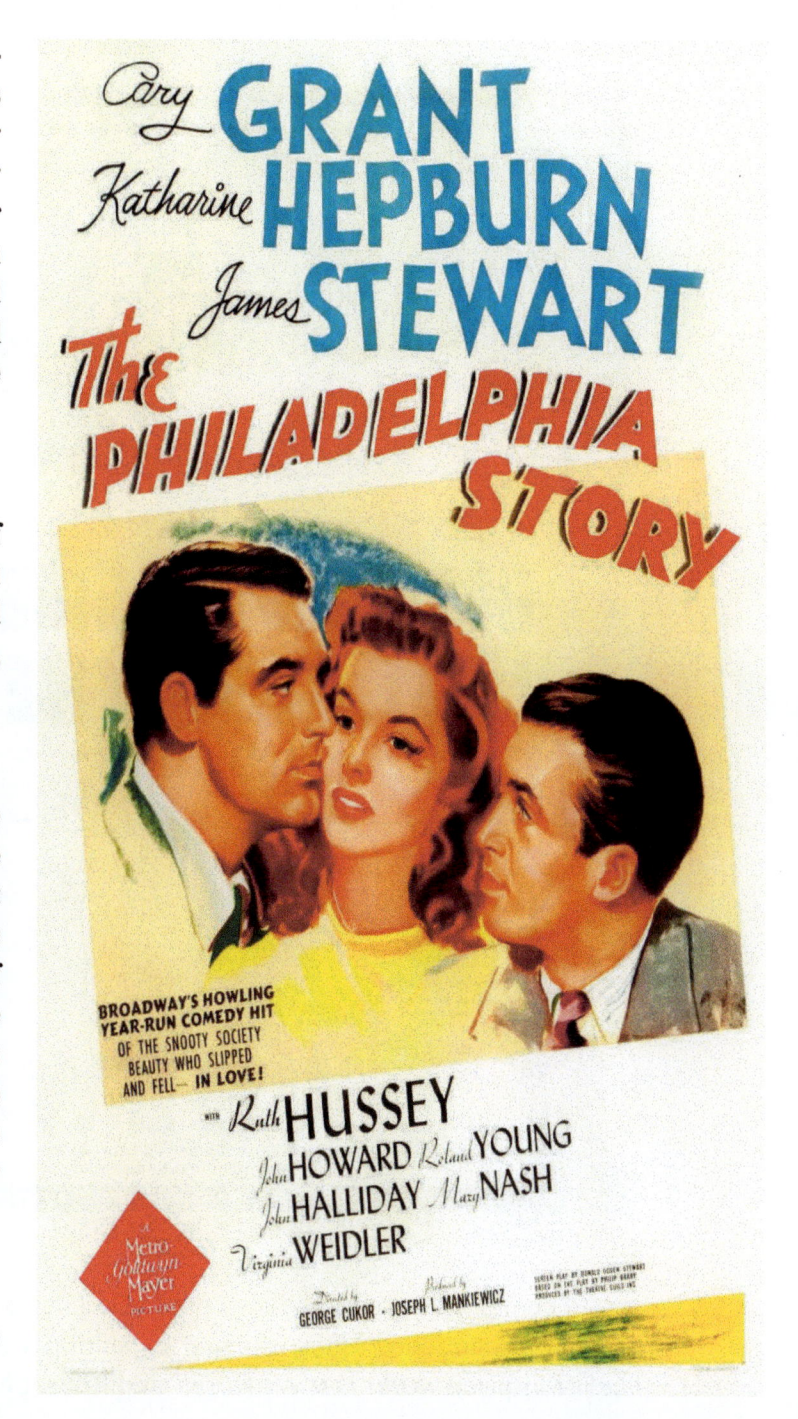

Katharine Hepburn

WE REFUSE TO DIE

Created independently of Fadiman and the WWB was *"We Refuse to Die,"* a one reel short of around 14 minutes produced under the working title *"Victory Short"* and released in the US on October the 22nd, 1942 by Paramount Pictures. Directed by William Pine, scripted by Max Shane and Produced by William C. Thomas, it was nominated for an Oscar in the category of "Best Documentary" at the Academy Awards in 1943.

The film commemorated the fate of the village through the eyes of Paul - a resident who returns following his death to tell Lidice's story.

"You are a free people," he begins. "If what I have to say gives you courage to remain free then my journey has not been in vain. The Czechoslovakian village of Lidice was filled with the sounds of peace - children's laughter, a blacksmith's hammer, holiday songs. Only 1,076 souls - small, unimportant," says Paul "But it was our home."

As Paul describes a grim reality of SS troops demanding that the men folk walk in-line to be executed, he hopes that the condemned men do not fall and wakes instead to the liberating realisation that the tragedy was merely a nightmare - because free people are always alert to the dangers of invasion.

The film was premiered at the *AAA Galleries* on the 12th of October and was coupled with the aforementioned Lidice themed exhibition where sculptor Jo Davidson unveiled his new Lidice inspired work *"Lest We Forget"* and Robert Nathan read his poem in tribute to the village.

MEN IN BLACK

The story of Lidice was a source for more popular fiction in the shape of *"Men in Black."* Born in 1894 in Bohemia, Otto Fürth was held captive in Russia and eventually escaped to Vienna, where he became an author. Emigrating to the United States in 1939, Fürth penned various plays, poems, and lectures. Following an invitation from members of the Writers' War Board, he was moved to write a novel about the Underground movement in Europe, his contribution towards raising awareness of the egregiousness of the Lidice atrocity. Due to his name, he wrote under the pseudonym Owen Elford—as was the case with *"Men in Black."*

Released in November 1942 by Albert Unger Publishing of New York at the purchasing price of $2.50, it is a concise novel which tells about the courageous struggle behind the backs of the Gestapo. The plot is nicely constructed, and though there is quite a bit of the usual cliché in it, the story has some original moments and considerable suspense. The subtitle, *"A Novel about Lidice,"* is somewhat misleading, since only the final scenes feature the assassination of the "Hangman of Bohemia," while Hitler's revenge on the people of Lidice is not mentioned at all.

Instead, primarily *"Men in Black"* tells us about a Viennese policeman, Anton Redtenbacher, who becomes a member of the Gestapo so that he can fight most effectively for the underground movement in Austria and Czecho-Slovakia. Owen Elford follows a regular black and white, good man vs. bad man format in his treatment of the plot and the characters. However, it is a sincerely written book, and the main character comes off convincingly.

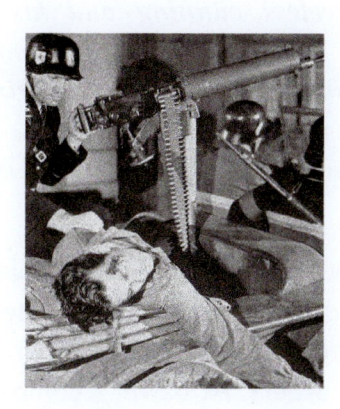

In early December 1943, cinema goers could watch three films about Lidice: We Refuse to Die, The Silent Village and Hitler's Madman (see images above) - which tells of a young Czech airman, Karel (Alan Curtis - right), who returns to his native village by RAF plane and parachute, hoping to save his people from the Nazis, of the difficulties he encounters, the unrest he incites which leads to the shooting of Heydrich (John Carradine - centre), the arrival of Himmler (Howard Freeman) and the terror which follows, the killing of Jarmila (Patricia Morison - right), Karel's boyhood sweetheart, and finally Karel's own escape to freedom to fight on till the end against the bitter domination of Nazidom.

The original story is by Emil Ludwig and Albrecht Joseph; the film was directed by Douglas Sirk. "John Caradine as Heydrich has to be seen to be believed!" said the Birmingham Gazette. Hitler's Madman was one of the more extreme examples of how the facts were bypassed in order to propagandise the Lidice tragedy.

THE DEAD LOOK ON

Gerald Kersh *1911-1968* was the author of several novels and short stories. Coming from a poor background and having worked in a variety of jobs, such as a cinema manager, bodyguard, debt collector, fish and chip cook, travelling salesman, French teacher and all-in wrestler, whilst attempting to succeed as a writer, Kersh's novels brought with them a refreshing honesty and integrity.

Dedicated to **'the murdered men of Lidice, and their memory,'** his third book, The Dead Look On, told the story of Lidice and its martyrdom in brutal fashion, **"setting down the grim record with strong feeling, but with a scrupulous care for the facts."** In Kersh's story, following the assassination of SS Obergruppenführer Max Bertsch, top Nazi General Heinz Horner flies in to Prague from Berlin to exact revenge on the Czech people.

He could well represent Himmler, as according to Kersh's description: *"... Horner was a thorough man, ambitious, precise, esteemed for his nerveless cunning and his cold inquisitiveness, his dogged obstinacy and hit pitiless energy. You would never have noticed him in a group of ordinary men. There was primness in the shape and set of his rimless spectacles on his nondescript nose; modesty in the cut of his small black moustache... Dull, colourless, plain, passionless, Heinz Horner sipped his tea and sat stiffly in the dead man's chair."*

Slowly, a noose tightens around the neck of a little village of four hundred and five people. For the purposes of the novel, it is called *Dudicka*. An abandoned motor-cycle is found near its boundaries. Other evidence is created to justify retaliatory action. With a map spread in front of him, Horner draws a neat ring round the village and issues orders. At dawn, a company of parachutists descends from the sky over the community, and a column of heavily armed motor-cyclists follows along the road, with armoured cars and trucks behind. Then, with menacing suddenness, the Nazis descend on the village. An acute sense of foreboding pervades over the villagers, as they realise this is not a routine inspection. Tensions grow as men, women, and children are segregated. Kersh spares none of the horror from his story, yet there is no sensationalism. His development of character makes for a deeper sense of pathos as he follows the grim drama through to its climax: the schoolmaster, Karel Marek; butcher, Otakar Blazek; glassmaker, the son and grandson of a master artisan, Jan Balaban; the old, somnolent mayor and his wife... Kersh salutes the faith and fortitude of the people of Dudicka, but he leaves the reader with, primarily, an unbearable sense of the nightmare evil, the immeasurable depravity and the mania of the oppressor.

The Liverpool Post's review from March the 2nd 1943, continued,

"Mr. Kersh neither exaggerates nor conceals the horrifying truth in this brief poignant tale. The war has already given us many appalling studies of the German war machine in action. When you read this one you will know that there could not be a worse. A writer who invented such events would be condemned. To imagine them would be an outrage on human feeling. To know that they happened is a nightmare, but we have to face up to the reality of such horrors, when our fellow beings have suffered them in the course of war and resolve that the humble martyrs of Lidice shall be avenged."

The book was released by Heinemann in early February 1943. Three different editions were made available: a leather-bound library edition costing 21s; a cloth bound, complete edition for 10s; and the shorter, paperbound version, containing only the first 704 pages of the full work, costing 6s. Though there was no gratuitous exploitation of the events at Lidice, there were questions at the time about whether such a hard-hitting retelling of the atrocity was appropriate so soon after the event.

Still, *The Dead Look On* remains a powerful indictment of humanity and leaves today's reader wondering how much the world has really moved forward.

GRAMOPHONE

Lidice was remembered in song in many American and British homes when Foreign Minister Jan Masaryk and Jarmila Novotná, the Czech soprano, produced an album of gramophone records called *"Songs of Lidice"* - **"... as a memorial of melody to the little village of Czechoslovakia which was destroyed by Nazi hate"** was how the Londonderry Sentinel announced the news on the 15th of June 1943.

Before Czechoslovakia had been invaded, Mme Novotná often sang these songs to the Foreign Minister's accompaniment while President Masaryk sat listening. **"Dedicated to the simple, 'immortal folk of that unhappy village who sang all these songs,' the collection is a record of the national culture which the Nazis seek to destroy, and which lives on."**

The Northern Irish newspaper went on to describe

"... another gramophone recording now popular in the United States is 'The Murder of Lidice,' by the well-known American poet, Edna St. Vincent Millay. Miss Millay's poem is read by Basil Rathbone and Blanche Yurka, against a background of the Czech and Slovak national anthems and folk songs."

Due to the popularity of the personalities involved and the highly emotive subject matter concerned, both packages sold well.

THE LAST STONE

One stage piece which seemed to underwhelm was *The Last Stone* by Emil Synek, a writer with a reputation in pre-war Czechoslovakia for popular drama. He produced the piece in Czech before it was translated into English by Charlotte Strauss and Hayter Preston.

It could be here that the problem lay - as the play seldom did the gravitas of the tragedy justice in terms of intensity, largely because the dialogue suffered from a monotony in convention.

In the play, Míla Reymonová (left), a Czech actress of the Prague National Theatre, takes the role of an Underground Movement leader in Prague. Produced in London in the autumn of 1944 by Edward Stirling of the English Players at the Phoenix Theatre, its performance followed a preliminary tour of the country.

The play opened on the 12th of September 1944 in front of a large audience, which included many Czechs who gave the play an attentive hearing and a friendly reception. A review, published in the Sphere a couple of days later, noted that:

"… from an aesthetic standpoint the dramatist, who had lived near to Lidice, must be praised for a certain detachment and objectivity in thus handling a theme on which he cannot but feel very strongly.

The same qualities are shown in the distinction which he makes between the character of Riemann, the captain, an aristocrat with at least some of the soldierly virtues, and that of the uneducated, brutal, and utterly ruthless local Gestapo chief. Another powerful message is in the form of Old Martin, the village schoolmaster and a humanitarian who puts the ethical case against murder and proceeds to save the life of the German captain in charge of the Lidice garrison."

However, it seems that overall, The Last Stone fell flat. While the review noted that Edward Stirling's adaptation was assured, the prominent British producer had created little in the way of excitement or startling effects; it also suggested that whilst Synek was to be a considered a dramatist of superior quality, he was not being shown at his best in this instance.

COCKPIT

An unusual production highlighted the continuing prominent profile of Lidice in the psyche of writers and audiences. Cockpit brought interactivity between actors and audience for the first time. An experimental play where the cast treated the audience as displaced persons - those you would find in the UNRRA camps across Germany. Bridget Boland's production opened in February 1948 as the coup was fomenting in Prague.

Although a critical success, as so often is the case, the play was a money pit, losing £4,000 over 58 performances at the London Playhouse. It then sank without a trace. The play features many characters from various theatres of war across Europe, one of those being the *Man from Lidice*, the original played by Paul Hardtmuth, an Anglo-German actor, and well known at the time for his cinematic work.

The British Officer and Sergeant speak to the Man from Lidice (Paul Hardtmuth). Joseph O'Connor plays Captain Ridley and Arthur Hambling, sergeant Barnes, in a scene from Cockpit at the Playhouse Theatre.

Cockpit was performed for the first time in 70 years when theatre director Wils Wilson took it to the Edinburgh Lyceum in October 2017. His adapted version received popular acclaim and on audiences had the thought-provoking effect intended.

ARTWORK

An exhibition of War Caricatures by Antonín Pelc and fellow Czech artist Adolf Hoffmeister took place at the New York Museum of Modern Art, 11 West 53 Street, Manhattan, on May the 11th 1943 as the first anniversary of the Lidice atrocity approached, closing on June the 13th - about a month later. President Beneš visited the exhibition on the 20th of May in the company of an entourage, including Czechoslovak Ambassador, Vladimir Hurban; Jan Papánek, Head of the Czechoslovak Foreign Department, and others. A large and imposing gouache drawing by Pelc simply titled *"Lidice"* dominated the exhibition and would emotionally affect many who cast eyes on it.

Following the show, the piece was displayed from a sizeable shop window outside New York City's Grand Central Station alongside Jo Davidson's Lidice inspired *sculpture "Lest We Forget,"* and several other drawings by the well-known caricaturist William Gropper. Pelc's drawing had been previously reproduced in a colour supplement for the Philadelphia Inquirer, at the instigation of the Writers' War Board - the Inquirer reported that the original would be on permanent display in New York's Freedom House. However, at some point the drawing was stolen - lost to the world.

The Museum described the exhibition thusly: **"These forty cartoons constitute a savagely brilliant attack on the Axis partners, principally the Nazis, impaling them on barbs of ridicule."** Upon completion, the display travelled across the United States and Canada, and was active until late summer 1944, appearing in Massachusetts, and the National Gallery of Canada in Ottawa.

THE PLAYWRIGHTS' DINNER

One criticism levelled against Fadiman and the members of the Writers' War Board was that their methods in the Lidice project were unethical. For many contemporaries, the words and narratives employed in the WWB's campaigning expressed a philosophy which incited Americans to hate all Germans and not only Nazis; and that consequently, its methods had an overtly polarising effect. The counter argument to this was that a strong, unambiguous message was needed during a time of war, lest the public lost their conviction or forgot why they were at war. Still, there was division within the WWB. Many colleagues aired concerns about the ramifications of strategies which openly propagated hostility towards the German people.

This dissatisfaction with the Writers' War Board's direction of travel flared up into a full-blown row at the first dinner of the PEN *(Association of Poets, Playwrights, Editors, Essayists, and Novelists)* in late October 1942:

Rex Stout and Clifton Fadiman did not intend to go back and instead appeared on behalf of the WWB to advocate more intensive *hatred* of America's enemies. In order to further fan American flames, Stout and then Fadiman, commenting on the Lidice Lives Committee, called on the writers assembled to generate an overt *hate campaign* against all Germans, not merely the Nazi leaders. Vehemently, literary historian and critic Henry Seidel Canby, a member of the WWB Advisory Council, took utmost exception to this type of enmity for one's fellow man, and soon there was a shouting and table-pounding match. Writer Arthur G. Hayes also made the most strenuous objection, calling the 'Board's position **"Hysterical."**

The 'Board, thus far, had been highly successful in distilling Lidice as a symbol of defiance against Nazi fury. But now, Fadiman was pushing for strategies which would promote general hatred of the German people; hatred of German people who in all likelihood would be sickened by the activities of the Nazis. This was seen by many to be unacceptable. The argument turned noisy and acrimonious, surprising for a group meeting which was usually uneventful. Robert Nathan, the poet and contributor to the Lidice campaign, and chair for the evening, had trouble keeping the speakers in order. But Fadiman insisted that he knew of **"… only one way to make a German understand and that's to kill them and even then, I don't think they understand."**

The debate concluded with no agreement, but it was indicative of the fact that over Lidice the 'Board could not expect unanimous support or appreciation.

Reporting for the Chicago Tribune, respected journalist Harry Hansen wrote:

"It appears that writers are dividing into little groups. The idealists, who want the United States to help the oppressed everywhere, are the largest; this is a natural attitude for authors to take. The haters are the noisiest - as always. The radicals also make use of authors for their purposes. Perhaps the most outlandish statement yet recorded is in Ernest Hemingway's calm declaration in "Men at War," that the Germans ought to be mutilated. This led John Chamberlain to reply that if America did this, it would not have a clear conscience for many years.

November 8th, 1942."

The shilly-shallying of the *"Playwrights' Dinner"* came as a hammer blow to key members of the Lidice Committee, which would soon wind down. The final decision to close down came in the face of survey findings by the National Opinion Research Center for November the 22nd 1942, which showed that a majority of US citizens believed that the German people should not be blamed for war atrocities. To restore harmony within the ranks of the 'Board, by the end of October 1942, the Lidice Committee decided that the propaganda angle of Lidice had virtually been utilised to its fullest extent; and so, it subdued its activities in order to preserve Lidice as a symbol, particularly since the 'Committee's projects had inspired numerous imitators. The public facing *"Lidice Lives"* Committee was officially dissolved in March 1943, in the belief that its task had been successfully accomplished. Fadiman was proud that the entire propaganda effect had been achieved for a cost-effective expenditure of $450, including travelling expenses. Reflecting on the project, Fadiman wrote,

"The word Lidice has meaning; it crops up continually and our record of achievements has been praised by responsible Office of War Information officials as one of the most effective single pieces of propaganda since the war started."

LIDICE: A UNIVERSAL MEANING

By the end of 1942, the Writers' War Board's special Lidice Committee had stirred up such a sense of moral outrage about the fate of the village that the very word *"Lidice"* had become associated with a thousand other words, quotes, thoughts, and memories which could warn or inspire: an unforgiveable procrastination; apathy in the face of a ruthless foe; a tremendous urge to defend; the creative energy to protect or fundraise...

"Lidice" carried an international message of a crime perpetrated by an Axis force on an innocent Allied community. These could be heard on the radio and read about in the press every day in the Western Hemisphere—it was a uniting force joining East to West, South to North, and would do much to draw the Southern American nations away from neutrality in their conduct of the Second World War.

A measure of how the importance of the village had deeply embedded itself into the United States' wartime culture is noticeable in the US press denouncements of horrors perpetrated by Nazi and Japanese troops against GIs and civilians. Each one a demonstration of a mindset deliberately moulded by Fadiman's Lidice committee. The habit of labelling atrocities or genocidal acts as *"Lidices"* was to continue right up to the Vietnam War when it was used reversely to describe a US attack on a Vietnamese village. That one simple word encapsulates the savagery of the act, the devastation, and the lack of contrition, such as this example detailing an attack on a Chinese village by Japanese troops, reported in the Bakersfield Californian newspaper on the 29th of April 1943:

JAPS SLAUGHTER CHINESE WHO AIDED DOOLITTLE RAIDERS

MORGENTHAU REPORTS NIP BUTCHERS MURDER WOMEN, CHILDREN IN CHINA COAST "LIDICE" AFTER AMERICANS BOMB TOKYO

SAN FRANCISCO, April 29. (U.P)

Japanese troops, emulating the Germans in the massacre of Lidice, slaughtered every resident, to *"the last harmless child,"* in Chinese coastal areas where many of Major-General James H. Doolittle's fliers landed after bombing Tokyo, Secretary of Treasury Henry Morgenthau, Jr. said last night. Morgenthau was notified of the slaughter by Generalissimo Chiang Kai-Shek of China in a cablegram arriving yesterday. He made it public in an address at the War Memorial Opera House.

"Just a few days ago," Morgenthau said, *"we learned, with horror, that the Japanese had taken some of those gallant fighting men (Doolittle's fliers), who were by all military law and precedent, prisoners of war, and executed them. Now, with a deep sense of shock and anger, I must bring you further news. I have here a cablegram which reached me this morning. It comes from Generalissimo Chiang Kai-Shek. Let me read it to you."*

The text of Chiang's cablegram follows:

"After they had been caught unawares by the falling of the American bombs on Tokyo, Japanese troops attacked the coastal areas of China where many of the American fliers had landed. These troops slaughtered every man, woman and child in those areas, let me repeat - these Japanese troops slaughtered every man, woman and child in those areas, reproducing on a wholesale scale the horrors which the world had seen at Lidice, but about which people have been uninformed in these instances."

"The dastardly execution of these American fliers, who were taken prisoners of war, has made it clear to all Americans that we face an enemy who knows no codes of law or ethics. The only language which such an enemy understands is that of the weapons of war, and in the bond campaign which you are pushing for the war effort, our people wish you all success."

Generalissimo Chiang made no mention of the number of Chinese slain by the Japanese, except indirectly in likening it to a reproduction *"on a wholesale scale of the Lidice massacre,"*

"We have work ahead of us," Morgenthau said. *"We have much to do."*

"Certainly, we now have a clearer idea of the nature of the enemy with whom we are dealing. If the Japanese will take special pains to march into a Chinese village, whose only crime is that of offering sanctuary to a handful of American fliers and wipe out that village to the last harmless child, we no longer need to ask what the Japanese would do on marching into a city like San Francisco."

Recalling that the Japanese fired on the Pacific coast (at Santa Barbara, California about a year ago), Morgenthau warned that if they returned, *"...they are not going to come with submarines and deck suns. Let's not fool ourselves. That's what we're up against."*

The network of writers, journalists, broadcasters, and personalities directly involved or associated with the Writers' War Board across the United States ran into the tens of thousands. News articles about Stern Park had been syndicated to every major newspaper across South and Latin America. Inevitably, through its international connections, the campaign in the North would attract support from kindred spirits in Latin America, the Caribbean, and the South. Now, many villages and communities across the Western Hemisphere wanted to bear the name of Lidice in some form or other.

Clockwise: "Lest We Forget" - Jo Davidson 1942; the actress Miss Madeleine Carroll was chosen to represent the Lidice Lives committee in receiving from sculptor Mr Jo Davidson his artwork representing martyrdom. The ceremony took place in the Associated American Artists Galleries in New York; Géza Szóbel, Slovak artist who attended the Fine Arts Academy of Prague before moving to Paris in 1927. With the invasion of Nazi Germany in 1940 he fought with the Czechoslovak forces in France, before reaching England by 1941; Antonín Pelc received his early education at Kutna Hora, a town famous for its Gothic architecture and rich monuments, and it was there he became interested in art, which he studied in Prague. The war left a deep impression upon his technique and artistic philosophy, determining his works' purpose for the duration of the conflict - and beyond.

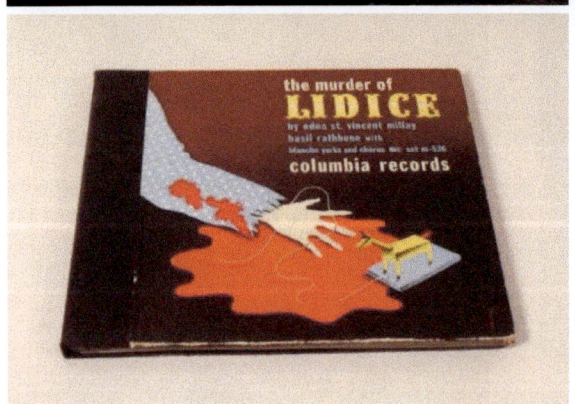

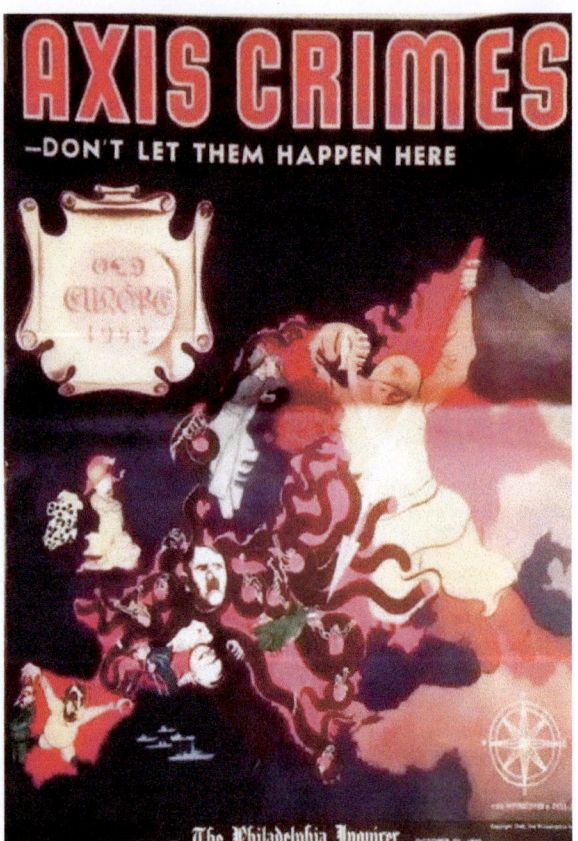

Clockwise: Edna St Vincent Millay – author of 'The Murder of Lidice'; Robert Nathan – author of 'Lidice'; An example of the kind of supplement appearing in the US press throughout 1942 and 1943 with the encouragement of the Writers' War Board - this time the Philadelphia Inquirer, published on the 22nd October 1942 and featuring illustrations by Antonín Pelc and Adolf Hoffmeister; Actors preparing for the NBS broadcast of Edna St Vincent Millay's 'The Murder of Lidice' set for 10:30pm on Monday, October the 19th, 1942 - Left to right: lead actor Paul Muni, director Wynn Wright, Peter Beauvais, Lotte Stavisky and Stefan Schnabel - of a cast of nine (the poem drew more public attention to the Lidice tragedy than any other single popular culture project throughout the war - on either side of the Atlantic. It was aired across the USA and then throughout the world in multiple languages); the gramophone release of Murder of Lidice with narration by Basil Rathbone.

Clockwise: Antonín Pelc made the "Lidice" gouache drawing (top centre) shortly after the horrifying news that the village had been razed to the ground.

The forcefulness of his painting helped many Americans understand the real face of Nazism, and a strong wave of disgust and solidarity arose not only among Czech expatriates but also among American citizens because of it.

(Bottom right) President Beneš visited the exhibition on the 20th May 1943 in the company of an entourage including Czechoslovak Ambassador Vladimír Hurban; Jan Papánek, Head of the Czechoslovak Foreign Department; and others; (bottom left) The New York Museum of Modern Art.

ACROSS THE AMERICAS

Whilst the activities of the Writers' War Board had been limited in terms of organised re-naming events, it would fulfil its crucial role of inspiring others to pick up the mantle of commemoration in assuring the eternal presence of Lidice across the United States. This force of will was to spread well beyond the nation's frontiers, attracting interest across the Western Hemisphere as free people who had seen the newsreel footage or heard the wireless broadcasts remembered the people of Lidice in their own communities. Between 1942 and 1945, a flurry of christening and re-naming ceremonies took place. Many of these resulted from the viral news coverage the Writers' War Board had created - the broadcasting of material in several languages on the wirelesses of most of the countries of the Americas. For some nations' governments Lidice presented an opportunity to show their massive North American economic and military neighbour that they too shared a pro-Allied stance following years of neutrality, even tacit favour for the Axis cause - as with Brazil, with its large German migrant population.

Colombia re-christened one quarter of the City of Medellin, *Lidice*. Ecuador re-named one of its finest squares in Quito, *Lidice Place*. Chile made several memorials to Lidice - a square in the port of Vina del Mar, a square in Santiago, and a promenade on the port of Esperanza. In April 1944, the Democratic Germans' organisation *Alemana Libre* of Santiago de Chile contributed 11,000 pesos towards the Lidice Memorial Fund, thus expressing its solidarity with the enslaved Czecho-Slovak people. The German antifascists, who during the war stood at the head of a European revolutionary broadcasting station, offered an appeal renouncing the Nazi regime in Germany and rejecting Hitler's tactic of involving the German nation in fascist crimes. **"If we rise, one and all, the Gestapo will no longer be omnipotent,"** said the appeal. Spanish antifascists living in New York during the war expressed their solidarity with Lidice in the information bulletin *Free Catalonia:* **"The tragedy of the tortured, heroic and immortal Lidice is now echoing in the hearts of the Catalonian people... Lidice, Czecho-Slovakia, Spain and all other nations now living under oppression are facing the years to come as brothers..."**

LIDICE - BRAZIL

Raimundo Magalhães Júnior, journalist, biographer, and playwright, was working as a foreign correspondent for the newspaper *A Noite* when he was sent on a journalistic mission to the United States for three years at the start of the Second World War. He was special assistant to Nelson Rockefeller in the office of the Coordinator of Inter-American Affairs, where he remained from 1942 to 1944. While in post he collaborated with writers at the New York Times, Pan-American Magazine, American Mercury, and Theater Arts, many of whom were contributors to the Writers' War Board.

Back in Brazil, he took part in the writing of the Brazilian-American magazine, which was published in English in Rio de Janeiro. Magalhães had been impressed by the media's effective propaganda response to the Lidice atrocity in generating greater levels of public enthusiasm for the US war effort. On the day of Villa de Parada's re-christening on the 10th of June 1944, in the Rio based newspaper *A Noite,* he explained the organisation behind the programme, following a re-counting of the events in Bohemia two years prior:

"... instead of destroying Lidice, the Nazis did nothing but immortalize her, multiplying her spirit in so many other Lidices, in so many other countries. It was from New York that the movement destined to perpetuate the mother Czech town came to the lands of our continent. The front from this initiative- distinguished personalities, artists, critics, politicians, and diplomats. I remember some of these personalities: Wendell Willkie, Pearl Buck, Lin Yutang, Paul Robeson, Paul Muni, Rex Stout, Louis Bromfield, Robert Nathan, Litvinov, Eleanor Roosevelt, Marian Anderson, Katharine Hepburn, Helen Hayes, Dorothy Thompson, Edna St. Vincent Millay and so many others who constituted the Lidice Lives Committee."

Magalhães went on to describe how the press, radio and cinema had mobilized for the occasion and the furore created by it. "I have never seen such a perfect synchronization of modern advertising elements: the Paramount film, the admirable "short" entitled "We refuse to die," from which they produced the hundreds and hundreds of copies, it represented a special contribution by cinematographer Adolph Zukor and was released simultaneously in every movie theater in New York. Edna St. Vincent Millay, America's greatest poetess, wrote a play in verse, "Lidice's Drama," radiated through millions of radios, in the masterly interpretation of Paul Muni, on NBC. This piece was then published in a book. At CBS, Joseph Schildkraut, Madeleine Carroll, and Eric von Stroheim staged another dramatic play. At the end of the broadcast, President Beneš, from London, spoke, thanking the tribute. Topics, articles, stories, drawings were published in every newspaper and magazine." He proceeded to outline *"Lidice Lives"'* wider aspirations, of how the committee was not satisfied with its movement in the United States alone:

"I wanted it to have a continental repercussion. Other countries were interested in the same campaign, so noble and so necessary. Lidice became a symbol of all the resistance of the oppressed nations and in her martyrs, all the victims of Nazism were glorified."

"At the request of this committee, I wrote from New York to Interventor Fluminense, Mr Amaral Peixoto, requesting that Lidice's name be given to a town in the State of Rio. Then, I gave his address to Mrs Rita Halle Kleeman, secretary of the Pen Club and member of the (Lidice Lives) committee, so that they would also write in the same direction. I didn't know much after that until I read in the news that, after the United States, Mexico, Uruguay, Cuba, and other countries have participated in this movement, we will also have *our Lidice*. The suggestion had been accepted. The imagination was late. But this delay was perhaps providential, because it will now, two years after the tragedy, give new repercussions to the glorious movement as keeper of the Czech bravery."

Magalhães rounded off with the following thought: "the spirit of Lidice is the sublime spirit of freedom, through which man affirms himself as a divine and not like a herding animal. The Lidice's spirit is the affirmation of human dignity and vertical species. There are the names of many men in the history of the martyrs to freedom. But it took this war and a people like the Czechs to inscribe the name of an entire city on this list."

Permission to re-name the former village of Villa de Parada to Lidice on Saturday the 10th of June 1944 was given by Ernâni do Amaral Peixoto. Appointed in 1937, after the establishment of the Third Brazilian Republic to the position of Federal Administrator to the state of Rio de Janeiro, Peixoto sought for improvements in the economic conditions of the municipality. In 1939, he began to work informally in the United States of America to bring Brazil closer to the Allies during the Second World War. Having developed pro-Allied contacts, in 1942 he supported student marches in favour of Brazil's entry into the conflict, organised a subscription among citizens of Rio de Janeiro to raise funds for the purchase of a ship for the Navy, as well as other campaigns to promote Brazil as an Allied force. During 1943 and 1944, he directed the supply service of the Coordination for Economic Mobilisation, an agency whose goal was to guide the national economy during the course of the world conflict. The re-naming occasion was promoted as an *"Expression of Love for Freedom and Justice,"* as the event was taking place within an ancient region of the municipality, right in the heart of Itaverá, symbol of the democratic spirit of the people of Rio de Janeiro, in the struggle against Nazi tyranny. According to *A Noite*, the occasion,

"...was a brilliant spectacle of civility and understanding people from all over the world. The Inborioso people of Itaverá knew how to understand perfectly, through the words of their speakers, the responsibility that fell to them when one of their villages was given the name of the heroic and deadly city devastated by the Nazi fury."

State Administrator Amaral Peixoto, accompanied by a party of guests, left Rio at 8.00 am. With him were Jared Colonel Hélio de Macedo Soares e Silva, Secretary of Traffic and Public Works of the State of Rio; Colonel Agenor Barcelos Feio, Secretary of the Interior and Justice; Capitio Joao Batista Vicima, aide to the administrator; Sr. Hermes Cunha, Director of the Department of Municipalities; and engineer, Saturrino de Brito, Director of the Department of Highways.

In addition, a large international delegation of dignitaries made their way from Rio de Janeiro to the happening - a mix of business leaders, ambassadors, and attachés. They included the former Czechoslovakian Ambassador to Brazil, Mr Vladimir Nosek; Ambassador José Maria Davila of Mexico; the Minister of Poland; Business Minister from Turkey, Mr Geraldo Mendes de Barros; Mr André Fasset, Belgian Embassy; Mr David Scott Fox of the British Embassy; Mr Fernando Digital, Counsellor of the Embassy of Mexico; Mr D. S. Sloper, Executive President and other members of C. Interalado; Prince Czartoryski of Poland; Consul F. Teixeira de Mesquita, representative of Minister Oswaldo Arant; plus, the Czecho-Slovakian military attachés, members of the Czech, Yugoslav and Polish colonies.

Following a detour to the ancient city of Rio Claro for a small unveiling ceremony, Administrator Peixoto and his entourage headed for Villa de Parada, the picturesque young village soon to be re-christened. The pastoral village was magnificently decorated with the flags of the United Nations. According to *A Noite*, the community was infused with a festive atmosphere as the special guests began to arrive:

"In the main square, the guests received their formal welcomes. This popular enthusiasm was also married to that of several Czech families, Yugoslavs and other nations who arrived transported in special trains to brighten the solemnity. It was a curious note among the many verified at this ceremony the fact that several young ladies from the Czech colony Icrem came with their characteristic clothing, a fact that contributed greatly to lend an exceptional colour to the already brilliant events of today. All of this resulted in the great homage that the people of Rio de Janeiro gave to the people of Czecho-Slovakia because, in inaugurating a city with the same name as the village sacrificed, it had in mind to honor its brothers who gave their blood in a holocaust for the freedom of the peoples."

Between wings formed by national flags held aloft by uniformed schoolchildren, the guests headed for the magnificent new official school building named *President Beneš*. The building had been built by the Government of Rio de Janeiro in the *"Czech style"* and was lauded as having **"the most modern facilities and capacity for 300 students"**. Here a memorial plaque, ordered by the Czech community of Brazil, was unveiled. The Czecho-Slovakian consul in São Paulo came over specially to deliver five hundred books to the school library. Before leaving the school, Administrator Peixoto examined an *Urbanization Plan* for the new Brazilian Lidice: there were plans for a new *Central Zone*, new residential districts, industrial zone, and working-class neighbourhoods.

The main ceremony took place in the town's central square, where, in front of the church, a monument was unveiled to commemorate the inauguration of the new Lidice. The music band of the Rio State Police Force performed the national anthems of Czechoslovakia and Brazil, and a plaque was unveiled, which read, in addition to other inscriptions, the following caption: *"Lidice must always be in the heart of Brazil as a symbol of freedom."* Federal Administrator Amaral Peixoto then said a prayer. Then spoke Messrs Vladimir Nosek; the Mayor of Itaverá; and Dr Mário Acioly, Secretary of the Brazilian Bar Association. Dr Acioly delivered to Nosek an honorary partner diploma from the Institute, awarded to President Beneš. Thanking this honour, Mr Nosek said that,

"... the President of Czechoslovakia would certainly receive, with the greatest pleasure and with great honour, this title that that institution had bestowed upon President Roosevelt and Minister Churchill."

Finally, Sr. Jorge Bico spoke on behalf of the people of the former village of Parada.

At the end of these ceremonies, the visitors were taken by car to the Coutinhos Canyon, a pleasant place found on the top of the Serra do Mar, from where Angra dos Reis and other picturesque spots on the coast of Rio de Janeiro can be seen. There, a barbecue was served. Finally, Peixoto and his delegation visited a public works scheme connecting the Rio São Paulo and Angra dos Reis Road, including the work being done on one of the large tunnels penetrating the ancient rock.

LIDICE – CUBA

On the first anniversary of Lidice's destruction, June the 10th 1943, the residents of Havana, Cuba, christened one of their city centre's squares *Lidice*. A college student who addressed the accompanying rally said: *"The Cuban people feel deep sympathy for today's tribute to the people of Czecho-Slovakia. The flames that gutted Lidice have become torches of freedom, the ruins of the buildings are now memorials of their grand tradition and the men, women and children who have fallen victim to that fury, are now the heroes of the national ordeal. The day that Lidice died for the world, it was reborn again in the minds and hearts of all friends of freedom."*

Later, on September the 12th, 1943, a suburban district of the town of Regla was re-christened *Lidice* whilst a coastal town, Caibarien re-named one of its streets *"Lidice Street"*. A mass rally marked the occasion, and a brochure titled *"A Tribute to Heroic Czechoslovakia"* was published.

LIDICE – PERU

Callao, a Peruvian seaside city and region on the Pacific Ocean, just outside the capital Lima, paid tribute to the memory of Lidice by re-naming one of its loveliest squares and unveiling a memorial in honour of the Czech village on the 20th of June 1943.

The campaign started in April with the regional broadcasting station Radio Collao launching a massive propaganda drive in connection with Lidice. Then, the station's director, in conjunction with a Peruvian senator, proposed the setting up of a Peruvian / Czechoslovak Organisational Committee. The Czechoslovak diplomatic representative Vladimír J. Polodna managed to organise a large commemorative ceremony for re-naming a part of the town of Callao to *Lidice*. An intensive media push took place in the run up to the event, with promotional leaflets being widely circulated, posters appearing in the streets, and a press conference being held.

The rally, headed by the President, Manuel Prado Ugarteche was attended by many leading Peruvians, cabinet ministers, representatives of the Senate and Parliament, diplomatic staff, army generals, clergy, delegates from Allied nations, the Mayors of Callao - de La Punta and Bella Vista, and also the entire Czechoslovak community in the country. Polodna did not have any official influence as the Czechoslovakian Embassy had been handed over to Germany in 1939; and so, his attendance at the event was in the role of *"diplomatic representative of the Czechoslovak Government-in-exile"*. The memorial bore the words: *Lidice Vivira Siempre - 10 Junio 1942*

LIDICE – URUGUAY

In 1943, Uruguay was returning to democracy following a cycle of authoritarianism that had begun years before, with the coup d'état by Gabriel Terra, who went on to set up a dictatorial regime, supported by the most conservative sectors of the society. His successor, Alfredo Baldomir, increasingly distanced himself from the excesses of his predecessor's rule by democratically reopening society. Baldomir also disassociated himself from Terra's foreign policy, steering Uruguay towards the Allies and away from its former Axis stance during the Second World War. In October 1942, a matter of months after the Stern Park inauguration, Baldomir signed a decree for the creation in Montevideo of a square with a memorial to commemorate the Lidice atrocity. In the local newspaper, he was quoted as saying:

"...it is a tribute to perpetuate the memory of a town that was destroyed by invading forces for having expressed their resistance to domination imposed by force." *(Municipal Bulletin, 1942).*

The *Plazuela Lidice* in Montevideo opened to the public at the end of May 1943. Attending the inauguration of the square were representatives of the new democratic government: the Vice President of the Republic; the Municipal Mayor of Montevideo; the Vice President of the Board Departmental; and some members of the Culture Commission.

In addition, present were diplomats from the Allied powers, such as Great Britain; delegates from the countries suffering from Nazi occupation, such as France, Italy, Greece, Poland, and Belgium; emissaries of the Spanish Republican Government-in-exile; the Ambassador of the Czechoslovak Government-in-exile; the President of the Czechoslovak Democratic Union; and some representatives of said community in Argentina.

The ceremony began with the performance of the national anthems of Uruguay and Czechoslovakia and ended with the singing of La Marseillaise. Speeches were made by the Municipal Mayor of Montevideo, the Czech ambassador, the delegate of the Czechoslovak Democratic Union, a representative of the Czech community in Argentina and a delegate from the Anti-Totalitarian Committee of Municipal Officials.

Uruguay's memorial to Lidice is made up of seven snow-white blocks with an arch carrying two bronze plaques. The first is a representation of St Martin's Church, surrounded by hens and diminutive houses with steep roofs, strange-looking trees, and a low mountain range in the background. The village of Lidice is represented in high relief, and is sub-scripted with these words: *"Evoking the martyrdom of the Czechoslovak village, devastated entirely in 1942 by the destructive forces of Nazism, Your Name is Remembered Here."* No less significant is the statement that partners the second plaque: *"The Czechoslovak community residing in Argentina to the people and to the Uruguayan authorities as a testimony of gratitude for the remembrance of Lidice's sacrifice."*

LIDICE – VENEZUELA

On May the 28th 1943, the New York Times reported how, as a result of a campaign conducted by the newspaper *Ultimas Noticias* and a petition of its residents, a newly built working class residential area in the middle of Caracas was to be called *Lidice* instead of the originally intended name Villa Amelia.

The ceremony, which took place on Christmas Eve, was attended by the Venezuelan President, Isaías Medina Angarita, and members of his government, and was described in the local press as **"one of the most moving and beautiful events ever held in the city."** It was also said to be the first case in South America of a municipal council building decent homes for workers.

LIDICE – PANAMA

Panama's Lidice lies in a coffee producing valley near to the town of Capira, about forty minutes from Panama City. Mount Trinidad, the eastern-most high mountain in the central highlands of the country, dominates the landscape. In the summer of 1943, the small community of Potrero, of the Capira District, was a mere six years old when Mayor Nincanor Subia instigated a campaign to have its name changed to Lidice. On the 31st of October 1943, a date which warmly resonates with the anniversary of Czechoslovak independence, the re-christening ceremony took place. The occasion was celebrated with a fiesta attended by hundreds of residents and neighbours, and the nation's entire Czechoslovak population.

Clockwise: Raimundo Magalhães Júnior, foreign correspondent for the Rio based newspaper A Noite who gained inspiration for the re-naming ceremony from a journalistic mission to the United States for three years at the start of the Second World War, where he collaborated with contributors to the Writers' War Board; Alzira Vargas, daughter of Getúlio Vargas (the President of Brazil) and Ernâni do Amaral Peixoto - permission to re-name the former village of Villa de Parada to Lidice was given by Piexoto, who had been given the post of Federal Interventor in the State of Rio de Janeiro in 1939; a photo from Saturday the 10th of June 1944 – taken in the main square at the re-naming ceremony of Villa de Parada to Lidice.

A Plaza dedicated to Lidice was opened to the public in Montevideo, the capital of Uruguay, at the end of May 1943. In attendance were the Vice President of the new Republic; the Mayor of Montevideo; and Allied delegates from Britain, France, Italy, Greece, Poland, Belgium, Spain, Czechoslovakia, and Argentina. Bottom - Just a year following the events at Lidice, on June the 10th 1943 the people of Havana, Cuba christened one of their city centre's squares Lidice. A college student who addressed the rally with these poignant words: "...The day that Lidice died for the world, it was reborn again in the minds and hearts of all friends of freedom."

PLANS FOR A NEW LIDICE

It was reported in the New York Times on February the 1st, 1945, that a construct of the resurrected Lidice was ready for shipment to London on passage to Czechoslovakia - in line with a brief that had been provided by the *Society for the Restoration of Lidice*. The press release came from Leopold Arnaud, Dean of the Columbia School of Architecture.

The model, the creation of the Czech architect Robert H. Podzemný, was due to be received in London by Dr Joseph J. Kalenda, Head of the Department of Public Works of the Czechoslovak Ministry of Agriculture, who authorised the project on behalf of his government. According to Podzemný, this plan of the new village revealed *"... the most modern architectural developments and would serve as a model for Czech architects resuming practice after the war."*

LIDICE MEMORIAL COMMITTEE

On Sunday the 13th of September 1945, came the announcement of the establishment of a Lidice Memorial Committee Inc. and its ambitious plans to create an impressive memorial in the shape of an open-air cathedral in the newly constructed village of Lidice built by the Czechoslovakian Government. The New York Times reported that the cathedral was to be built **"on a hill overlooking that village."** The committee, whose address was listed as 79 Madison Avenue, was headed by Henry Schwanda, and would seek to raise a building fund of $1,500,000 as *"a gift of the American people to the people of Czechoslovakia."*

Serving Czechoslovakia in an honorary capacity on the committee was Jan Masaryk, Foreign Minister; Vladimir Hurban, Czechoslovakian Ambassador to the USA; Jan Papánek, Minister Plenipotentiary, and Consuls General Karel Hudec and Joseph Hanc. According to reports, the Czechoslovak Government had approved the plans for the village planned by the aforementioned Leopold Arnaud and Robert H. Podzemný of Columbia University's School of Architecture in July; and a brochure distributed by the Lidice Memorial Committee said that the cathedral design would be the work of the sculptor, Mario Korbel:

"The ruins of the old Lidice will remain untouched as a cemetery for the bones of the innocent martyrs and the ashes of their homes," it explained, **"On one side of the valley will spring the new, modern Lidice; on the other, and facing it, will stand this memorial: both city and memorial tangible and eternal witnesses to Czech labour and universal brotherhood."**

The open-air cathedral was to rise 250 feet above a colonnade-enclosed Court of Nations. Flanking an *Altar to Freedom* would be windows of cobalt blue glass and at each side a column supporting a guardian angel. Each column of the colonnade surrounding the cross-shaped court before the altar would commemorate a martyr of Lidice. This was to be the *Colonnade of Cities*, with each column being dedicated to a historic city, town, or village of Czechoslovakia. Carved over each column would be the coat of arms of the town and a bas-relief of that town's most important historic event. In a message to the committee, Edvard Beneš declared that,

"The Lidice memorial will be a beautiful tribute, and I sincerely wish you to bring it about so that the martyrdom of Lidice will be remembered forever in the history of mankind."

The committee also included film producer, Messmore Kendall, and Chief of Finance and Industry at the Office of Commercial and Cultural Relations, Joseph C. Rovensky, as Vice Chairmen; businessman and philanthropist, William Ziegler Jr. as Treasurer; William Kostka as Secretary; and the poet and novelist, Joseph Auslander, as Associate Secretary. At the end of October, the campaign had grown in stature by attracting former members of the Lidice Lives committee to the group, as the New York Times reported on the 30th October:

"The National Honorary Committee of the Lidice Memorial Committee, registered at 420 Lexington Avenue, New York 17, has several prominent American writers and authors as members. Included in the group are Louis Adamic, Faith Baldwin, Clifton Fadiman, Dorothy Canfield Fisher, Langston Hughes, Will Irwin, Walter Lippmann, André Maurois, Emma Mills, Quentin Reynolds, Rex Stout, Migrk Van Doren, Lin Yutang and Elmer Rice. The committee is conducting a campaign to raise $1,500,000 to construct an open cathedral on a hill overlooking the site of the village destroyed by the Germans."

In the end, the ambitious American idea of a colossal memorial dedicated to the Lidice victims sited in the village ended in scandal, as promises of funds remained unfulfilled. Following the Prague coup of February 1948, the hardening of East – West communication arteries meant exchanges became openly frank and a direct accusation of embezzlement was levelled at William Kostka, Chairman of the US Lidice Memorial committee. Kostka's response was reported in the *Bakersfield Californian* on Wednesday the 1st of June, 1949:

A Denver man today branded as false charges by a Czech official that Americans squandered five million dollars contributed to rebuild the war-smashed village of Lidice. Jan Vodička, secretary general of the Union Fighters for Freedom in Prague, was quoted as saying

"Not one dollar of the money has been applied to the cause it was meant for." **Vodička reportedly said the fund was collected among** *"Our compatriots in the United States and from the rest of the American public."* *"Thirty per cent was taken by the collectors,"* **he declared,** *"and nearly 70 per cent by the administration."*

William Kostka, former managing director of Look magazine and now a public relations counsellor in Denver asserted the sum collected was actually $5000. Kostka, who was secretary of the Lidice memorial committee, said the campaign was called off on his recommendation. He explained:

"I was asked to be secretary although I am a second-generation Czech. I suggested that before a collection campaign started, we ought to know what would be done with the money." **Kostka said he made a trip to Europe early in 1946 and found that Communist-dominated officials in Prague** *"would be glad to take the monies but would not permit a memorial."* **He said about $5000 came in without solicitation and is held in trust in New York. It will probably be used, he said, for Czech refugees.**

A NEW LIDICE

U.N.R.R.A.

A pooling of resources had won the war. A pooling of resources was now needed to help win the peace. The first combining of United Nations resources in the pursuit of peace was represented by the United Nations Relief and Rehabilitation Administration.

UNRRA was a United States led initiative under the auspices of the United Nations. Set up in Washington D.C. on the 9th of November 1943 at the White House, it was signed off by Franklin D Roosevelt along with 44 signatories representing nations throughout the world *(this was later extended to 48).*

Correspondingly, the principal contributors to an aid package worth $3.7 billion were the Americans - who put $2.7 billion into the kitty, with bankrupt Britain somehow coughing up $625 million, and Canada donating $139 million - these three were the investors in the programme. However, many nations took part in other ways, helping in kind with exports of raw materials and foodstuffs. For example, South Africa supplied coal; India, peanut oil, and jute; Australia and New Zealand, raw wool, and foodstuffs; Brazil, livestock, food, and textiles; Cuba, sugar; the Dominican Republic, corn; Peru, beans, and fish; Uruguay, blankets, and cheese; Iceland, fish. and other stuffs—even Argentina, though not a member of UNRRA, contributed 150,000 tons of grain for use by UNRRA in the spring of 1946.

Though largely spared the ravages of conflict, due to her inevitable interdependence with others for her markets and supply chains, Czechoslovakia was as poverty-stricken as much of the rest of Central and Eastern Europe. Despite the hopes and wishes of Dr Beneš and Jan Masaryk, to perform a balancing act between East and West in order to preserve the liberal freedoms and prosperity for Czechoslovakians in the spirit of the original republic, she would soon be sliding inexorably towards a Soviet style planned economy involving the nationalisation of many of her sectors; and the increasing domination of Communist representatives within the - still democratically elected Parliament. All this validated by the nation's *"gravedigger of democracy"* Zdeněk Fierlinger, a so-called Social Democrat who openly favoured the Communists and their leader Klement Gottwald within Parliament.

Nonetheless, despite ominous signs, in London on the 26th of February 1945, Czechoslovakia's funding from UNRRA was agreed at a meeting between Jan Masaryk, acting as Czechoslovak Minister for Foreign Affairs, and Frederick Leith-Ross, Deputy Director-General of UNRRA. Delicate details were negotiated on the 12th of April, with six Supplementary Agreements on Welfare; Health; Agricultural Rehabilitation; Rehabilitation of Industry and Public Utilities; and Displaced Persons and non-Czechoslovak Displaced Persons and was signed by Hubert Ripka, Czechoslovak Minister of Foreign Trade, and Mr Edward Rhatigan, Deputy Director General of the European Regional Office of UNRRA. With the completed contracts pledging **five years** of funding from the United Nations agency this meant that the Košice Czechoslovak Government, led by Zdeněk Fierlinger could move forward with its economic plans, such as the extension of nationalisation, assuaging fears concerning the fragile nature of the state's finances, which showed a large budget deficit.

Although a sub-committee decided on the 23rd of February 1945 that Czechoslovakia was "at this time not to be in a position to pay", an agreement was signed in London on the 26th of February; Sir Frederick Leith-Ross signing for UNRRA and Foreign Minister Jan Masaryk for Czechoslovakia. Masaryk said that the Soviet Union had informed his government that Black Sea ports would be available to receive supplies and inland transport would be provided. UNRRA H/Q was informed by the London Office that the Ministry of War Transport would make available 5,000 to 5,500 tons of shipping space for UNRRA supplies to Czechoslovakia.

The first shipment from the UK to Constanţa, Romania, left in March with medical supplies, food, agricultural machinery, pesticides, veterinary supplies, footwear, and lorries. Hearing that 19,000 long tons of relief supplies for Poland and Czechoslovakia were unloading their cargoes at the port of Constanţa on May the 22nd, Masaryk sent the following message to UNRRA Director General, Robert Lehman,

"I would like to join personally my government in expressing to you my thanks to UNRRA for the very timely help which now arriving on Czechoslovak territory. May I add the expression of my sincere admiration and friendship."

Photograph - taken on the 23rd of February 1944 in London shows Masaryk informing the Czechoslovak State Council about his participation in the UNRRA conference in the USA. Credit ČTK

At first, the problems for Czechoslovakia accessing aid involved its landlocked nature: the long distances from the ports where supplies could be unloaded, and the need for transportation over the long overland route. The first shiploads of supplies had to be routed via the Port of Constanța, Romania, while distributors awaited the reopening of the ports of Hamburg and Bremerhaven to allow access to full-scale aid. Upon reaching Czechoslovakia, all supplies were sent to the main UNRRA distribution centre of Plzeň.

Despite the teething troubles, the Czechoslovak Mission was one of the most successful examples of economic resurrection. By the 1st of January 1947, a total of $224,586,000 worth of supplies (equivalent to $2.8 Billion in 2022 prices) had been shipped to Czechoslovakia. Whilst half of these shipments consisted of foodstuffs, many contained raw cotton and raw wool to help rejuvenate the nation's textile industry. UNRRA also imported thousands of trucks, acquired principally from surplus military stocks. The Czechoslovak Government also used funds derived from the sale of UNRRA supplies to maintain children's nurseries and other welfare institutions and services.

The positive regard for the programme was stated clearly on November the 6th, 1946 in a statement to the National Assembly in Prague when, in celebration of UNRRA's third birthday and the agency's impact on Czechoslovakia, Food Minister Václav Majer stated:

"For us Czechoslovaks, UNRRA has not been purely material aid. The Czechoslovak people consider UNRRA to be the first major step towards economic cooperation of nations. Humanity longs for a lasting peace. We all know that it is not individuals, nor individual nations or states that can establish peace, for as President Beneš put it once very beautifully: 'Peace is the common aim of all,' therefore it is not only the political agreement that must underlie a lasting peace but also sound economic foundations. It is a question whether people are capable of creating such an organisation. UNRRA is a clear answer that they are, for it is UNRRA which first united the nations of the world for mutual assistance and economic cooperation with practical results. Only history can evaluate the significance of UNRRA, not only in the fight against need, hunger, and poverty but also for the better understanding among nations."

"We all sincerely wish that the ideas, in the spirit of which UNRRA was created, should win forever not only lasting peace but happiness and prosperity for humanity."

Certainly, for the returning women of Lidice, the critical work of UNRRA was its devotion to the task of detecting, rehabilitating, and repatriating displaced people *(simply abbreviated to DPs at the time)*—including the thousands of unaccompanied children. Of UNRRA's workforce of civil servants and highly specialised staff, which exceeded 12,000 in January 1946, approximately half were dedicated to the crucial role of retrieving people who had been transferred to Germany and Austria, predominantly, helping them move back to their homelands where possible; for example, forced labourers or *"Germanised"* minors adopted by Nazi parents.

In March 1947, Ruth Feder, correspondent for UNRRA's *Team News Magazine - Operations Europe* - responded to growing interest in the fate of the Lidice children. She had some positive news. According to her, **"approximately 35 Czechoslovak children found by child search officers of UNRRA and the Czechoslovak Red Cross in Germany are being collected at the Prien am Chiemsee International Children's Centre, awaiting transport home. UNRRA search officers also list 76 other presumed Czech children who are currently being checked** as to nationality." The majority of the youngsters were discovered in German homes where they had been placed for *Germanisation* and the probable adoption by an SS child-placing organisation. The others were in orphanages, monasteries, and similar former Nazi German institutions. Most of the children had been encouraged to abandon their mother tongue and the fact that they were of Czech nationality. In addition, several had been told that their parents were dead, although later this was proved untrue.

Two members of the Czechoslovak Red Cross, Joseph Ondráček of Kladno, and Václav Vondráček of Prague, collaborated with members of the UNRRA search teams throughout Germany in tracing the clues which led to the discovery of the youngsters: Ondráček was sent to Germany in 1945 by the Czechoslovak Ministry of the Interior, before formal search operations had been started by UNRRA. His assignment was specifically to find the children who had been deported from the villages of Lidice and Ležáky after the towns were razed. In the course of their preliminary searches, Ondráček travelled to Poland five times. His chief clue consisted of the postcards that had been written by the Lidice children at the behest of the Gestapo in order to allay the youngsters' fears - these had been smuggled out of Łódź by a nun. Since July 1946, Ondráček and Vondráček had been assigned by the Czechoslovak Red Cross to work as members of the UNRRA child search teams in Munich and Regensburg, respectively. While detailed particularly to search for Czechoslovak children, their efforts resulted in uncovering clues leading to the discovery of kidnapped children of other Allied nationalities.

UNRRA's search records showed that those children selected for *Germanisation* were sent for a period of training to a *Kinderheim*. Here they were usually mixed with German children. When they had learned to speak German, they were assigned to families of SS men. Their names were changed to Germanic ones and, in many cases, the prospective foster family was told that the children were orphaned Aryan youngsters whose parents had been killed during a bombing. Search efforts for the children were further complicated by the fact that of all the youngsters brought to Łódź, in line with the treatment of the village the records of the Lidice children were ordered to be completely destroyed, even the name cards pinned to their clothing were ordered burned. But they prevailed.

The New York Times, reported on the 3rd of April 1947, how 17 children from Lidice were about to be returned home:

UNRRA Reports Group on Way Home from Bavaria

PARIS, April 2 (AP) - Administrative headquarters for the United Nations Relief and Rehabilitation Administration's displaced persons operations said here tonight that seventeen children from Lidice were among a group of thirty-five Czechoslovak children who have left the Prien international children's center in Bavaria on their way home.

The children were found, dispersed in Germany, after an intense search by officers of the UNRRA and the Czechoslovak Red Cross.

The following month, on the 3rd of May, an article called *"Children Who Have known No Childhood"* by the photojournalist and later editor of the New York Times, Gertrude Samuels, appeared in the newspaper and in UNRRA's *Displaced Persons News - Europe Edition* - for that month. She commented:

"Of all the survivors of the Hitler era in Europe, perhaps the most tragic and the most desperate are the *"unaccompanied children"* - the orphans of the ghettos, concentration camps and slave labour forces who lost every precious thing except their lives. In the American zone of Germany, living still within a few kilometres of prison camps which now hold their old torturers, are some 6,200 of them. To Aglasterhausen, with its specially constructed nursery and workshops, have been brought many of the war's *"hidden"* children. For the past year, teams of UNRRA welfare officers, working with interpreters, have been making the search landkreis by landkreis, working with captured enemy documents and police and institution records, and often without any clues at all for children kidnapped from their native countries. They have gone into German homes, hospitals, orphanages, talking with youngsters who, with a little prodding, remembered an earlier home, another language. The Munich area alone has records of 1,500 such children. Seventeen children from the razed town of Lidice recently were found and returned. And in Heidelberg, teams sponsored by Red Cross are presently searching for 700 Czech children thought to be hidden in German families."

These days, like so many other organisations from the mid-twentieth century, mention UNRRA to the majority of people and they will stare back at you in ignorance of its existence. Yet, in the few years that it ran, the United Nations Relief and Rehabilitation Administration transformed the lives of millions of people, undoing the carnage and chaos of the Second World War, both directly through the emergency relief it supplied and indirectly through the economic stabilisation and improvements it brought about.

UNRRA's mission in Czechoslovakia gave the country the ability to manage its transition from a mixed market, socially democratic economy, into a planned communist state without the intervention of the Soviet Union; and it was these few years of sound application of UNRRA aid that allowed Czechoslovakia to recover more quickly than other afflicted countries. UNRRA provided the economic stability and breathing space for Prime Minister Zdeněk Fierlinger and the communist leaning Košice Czechoslovak Government, to proclaim with some degree of assurance that the building of a new Lidice would be a **NATIONAL** project and not one sponsored by the Soviet Union, the USA or even Britain. On Friday the 23rd of May 1947, it was reported in the Derby Daily Telegraph how the Czechoslovak Government had agreed to an initial budget of £250,000 to fund the Lidice building project.

DECLARATION

Ostensibly, the situation *immediately* after the war seemed favourable for developing contacts between Britain and Czechoslovakia - there was complete cooperation between the freshly coalescing political establishment in Prague and the British Lidice Shall Live committee. In most cases, the mediator was the Czechoslovak Embassy in London. Contact between the Lidice Shall Live committee and the founding committee, which was to lead to the full Society for the Reconstruction of Lidice took place in 1945 with the help of the Secretary of the British-Czechoslovak Friendship Club, the redoubtable Frank Hampl, and the Czechoslovak Member of Parliament Julius Firt, a former member of the Czech Government-in-exile and contact at the London office of the Lidice Shall Live Committee.

On June the 10th 1945, some 100,000 people gathered on the gentle slopes of Lidice to attend the first commemorative event. They came as pilgrims, as organisations, as families, and as individuals. Czechoslovakian resistance fighters from both world wars came together with the soldiers, partisans and the other fighters who had put their lives at stake during the last days of the war, during the Czech national uprising which had manifested in cities, towns, and villages, and on the barricades of Prague. Kladno miners and steelworkers came to pay their last respects to their colleagues. There, from a makeshift grandstand, constructed to host the many governmental and international dignitaries, the Minister of the Interior of the National Assembly, Václav Nosek declared the following in his statement to the crowd:

"... there can be and will be no appeasement between the world of fascism and darkness and that of democracy and freedom: only one 'relationship can be there - that of struggle, a struggle for life and death, a struggle until the final victory..."

What would come as a shock to a sizeable proportion of the crowd would be the announcement that the Government of the Republic of Czechoslovakia was about to start building a new Lidice, as Nosek continued:

"The 10th of June 1942 saw the village of Lidice in the Kladno political district destroyed and razed to the ground... the name of the village was to have been erased forever. This atrocious crime marks one of the hardest periods in the Czech nation's life. It enraged not only the people of Czechoslovakia but of all freedom-loving nations.

To redress this tragedy, the Government of the Czechoslovak Republic made a solemn resolution at its meeting on the 6th of June 1945, to build a new Lidice. As the Minister of the Interior, I announce that we will renew the village of Lidice in the liberated Czechoslovak Republic in its original boundaries, along with its historic Czech official name."

Worldwide condemnation and goodwill had stirred the intention to build the village of Lidice anew the instant it was destroyed, while the welcome economic intervention of UNRRA added extra reassurance and stability to the project. But in dealing with the practicalities of realising the vision, it was left to the re-emerging Czechoslovak Government to create some vehicle for managing the sensitive and complicated processes involved in the resettling and rehabilitation of survivors, as well as the construction of a new community. Whatever this organisation was would have to protect Lidice's survivors and renew the village.

To these ends, two organisations were set up: a short-term *Preparatory Committee of the Society for the Restoration of Lidice* and a *Local National Committee of Lidice*. The Local National Committee of Lidice, whose first Chairwoman was Helena Leflerová, was run like a town council and included other Lidice women - it held a seat at the District National Committee at Kladno and pursued the usual municipal and economic agendas. The Preparatory Committee had five members: the Minister of the Interior of the National Government, Václav Nosek; Ladislav Kopřiva, Chairman of Zemský of the National Committee in Prague; Jaroslav Mildorf, Chairman of the District National Committee in Kladno; Helena Leflerová, Chairwoman of the Local National Committee of Lidice; Anna Hroníková as a representative of the Lidice women; and František Knor, who was also appointed to the position of Secretary General.

The Preparatory Committee's main task was to take part in the preparation of the law founding the Society for the Restoration of Lidice, to take care of the returned Lidice women and children and to start providing ground work related to the reconstruction of the community in terms of legal and technical aid.

The construction of a new Lidice was a significant international undertaking. Such had been Lidice's profile during the war, the new Government of Czechoslovakia realised the entire world would be scrutinizing its handling of the matter. On the 1st of August 1945, the National Committee in Prague made the decision to invite tenders for the construction of a new village, setting the deadline for submissions at the end of October. Besides housing, planners were looking for an agricultural boarding school focused on collective farming, a church with a presbytery, a primary school, a hotel with a large garden and garages, administrative buildings, a car park, a library, and a museum, not forgetting the British miners' idea for the international research institute for safety in mines - to be included into the designs for the community.

In all, 58 designs were sent and shown at the *Museum of Decorative Arts* in Prague. This led to another round which took place the following year and was announced by the Local National Committee on the 10th June 1946. The jury included experts and some of the Lidice women. In July 1946, the jury chose the three best designs, awarding prizes to the architectural studios of Václav Hilský, Richard Podzemný and Antonín Tenzer; František Marek and Zbyněk Jirsák; and Jaromír Krejcar, respectively. At that point 150 new houses were planned. Now, in addition to the first proposals, there were plans for a new post office, a police station, a shopping centre, a playground, a new cemetery, as well as buildings to host the residents' indoor events and cultural activities.

CREATING A NEW VILLAGE

The Society for the Restoration of Lidice was set up to ensure the plans for Lidice became reality, and it had strong British connections through some of its members' historical wartime links within the Czechoslovak Government-in-exile and the Lidice Shall Live campaign. It was established by law in September 1946 and its activities were regulated by government directive. It was the administrative vehicle for managing the creation of the new village and caring for the needs of survivors returning home. Its aspirations were ambitious, but primarily the state wanted to provide Lidice women and children with as comfortable a living as possible.

The law went through the usual parliamentary procedure, but due to the symbolism of Lidice and the promises given and claims made by key figures, there was an emphasis placed on pushing ratification through so that formal building of the new Lidice could begin promptly. Nonetheless, it was September the 13th, 1946, before the Society for the Restoration of Lidice was formally set up with its registered office in Klimentská Street, Prague. And the subordination of the Company to the Ministry of the Interior was an absolute prerequisite in ensuring its successful foundation.

A government decree, adopted on October the 18th, 1946, set out in detail the statute of the Society for the renewal of Lidice. It described its principal aims and objectives:

"The purpose of the Society is primarily to build Lidice, to give a new home to Lidice women, returning from concentration camps, and their children within the community, as well as the inhabitants *Lager*, if they return, take care of the memory of the victims of Nazi atrocities... and to restore Lidice so that they become a permanent symbol of the union of all democratic forces that co-built international unity to overcome fascism."

The Society's breadth of responsibilities was vast for a fledgling association of volunteers charged with the unique challenges of supplying a duty of care for the victims of an atrocity and building back their community from scratch; and all this under the watchful eye of an inquisitive international community. Actually, the Society for the Restoration of Lidice had several fundamental goals and tasks: to supervise the construction of a new municipality; to provide aid to the returned citizens of Lidice; to develop and support contacts with foreign committees formed to help Lidice; to pay attention to the promotion of the Lidice monument; and to care for other destroyed villages. In December 1946, the Society officially started its work. Minister of the Interior and Chairman of the Society, Václav Nosek opened the first session of the executive with a speech. He announced that the new Lidice would present a symbolic warning to the world. In 1949, one could read in the newspaper, Rudé Právo that the new Lidice was:

"... growing again from its foundation to illustrate our constructive efforts by the bright red colour of its roofs and the raw smell of mortar and lime."

"The world of the new, the future, was represented by the new Lidice; the world of the old, scarred by Fascism and Nazism, that was the old Lidice"

The new Lidice would not be allowed to become an uneventful, ordinary village that few people would visit. The press and the official writings would present the new Lidice as a model socialist housing development, the first of its kind in Czechoslovakia.

That is how the Košice and future Communist led Czechoslovak Governments would present Lidice. In June 1947, the Society for the Restoration of Lidice imparted their optimistic vision to journalists at the *5th Lidice Anniversary Event*, which saw the laying of the village's foundation stone. Employees of the Society and people at the relevant ministries expected the fast completion of the houses in the new village, which was to be enhanced by the construction of public facilities and the final landscaping of the memorial site. However, the rebuilding of Lidice proved to be a slow process. Many legal issues were protracted, including the purchase of land and probate proceedings. It took a long time for survivors to stop searching for missing Lidice friends and relatives, and reluctantly concede their death; and especially so in the case of children, as their mothers clung on to the hope that they would still be found. Another issue was the purchase and appropriation of plots of land that belonged to inhabitants of neighbouring villages, which were then meant exclusively for Lidice survivors.

Housing work could be held up for promotional purposes or more often because it was being done by young, inexperienced volunteers. Reconstruction of Lidice was declared a *Construction Project of Youth*, a mission enthusiastically taken up by the younger generations of all nationalities. During the *First World Youth Festival* held in Prague in 1947, seventeen thousand young people converged on the capital and many foreign delegates took part in the first stage of the Lidice building project. Young people built new roads, dug foundations for new family houses and restored the surroundings of the former village. Newspapers would run articles praising the help Lidice received from the young people of the nation and its student supporters from overseas. In the period from May the 8th, 1947 to October the 28th, 1948 - 600 young people from Czechoslovakia and abroad co-operated on the project. However, for all the goodwill shown by volunteers, their efforts replaced the work of experts and experienced artisans. Eventually, there were criticisms aimed at the poor state of the construction site and a recognition that the progress being achieved was inadequate for the expectations being expressed at home and abroad.

Václav Nosek at the Ministry of Interior responded. He considered the Society for the Restoration of Lidice ineffectual as the body to manage the building of the new village: the results were too inexpert and arriving too slowly. The Society could not exert enough influence to be able to make noteworthy progress. The government intervened and made changes in 1948. It delegated the Society's supervisory powers over to the Regional National Committee in Prague. Specifically, responsibility for the quality and rate of construction of Lidice was brought directly under state control. Meanwhile the Society's role became increasingly peripheral, focused on liaison work, with its wide network of contacts at home and abroad, and the promotional work it published.

The Society for the Restoration of Lidice had also managed the anniversary day of the Lidice tragedy. This was already becoming a truly important day, publicly commemorated every year. The task of programming this big and purposefully grand gathering was taken from the Society. It finished preparations for the manifestation marking the 5th anniversary in 1947 and then retired to a mere advisory role regarding the programme. Instead, the organising responsibilities were assumed by the *Union of Freedom Fighters* and the *Czechoslovak Peace Defenders Committee*, where the Lidice women were also represented.

With these organisations at the helm, an ideological narrative based around the village increasingly dominated the commemorative one from 1948 onwards. That it was the case is shown by a quote from the annual meeting in 1952:

"Dignified commemoration of the Lidice victims and strengthening of the fight for global peace. The fight against the perpetrators of the obliteration of Lidice, against neo-fascist and revanchist efforts, supported by the American imperialists, that pose a threat again to our freedom and independence; the fight for collective security, unification, a peaceful and democratic Germany; paying tribute to the 10th congress of the Communist Party of Czechoslovakia, the leading constituent of the National Front and the second fight for our liberation." - Somehow, although listed first, the *commemorative aspect* of the event was swamped by an increasing emphasis on Communist unity in the fight against fascist expansion, in order to maintain world peace.

On June the 10th, 1945, some 100,000 souls converged at the site which for the past three years had symbolised both grief and defiance. Earth covered the mass grave of the Lidice men. A week earlier, a memorial had been unveiled there, erected thanks to a collection by Soviet soldiers. It carried the inscription: "To the citizens of Lidice, victims of the German Nazi occupiers, from Red Army soldiers, sergeants and officers of the unit of the Hero of the Soviet Union, Colonel Pankov." In fact, Colonel Pankov addressed the rally: "Why have the men of Lidice been murdered and their wives and children dragged off? For the single reason alone that they had been the sons and daughters of a free nation who would not betray their freedom. The whole civilized world has taken into its memory the name of Lidice, and will never forget its martyrs..."

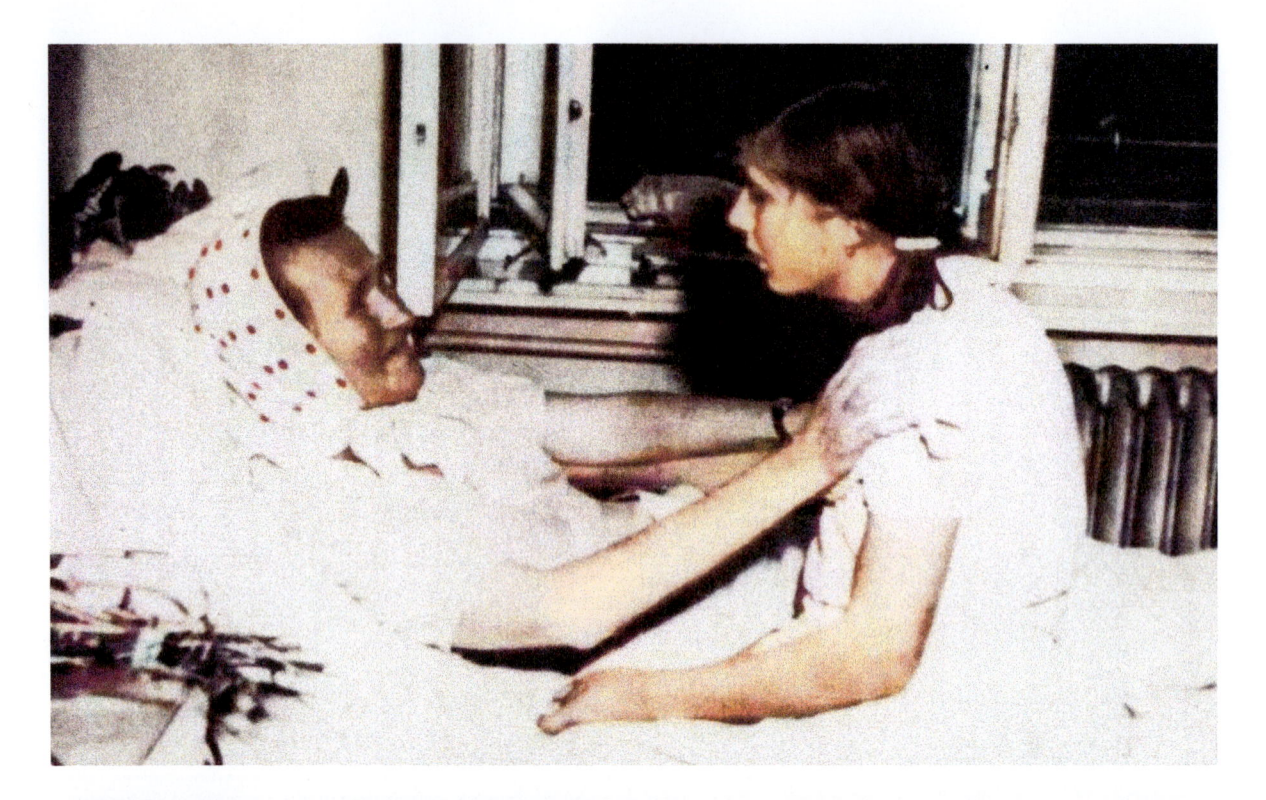

Top: Marie Doležalová a child of Lidice chosen by the SS for Germanisation is reunited with her mother in Spring 1947. Unfortunately for some of the returning children there was a difficult period of adjustment as they had often lost the ability to speak Czech whilst their parents found it difficult to speak German; more often than not their German parents had treated them with kindness, yet Czechoslovak society in the late 1940s renounced all German citizens for the crimes of Nazism. Bottom: President Dr Edvard Beneš (left) speaks at the first Lidice Commemorative ceremony on the 10th June 1945. To his left sits Prime Minister Zdeněk Fierlinger of the communist leaning Košice Czechoslovak Government. Beneš's speech was highly incendiary as he incited Czechoslovaks to take out revenge on Sudeten Germans: "Let us not forget that the leading instigators, accomplices and executioners of these crimes were Bohemian Germans".

Clockwise: The 10th of June 1945, the first Lidice commemorative gathering. Václav Nosek, Minister of the Interior announces the building of a new Lidice to the crowds Credit ČTK; December 1946, Václav Nosek announced at the first session of the new Lidice project that the village should be a symbolic warning to the world, and should not be allowed to become an uneventful ordinary village that few people visit, and that the press and the official writings will present the new Lidice as a model socialist housing development; Helena Leflerová spent much of the war in Ravensbrück concentration camp along with many Lidice women. On returning to the village, she became involved in politics. In 1945, she became the Chairwoman of the National Local Committee in Lidice and a member of the commission for the renewal of the village. After the elections in 1948, she was elected to the National Assembly in Prague as the Communist representative for the Kladno constituency.

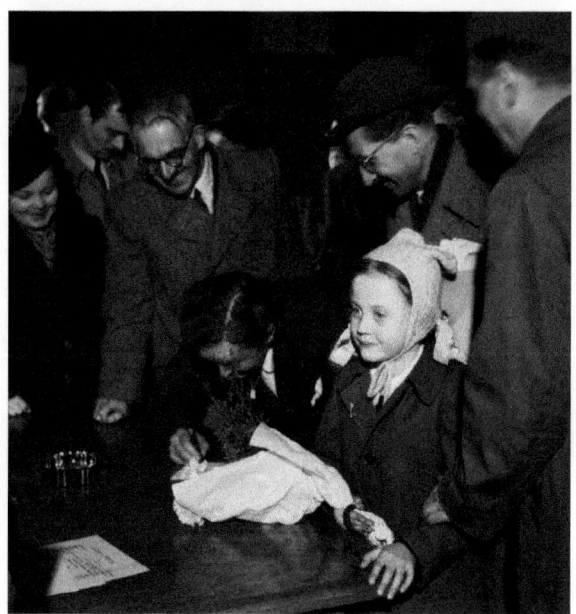

Clockwise: The 10th of June 1945 and President Edvard Beneš takes part in an event to commemorate the victims of Lidice on the occasion of the 3rd anniversary of the destruction of the village. Photo includes Beneš (middle), and to his right and left - the Minister of National Defence, Ludvík Svoboda, and the head of the military office of President Beneš, Oldřich Španěl; Minister of the Interior, Václav Nosek; President of the Lidice National Local Committee, Helena Leflerová with General Bohumil Boček at the first national pilgrimage to Lidice, which took place on June the 10th 1946. Helena Leflerová holds the Czechoslovak War Cross (Československý válečný kříž) 1939 - 1945, which she received on behalf of the village of Lidice; The direct work of UNRRA: Photographs taken on the 3rd of April 1947 showing the return of two Czechoslovak children found by UNRRA search workers; the children were tracked down in the French and American German zones and brought together at the UNRRA camp in Prien near Munich. Photographs show part of the arrival and registration of 31 children at Wilson Railway Station, Prague - they include Hana Špotová from Lidice registering her daughter Hana - who had been taken to Nazi Germany to be "Germanised" when her village had been razed; and the boy Koller from Nebahov near Prachatice, held by an UNRRA relief worker. Photo credits - ČTK

Clockwise: As Director of UNRRA, Fiorello LaGuardia made an official visit to Lidice, along with US Ambassador to Czechoslovakia, Laurence Steinhardt on August the 8th, 1946; A survivor shows LaGuardia photographs depicting the Nazi atrocity. Also pictured is Laurence Steinhardt, US Ambassador to Czechoslovakia (next to LaGuardia smoking a pipe), and Václav Majer, Czech minister of Food (right); Fiorello LaGuardia and Laurence Steinhardt. LaGuardia, in his speech to the people of New York on the 10th June 1945 said: "It is just three years ago that the cowardly, brutal massacre of Lidice took place. I notice that in today's papers and also in radio talks, it is referred to as the third anniversary of Lidice. To me it is the twelfth anniversary. It was just about twelve years ago that the Hitler regime came into power. It was then that massacres, pogroms, oppression, and persecution were first conceived and initiated."

MODEL SOCIALISM

Czechoslovakia's alliance with the Soviet Union had already been declared in the Treaty of Friendship signed in 1943 and continued to solidify throughout the Košice National Front Government between the 3rd of April 1945 to May 1946. Proclaimed admiration for all that was Soviet and above all—Stalinist - was becoming ubiquitous and would soon permeate the whole of society. Given its status as the village where the good of socialism defeated the evil of Nazism, it was no surprise that in Lidice suitable words could invariably be found to express impressively one's love for the Soviet Union; and the subservient displays of gratitude were to become more commonplace following the fateful coup d'état of February 1948. There were always plenty of relevant opportunities to pay respects to the Soviet Union, be it an anniversary celebrating the end of the war; Stalin's birthday, the 18th of December; or, in 1953—Stalin's death on the 5th of March. Ornate, effecting but obsequious expressions of appreciation were part and parcel of such speeches and were not out of the ordinary.

This was the position the embryonic Lidice Mk II found itself in, as the village which stood up to Nazism with the aid of Socialism. With the world dividing, Czechoslovakia sat indisputably at the side of the Soviet Union - liberators of Prague and Lidice. Czechoslovakia announced her place in *"the camp of progress and peace"* - which is how the *Eastern Bloc* liked to refer to itself. Progress, peace, love, gratitude, freedom, democracy, work without worries - all were symbolised by the Soviet Union and her leader. Gratitude for such security would be state fostered for decades, seen and heard ubiquitously, even in everyday life, like work or school reports or something oblique like waste paper management.

By 1952, the responsibility for the construction of the new village had passed over to the state and the Lidice National Committee wrote a letter of thanks for the change. The version addressed to the Central Committee of the Communist Party of Czechoslovakia holds the explanation that the new Lidice could only come into existence and life could only be happy thanks to the work of the working class and thanks to the fact that they...

"...live in a country that took the socialist way that, under the leadership of the Soviet Union, fights for that there should be no destroyed villages, cities and innocent lives in the world."

For the people of Czechoslovakia in the 1950s, if there was an occasion that could be universal besides the end of the Second World War, it would have been Czech Independence Day or the celebration of the 1917 October Revolution. In November 1959, Lidice citizens took part in celebrations to mark the 42nd commemoration of the Russian Revolution. It was a display of fraternity and loyalty towards the people and Government of the Soviet Union:

"On the occasion of the 42nd anniversary of the October revolution, we, the citizens of the newly built Lidice, send our greetings to all the Soviet people, who were the first to rise against the capitalist system and show to all people round the world a new way of building a democratic state in the spirit of peace. ...Increasing our efforts in the fight for socialism and peace at all fronts, we proudly claim allegiance to the historic legacy of the October revolution and send impassioned greetings to all Soviet people, their Communist Party, and its Lenin Central Committee; "With the Soviet Union forever!"

It was important that Lidice was seen to be a model *socialist village* as far as the hard-line Governments of Zdeněk Fierlinger, Klement Gottwald, Antonín Zápotocký, Antonín Novotný, Ludvík Svoboda, and Gustáv Husák were concerned as the village was intended to become completely synonymous with *loyalty to* Communism. But contradictions can be found in the documents of the post-war history of Lidice, regarding what was claimed on behalf of all the Lidice inhabitants or Lidice as an entity on the one hand, and the way it was in reality at cultural and propaganda events that were supposed to be attended by everybody. For example, officers of the Local National Committee often complained about the insufficient attendance of local citizens at rallies to celebrate Soviet leaders. Some events enjoyed satisfactory participation, others less so. Many residents paid lip-service to Communism and did what they had to do to get by.

The operational area the Society for the Restoration of Lidice mostly worked on up until its own demise was *"international liaison"* with those friends, associates, and societies abroad who had helped Lidice. Of these, the most important was Dr Barnett Stross, the Lidice Shall Live Committee, the Lidice Lives Committee in the USA, and other associated contacts. There were also a substantial number of communities that bore the name *Lidice* in honour of the original village, wishing to contact the resurrected community, as well as parents of young daughters writing to tell the Society of their inspiration.

THE INAUGURATION OF THE VILLAGE

In 1946, with the amount raised by the Lidice Shall Live movement surpassing £30,000, a delegation from the Society comprising Helena Leflerová, Mayor of Lidice; František Knor, Secretary of the Society for the Restoration of Lidice; and Václav Babuška, Czechoslovak Minister for Education, was invited to Britain for the celebrations. Whilst in Britain, the Society reciprocated by inviting a delegation of the Lidice Shall Live Committee to the 5th Lidice anniversary commemorations. At some point, the campaign executive decided that this would offer the most appropriate time and place to present the grand total amount of funds collected to the people of Czechoslovakia.

Before flying out from Northolt Airport on Friday, June the 13th 1947 Dr Barnett Stross commented, *"I think it very moving that something we created in the difficult days of 1942, as a symbol of resistance against tyranny and barbarity, now comes to fruition."*

Accompanying Stross, Will Lawther said, *"We see in the rebuilding of Lidice the blossoming of our original concepts that we should build a symbol of stability and peace and of international freedom."*

Lidice's foundation stone was laid on Sunday the 15th of June 1947. A considerable British delegation attended, headed by Dr Stross and Will Lawther, and comprising 21 community and civic leaders from across the nation's coalfields and councils. Mineworkers' leaders included: *Arthur Horner, National Union of Mineworkers; Harold Lockett and Arthur Baddeley, now acting on behalf of the Staffordshire section of the new National Union of Mineworkers; Abe Moffat, President Scottish Union of Mineworkers; Jim Bowman, Vice-President Mineworkers' Federation of Great Britain; George Jones, Secretary Midlands Mineworkers' Federation; Alf Davies, President South Wales Miners' Federation; Joe Hall,*

President Yorkshire Mineworkers' Federation; the Lord Mayor of Stoke-on-Trent, Harry Leason; the Mayor of Coventry, George Briggs; Coventry Alderman, G. E. Hodgkinson; Coventry Town Clerk, Mr Charles Barratt; Cllr Charles G. Spragg, President National Federation of Building Trades Operatives, Midlands Area; Harry Baker, Secretary Birmingham Trades Council; Rev. E. Walton, Chairman British-Czechoslovak Friendship League, Derby; Lt. Col. David Bourner, Midland Regional Secretary, British Legion; Mr and Mrs Julius Jacobs, Secretary London Trades Council; Mr and Mrs William Kirkwood, Secretary Scottish Friends of Czechoslovakia; Mrs Olive Stross; Mrs Will Lawther; and Frank Hampl, Honorary Secretary of the Lidice Shall Live fund.

The visiting delegation undertook an exhausting schedule during their week's stay, which included visits to the ancient spa towns of Mariánské Lázně, Karlovy Vary, and Františkovy Lázně; visits to the Kladno mines; a tour of Pankrác Prison; laying wreaths at the Tomb of the Unknown Soldier and the tomb of Tomáš Masaryk, as well as all the requisite civic functions with the Lord Mayor of Prague, Dr Václav Vacek; Minister of the Interior, Václav Nosek; and Minister of Foreign Affairs, Jan Masaryk.

On Sunday, the party left their hotel at 1pm to reach Lidice with more than enough time for the 2pm programme to start.

At the event, Dr Stross presented to the Czechoslovak Minister of the Interior, Mr Václav Nosek, a cheque for £32,375 raised by the Lidice Shall Live movement. In response, Dr Vladimir Clementis, Czechoslovak Foreign Affairs Secretary, said that

he hoped the new Lidice would be a lasting symbol of British-Czechoslovak friendship.

The Lord Mayor of Stoke-on-Trent, Alderman Harry Leason, extended greetings of great solidarity from the city at the ceremony, saying,

"Many of you know that the citizens of Stoke-on-Trent were the first to say, "Lidice shall live." My action at this moment means that I am making on their behalf a bond of everlasting friendship with the sincere hope that all who live in this town in the future will have a life of peace, happiness and prosperity."

The *laying of the foundation stone* dedication service, which had been carefully planned, was interrupted with breath-taking effect when a severe thunderstorm symbolically swept the barren plain of the commemorative ground half-way through the ceremony.

It was as though the new and old of Lidice had communicated in an ethereal, magnetic space for a moment in time, and saw thousands of spectators scurrying for shelter. Eventually, with an umbrella held over his head, Vlado Clementis tapped the marble stone with a silver-headed hammer to inaugurate formally the village. Unfortunately, due to the weather conditions, a *"freedom fire"* which was to be ignited to celebrate the recreation of new life was never lit as the rain soon filled the black-draped cup prepared for it.

Later, at 8.30pm, the delegation was dined at the legendary Barrandov Terraces which overlook the River Vltava.

On Friday the 20th of June, at a special event at Černín Palace in Prague, Jan Masaryk made investitures of the Midlands delegates. Those receiving awards included Dr Barnett Stross MP and Will Lawther, Chairman and President of the Lidice Shall Live campaign respectively, both of whom were presented with the Commandership of the Order of the White Lion of Czechoslovakia (Class 3).

Altogether, including Stross and Lawther, eleven delegates were invested with an award from Jan Masaryk. Awardees Masaryk invested with the Order of the White Lion of Czechoslovakia Medal (Class 1) included all three members of the Coventry delegation: Alderman G. E Hodgkinson; the Mayor of Coventry, George Briggs; and the city's Town Clerk, Charles Barratt. William Kirkwood, Czech Vice-Consul at Aberdeen, received the medal, as did Rev. E. Walton, the Chairman of the Derby Czecho-Slovak - British Friendship Club, and David Bourner, leader of the Nottingham Lidice Shall Live campaign. Three more delegates were decorated—the delegation from Stoke-on-Trent, comprising Lord Mayor Alderman Harry Leason; Mr Harold Lockett, President of the North Staffordshire Area of the National Union of Mineworkers (NUM); and Mr Arthur Baddeley, former President of the North Staffordshire Miners' Federation and now Area Secretary of the NUM. The Derby Telegraph, on the 24th of June, described the medal as being made of,

"... virgin gold and is valued at £22. It is awarded only to foreigners, and so far, there have been only 150 recipients."

On his return, Barnett Stross gave an interview to a local paper; he described the event in his inimitable manner:

"To us in Hanley and throughout North Staffordshire it had an especial significance. It was the coming true of our five-year-old dream. The part which the British miners have played in this was magnificent, but it is important to realise that the rest of the community also contributed greatly.

I stress this, because, as Jan Masaryk said, the "Lidice Shall Live" movement is the most powerful instrument we have for bringing our two nations together and is not sectional or narrow in any way."

"Of the original village, there is nothing left. Even the gravestones of Lidice's original cemetery had been hacked to pieces and buried. The village pond was filled in, and the stream which fed it diverted. There is just an open valley, with a garden which is the common burial ground, and the wooden cross which was put up by the advancing Russians."

"The ceremony itself was unbelievably impressive. The terrifying storm made it seem that the elements were determined to take part. Just as I was using the phrase "the living and the dead" *(in his speech)* the atmosphere seemed breathless - then the most tremendous wind swept across us."

A MUSICAL TRIBUTE FOR THE FESTIVAL

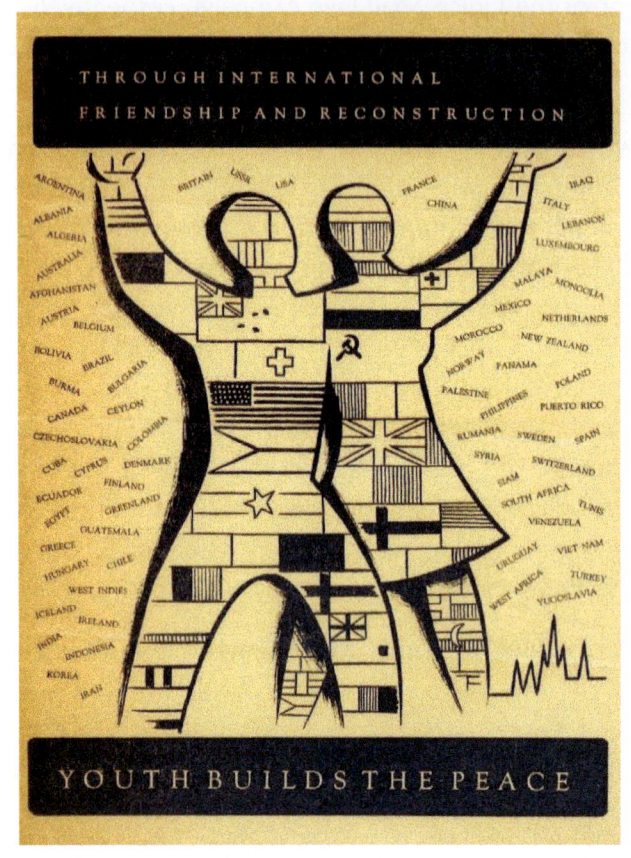

Following Dr Barnett Stross and the British Lidice Shall Live delegation in their pilgrimage to Lidice were eminent composer and conductor Alan Bush and his Workers' Music Association (WMA) Singers. Bush had established the WMA in 1936, and they were visiting Czechoslovakia to participate in the First International Youth Festival hosted in Prague.

The programme of events set to last four weeks, launched with more than 17,000 young people from 72 countries, gathered together under the slogan "Youth, Unite in the Fight for a Firm and Lasting Peace!" on the afternoon of July the 25th, 1947, at Prague's Strahov Stadium.

Here the festival was officially inaugurated to a proud fanfare of trumpets, and the blue flag of the World Federation of Democratic Youth was raised for the first time.

The Workers' Music Association Singers contributed to the BBC *"Britain Sings"* transmissions to Europe and overseas for the duration of the war and had built up an excellent reputation for themselves with their performances of songs from the Resistance Movements and of the national songs of the Allied countries. Their choir was now to meet its unseen audiences on the Continent who, throughout the conflict, listened to those BBC broadcasts, knowing that discovery meant almost certain death. Meeting up would be a humbling moment. Under their conductor, Alan Bush, the well-known musician and composer, the choir gave concerts of representative English music and youth songs, sprinkled with a selection of international and partisan songs. But in early August the players also performed at Lidice a tribute specially written by Alan Bush to commemorate the martyrs of the village.

'Lidice' for Unaccompanied Mixed Chorus portrays the destruction of the village. Alan Bush's tribute website describes it thus: **the music starts low and quietly in B Aeolian. The music is profoundly sad, but without a trace of sentimentality or self-pity. It ends with a beautiful, original cadence, the final chord being in B major.** The words are conceived by John's wife, Nancy. I have in my possession one of the original scores. It is not difficult to imagine a choir of British school children repeating the performance one day - it's never been performed in Lidice since 1947 as far as I'm aware. Due to his post-war associations with communism and the Warsaw Pact countries, Alan Bush was shunned by the BBC, who treated him as *persona non grata* in a form of British McCarthyism from the mid-1950s.

MINING INSTITUTE – HOPES FADE

The concept that Lidice could save more lives than it lost through the creation of an international mining research institute in Lidice seemed increasingly appealing to Dr Stross as it became clear that the funding raised by the movement would be insufficient to construct an entire village, and in any case the Czechoslovak Government would be looking to support the building of the village themselves. Indeed, throughout 1946—1947, references in the British papers would refer to the fund to build the mining centre in Lidice, as opposed to the whole village. In an interview with the local paper in Staffordshire, he spoke excitedly about the appeal:

"… **now to be made to the miners of every country to support the proposal to create in the new Lidice an International Miners' Institute, at which there will be research into mining industrial diseases and mining practice with a view to ensuring better health and greater safety in the industry throughout the world. The results of the research would be made available to every country, and it is emphasised that every country must therefore be asked to help in setting up the Institute. The British fund will be devoted to that purpose. Russia will be asked to join in. Professor J. B. S. Haldane has offered to give to the Institute the library of books: on mining practice collected by his father, who was an authority on the subject.**"

Professor Haldane had been a supporter ever since he had heard about the vision for the mining institute in 1942. And it was then that he had first approached Stross. A First World War veteran, Jack was credited by Arthur C. Clarke as "**perhaps the most brilliant science populariser of his generation.**" According to a Cambridge student, "**he seemed to be the last man who might know all there was to be known.**"

The full name of the intended mining institution proposed by the Lidice Shall Live campaign was the *Lidice International Mining Institute*. Lidice was a symbol of many things. For the people of Britain, the often-used fact that some Lidice men had worked in the nearby Kladno mines and steelworks came into focus. This aspect of Lidice being a miners' village had been put on a pedestal soon after the obliteration of the village. Rebuilding it as a modern village with the very best of housing and facilities became one of the primary features of the fund-raising campaign in the UK. British miners, headed by an executive of Hugh Leese, Will Lawther, George Jones, Arthur Baddeley, Fred Hancock, and others, forged the Lidice Shall Live movement on the back of it. It was part of their vision for a nationalised coal industry.

Following the war, the Committee for Organisation of the International Mining Institute was set up in Czechoslovakia in December 1946 for the purposes of developing the centre. The establishment of the institute was also put on the agenda at the International Miners' Conference in Geneva. The Czechoslovak committee consisted of the following members: František Kropáč, Ministry of Interior; Jaroslav Härtl, Ministry of Industry; Václav Babuška, Ministry of Education; František Kropáček, Ministry of Social Care; MUDr Theodor Hlavák, Ministry of Health; František Knor, Society for the Restoration of Lidice; and František Malík of the Central Union Council.

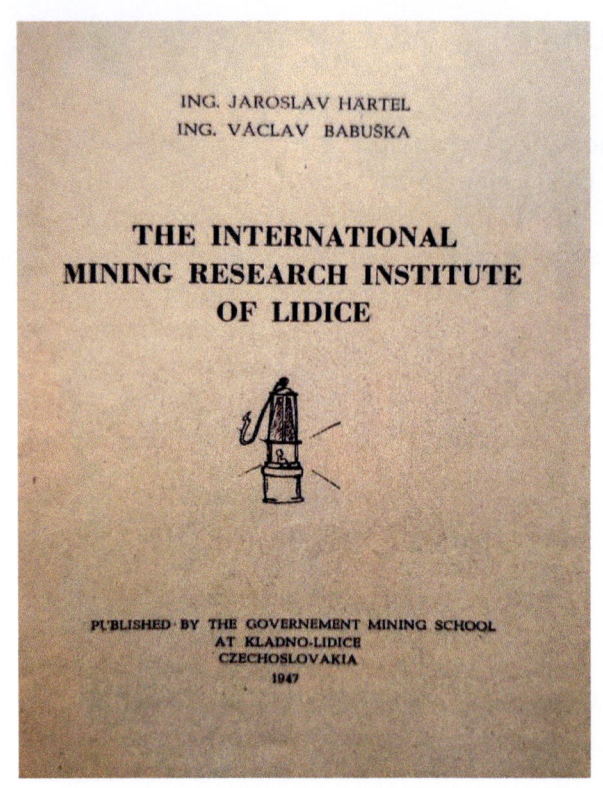

The institute was meant to consist of four departments the purpose of which would be to monitor working conditions, conditions of machinery, compliance with rules and regulations, and to organise training courses.

As part of the institute, junior and senior mining schools were planned to be established at Lidice. Prior to the construction of the schools, however, it would have been necessary to close down or transfer the mining school in Kladno, the headmaster of which, Václav Babuška was a member of the committee.

In the end, good reasons were found to keep the school at Kladno - as homes needed to be built first, the institute was some way off being built at Lidice. Most significantly, Ostrava Czechoslovakia's principal mining region was lobbying for a mining institute there.

The visions of Lidice rebuilt as a *"model mining village"* with a scientific mining research centre which stirred the miners of North Staffordshire to rise-up in empathy with their Czech counterparts in 1942 were now being usurped by soberness and pragmatism. The lack of enthusiasm to look for solutions but to point out instead irresolvable problems mask the much deeper, more fundamental geo-political shifting of Czechoslovakia's relationship to the West, mirroring the British Government's growing antipathy towards the Eastern Bloc.

As political and financial obligations towards the US drew the UK inexorably and overtly anti-Soviet, so the Society for the Restoration of Lidice put the failure of the negotiations on the establishment of the International Institute for Mining down to **"*deteriorating international relations and British members of the committee becoming disinterested in the co-operation."***

THE KERNEL OF EXCHANGE

During the visit to lay the foundation stone for the new Lidice, the invitation was extended to the British delegation by the Czechoslovak Minister of Information for 100 workers, (*miners and others*) to visit his country for free spa treatment as a way of reciprocating the help that Czechoslovakia had received from British workers. The selection was expected to be conducted jointly by the British-Czechoslovak Friendship League and the new National Union of Mineworkers, and they would be drawn from areas in which the Lidice Shall Live campaign operated most prolifically.

Making clear the intention that this was to be a long-lasting friendship, the British delegation invited a Kladno miners' band to tour the British coalfields. The band was led by Ladislav Huřík, the son of the former band-master, Vojtěch Huřík - one of the men executed in Lidice. After the war, Ladislav had taken on the role his father had played, first in the locale of Buštěhrad and

Kladno, but then further afield. The songs which Ladislav had greeted the recent British delegation with - *"God Save the King," "Auld Lang Syne," "Annie Laurie"* and *"Tipperary"* were so warmly received that it was arranged for the band to come to Blighty that autumn. There, around the industrial communities of England and Wales, he and his band-members were to be heartily received.

As the world moved inexorably towards 1948, and ever widening schisms, these exchanges further deepened relations between the peoples of the United Kingdom and Czechoslovakia, regardless of the growing cynicism and increasing distancing of relations at a governmental level…

THE 1947 DELEGATION TO BRITAIN

On the 24th of April 1947, Mr Josef David, President of the Czechoslovak National Assembly, commenced a fortnight's tour of Great Britain. On May the 1st, Staffordshire's Evening Sentinel reported on the tour and how Mr David *visited* Stoke-on-Trent on Wednesday, April the 30th along with a party of his Czechoslovak Parliamentary colleagues. He dropped in at Shelley Potteries, Fenton, before moving on to other venues, including a special reception at the civic chambers in Stoke. Later, they left Stoke-on-Trent for Weymouth, where they inspected a Royal Navy shipyard and boarded a destroyer. The rest of their programme before they left for home on May the 9th included participation in the London Trades Council's May Day demonstration in Hyde Park, a tour of London's dockland, a visit to the BBC to record their impressions of their stay and a luncheon with the Prime Minister, Mr Attlee MP.

Speaking through his interpreter, Mr Fišera, he said,

"We have visited Stoke-on-Trent with great pleasure because this is the place where the fund "Lidice Shall Live" started in 1942, when President Beneš came here. First of all, we have come to thank all the inhabitants of your city and county for the help and friendship shown to us then… Here I am reminded of my native Ostrava, which is very similar, being the centre of big industrial plants and coal mines."

Referring to the visits which his party paid to the Shelley Potteries at Fenton, and the Barlaston Works of Josiah Wedgwood and Sons, Limited, Mr David said they had been impressed by their most modern installations and the hygienic conditions:

"In Western Bohemia we have old established potteries centred near the famous spa of Karlsbad, now called Karlovy Vary. This industry was very much destroyed during the war and only recently has reconstruction been completed. Your china and other pottery products are really most excellent. We admire especially the hand painted examples. One can see that the girls responsible for this work have real artistic skill."

Speaking of the visit which the party paid to the Meaford Power Station, then under construction, Mr David said: **"We are faced with similar power and electrical problems in our country. But we are not making progress as quickly as you are here."**

The party had tea at Meaford, where the Lord Mayor of Stoke-on-Trent, Alderman Harry Leason, after welcoming the visitors, explained that one of the necessities in Britain was producing more electricity. At Meaford, they had the reputation of making greater headway than at any other similar location in that undertaking. Mr Favell, Chief Engineer, and General Manager of the Meaford Scheme, said that about 900 men had been employed there for two years, and that it was hoped to have the wheels going round before the end of the year.

On the last day of the visit, the delegates visited Buxton. On returning they were entertained in the Lord Mayor's Parlour at Stoke Town Hall, and here Mr David, on the guests' behalf, thanked the Lord Mayor and the city for the hospitality extended to them, and for the gift of a Wedgwood vase. He referred in particular to the Lidice Shall Live campaign launched in the Potteries. "Because of it," he said, **"Lidice had become the symbol, not only of Czechoslovakia's sufferings, but of the fight of all liberty-loving nations against Nazi aggression, barbarity and vandalism."**

The delegation visiting the Potteries, besides Mr David and Mr Fišera, was Mr Komzala, Mr Viboch and Professor Bělehrádek. The party was accompanied by Mr Ellis Smith, MP for Stoke, and Dr Barnett Stross, MP for Hanley.

THE 1947 SPA VISITS

On June the 16th 1947, the Yorkshire Evening Post argued how the visit to inaugurate the new Lidice was helping to develop links by reporting how the Czechoslovak Government had invited 100 British union members for a four-week stay in the autumn to a spa in Czechoslovakia and was encouraging Czech companies to participate in the entertainment of the delegation:

"100 workers from Leeds, Aberdeen, Derby, Birmingham, Leamington, Coventry, Crewe and Stoke-on-Trent will visit Czechoslovakia as guests of the Czechoslovak Government. As a result of the visit of the British organisation at the laying of the foundation stone of the new Lidice, an invitation was extended by the Czechoslovak Government through Lawther and Stross. Candidates were to be selected through the British-Czechoslovak Friendship League."

Later, in September, the Evening Sentinel in Stoke-on-Trent reported on the results of the stays, relaying news from Albert Bennett, Secretary of the North Staffordshire Trades Council, and liaison officer with Czechoslovak Union leaders. Bennett reported on the experiences of North Staffordshire Trade Unionists included in a party of 100 British workers on a month's holiday as guests of the Czechoslovakian TUC. Mrs Enid Hancock, of Talke, describes visits to Lidice and Prague and other centres of interest. While in Prague Mrs Hancock was a member of a party invited to an informal gathering as the guests of the Government, at which they were introduced to many representatives of public life, including the President of the Constituent Assembly, the Deputy Prime Minister, and the Minister of Health:

"Everyone was grand to us. The Czech people, I am sure, feel they cannot do enough for us. Whatever we wanted, we were able to get."

RETURN OF JOSEF HORÁK AND JOSEF STŘÍBRNÝ

Returning to the barren wasteland of Lidice following the war were the two RAF Flight Lieutenants - Josef Horák and Josef Stříbrný. Both faced for the first time the grim realisation of what they had known for three years. Unfortunately, they found themselves shunned by many as being passively complicit in the destruction of the village, even though both had played particularly effective roles as campaigners for the Lidice Shall Live campaign. Notwithstanding the stonewalling and awkwardness the men were to experience, both took part in activities to secure good relations in the renewed village and were active in its reconstruction, for example in the Local National Committee and in the Society for the Restoration of Lidice.

However, Josef Horák's and Josef Stříbrný's efforts to be allowed to live in the new Lidice were to be unsuccessful. Gabriela Literová in her 2010 thesis in her interviews with village inhabitants suggests many women continued to perceive them as the culprits of the tragedy and treated them as such. According to the petitioners, the interpretation of the law on the establishment of the Society for the Restoration of Lidice stated that they were not entitled to a house in Lidice as the Lidice atrocity had not resulted in their persecution. With the help of František Knor, General Secretary of the Society throughout 1947 till 1948, Horák and Stříbrný lived hoping their problem could be solved satisfactorily. However, the matter soon became academic, surpassed by the issue of mere survival for anyone in Czechoslovakia with past or existing connections with the West.

1948 arrived and like many other pilots who fought on the Western Front - Josefs Horák and Stříbrný were considered undesirables by an increasingly Communist dominated Beneš regime. Stříbrný was demoted from the air force to the army, discharged from the army, accused of anti-state statements, subversion of the republic, and assault of a public official. He was then arrested and imprisoned. Only the pleading of his cousin Anna Hroníková from the Lidice Women's Association could release him in February 1949 from an extended prison sentence. He married his fiancée, Radka, and two children were born to them. He moved to Písek, where he lived peacefully working as a painter in a factory.

It was clear to Horák that like Stříbrný not only would he be expelled from the army but also be brandished a criminal. He took the only measure available to him: for the second time in his life, Josef Horák left his homeland. This time it was to be with his wife and sons in the UK, where he re-joined the RAF. Sadly, on January the 18th, 1949, during a routine training flight in severe weather, Josef's plane crashed 1.5 km north of Chipping Sodbury. He died of his injuries. Following the Velvet Revolution, in the 1990s the names *Red Army Street* and *Václav Nosek Street* changed to *Josef Stříbrný Street* and *Josef Horák Street* in tribute to the two men in part recompense for the suffering they had suffered at the hands of the Czechoslovak Government in their attempts to placate tacit, but very real Soviet demands.

THE FIRST HOMES

The first houses of Lidice were erected in May 1948; they featured four designs, each offering around 100 square metres of accommodation. All were well equipped by contemporary standards. By Christmas 1949, the first women from Lidice were handed the keys to their new homes, and this was widely reported by the Czechoslovak press. But it was a gradual process of re-housing, nonetheless. In 1951, fifty homes were inhabited with another twenty-nearing completion. Meanwhile, still another 83 women were living in temporary accommodation in the neighbouring city of Kladno, waiting for their new homes. They too joined the residents in creating the future Lidice by planting trees and shrubs in the north-eastern section and starting an orchard on the southern side of the slope. They initiated construction of the main street leading towards the future square and planted linden trees along the pavements. They even created the beginnings of a playground for future generations.

By the decision of the government, the Society for the Restoration of Lidice was dissolved on the 31st of March 1959, but the real liquidation of the property, the transfer of the archives and the employees to the Local National Committee at Lidice dragged on till 1960.

A governmental promotional photo shows a mother and daughter enjoying time together in one of Lidice's first new homes, Christmastime 1949.

Clockwise: General clearance and construction work being carried out by Lidice women, photographed on the 9th of May 1947, a month before the second commemorative gathering and inauguration of the new village; On Sunday, October the 17th, 1948 - 100 members of the Prague Castle Brigade moved to Lidice where they worked with the women of Lidice on clearance work at the main entrance to the village; Photograph taken on June the 12th, 1949, the day of the 4th commemorative event was the first under a fully established dictatorship; it was organised by the Union of Freedom Fighters, having taken over responsibility for the day from the Society for the Restoration of Lidice. Promotional literature for the day included the following line: *"the burning of this settlement will be manifestly remembered in Lidice, which the German occupiers first brutally murdered and then razed to the ground."* Photo Credits - ČTK

British delegates at the start of the commemorative ceremony, left to right: Mrs Olive Stross and Mrs Will Lawther; Dr Barnett Stross, Chairman of the Lidice Shall Live campaign; Harry Leason, Lord Mayor of Stoke-on-Trent; Frank Hampl, Secretary of the Lidice Shall Live Campaign; Julius Jacobs, London Trades Council; Mrs Julius Jacobs; Mr William Kirkwood, Czechoslovak Vice Consul; and Will Lawther, President of the National Union of Mineworkers.

Left to right: Hubert Ripka, Minister for Foreign Trade; Václav Nosek, Minister for the Interior; unidentified woman; Václav Vacek, Mayor of Prague; Vlado Clementis, Vice-Minister of Foreign Affairs

The ceremony saw a queue of delegates from several continents make speeches hailing the achievements of those involved in resurrecting Lidice from the ashes of the past.

A NEW LIDICE   The Path to Lidice

Clockwise: Tapping of the Lidice foundation stone ceremony - divine blessing; Harry Baker, Secretary of the Birmingham Trades Council taps the stone overlooked by Arthur Baddeley, former President of the North Staffordshire Miners' Federation; Flight Lieutenant Josef Horák of the Society for the Reconstruction of Lidice takes members of the British Lidice Shall Live campaign on a tour of the memorial site pointing out the devastation; image 4 - outlining the plans for the site and new village; image 6 - in discussion with miners' leaders and Dr Barnett Stross.

Top - a photograph of the Lidice Shall Live delegation taken just off Prague's old town square; bottom - possibly taken at the commencement of their stay, by way of introductions at Prague Civic Chambers. Foreground to the right Cllr George Briggs, Lord Mayor of Coventry; centre Harry Leason, Lord Mayor of Stoke-on-Trent; left unidentified man - possibly William Kirkwood - Czech Vice Consul? In the background: to the left, man with glasses, moustache and hands crossed, Colonel Bourner - Leader of the Nottingham Lidice Shall Live campaign; to the right, man with glasses, placing pen in breast pocket, Dr Barnett Stross - Chairman of the National Lidice Shall Live movement.

Top: Dr Barnett Stross makes his speech at the Lidice inauguration event on the 15th of June 1947. Later, back home in Stoke-on-Trent he told reporters: **"It is not often that the dead and the living participate in the same ceremony. Just as I was using the phrase "the living and the dead" the atmosphere seemed breathless - then the most tremendous wind swept across us."** *Bottom: Promotional photograph for Lidice showing a mother and two children enjoying a sunny day with the new housing estate in the background - which was finally completed by 1960.*

```
PROGRAMME OF DELEGATION TO ATTEND OFFICIAL LAYING OF
       FOUNDATION STONE OF LIDICE, June 15th 1947.
              Departure by 'plane June 13th.
              ---------------

Friday June 13th.
              Arrival Prague official welcome by Mr. V.
              Nosek, Minister of Interior on behalf of
              the Czechoslovak Government.
              Departure by car to Hotel.

Saturday June 14th.
              Tour of Prague.  Visit to the Pankrac Prison.
              Evening: Opera Performance.

Sunday June 15th.
              Morning Free.  At 1 p.m. departure to Lidice.
              2 p.m. beginning of ceremony.  5 p.m. re-
              turn to Prague.  8.30 p.m. Dinner at Barandov.

Monday June 16th.
              Between 11 - 12 a.m. visit to Lord Mayor of
              Prague Dr. Vacek.  Laying of wreath on tomb
              of Unknown Soldier.
              Evening:  Reception with members of the Govern-
              ment present.  If weather permits it will be
              held at Valdstyn Gardens.

Tuesday June 17th.
              10.30 a.m.  Meeting in the Hall of the Ministry
              of Interior.  12.30 p.m. Visit to museum then
              to Vyschrad, Lany and to tomb of T.G.Masaryk.

Wednesday June 18th.
              Visit to Mines in Kladno and the Kable Works.
              Taking the whole day.

Thursday June 19th.
              Departure by car to Marianske Lazne, Karlovy
              Vary and Frantiskove Lazne.

Friday June 20th.
              Return to Prague.
              Evening Dinner in honour of the Delegation
              given by the Minister of Foreign Affairs.

Saturday June 21st.
              Departure for London by 'plane.

              ---------------------------
```

The itinerary of the Lidice Shall Live delegation during their visit to inaugurate the new village on the 15th of June, 1947 - including visits to the ancient spa towns of Mariánské Lázně, Karlovy Vary and Františkovy Lázně; visits to the Kladno mines; tour of Pankrác Prison; laying wreaths at the tomb of the Father of Czechoslovakia - Tomáš Masaryk, as well as functions with the Lord Mayor of Prague, Dr Václav Vacek; Minister of the Interior, Václav Nosek; and Minister of Foreign Affairs, Jan Masaryk

Clockwise: On Wednesday the 23rd of July 1947, just two days prior to the launch of the World Festival of Youth and Students in Prague, an international youth delegation was welcomed to Lidice; The young men and women offered their support to the building works taking place and pledged their assistance to help see the project through to a successful outcome; Chairwoman of the Lidice National Committee, Helena Leflerová addresses the students. The First World Youth Festival brought together 20,000 young people at a time when the world was still reeling from the aftershock of the Second World War. The programme of events saw 1,337 athletes from 27 countries taking part in 75 sports events; 100 groups and 3,500 artists performing 279 concerts of classical and folk music; and a daily festival journal printed in four languages. Photo - credits ČTK

Alan Bush conducting the first performance of 'Lidice' (1947)

The WMA would perform at several International Youth Festivals alongside Alan Bush. Its aims remain, "...the composition and performance of music with special regard to that which expresses the ideals and aims of humankind towards the improved organisation of society, music which exerts an influence against social injustices of our present society and music which encourages and reflects the activities and aspirations of the labour and peace movements for a new society." The performance at Lidice was filmed and clips of it can be seen on a documentary made by Anna Ambrose in 1983 called "Alan Bush - A Life". The film can be viewed freely using the BFI's online player.

A NEW LIDICE

The Path to Lidice

On the 12th of June 1949, the regional committee of the Union of Freedom Fighters organised a demonstration of the Lidice construction plan, which involved opening up the first completed Lidice house to the public. The ceremony was attended by Minister of National Defence, Ludvík Svoboda; Chairman of the Society for the Reconstruction of Lidice, Minister of the Interior, Václav Nosek; Deputy Chairman of the National Council, Anežka Hodinová-Spurná; Mayor of Prague, Václav Vacek; and other public figures. The first houses, erected in May 1948, featured four designs, offered around 100 square metres of accommodation, and were well equipped by contemporary standards. By Christmas 1949 the first women from Lidice were handed over the keys to their new homes. Two years later fifty homes were already inhabited and another twenty were nearing completion. Photo - Credit ČTK

Top left and right, Lidice residents in their new homes, photographed in the mid-1950s: Marie Šupíková, née Doležalová with daughter - secretary of the Lidice Local National Committee from 1970 to 1986; and Marie Jarošová - secretary and chairwoman of the committee throughout the 1950s and 60s.

Clockwise: Photograph of the supermarket in Lidice taken on the 13th of January 1961. Photo - Credit ČTK; Václav Nosek, who had passed away in 1955, had pledged that the events which had taken place at Lidice in 1942 would not be forgotten and would serve as a lesson for mankind. By 1960 most of the facilities set out in the original plans for the village were in place and Lidice was functioning as the model socialist village. The Rose of Lidice - which was sold across Czechoslovakia and beyond, grew in status throughout the 1970s and 80s, along with visitor numbers.

THE WINDS OF CHANGE

LOANS AND OBLIGATIONS

The Allied victory over Nazi Germany was secured, but conflict had left the British people exhausted and the nation financially crippled. To keep going, between 1939 and 1941 Britain had liquidated most of its overseas holdings, sacrificed most of its export trade and borrowed to excess. The national feeling was that Britain had stood up for what was right in order to protect and safeguard the future of all humanity, while all around sat still. Because of these sacrifices by 1945, the UK National Debt had tripled and external borrowings were the highest in the nation's history - more than £140 billion in 2022 prices. To compound matters, by September 1945, with the war with Japan now complete Lend-Lease - the US programme of assistance that provided food, oil, and materials to Britain throughout the war abruptly stopped.

Winston Churchill could only offer more austerity, but the people desired change. On the 5th of July 1945, Clement Attlee's Labour Party swept to power in Britain with a manifesto that promised to provide sweeping reforms to its Industry, Education, Housing, Transport, Welfare and Health sectors, including the establishment of a *National Health Service*, based on the recommendations of Sir William Beveridge in his 1942 report *'Social Insurance and Allied Services'*.

To pay for the reforms, economist John Maynard Keynes warned Britain faced a serious situation: only a grant from the USA would assuage severe costs on the British people. Not to fund the changes meant destitution or *"Starvation"* for Britain - certainly, the continuation of strict wartime rationing and the inability to bring in the programmes promised in the manifesto. To borrow funds or *"Temptation"* entailed financial and political obligations towards the USA stretching long into the future. Instead, with the United Kingdom facing monetary collapse thanks to ruinously high debts and its foreign exchange reserves drained by the demands of opposing the tide of Nazi aggression alone, Keynes suggested the Cabinet opt for *"Justice."* In this option, it was hoped that Britain's valiant fight would count for something with her Allies across the pond. When Keynes met with negotiators in Washington, it soon became obvious that it did not.

There was a fundamental misapprehension of the situation on the part of the British. The years of conflict had been good for the population of the USA. Kick-started by the Keynesian influenced *New Deal*, the economy was boosted by a mix of defence contracts and consumerism during the war years, such that America's GDP had more than doubled by 1945. However, despite the claims of Keynes, the British Cabinet and many British people, a majority of Americans felt that twice in one century they had ridden to the rescue of Europe, at great personal cost and sacrifice to their nation. There was the viewpoint that thousands of American GIs should not have died just to restore Britain's old imperialist status quo. If anything, they believed it was Britain that owed America a debt of gratitude. It was not looking good; but the British people would not stand for *"Starvation."* Having failed to secure a grant from the USA to put in place the Welfare and Health reforms outlined in their manifesto, and desperate for cash, on the 5th of December 1945, the British Government finally succumbed to *"Temptation"* and reluctantly approved the best offer John Maynard Keynes could secure from US negotiators: $3.75 billion at 2% with plenty of small print thrown in. This was no free handout, and was eventually paid back, with interest on the 29th of December 2006. Rationing and austerity continued well into the 1950s.

A NEW WAY OF THINKING

In the Spring of 1946, Dr Barnett Stross put his views concerning Great Britain's future relations with Czechoslovakia and the Soviet Union succinctly and frankly in a letter, published in English in *The Weekly Bulletin*, a publication printed by the Czechoslovak Ministry of Information in Prague. The letter commended the inauguration of the Prague branch of the British-Czechoslovak Friendship League and referred to the intimate rapport and understanding that had developed between the two countries during the war years - it mentioned the formation of the Friendship Clubs that had grown in number across Britain; and the Lidice Shall Live movement - which was still receiving funds. Dr Stross explained the future working objectives of the Friendship League and included an intriguing caveat post scripted to the message:

"We cannot forget that Czechoslovakia lives on the borders of the USSR. and that friendship between them will make for stability and peace in Eastern Europe. No one has any doubt that such friendship is certain and must indeed become permanent. We must remember, however, that Czechoslovakia has old cultural ties with us and is therefore uniquely placed to act as a friend of both countries and both peoples."

"It is in the cause of future peace that the League now works. Its functions must be utterly simple and frank, weaving innumerable and delicate strands in the warp and woof of European peace until the garment is complete and indestructible."

Thus, Barnett Stross openly rejected what would become an official pro-US / anti-Soviet, British Governmental stance, led by Ernest Bevin months later. It was clear that Stross intended for the League to expand its operations, not wind them down, as it continued developing relations with Czechoslovakia and those nations associated with it - in the name of peace.

ALTRUISTIC *LEVELLING UP* OR ECONOMIC IMPERIALISM

Although Britain's Labour government, headed by Clement Attlee was elected with a desire to develop progressive relations with the Soviet Union and her allies, it soon became clear that, as far as Stalin was concerned, Attlee's brand of Socialism deserved a greater degree of contempt than Churchill's capitalism. Because, for Stalin, the socialism of the Labour Party was dishonest: its conning of the public into believing the Government was acting in its interests was more despicable than the pure, laissez-faire philosophy of free markets and minimum state intervention.

In March 1947, in an address to Congress which paved the way ahead for McCarthyism in the early 1950s, US President Harry S. Truman announced a set of policies committing the United States to opposing Soviet expansionism. It would come to be known as the Truman Doctrine. At home, it meant his Executive Order 9835 of March the 21st, 1947, required that all federal civil-service employees be screened for *"loyalty"*, with signs of *"disloyalty"* to include:

"... membership in, affiliation with or sympathetic association" with any organisation determined by the attorney general to be "totalitarian, fascist, communist or subversive"

or advocating or approving the forceful denial of constitutional rights to other persons or seeking "to alter the form of Government of the United States by unconstitutional means."

Internationally, it meant rewarding those countries who backed US foreign policy and punishing those perceived to be against or undermining it. Throughout the rest of 1947, this thinking infiltrated its way into British political society, establishment, and its press and media. Hence, though the foundation of the NHS was announced as a Socialist invention, the rules of the game began to change incrementally following the signing of the US deal so that from 1947 many of those within the Labour Party labelled as "Socialist" increasingly found themselves marginalised and pushed to its periphery. Over the decades, those with past links to communism or the full state control of industry and markets were cancelled or even made an example of in the press.

With no European power left unscathed following the war, economic stagnation created a vacuum across the continent, and the US Government recognised the threats and opportunities which lay before it. In 1946, the potential for social unrest and the creeping expansionism of Communism into the West still existed across Central and Eastern Europe, even accounting for the successes of UNRRA in bringing people back home and helping to rebuild their communities. Though commitments had been for five years, funding to Czechoslovakia ground to a halt in 1947. Instead, soon efforts were made to revive the stricken economies of Europe through the *European Recovery Program*, commonly called the *Marshall Plan*, after its creator US Secretary of State George C. Marshall; an overtly US package of support which transferred over $13 billion in economic recovery programmes to those countries of Europe most impacted by the war. Launched on the 3rd of April 1948, it provided the British economy with $2.7 billion worth of free aid, allowing it to haul itself out of severe austerity and properly implement its reforms.

The task at hand for the Attlee Government was simple during the remainder of the 1940s: to keep the United States happy by ensuring that obligations towards her were met and maintained. Britain *should be and be seen to be* anti-communist in her foreign policy, promoting capitalism and the free market, and supporting her benefactor whenever called upon for support against new Allied enemies—specifically the Soviet Union and her satellites. For several members of the new British Government this last requirement must have felt like an ultimatum, even a bridge too far, as the ideas which brought them into politics in the first place were inspired by the Russian October Revolution of 1917. Now, rather than a vision based on a redistribution of income to create a more equal society, Attlee, Bevin, Cripps, Dalton, Wilson, Stross and other MPs were being forced down a road contrary to their economic sensibilities.

ALIENS

International squabbling was about to collide with the campaign to rebuild Lidice, which had grown so formidable during the years of conflict, garnering such emphatic support from all sectors of British society. The successful conclusion of the War in Europe meant the Flag Days, so successful during those darker days, the times before Stalingrad, were received with limited enthusiasm. The events and activities organised around the country to raise funds for the Lidice renewal committee or wounded Czech veterans by activists in the Lidice Shall Live committees and Czecho-Slovak – British Friendship Clubs generated less interest. British feelings towards the Soviet Union and anything associated with it were deteriorating progressively, as the war of words amongst the world's leaders amplified.

Now *"Nazi Germany"* was dead. The British Government had accepted help from the US to the tune of $3 billion of Marshall Aid and $4.5 billion of loans at 2%. It was desperately needed, but it signalled a massive national, long-term obligation. The people of Britain had contemplated which side of the fence their bread was best buttered, and for most, the choice was clear: they concluded it was the side of the United States of America. Fundraising for Soviet friendly projects became an increasingly peripheral, and lonely, activity.

In January 1948, the British Government went on the attack and launched a more belligerent propaganda policy designed to **"oppose the inroads of communism by taking the offensive against it."** The campaign was spearheaded by Ernest Bevin, Secretary of State for Foreign Affairs, and outlined in a paper presented to the Cabinet on January the 8th. It stated that since the end of the war, Soviet propaganda had conducted **"a vicious attack against the British Commonwealth and against Western democracy."** Bevin did not propose a simple defensive pact; it was not enough to reinforce the physical barriers which reinforced Western civilisation:

"We must also organise and consolidate the ethical and spiritual forces inherent in this Western civilisation, of which we are the chief protagonists. The time had come to pass over to the offensive and not leave the initiative to the enemy but make them defend themselves."

It also claimed that Britain as a European social democratic government should take the lead in uniting the forces of anti-communism: **"This in my view can only be done by creating some form of union in Western Europe, whether of formal or informal character, backed by the Americans and the Dominions."**

COUP D'ETAT

Whilst Britain benefitted from $3 billion of aid from the *Marshall Plan*, Czechoslovakia, along with other Eastern European nations, was forced to go without. Stalin had seen France, Italy and Greece reject Communism and was not prepared to let his immediate neighbours slip through his fingers.

When, in 1947, President Beneš notified the Generalissimo of Czechoslovakia's intention to renew her pre-war military alliance with France, a country that, like Czechoslovakia, had suffered severely because of her proximity to Germany, the President's letter received a lukewarm response. Soon afterwards, on the 5th of July, while political negotiations between Poland and Czechoslovakia were taking place in Prague, the invitation to attend talks in Paris on the *European Recovery Program* was extended to all war-devastated European countries at the suggestion of the United States' Foreign Secretary, General Marshall. When Mr. Masaryk asked his views, the Polish Prime Minister, Józef Cyrankiewicz, who was in Prague, replied that Poland was most interested in the Marshall proposals and would also send representatives to Paris. This statement passed to the Czechoslovak Government, which met on the 7th of July. After discussion, it was voted unanimously that Czechoslovakia would accept the invitation.

Poland did not react as quickly and on the 9th of July, it was evident that Czechoslovakia was the only country behind the *Iron Curtain* that had agreed to take part in the conference in Paris.

The same day a Czechoslovak Governmental delegation, headed by the Prime Minister, Klement Gottwald, and the Minister of Foreign Affairs, Jan Masaryk, left for Moscow to discuss pending political problems and to pave the way for a new commercial treaty with the Soviet Union. Dr Drtina, the Minister of Justice, accompanied them in place of Dr Ripka, the Minister of Foreign Trade, who had suddenly been taken ill - perhaps he had an inkling of what was in store for them!

It was Thursday, the 10th of July, and the audience with Marshal Stalin had been arranged for 9.30am. Masaryk and Drtina met half an hour earlier in one of the rooms of the State residence put at their disposal, but Gottwald was late. They became impatient as the minutes passed, so Masaryk sent a message to Gottwald's apartments, enquiring if everything was all right. The Prime Minister's secretary came down and profusely apologised, explaining that the meeting had been postponed, but he had omitted to inform them. At that minute Gottwald entered, and according to Josef Josten in his book *Oh My Country*, he seemed,

"... in the best of spirits. *'All has gone well,'* he announced to Masaryk, who still had no idea what the Prime Minister was talking about or what had given him such satisfaction. *'We shall not need to go to Paris. We shall get all we want from the Soviet Union. The Generalissimo has just told me so!'* When Mr. Masaryk had recovered from his surprise and annoyance, he turned to Dr Drtina, ignoring Gottwald, and said: *'It seems there is not much point in our being here at all. I may as well hand in my resignation!'"*

In the Kremlin, their reception was cold and the discussion was one sided. Marshal Stalin had the newspapers of the world displayed on his table and pointed out two-inch headlines: "Prague losing her ties with Moscow," "Breach in the Eastern Bloc," and others, just as the more sensational overseas newspapers had happened to report Czechoslovakia's decision to go to Paris.

"In these circumstances, gentlemen," said the Marshal, after a long discussion on Czechoslovakia's economic situation, *"it is for you to decide whether you consider the pact of friendship and mutual aid between our countries valid, or whether you prefer to go to Paris. I suggest you discuss it with your government and let me have your answer later today."*

On his return to Prague airport in response to journalists' enquiries, Masaryk declared,

"I left as a minister of a sovereign state but have come back as Stalin's lackey."

From that moment on, Czechoslovakia became increasingly *Sovietized* as moves were made to set up a puppet state, mimicking the behaviour of the *Motherland*. In Prague, during the winter of 1947–48, rising tensions between the Communists and other parties, both in the cabinet and in parliament, led to bitter conflict. Masaryk and Beneš knew the score, that there was no way back. All traces of support from the West would be lost. Czechoslovakia would be sucked under the umbrella of Soviet hegemony, with nothing to halt the process, as a larger drop of water absorbs the smaller. Both statesmen would lose all hope for the nation and would die during the fateful year of 1948 - Masaryk under mysterious circumstances.

Václav Nosek, a former member of the British-based Czech Government-in-exile, who was seen as one of the *good Communists* in London, and the prime mover behind the construction of a new Lidice was also a principal agitator at grass roots level and within industry, ruthless in the pursuit of the Communists' manifesto and willing to implement totalitarian methods. And he was brazenly candid about it, once announcing at a speech in Brno in October 1947 that he was happy to apply the techniques of the Nazis to the Communist cause in order that the Czechs out-Gestapo the Gestapo:

"We are accused of *Gestapism*. I do not deny it. On the contrary, we shall show our opponents that we can do this better than the Germans." he said.

With this ideological thinking at work in 1947, it is easy to extrapolate how the groundwork was being prepared for the political weaponisation of the future village of Lidice by an increasingly hard line, Stalinist government. In February 1948, Chairman of the Lidice National Committee, Václav Nosek, acting in his capacity as Minister of the Interior illegally attempted to remove all remaining democrats and other non-Communist personnel from the Czechoslovak police and intelligence services. Many saw this as a move towards subjugation - the Communist Party of Czechoslovakia (KSČ) using the security services as instruments of tyranny.

Seeking retribution, on the 12th of February 1948, in Prague, the non-Communists in the cabinet urgently demanded punishment for the offending Communists in the government and an assurance that they show loyalty to democracy. Nosek, backed by Prime Minister Klement Gottwald, flatly refused. Instead, he and his fellow Communists threatened to use force and, in order to coerce colleagues in parliament, appealed to groups of activists and their supporters across the nation to mobilise in support of the Communists' aims. On the 21st of February, twelve non-Communist ministers resigned in protest after Nosek refused to reinstate eight non-Communist senior police officers in defiance of a majority vote of the cabinet in favour of doing so. President Beneš initially rejected their resignations in the hope that Prime Minister Gottwald would either back down, resign, or call new elections. But by then it was too late: there was no pretence at following the democratic process.

On the 25th of February 1948, fearful of civil war and Soviet invasion, Dr Beneš capitulated. He accepted the resignations of the non-Communist ministers and appointed a new government in accordance with Communist Party demands. The Communist Party's takeover of Czechoslovakia was complete.

Thousands of people fled the country as the Communists began tightening their grip on power. Non-communists were fired and hundreds were arrested. The National Assembly, which had been freely elected two years earlier, quickly became a rubber-stamping machine, making a mockery of democracy by handing the autocratic President Gottwald and his Government a 230-0 vote of confidence. The loss of the last remaining democracy in Eastern Europe came as a profound shock to millions. For the second time in a decade, Western eyes saw Czechoslovak independence and freedom snuffed out by an oppressive dictatorship intent on dominating a smaller country.

The ripple effects had serious ramifications for the whole of Europe, one of a series of momentous events which sealed the fate of East - West relations for decades to come, as it contributed to an increase in mutual distrust and cynicism, we today label the Cold War. Britain, facing financial ruin, now saw every vindication in its growing loyalty towards the US, measured by its speedy adoption of the Marshall Plan. Through Ernest Bevin's active foreign policy, Britain openly upheld the establishment of the West German state and backed measures to keep communists out of power in Europe's most vulnerable post-war nations. Within a year, Bevin pioneered a system of collective security and due diligence across the Western powers that would function as a deterrent to the perceived ever-pressing Soviet threat. The result was the *North Atlantic Treaty Organisation* or NATO, and its signatories were all the major Western powers including and backed by the USA. The day of its founding signalled the moment the *Iron Curtain's* descent was complete. It would not rise again until the Velvet Revolution of December 1989.

For several years, the welfare of Czechoslovakia had grown central to a high-profile British wartime cause due to national remorse associated with the Munich Agreement, a debt of gratitude related to the Battle of Britain, and a genuine empathy towards the Czechoslovak people, who shared similar Western and in particular, British sensibilities. An expression of much of this kinship could be found in the Lidice Shall Live campaign. When many leading Czechoslovak émigrés announced their concern at the nature of the Prague coup, there was a galvanising of anti-communist sentiment in Britain, and within Government especially, which led to calls for Britain to adopt a more offensive propaganda policy. "Murder in Prague" wrote the Daily Herald's Michael Foot as he lamented the most **"tragic week since the end of the war."** On the 3rd of March, the Labour Party's National Executive Committee issued a fierce condemnation of Soviet actions stating that Czechoslovakia had **"fallen victim to aggression from without aided by treachery from within."** The concern for many onlookers was, if the Russians could do this to one European democracy three years after the end of the war, there was little to prevent them from doing it to other European countries, and notably in Western Europe.

Czechoslovakia's Communist Government soon found itself in economic, social, and political trouble. It became necessary to find scapegoats who could be made responsible for falling living standards and the failures to achieve set targets. Over a number of years, waves of recriminations and prosecutions resulted. First, the regime focused on enemies outside the Communist Party. Later, with direct Soviet involvement, it looked inward, purging those considered suspect within its core. Through provocation and the spreading of disinformation about targeted individuals by the State Security - *StB*, many elected representatives, some with hitherto unblemished party records, were prosecuted, found guilty in filmed show trials, and summarily executed. Altogether, 180 politicians met their fate in this way, including several former members of the Czechoslovak Government-in-exile.

One especially relevant case was that of Vladimir (Vlado) Clementis who, in his capacity as Deputy Foreign Minister, had accepted the cheque for £32,375 from Dr Barnett Stross and the Lidice Shall Live campaign, on the 15th of June 1947. Clementis was one of 11 condemned to be hanged on the 3rd of December 1952 after being convicted in a show trial along with 14 others. His ashes were scattered on a road and Lída, his wife, received just her husband's two pipes and tobacco.

This was the new Czechoslovakia Barnett Stross was engaging with. It was a state that was creating adversaries in Britain and the West. Those perceived to be apologists for the actions of the Czechoslovakian state were, by association, suspect, too. The British-Czechoslovak Friendship League sent Klement Gottwald a telegram of congratulations on his election as President of Czechoslovakia on the 14th of June 1948 and assured him that,

> *"... it would continue in its efforts to bring about still closer friendship and understanding between Great Britain and Czechoslovakia."*

The message carried the signature of Dr Barnett Stross, the then Chairman of the League. With an appreciation of Dr Stross, this was a perfunctory invitation for increased dialogue between the British-Czechoslovak Friendship League and the new hard-line communist dictatorship. As Chair of the 'League, Stross used his position to protest against human rights issues in the country. **"However, this cut little ice with MI5: Stross was on the left of the Labour Party, an émigré and thus a natural target for the security services."** From this time forward until his death, Dr Barnett Stross would become a constant source of interest to Britain's security services, through his work keeping Britain's links with Czechoslovakia alive.

The new order ushers in a complete syncopation of politics, industry, society and living with the words of the Czechoslovak Communist Party song Kupředu Levá, Zpátky Ni Krok! *("Forwards Left, Not a Step Backwards!")* displayed above the doors and factory gates of industrial plants, and all manner of civic buildings, schools and hospitals.

The time has come and it smells of hope, the sun of freedom rains down from the clouds.
Forward comrades, look, the promised land, where there are no masters nor beggars.
Where a sky of peace above our heads is curving, where man is no longer wolf to another man.
Forward comrades, look, the promised land, that the poor searched for from the dawn of time.

Into a herd in our faith, we shall our hearts unite, man by man, side by side, we will arrive, we will arrive!
It is time, it is time for every one of us to lend a working hand, there, where our strength is mustered, there the world shall move!
Into a herd our hearts unite to form one solid block!
Forward, left, forward, left, not one step back!

On the side he is, he who is deaf and blind, he who doesn't go with the people, returns back.
Forward comrades, look, from eastern steppes, spring wind blows into our sails.
Now in the unison of work let us hold hands and let the song of the people reach to the stars!
Let us raise higher the banner of revolution and against enemies an iron fist.

Into a herd in our faith, we shall our hearts unite, man by man, side by side, we will arrive, we will arrive!
It is time, it is time for every one of us to lend a working hand, there, where our strength is mustered, there the world shall move!
Into a herd our hearts unite to form one solid block!
Forward, left, forward, left, not one step back!

Top - The Marshall Plan (or European Recovery Program) was an American initiative which transferred over $13 billion in economic recovery programmes to Western European economies following the end of the Second World War. Although offered participation, the Soviet Union rejected the plan and blocked Eastern Bloc nations, such as Czechoslovakia, Poland, and Hungary from accessing the funds. Instead, the Soviet Union set up the Molotov Plan which later expanded into the Comecon. Bottom - The nightmare vision of the totalitarian state was perfectly portrayed in George Orwell's seminal work 1984 - illustrated in reality here in this photo - taken on the 21st of February 1948. On the original, one of the chief architects of the coup d'état, Vladimir Clementis, executed for having links to the bourgeoisie, stands next to Czechoslovak President Klement Gottwald. When Clementis was imprisoned in 1950, he was erased from the photograph.

WHITEHAVEN LIVES

This shift in the British Government's attitude towards Czechoslovakia was nowhere better illustrated than in the collapse of the Czechoslovak-British aid project for the victims of the Whitehaven Mining Disaster, where it would seem an action by Czechoslovak miners to support the bereaved families of British miners killed underground became the victim of controversy and political game-playing following the Prague Communist takeover in February 1948.

On August the 15th 1947, 104 miners lost their lives in a pit explosion at the William Pit coal mine in Whitehaven, Cumbria. On the 27th of September, Evžen Erban, Secretary General of the Czechoslovakian Central Council of Trade Unions, announced a proposal for a Czechoslovak supported miners' recreation home in Britain in commemoration of the victims. Mr Erban said that under the proposal, Czechoslovak miners and other workers would do an extra hour's work and give the additional pay to the fund for the building. The scheme was reminiscent of the Lidice Shall Live campaign. Erban called on all workers throughout Czechoslovakia to do this,

"... honour to the men who gave their lives in the battlefield of industry."

Additionally, the Secretary General announced that free scholarships would also be provided for the children of affected families, who would like to study in Czechoslovakia, and invitations extended towards bereaved wives and children for them to receive treatments in Czechoslovakian spas and for the costs to be subsidised. All details of the plan were to be arranged in co-operation with the National Union of Mineworkers. As far as Evžen Erban and the Czechoslovak Central Council of Trade Unions were concerned, this was a reciprocal, empathetic gesture for the £32,375 collected in Britain subsidising the creation of a new Lidice—a campaign spearheaded by British mineworkers.

It was reported on the 26th of January 1948 how Will Lawther was co-operating on the project with the Czechoslovakian Trade Union Council and that, true to their word the trade unionists had indeed raised about £40,000 for the widows and orphans of the Whitehaven Pit Disaster the previous year, **"a reciprocal gesture for the kindness shown towards the victims of Lidice"**, it said.

Erban and Lawther planned to meet to discuss how the money could best be spent. There were three ideas: holidays and spa treatments in Czechoslovakia for Whitehaven widows and orphans; scholarships in Czechoslovakia for the orphans; and building homes in Britain which they could occupy, and which would later be used for old miners and their wives.

During a time of great upheaval in Czechoslovakia, General Secretary of the NUM, Arthur Horner, along with two other representatives of the union, travelled to Prague in early February 1948 to discuss the Whitehaven plans in person. Satisfied with the way the scheme was working out in practice, the authorities in Prague decided that the Czechoslovak holiday tours should be sold to *"progressive"* Britons for £37.10 a head and that part of the proceeds donated to the Whitehaven Fund. It was agreed that the business would be run by the company *Progressive Tours* since they already had expertise in organising package holidays behind the *Iron Curtain*. For a nation being strangled by the grip of communism, it was quite a *free-market* venture.

On the 19th of December 1949, an industrial correspondent for the Belfast Telegraph wrote,

"The sum of £40,000 collected by Czech miners two years ago for dependants of 104 miners killed in the Whitehaven pit disaster in August 1947 has still not reached Britain. Miners' leaders think that it never will,"

Difficulties had arisen since the Communists seized power in Czechoslovakia. The Czechoslovak miners wanted half the cash devoted to widows and orphans, and half to offering spa treatment in Czechoslovakia for disabled British miners. But Sir William Lawther, now President of the *National Union of Mineworkers*, said: **"We have told the Czechs that the idea of British miners going there for treatment is impracticable. We have suggested they send the money here for the Whitehaven dependants."**

Sir William denied that the change of Government in Czechoslovakia had anything to do with the NUM's attitude. The report continued that Communists had alleged that the union was afraid to let its members discover **"how well the Czechoslovak miners live under a nationalisation policy which encourages workers' control at all levels."** According to British reports, the leaders in Prague announced subsequently that the country's sterling currency reserve would not permit this amount to be transferred to Britain, and they offered to use the money to provide holidays in Czechoslovakia for miners and their families instead.

A note sent from the Foreign Office to the Treasury on the 5th of February 1950 described a typical holiday as including transport by air from London to Prague for a fortnight's stay, whereby the participants would enjoy five meals per day. They would have the opportunity of visiting the surrounding districts besides seeing the Prague. The Czechoslovak Trade Union Movement would make no special charges for the administrative costs connected with the realisation of the scheme. The British NUM, for its part, pledged to obtain permission from the British authorities for the landing and taking off of the specially chartered Czechoslovak planes.

Unsurprisingly, government officials in Britain soon realised the pro-communist propaganda potential of the holiday-in-Czechoslovakia idea. Staff at the British Embassy in Prague had no illusions about how the tours could improve sentiment among the holidaymakers for the increasingly autocratic Communist dominated Czechoslovak Government, and how this could spread through their families, friends, and colleagues on their return home. As written in the British Embassy's report to the Foreign Office,

"... the Czechs, no doubt, will do everything to persuade the visitors that Czechoslovakia is a workers' paradise. Nor should they have much difficulty in doing so if they lock them up in a series of delightful mountain resorts and surround them with engaging young communists of both sexes."

In due course, the promise of funding for the Whitehaven dependents materialised; it was reported on April the 6th, 1956, by the Lancashire Evening Post how:

"In the near future each surviving widow and adult dependant of the 104 miners who lost their lives in the William Pit Whitehaven, disaster in August 1947, will receive a lump sum of £100 and each child under 16 at the time of the disaster-there are 189—will get £10 each."

It was affirmed that the money would come from the Czechoslovak trade unions whose members had worked an extra hour to honour the memory of the lost miners. It had taken over *eight years* to have the funds transferred to England because of currency difficulties. Now, finally, here was confirmation that about £33,060 would be available for distribution amongst dependents by the end of the year.

"Apart from the lump sums, Mr Tom Stephenson, secretary of the Cumberland Miners, announced this morning that it was proposed to give the 64 widows and adult dependants who have not remarried a pension of 30s each a week for the next three years and 97 children who are still under the age of 16 will get 7s. 6d weekly during the same period."

"The payment of the initial lump sums will cost the fund £9.800 in respect of the adults and £1.890 in respect of the children, a total of £11.690. While the annual cost of the weekly payments will be £6.883 10s. In the three years, during which these payments will run, more than £20.650 will be distributed, and leave in the fund about £720, which will be used for the payment of fares between West Cumberland and London for those dependants who wish to take advantage of the holidays which are offered by the Czechs to use up the remainder of the fund, some £19,600 which they continued to hold."

"Mr Stephenson said that in the near future he would call a meeting in Whitehaven of the widows and dependants to tell them of the details of the scheme and hear any suggestions which might be put forward. With him on that occasion will be Mr J. Hewitt, president of the Cumberland Miners; Mr R. Beattie, the Haig Pit representative; Mr A. Lee, representative of the Ladysmith Works; and members of the council from the Whitehaven area. It is not known precisely when the share-out will begin."

Any trip to Czechoslovakia invariably included a visit to Lidice. Sightseers were taken to both the new village and the few scarred remnants of the commemorative site - the symbol and pinnacle of Nazi brutality towards Czechs during the Occupation. For many British people with their own memories of the Second World War so clear in the mind, this would have come as a shocking cultural reality.

In 2008, a man named Joe Hewer, a beneficiary of the Czech funded Whitehaven scheme, recalled his experience:

"I visited Czechoslovakia in 1956. I was nine years old, and we went to Lidice, a place I will never forget. I'm 61 now. I was with a party of miners' widows and orphans as guests of the Czech miners. My father and 103 other miners were killed in an explosion in the William Pit disaster at Whitehaven in Cumbria on 15 August 1947. Czech miners contributed to a fund for the miners' dependants. We travelled to London and then on to Dover. We crossed the Channel to Ostend and then continued by train to Czechoslovakia. We stayed in a beautiful town called Mariánské Lázně.

I will never forget our visit; the people were so kind and friendly to us all. We had two days in Prague and I remember visiting a youth camp by a lake in a woodland setting. We played games with the children and had our meals with the Czech youngsters. When it is near the anniversary, my memories of Czechoslovakia always come back to me. Thank you for everything you did for us all."

William Pit, Britain's oldest under-sea mine, at 5.40pm on Friday, August the 15th; with 117 men working below, an explosion occurred. Several heavy falls of rocks trapped over a hundred colliers. By Saturday afternoon, following the efforts of rescue parties, fifty dead bodies had been located and the National Coal Board announced there was little hope of any trapped men being found alive. Although men miraculously escaped death, the total number of fatalities numbered 104. Clockwise: relatives of the trapped men sit by the pit head waiting for news; rescue workers laden with special equipment preparing to enter the dangerous workings of the pit in a desperate attempt to save colleagues; Evžen Erban, General Secretary of the Revolutionary Trade Union Movement in Czechoslovakia and a left-wing Social Democrat; an ambulance takes three men, miraculously escaped from the workings to the hospital.

THE FORGOTTEN FACTOR

On Sunday, June the 20th, 1948, something significant happened at Victoria Hall, the birthplace of the Lidice Shall Live campaign. The event typified the change in direction the nation was taking. A mere three years prior, the flags of Czechoslovakia and the Soviet Union were warmly embraced in the auditorium. Now their presence could have been met with disquiet, even alarm, in some quarters.

The occasion marked a sequel to a run of performances which had happened 14 months earlier at Burslem's Queen's Theatre, of the *Moral Re-Armament* industrial teamwork play, *The Forgotten Factor* by Anglican priest and author, Alan Thornhill. During the war, the play had been used with remarkable success to maintain production levels across British coalfields. The drama emphasised the need for managements and unions to work together on the basis of *'not who is right but what is right,'* in order for both to survive. Now the play had been re-embraced by the Attlee Government to improve industrial relations and output, to keep communities alive at an hour of extreme national economic struggle. But it was about more than that. The Government wanted workers to shift their allegiances towards the West, to see socialism as more belligerent and capitalism as more benevolent, in line with Bevin's Foreign Policy. It was time for workers to be content with what they had and to cooperate with employers and the owners of capital — the British Government.

The Victoria Hall rally was about the North Staffordshire Area of the National Union of Mineworkers highlighting what results had been achieved through the presentation of The Forgotten Factor to various coalfields. *(See appendix)*. Besides delegations from the South Wales, Scottish, Lancashire, South Staffordshire, Leicestershire, and Warwickshire coalfields, in addition to North Staffordshire there were guest mineworkers' representations from France, Holland and the Ruhr to make the occasion international in its scope. Italy was represented in the person of Mr Umberto Celosso, Secretary of the Saragat Socialist Party. But this time, there was no contingent from the Soviet Union or Czechoslovakia.

It was an afternoon of speeches. Some contained personal testimony to a new found outlook on life, all stressed the need for greater co-operation in the home, at work and in world affairs to develop true understanding and successful teamwork. The greatest applause was given a 59-year-old German - August Halbfell, Minister of Labour for North Rhine-Westphalia, a province of 13.4 million people, who spoke as a miner and as a politician:

"When you hear Germany talked about even to-day, you will think of the horrible Germany which brought so much unhappiness to the whole world. But I ask you not to forget that alongside this terrible Germany, there was another Germany - a Germany that was ready to fight for the friendship, affection, and teamwork of the world. During the days of Nazism, this other Germany fought against Nazism and hundreds of thousands died in concentration camps and on the scaffolds. Several of our delegation, including myself, have had the opportunity to show in concentration camps that they were ready to suffer for those ideals. And yet, as we look around in the world, we see that hatred is still a real passion. What we ask to-day is that there should be an understanding of a beaten people, and a poor people and of a broken economy. If hatred remains alongside hatred, it can mean fresh suffering for mankind."

Chairman for the rally was Harold Lockett, former President of the North Staffordshire Miners' Federation, holder of the Czechoslovak *Order of the White Lion* and now the President of the North Staffordshire Area of the National Union of Mineworkers. Lockett told the audience of 2,000 that unless they were prepared to stand up for the things that would bring peace to themselves and their own homes, there was little chance of getting peace among the nations. Mr Bill Yates, President of the Victoria (Biddulph) Colliery Branch of the NUM, gave the first of a number of two-minute addresses by mineworkers under the title of *The Miner Speaks*. Yates spoke of the impact on himself and on workmates of the play *The Forgotten Factor* and said he was struck to find that all people were regarded as equal. He only regretted that the Russians were absent.

Among others who addressed the rally were Mr Horace Holmes MP, Parliamentary Private Secretary to the Ministry of Fuel and Power; Mr W. Brough, Under-Manager Long Lane Colliery, Wigan; M. Frank Smith, Leicestershire Coalfield; Mr Bill Sperring, President of the Deputies Association of South Wales; Mr A. H. J. Kramers, Inspector of Personnel, State Mines, Holland; Mr Joseph Sauty, Secretary C.F.T.C. Miners Northern Coalfield, France; Mr Frank Painter, President of the Warwickshire Area, NUM; Mr Fred Copeman, one-time Commander of the International Brigade, former Communist and now a member of the Labour Party; and Mr Peter Howard, author; the Makinac Singers; the Wolstanton Colliery Choir; and the Pare and Dare Colliery Band, Welsh champions.

DISINTEGRATION

Besmirching the post-war, London based Lidice Shall Live Committee and the British-Czechoslovak Friendship League inevitably meant retrospective criticism of the wartime fundraising effort. Worse still, it cast a shadow over the national Lidice Shall Live movement, implying that there were ulterior motives at play and a degree of manipulation involved in persuading hard working miners and other working-class people to cough up for a communist cause. Most of all, it suggested a deep insincerity at the very heart of the operation and its leading campaigners.

FRANK HAMPL

It was now 1948, and six-years prior Frank Hampl, a German Jew who had escaped the Holocaust with his family by the skin of his teeth, had been helping to transform the Lidice Shall Live campaign from a parochial fundraiser to a full-blown international movement. At the time—1942-1945—Hampl's involvement suited the Coalition Government's interests perfectly. Now he was fulfilling another function for the British Government: he was on a charge of espionage at a time when Britain needed to show its Cold War credentials, that it was prepared to prove its commitments to the USA. He was at the point of being deported.

Dr Barnett Stross called to see Mr Chuter Ede, the Home Secretary, on the 21st of July to plead the case of the 41-year-old Hampl, who was by then Secretary of the British - Czechoslovak League. Colonel George Wigg, Labour MP for Dudley, who accompanied Dr Stross, told a reporter that the Home Secretary had stated that the charge against Mr Hampl was concerned with the passing, either wittingly or unwittingly of a letter as a result of which extremely valuable information prejudicial to Great Britain had got into the hands of an unnamed foreign power.

According to the Gloucester Echo on the 21st of July, Mr Hampl said:

"It is quite clear this was a deliberate 'frame-up,' not against me as Frank Hampl, but against me as Secretary of the British - Czechoslovakian Friendship League, which is working successfully for better relations between the two peoples."

Colonel Wigg said that the person who had collected the letter was still "walking about the country," and that the man who had left the letter was a Czech in "an official position."

In the House of Commons on the 30th of July, on the matter of the deportation, when the subject of Mr Hampl's reputation was raised, Mr Kenneth Younger, Parliamentary Under Secretary for the Home Office, declared:

"I resent the ready assumption that the Home Secretary and myself are willing to take part in some plot against British Czech relations or are dancing like marionettes as some hidden hand jerks the strings."

To which Hampl later replied,

"Mr Younger referred to my anti-Nazi record and said the Home Secretary wished to see good relations between our two countries. These are two matters that I feel deeply about. I shall continue to work for friendship between our two nations. I would also like to express my gratitude for the fair treatment I have received from the British press."

George Wigg MP, who had raised the matter in Parliament, said he had known Hampl for ten years and considered him to be an honest, upright, and honourable man, as well as a great friend to Britain in her darkest days. The Socialist Government, he warned, ought to be *very careful* how it oversaw an order like the Aliens Order, which was adopted by the most reactionary House of Commons of modern times.

Younger reiterated the Home Secretary's decision that it was not in the public interest that certain persons should remain in Britain, one of the persons involved being Mr Hampl. "It would not be right in this or in other cases to ask the Home Secretary to disclose all the information which is available to him." He denied that there had been a frame-up.

On the day of his deportation, on the 2nd of August, Frank Hampl said,

"I shall try to come back, but that does not depend on me. I came to Britain in 1939 and have worked unceasingly for better relations between our two countries. I am grateful to those MPs who did their best in order to vindicate the charges made against me. These charges I refute. My only aim was to work for better relations between the British and Czecho-Slovak people. I am the victim of a conspiracy of certain elements who would besmirch the good name of anti-Fascist refugees."

Asked about his plans, Mr Hampl said he did not know what they were. "I am absolutely in the air." he added.

WILL LAWTHER

Britain's mining industry was nationalised on July the 6th, 1946. Its miners were represented by the National Union of Mineworkers. Will Lawther, one of the principal leaders of the Lidice Shall Live campaign, was still at the helm as President of the new national executive. In line with British Government policy, Lawther felt an immediate inclination to walk away from anything to do with communism. The old Mineworkers' Federation of Great Britain had already played its part for socialism, in terms of *Aid for Manchuria, Spain, Russia*, and presently Lidice was being built anew following the miners' movement's contribution of £32,375 - presented to Václav Nosek on the 15th of June 1947.

But 1948 was an awkward year for the NUM's membership, the sensibilities of which displayed a historic inclination towards the Soviet Union, to the inconvenience of the Attlee Government. Many members remembered the £1,000,000 of aid received *from* the USSR during the protracted national coal disputes of 1921 and 1926 and still felt a debt of gratitude for the sacrifices and achievements made *by* the Red Army in destroying the Third Reich. In fact, Lawther clashed repeatedly with Arthur Horner, General Secretary of the NUM, and someone diametrically opposed to Lawther in his attitude regards the British Government's foreign policy. It was to cause serious trouble for the union and general unrest in the nation as a whole. Lawther had warned striking French miners that they could expect no help from the British miners, since the policy of the National Union of Mineworkers was against strikes and in favour of conciliation and negotiation. Mr Horner, on the other hand, was in Paris giving moral support to the French Communists, who were encouraging the miners' strike in France. Lawther let his views be known in the Sunderland Echo on the 14th of October 1948:

"It is tragic. Mr Horner, incidentally, has let out in Paris a well-kept secret that the USSR sent £1,000,000 to help the British miners in the strikes of 1921 and 1926. British miners, when they reflect on the state into which the world has been brought today by Communist Russian policy, with civilization itself imperilled by the threat of another world war, must have some uneasy qualms of conscience at having accepted aid from such a quarter."

On Monday the 21st of March 1949, the Guardian reported on Barnett Stross's reaction, as Chairman of the British-Czechoslovak Friendship League, to accusations made by the League's former President, Sir William Lawther *(he had recently been knighted)*, that the reason he had disassociated himself from the British-Czechoslovak Friendship League was because it had degenerated into nothing more than a political tool:

"To me, quite frankly, the League has descended to nothing more than a stooge of the Cominform and I cannot understand how any Britisher can so far forget the tremendous sacrifices which were made by our Czech colleagues in the days when the League was founded, to link them up with many of its members to-day, who were associated with the destroyers of Czechoslovakia."

Dr Stross described this reason as **"pernicious nonsense,"** and accused Lawther of being influenced by the nationalist Lord Vansittart, who, in a House of Lords speech, had made defamatory remarks about the activities in Great Britain of a Czech Embassy official and of Frank Hampl, the former organiser of the 'Friendship Club and Treasurer of the Lidice Shall Live Committee in Stoke-on-Trent. Stross continued in his attack on Lawther's position:

"The Executive Committee of the League wish to place on record their amazement at the accusations contained in your letter. They have been unaware of receiving any assistance, criticism, or advice from you at any time since 1945. As late as June 1947, you were able to allow yourself to go to Prague with other members of the "Lidice Shall Live" organisation and of the British Czecho-Slovak Friendship League in order to receive a decoration from the Gottwald Government. Our aim remains as always: the promotion of friendship between the ordinary folk of both countries. Your ridiculous view, that the League is influenced by the Cominform, is, at best, a piece of gross impertinence. The only condition of membership is the desire for joint friendship."

Arthur Horner and Will Lawther in more amicable times, in their roles as President of the South Wales Miners' Federation and President of the Mineworkers' Federation of Great Britain respectively, about to go in to a meeting with colliery owners on March the 8th, 1944.

Lídice Calixto Moraes – Roses - 2022

THE ROSE GARDEN

On Thursday, September the 3rd, 1942, in the Evening Sentinel, a poem by Elizabeth Williams prophetically appeared posing the question of what might come next for the wasteland at Lidice if it were to ever fall back into Allied hands:

> *The rose roves back through centuries, and fields near Philippopolis*
>
> *Breather through Bellona's mysteries, the perfumes of an earlier Greece,*
>
> *"In Flanders field the poppies blow," brave banner of an earlier youth*
>
> *Who fought, and thought in fighting, so, to salvage, honour, faith, and truth,*
>
> *In England now moon-daisies flower, soon vetches' blue will claim the eyes-*
>
> *But o'er the waste of Lidice, what flower shall rise?*

MAD WORLD

At the start of the 1950s, a severe mutual distrust began to freeze East-West relations, and international communities feared the start of a fresh global conflict. A rise in tensions between the *Super Powers*, combined with a proliferation of atomic bombs on each side, meant the world lived in terror of what it could do to itself. The 1950s brought with it a new age of scientific and technological advancements, making it possible to kill far more people and devastate far more land mass with a single device. The era of *mutually assured destruction* or MAD had arrived. It was here to stay.

The Soviet Union had its RDS-6 - Reaktivnyi Dvigatel Specialnyi *(Special Jet Engine)*, which was exploded on August the 12th 1953, with a yield of 400 kilotons. This was a deliverable H-Bomb which threatened the USA. A heightened state of tension in the United States during autumn and winter of 1953-1954 saw frenetic efforts by America's scientists to catch up. They did so on the 1st of March 1954, when they tested a deliverable H-Bomb on the tiny Bikini Atoll in the Marshall Islands. The test codenamed *"Castle Bravo,"* which was intended to send a message of deterrence to the Soviet Union detonated with devastating effect, exploding with a force equivalent to a thousand Hiroshimas, creating a crater over 2km in diameter and sending a radioactive mushroom cloud 40km tall, with a blast range of 100km, into the atmosphere.

The impact of *"Castle Bravo"* sent shivers down the backs of the nations' leaders and ordinary people alike as fears for the future of humanity reached a higher state of alert. Internationalists like Dr Barnett Stross MP held deep-rooted ideological interests in creating a more peaceful world and felt a compulsion to act. His first chance came at a House of Commons debate on the nuclear tests taking place. Stross seconded a motion from Ellis Smith, MP for Stoke-on-Trent South, demanding Parliament discuss Britain starting **"immediate talks"** between the Soviets and the Americans to end the nuclear tests. It transpired that the proposal, which had the support of 120 fellow MPs, was withdrawn for the sake of unity to ensure a similar motion by the now leader of the Opposition, Clement Attlee MP, was carried.

The debate which took place on the afternoon of Monday the 5th of April 1954 was over a sincere request for the Prime Minister of Great Britain, Sir Winston Churchill to be an intermediary and facilitate a meeting between US President Dwight D. Eisenhower and the new Soviet President Georgy Malenkov. But Churchill prevaricated over the need for talks, arguing instead that the British Government was powerless to intervene to stop hydrogen bomb tests and that it would be unwise to propose consultation. In fact, it was Churchill's judgement that the world was a safer place for the nuclear tests taking place at Bikini Atoll:

"I believe that what is happening, what has happened and what is going to happen in the Pacific increases the chances of world peace more than the chances of world war." The Prime Minister also believed that **"we had time, though not too much time, to consider the problems."** Following a test which had detonated erroneously 15 megatons instead of the intended six, seriously irradiating many thousands of people thought to have been safe, Churchill added:

"I shall not ask the United States Government to stop their series of experiments, which will go on throughout April. After full consultation with our technical experts, I can repeat the assurance which I gave, "that there is no foundation for the suggestion that these explosions are 'incalculable,' in the sense that those making the tests are unable to set limits…"—even if not exact limits— **"to the explosive power of the bomb, or to calculate in advance what the main effects will be."**

"If it were proved, for instance, that a very large number of hydrogen explosions could, in their cumulative effect, be detrimental to the health, or even the life, of the whole human race—without any need for a declaration of war upon itself—the effect would certainly afford a new common interest between all men, rising above military, political or even ideological differences. That aspect, the biological aspect, must certainly receive the constant study of scientists in every country. I am assured by our scientists, I may say, that the remainder of the series of experiments contemplated in the Pacific could not possibly affect appreciably such an issue, as some of these biologists have led us to suppose."

Sir Winston's response was received with a cocktail of bemusement, disappointment, and alarm by many, not least Dr Barnett Stross, who made a cutting observation about the weight of responsibility incumbent upon politicians during the nuclear age:

"I was influenced by hearing one part of the speech of my hon. Friend, the Member for Leek (Mr Harold Davies), who said that there might be a dearth of lamp-posts. He did not mean, I gather, that the lamp-posts would be atomised and there would not be enough light available for us. *My hon. Friend thought that politicians, like ourselves, including Foreign Secretaries all the world over, would have to rest on lamp-posts and dangle from them."*

Then, in acknowledging the advancements in science and technology that had led them to the debate, he suggested a re-examining of human values and sensibilities in order that the awe-inspiring tools science had gifted man could be managed responsibly. He submitted:

"This is an atomic world, and an atomic world means that we are using cosmic power and that the dreams of the alchemists have come true. It means that matter is turned completely into energy. It is something that 30 or 40 years ago we were only beginning to dream about. Now, we are doing it. If we use cosmic force, we use the very power that keeps the sun alive and, through its energy, heat, and light, keeps everything as it is. If we have

such powers, can our old morality and our old political forms match up to them? We have had in the House tonight a definite attempt and an admission from all sides, except by the Prime Minister, to accept that we need a new morality and that there are different ways in which people have tried to approach it. But whatever that morality means, everybody has admitted that it means tolerance, patience, pity and compassion."

CONCEPTION

The motion put forward agreed to –

Resolved, That this House, recognising that the hydrogen bomb with its immense range and power as disclosed by recent experiments constitutes a grave threat to civilisation and that any recourse to war may lead to its use, would welcome an immediate initiative by Her Majesty's Government to bring about a meeting between the Prime Minister and the heads of the Administrations of the United States of America and the Union of Soviet Socialist Republics for the purpose of considering anew the problem of the reduction and control of armaments and of devising positive policies and means for removing from all the peoples of the world the fear which now oppresses them and for the strengthening of collective peace through the United Nations Organisation.

But Churchill's attitude had unnerved Stross. He may have been an asset for the nation in times of war, but it was against his lack of statesmanship in times of threatened peace that Dr Barnett Stross and the Lidice Shall Live committee decided they needed to act for the sake of international relations. In association with the national British-Czechoslovak Friendship League, they started an action designed to promote the idea of peaceful global co-existence. A matter of weeks after the Commons debate, Stross offered a proposal to create, in Lidice:

"... a Rose Garden of Friendship and Peace. Free from political, religious or racial pressures, disputes and preconceptions, the garden would grow from one root and thus satisfy the fundamental human desire for the peace and togetherness of all inhabitants of this planet."

This was a serious attempt at fashioning a space that would unite ideologically people of all nationalities, political creeds, and faiths in their opposition to war and their resolve to prevent atrocities and genocides.

The intention of creating a rose garden was reported in the British press as early as the 10th of June 1954 - as the Newcastle Journal's Peter London wrote:

"I met a man yesterday who is trying to ensure that a corner of a certain foreign field shall be forever England. The field has an ominous, doom-laden name: Lidice; the formerly unknown Czech village that 12 years ago today became a symbol of the unrestricted ferocity and bestiality of the Nazi system. But Dr Barnett Stross, mild-mannered MP for Hanley, is planning to fly between 3,000 and 10,000 rose trees out there to create a typical British rose garden at the approach to the great open space where the Nazi victims lie buried."

"The roses will remind the people of both lands of the friendship that cemented us together in common struggle."

"... says Dr Stross, who is Chairman of the Lidice Shall Live Committee. He tells me that the Archbishop of York and the Archbishop of Wales are among those who have agreed to sponsor the appeal for the trees which the committee is launching. With the aid of £34,000 contribution from this country - mainly contributed by miners, Lidice has now been re-built."

The Birmingham Post reported how on Thursday July the 15th, 1954 from offices in Westminster, Dr Stross launched a public appeal for funds to purchase rose trees for a Lidice International Garden of Peace and Friendship. He emphasised only the modest sum of between £2,000 and £3,000 would be needed. This would pay for between 5,000 and 10,000 rose bushes and standards. The Czechoslovakian authorities would meet the bulk of the expense. The garden would sit half-way between the new Lidice and the site of the old village. Dr Stross announced he would be hoping to procure the services of Mr Harry Wheatcroft, a prominent authority on roses, whose nurseries in Ruddington, Nottinghamshire, grew millions of roses and propagated many new varieties across many acres each year. Some bushes and standards would be used by Czechoslovakian horticultural research workers to develop a new prize rose called the "Rose of Lidice." Dr Stross explained his idea in the following manner:

"This village and its rose garden are in a way an example upon which our civilization can firmly rely for hope, love and peace are pillars strong enough to support the high sky above."

Several Midland MPs had associated themselves with the appeal, including Mr George Wigg (Dudley); Mr John Baird (Wolverhampton N.E.); Mr Harold Davies (Leek); Mrs Harriet Slater (Stoke-on-Trent N.); Mr Ellis Smith (Stoke-on-Trent S.); and Mr Stephen Swingler (Newcastle-under-Lyme). Several trade unions agreed to support the campaign, and so did the Archbishop of York, Dr Garbett; and the Chief Rabbi, the Very Rev. Israel Brodie.

Dr Stross concluded the Westminster press conference by stating:

"It is difficult to talk of symbols of peace of this nature, but if I were asked the value of this garden, I would simply reply that every rose which is added to it may mean one atom bomb the fewer in the future."

MAKING IT HAPPEN

The initiative was sincerely welcomed in Czechoslovakia. At last it was possible for East and West to co-operate on a project designed to *ease* international stresses and draw close the ever widening geopolitical chasms which had been splitting apart since 1945. An imaginatively titled sister board called the Committee for the Founding of the Rose Garden was set up in Czechoslovakia by the renowned Czech philosopher and theologian Prof. Josef Lukl Hromádka. Besides co-operating with Stross and the British Lidice Shall Live Committee, Hromádka was to organise the garden's practical formation, attract international support and seek contributions for its creation. But his committee was pressed for time: it had about eight months to make plans and start on-site works, which were meant to be completed in June.

With the idea formally adopted in February 1955, this left an incredible workload at the feet of Stross's colleagues, with the developmental tasks beginning promptly. To speed things up, volunteers poured in from the Prague and Kladno region.

By 1954 the National Secretary of the British-Czechoslovak Friendship League was Lou Kenton - a veteran anti-fascist campaigner who had taken part in the disruption of the British Union of Fascists' rally at Olympia in June 1934 and resistance to the BUF in the Battle of Cable Street in October 1936, before enlisting as a volunteer to fight in the International Brigade in the Spanish Civil War. Kenton had joined the Lidice Shall Live movement in 1942 and ran the company *Progressive Tours,* which sold holidays to Czechoslovakia.

Kenton was keen to see Dr Stross's proposal succeed and, in the autumn of 1954, took on the mantle of writing to prominent rosarian, Harry Wheatcroft, to discover whether he would indeed be willing to help plan the rose garden proposed for the outskirts of the rebuilt Czech village - and to supply it with the necessary quantity and types of roses.

Harry Wheatcroft was someone who shared the sensibilities of Stross and the Friendship League and he agreed to meet up with Kenton in London at the Royal Horticultural Hall, where he was exhibiting at one of the fortnightly shows of the Royal Horticultural Society. Lou explained exactly what was needed, and as he went on, the rose expert grew increasingly enthusiastic about the project and its purpose. Harry takes up the story:

"Kenton was the group's organising secretary and had come to me for two reasons. He felt that large numbers of 'Peace,' a variety of truly great distinction which we had introduced into Britain, should be planted in the Garden; and a point which I felt was most flattering: someone in the nursery business had suggested that the inspection and despatch of the large number of trees involved could best be handled from Ruddington."

Harry was sent details of the site: the type of soil, the climate, and all the other necessary data required before one can plan a rose garden, before flying over to Czechoslovakia to look at the site in late 1954 with Honorary Chairman of the British Lidice Shall Live Committee, Julius Jacobs. Whilst there, he discussed details with Czechoslovak colleague František Marek and other members of the Committee for the Founding of the Rose Garden, and of the Lidice house building programme.

Originally, Wheatcroft's idea was to have a circular pattern of beds with a central bed of about three hundred bushes of the "Peace" variety. However, as Wheatcroft explained,

"... the scheme progressed more quickly than I did. Long before the time came to despatch the plants, there had been two developments. In the first place, I learned that many thousands of roses had been ordered in England alone; moreover, the idea had spread abroad, so that what had begun as a purely British effort was now involving countries all over the world - in the end, roses came from thirty-five of them.

"First of all, I thought that all the roses from Britain should be planted together in the same way, all those from France, all those from Germany, and so on. However, as the scheme grew bigger and bigger, it was obvious that even this would not be satisfactory, and that the best way of planting the garden would be to have the bushes grouped according to colour rather than country."

"Only in Lidice itself were all the details of the scheme known, so the final lay-out of the garden was turned over to Mr. Marek, the local architect who had planned the new village, and who was able, I must say, to make a most excellent job of it."

DONATIONS GRATEFULLY RECEIVED

Throughout the autumn of 1954, Dr Stross's public appeals kick-started a wave of generous donations which were to see individuals, trade unions, civic leaders, businesses, and corporations throw off political allegiances in a quest for a wider vision of international fraternity without barriers. By this time, a collection centre had been set aside at Wheatcroft's Nurseries near to Nottingham. Harry and brother Alfred Wheatcroft agreed to nurture the roses until they could be given a clean bill of health by the Ministry of Agriculture and then sent to Czechoslovakia by plane.

Stoke-on-Trent City Council decided to support the proposal to send rose trees at a meeting on Thursday July the 1st 1954 when Alderman George Parton successfully moved a resolution reversing a decision of the Parks Committee that no action be taken by recalling that the movement for the reconstruction of Lidice after the war was started by North Staffordshire miners, who contributed a substantial sum towards the fund. He added,

"It is far better to send them roses than to send them bombs… Someone has said that they are Communists, but the truth is they are under the yoke of Communism and they cannot shake it off. Why should we desert them now?"

Former Lord Mayor Alderman Harry Leason, who seconded the motion, said **"anything which could be done to cement the friendship between the two countries should be supported."**

On Friday the 12th of November 1954, The Western Mail and South Wales News reported an update:

"Roses from Cardiff Corporation parks department nurseries will soon be blooming in Czechoslovakia as part of a memorial to the people who died in the village of Lidice razed by the Nazis. Yesterday, the city parks, baths and cemeteries committee yesterday approved a request from the 'Lidice Shall Live' committee to donate rose plants for a memorial British rose garden for the rebuilt village of Lidice."

On Thursday the 9th of December 1954, The Birmingham Post reported how a concert in aid of the appeal was held at the Royal Society of Artists Hall in New Street the night before. Dr Stross, who was in attendance, explained how three thousand rose trees had already been assured and that Coventry, one of the first places to promise trees, was to send 1,000. He stated,

"The village had been rebuilt and was now the loveliest village in Europe for workers to live in and it now remained to go over the Iron Curtain, not to plant destruction but to plant roses there."

The concert received the patronage of the Lord Mayor, the Bishop of Birmingham, and the Chief Minister of the Hebrew Congregation; and was organised by the Birmingham committee of the Lidice Shall Live movement; performances included folksongs by the Clarion Singers, Czechoslovak dances by the Avoncroft College Folk dancers, songs by Eric Holmes (baritone), and by Brenda Griffith (soprano) and a violin recital by Stanley Wiesbard with Brian Priestman at the piano.

The Ripley and Heanor News reported how on the 21st of April, in response to an invitation by the Derbyshire branch of the National Union of Mineworkers, the General Secretary, Mr Arthur Horner, presented on their behalf a cheque for £50 to Czechoslovak officials in London to buy rose trees for the Lidice Memorial Rose Garden.

On the 1st of April 1955, The Birmingham Gazette's Anthony Hancox reported how smoothly the campaign was moving with The Midlands responding to Dr Stross's call:

MORE than a thousand rose trees cultivated in the Midlands will this summer blossom at Lidice, the Czechoslovakian mining village, which was wiped out by the Nazis in 1942. The trees from Coventry, Wolverhampton and Stoke-on-Trent will be among more than 5,000 contributed from all over the country to establish a British Garden of Friendship and Remembrance at Lidice. Blitzed Coventry is one of the biggest donors to the scheme: the Corporation is to send 1,000 trees. They are to be reds and yellows of the Polyantha variety, grown at the Corporation's Canley nursery. Wolverhampton Corporation is to send 50 trees and Stoke Corporation 100.

"The list of monetary contributions from private individuals includes a large number from the Midlands, among them the proceeds of a concert held in Birmingham."

DISRUPTION & THE DEMOCRATIC EXILES

The vulnerability of Barnett Stross's campaign of creating a Garden of Peace and Friendship in Lidice to attack from forces determined to see the termination of British-Czechoslovak relations, was highlighted in the Birmingham Post, when it reported on a raucous meeting in London the evening of Thursday the 21st of April 1955. Organised by the Lidice Shall Live Committee at the Friends' Meeting House, Euston Road, the purpose of the gathering was for the committee to meet official delegates from Czechoslovakia and symbolically hand over roses collected for the Lidice Garden of Peace and Friendship to be opened in June.

The meeting was thrown into uproar when around 200 protestors describing themselves as the *Czech Democratic Exiles* forced their way into the auditorium to make their point, leaving the Czechoslovak delegation on the stage staring in consternation as their exiled countrymen struggled with stewards and members of the audience. By 7pm, the demonstrators were seated in the main part of the hall. Dr Stross tried to speak but was shouted down by the Czech exiles. Standard bearers at the back of the hall had unfolded inscriptions such as **"FREE ELECTIONS IN CZECHOSLOVAKIA!" "RESTORE FREE TRADE UNIONS!"** and **"END SLAVERY IN CZECHOSLOVAKIA!"** A few moments later, a young Czech woman stepped onto the platform with a bunch of five roses in her hand. Addressing Dr Stross, she demanded:

"I want the delegation to put the first rose on the grave of the martyrs of Lidice, the second on the grave of President Liberator T. G. Masaryk, the third on the grave of the executed woman deputy, Dr Horáková, the fourth is for the imprisoned Archbishop Beran, and the fifth for the entire suffering people of Czechoslovakia."

Dr Stross accepted the roses while loud applause rang round the hall. On the platform were the Czechoslovakian Chargé d'Affaires, Mr M. Ruzek; Professor Hromádka, Prague University; Madame Helena Leflerová, Chairwoman of the Lidice Local National Committee; Bishop Miroslav Novák, of the Church of Czechoslovakia; and Mr Andrej Bagar of the Bratislava Academy of Music. British speakers who had been prepared to address the meeting included the Lord Mayor of Coventry, Alderman John Fennell, and the General Secretary of the National Union of Mineworkers, Mr Arthur Horner.

Police were called and a uniformed officer, Superintendent J. R. Wray, averted further incident by going to the platform and announcing that the chairman had closed the meeting. The audience were invited to disperse, and around 500 people, together with the gate crashers carrying their banners, quietly left the building.

The Friends House, Euston as it would have looked at the time of the meeting. Things had been so out of hand that Coventry's Alderman and Mrs Fennell, both more than 70 years of age, had to leave the building by a side entrance. Because of the demonstrators Fennell took the precaution of removing his badge of office and handed it for safe keeping to his chauffeur, Mr Powers, who had then driven the official car away. As a result, Coventry's civic heads had to ride in a private car from the building to the Czechoslovakian Embassy.

Afterwards, Dr Stross revealed that he had received an anonymous letter written on a printed leaflet calling on Czechs to demonstrate. He said he was going to pursue the matter:

"I am certainly going to let the Home Secretary have a full account of this if only to let him know what magnificent police he has got. I also think the Foreign Secretary ought to know what happened. My colleagues, MPs, with me were horrified. We are not used to this sort of thing in Britain. When I saw that the meeting was going to be of a pretty fantastic, maybe violent nature, an inspector with five or six sergeants and constables arrived and they were wonderful."

There had been more angry scenes at a Press conference in the Palace of Westminster that afternoon when journalists, representing the Czech exiles harried one of Dr Barnett Stross's guests about the article *"What I Have Seen,"* an editorial published in the Czech newspaper *Rudé Právo* in 1952. The journalist claimed that the pieces were untrue and asked Leflerová if she intended to write any more untrue columns after her present visit.

Through an interpreter, Madame Leflerová denied that what she had written was biased against Britain and said she had a great affection for the British people. Other journalists joined in and there was commotion when Dr Stross closed the conference, protesting that he would not allow the guests to be **"subjected to offensive and inquisitorial questioning."** Dr Stross said it was in the worst possible taste to make a political issue out of a non-political matter like a rose garden.

News materialised in the Coventry Evening Telegraph of a news-sheet being circulated containing allegations that the scheme for the rose garden was being organised by a traitorous, insurgent group called the *"British-Czechoslovak Friendship League."* According to the publisher, this was a body proscribed by the Government. The information had been sent to the Lord Mayor of Coventry, but he did not have time to study the news-sheet before going to the ceremony in London.

The news-sheet, in all likelihood, was the same as that received by Stross and came from the *"Free Czechoslovakia Information"* setup run by Czech émigré democratic journalist, anti-communist activist and advocate for freedom and human rights - Josef Josten. His information leaflets, bulletins, and newsletters later re-named *Features and News from Behind the Iron Curtain and Czechoslovak Magazine*, which he published were intended not only for the exiles themselves but also for the British, American, and other authorities and intelligence services, to which he supplied propaganda to fight the totalitarian regime in Prague.

Based on reports, the news-sheet in question contained *"useful"* information, including the time and location of the ceremony. Although proscribed by the Labour Party, the newsletter accused Stross of exploiting the Lidice Shall Live campaign in order to campaign on a Communist Party manifesto.

"… it would enable Dr Barnett Stross, Labour MP, Stoke-on-Trent, to address the meeting without being censured by his party." Mr Julius Jacobs, the chairman of the meeting, is described as **"being of the London District Committee of the Communist Party."**

Also included in the news sheet were extracts of what Madame Helena Leflerová, post-war Mayor of Lidice, wrote in the newspaper, *"Rudé Právo"* giving her impressions of Britain after a visit which included Coventry, Stoke-on-Trent, and London in 1952 *(see appendix)*.

ANONYMOUS ATTACKS

A mere six weeks before the Garden of Peace of Friendship was due to be opened to the public, on Saturday the 30th of April 1955 a mysterious author published the following piece in The Chronicle and Advertiser, a regional newspaper with a West Midlands readership:

"A Corrupting Influence at Work

ONE of the gravest charges that can be laid at the door of Communism is that it holds nothing sacred in its unending quest for its own advancement.

Nothing, if it can in any way be used to spread the creed, is safe from the contaminating influence.

There was once, for instance, a village in Czechoslovakia called Lidice.

The story of the utter destruction by the Nazis as a 'reprisal' during the last war and the slaughter of the entire population already has its place in history.

A Lidice Shall Live movement came into being, supported in this country by a great number of people who were actuated only by the most praiseworthy motives - a deep and sincere sympathy for the victims of a tyranny we, too fought so long and so bitterly, and a determination that they should not be forgotten.

The innocent plan for an English rose garden in Lidice flourished - a plan which had numberless well-wishers as well as its many active supporters.

But here again Communism saw its opportunity and, as always, was not slow to take it, with the result that today communist influence has tainted a fine ideal and is using it for its own ends.

Few will condemn the underlying principles of the scheme. Many, on the other hand, will feel the gravest concern that this corrupting influence can make itself felt in a movement so non-political in its nature and so worthy in its concept."

A month later, as a consequence of the increasing discord caused by a worsening geopolitical situation and the events of the 21st of April and its fallout, was the decision by the new Lord Mayor of Coventry, Alderman Thomas Henry Dewis not to visit Lidice to inaugurate the Garden of Peace and Friendship. Dewis told The Coventry Evening Telegraph on the 30th of May: "I am not going. I have already made that clear. If they still want to send someone, they will have to find someone else." Alderman Dewis did not explain the reasons for his choice.

A letter from Dr Barnett Stross, published as a right to reply, in response to claims made by one Cllr Clews at a meeting of Coventry Council on the 1st of June 1955 was printed on the 11th of June in the Coventry Telegraph:

"It has been brought to my attention that during the council's debate on June the 1st, one of the Councillors, Mr R Clews, made a statement as to the formation of the 'Lidice Shall Live' Committee in Britain.

Cllr Clews declares that it was formed immediately after the war 'by a section of people not in Czechoslovakia.' The facts are that the 'Lidice Shall Live' Committee was founded in Stoke-on-Trent by the people of North Staffs, and the first reference to its formation was made by myself two days after the destruction of Lidice in June 1942.

The 'Lidice Shall Live' Committee was entirely a British organisation, supported by men and women of all walks of life, and of all political persuasions, or of none. Our present Prime Minister was kind enough to lend his name as president of the Leamington branch throughout the war and for years after.

One of the most impressive meetings of all was held in Coventry during the war, and I find it somewhat bizarre that anyone holding a position of responsibility in Coventry should so soon have forgotten this memorable occasion.

Cllr Clews also states in the Council Chamber that there was no counterpart of the 'Lidice Shall Live' Committee in Czechoslovakia. This statement is also entirely inaccurate. The sister committee was founded in Czechoslovakia in 1945, as soon as the Nazis had been driven out of that country.

May I say lastly, that all those who inaugurated the 'Lidice Shall Live' movement throughout Britain are aware of the fact that it has no association with Governments or political parties. The presentation of the Rose Garden, like the original movement for the rebuilding of the village, is a gesture made by the peoples of this country to the peoples of Czechoslovakia. Any attempt to imply sectarianism or party-political motives is not only untrue, but entirely unworthy.

(Dr) B. STROSS - Chairman "Lidice Shall Live" Committee"

Josten, who would not let the matter rest, countered with his own letter published in the Coventry Telegraph on the 23rd of June:

"Lidice Committee DR BARNET STROSS, MP,

You may be right in claiming that the Lidice Shall Live Committee was established in Stoke-on-Trent as far back as June 1942. It was meant to be a people's movement without party affiliation, which would attempt to make up for Nazi atrocities committed on a defenceless democratic people. This is why the present Prime Minister, Sir Anthony Eden, associated his name with it, together with many others, genuinely interested in freedom, justice, and peace.

Where Dr Stross is wrong is in omitting to mention that the post-war reconstituted 'Lidice Shall Live' Committee was after 1948 turned into a formidable Communist propaganda tool. Dr Stross himself was chairman of the British-Czechoslovak Friendship League, of 'Lidice House,' London, of which his predecessor, Sir William Lawther, on his resignation, declared:

"To me, quite frankly, the League has descended to nothing more than a stooge of the Cominform and I cannot understand how any Britisher can so far forget the tremendous sacrifices which were made by our Czech colleagues in the days when the League was founded, to link them up with many of its members to-day, who were associated with the destroyers of Czechoslovakia."

The League as such is now proscribed by the Labour Party. Its chairman, Mr Julius Jacobs, is secretary of Dr Stross's 'Lidice Shall Live' Committee. The official headquarters of the latter is in the Friendship League building, 'Lidice House' London. Dr Stross is well aware of the fate of the people who, as Czechs, were connected with the original wartime 'Lidice Shall Live' Committee.

Just to mention a few: President Dr E. Beneš, who attended the inaugural meeting, died prematurely after the Communist coup: Dr Drtina, former Minister of Justice, attempted suicide, and is crippled for life; Jan Masaryk committed suicide. Many former members of the committee are now-in-exile, and most of those who stayed in Czechoslovakia are in prison or in concentration camps, including those whom Dr Stross thanked for their efforts to investigate and expose the Lidice crime. They formed what might be called the Czechoslovak counterpart of the British 'Lidice Shall Live' movement.

What was their crime? They were not Communists, but democrats, disciples of Masaryk and Beneš.

JOSEF. JOSTEN (Editor, Information Service of Free Czechoslovakia).

Referencing the formal accusation that he had recently made concerning the Czech heroes now lost to the coup d'état, Josten stated in the press: *"Dr Stross and others like him who are now going to Czechoslovakia will shake hands with their gaolers and executioners."*

Stross was to lock horns once more, with Josten and his Free Information Service following the inauguration of the rose garden. Josten suggested he was an apologist for the Czechoslovak Government and of not doing enough to protect those with connections to Britain. However, the aims of most of his attacks were to embarrass rather than to accuse.

THE CASE OF MRS ŠIŠPERA

Mrs Šišpera had been in Czechoslovakia since the end of the war. As Miss Phyllis Clarke of Thurston, living near Bury St Edmunds, she had married a Czech airman, Jaroslav Šišpera in England in 1941. She had met him while she was in the Auxiliary Territorial Service. Just before the Communist coup, she wrote to relatives requesting money to enable the family to return home - she had two girls and a boy. It could not be sent in time. In 1950, Mr and Mrs Šišpera made a last-ditch dash for freedom. They were caught and imprisoned.

Having had the matter brought to his attention, with the permission of the Czechoslovak Government Barnett Stross went to see the detainee on Saturday, the 25th of June 1955, along with several of the British delegation who had attended the inauguration of the rose Garden of Peace and Friendship. Phyllis Šišpera told him and the other members of the party about her experiences and confirmed newspaper reports of her imprisonment and the treatment she had been receiving. She said the Czech authorities had recently told her she was free to leave the country, but that her three children would have to stay. Dr Stross said that this was totally unacceptable and that he had discussed the whole question of British wives living in Czechoslovakia with the relevant Czechoslovak Government Minister. Days later, fuelled by Josten, The Daily Herald's Alan Taylor produced a scathing article on the 29th of June 1955, criticising British-Czechoslovak cooperation when there were significant issues with the relationship between the two countries.

"Lidice was the scene of one of the worst German war crimes. Men and women of this Czech village were massacred by the Nazis. The houses were levelled to the ground. It is right that British Friends of Czechoslovakia should send roses for remembrance to Lidice. Perhaps it is right that 20 British people, including three MPs, should go over to present the roses in person. Roses for Lidice are a protest against terror, whether by Germans or anyone else. They are a protest that harmless individuals must not be sacrificed for reasons of State. But when the British rose-bearers got to Czechoslovakia, they were faced with another act of tyranny. They were faced with Mrs Šišpera, mother of three children, who has committed no real crime. Born in England and married a Czech, she has suffered imprisonment and privation for trying to leave the country *'Illegally.'* Freedom isn't buried with the dead at Lidice ... even though it seems to be buried among the living in Prague. And those MPs would have honoured liberty better if they'd given the roses to Mrs Šišpera ... the woman who suffered because she tried to find it."

Mrs Šišpera was released three weeks later on the 16th of July and allowed to return home with her three children.

CREATING THE GARDEN

Thanks to the work of the respective British-based and Czechoslovakian based committees actively seeking supporters, the peace initiative found popularity with all political sensibilities and interest spread all over the world. Nations across Europe, Asia and the Americas found inspiration in the idea, joining the project through their respective Peace Committees. Other countries keen to take part included East and West Germany, France, Belgium, Luxembourg, Venezuela, Canada, China, Cuba, Brazil, Romania, Vietnam, and Hungary. Many sent flowering trees or shrubs representative of their country. It was thought that the flower beds would extend over 16 acres of parkland with the British contribution as the centrepiece. Befitting the gravitas of the tragedy that struck Lidice 13 years before, the organisers hoped they would create not just one of the largest floral displays on earth, but a powerful international statement against all weapons of mass destruction whose message all world leaders would feel compelled to follow.

As mentioned, the architect of the rose garden was František Marek, the leader of the architectural team working on the development of the whole Lidice building site. Meanwhile, horticultural responsibilities were taken care of by Bohumil Kafka. It was difficult to figure out the extent of the garden and the layout of the rose beds because roses were continually arriving from all corners of the world throughout 1955; in fact, they kept coming well past the official opening! And it was not just roses that were received: lilacs from Oradour sur Glane, France; tulips from Putten, the Netherlands; orchids from Venezuela; olive trees, myrtle plants and laurels from Greece; palm seeds from Cuba; just a representative sample of the vast selection of flowers, herbs and succulents which were turning up on a daily basis.

On April the 14th, 1955, a technical commission met in Lidice to ensure the construction of the Garden of Peace and Friendship. Photograph gives an overview of the site on the 15th April. Photo – Credit ČTK

Construction works started on the 14th of March 1955. Approximately 10,000m2 of soil was first removed so that the water pipes of the irrigation system could be laid. Then, the entire area, which slopes gently towards the memorial ground, was converted into terraces. The beds were covered with humus, fertilizer, and peat. Frustratingly, given the constraints which already existed, poor weather conditions necessitated putting the roses into flowerpots and later a makeshift nursery on a neighbouring field. As time ran out, help came in from various groups of voluntary workers, amateur gardeners from Kladno and Prague, and some of the Lidice women. By the time the garden could be opened, there were 17,000 rose shrubs planted on three hectares of land. Highlights of the garden still include a fountain featuring a sculpture called *"Peace"* by Karel Hladík and the stone semi-circle by Bedřich Stefan, which bears the names of towns and cities similarly affected by the Second World War.

Early in the spring of 1955, Wheatcroft's had to despatch the roses. They supplied about 5,500 bushes, including 300 of the *"Peace"* variety and 250 or more of about forty other kinds. About 1,500 came to them from other sources, for example 600 polyanthas from Coventry, hundreds from Stoke-on-Trent, and various supplementary contributions from Hull, Brighton, Cardiff, Barnsley, and other British communities. All required correct inspection, vetting, and correct packaging before shipment. By April, Harry Wheatcroft's Nurseries had sent off 7,000 plants to Lidice, while another 10,000 or so had been shipped direct to Lidice by other countries taking part in the scheme. Other British contributions included three quarters of a ton of English grass seed and the rose varieties *"Independence"* and *"Happiness."*

OPENING THE GARDEN

The Garden of Peace and Friendship was opened on the 19th of June 1955. People poured to Lidice from far and wide to see the spectacle. Dignitaries were present from around the world, including Jawaharlal Nehru, Prime Minister of India; as well as other leaders from both sides of the *Iron Curtain,* including the Soviet Union, Italy, Hungary, East and West Germany, the USA and Poland. Dr Barnett Stross led a large British delegation, which included Harold Naylor, the Lord Mayor of Stoke-on-Trent; William Isaac Thomson, Deputy Mayor of Coventry; as well as other civic leaders and delegations of miners from around the country.

It was a hot and cloudless day. The villagers and organisers made an early start so that as the first guests began to arrive at 8.30am they found the preparations for what would be an impressive ceremony just being completed. The flags of the thirty-five contributing countries fluttered in the light breeze, while the gathering crowds were directed to their places by scores of young boys and girls, many of them students, dressed in the blue berets and overalls of volunteer marshals. Photo credit ČTK

The next day, the Czech newspaper Rudé Právo published an article about the inauguration. It described how the many dignitaries and friends from visiting nations laid flowers at the common grave of the executed Lidice men. These representations included the Lord Mayor of Stoke-on-Trent, Cllr Harold Naylor; and Miss Helene Walker, representing the Clerical and Administrative Workers Union, who placed a wreath for Britain, before an introductory address delivered by Prof. Hromádka at the open space of the Rose Garden. This was followed by the main speech presented by the Deputy Mayor Helena Leflerová.

Then, came the turn of the representatives of the foreign delegations, mentioning names such as Stalingrad, Coventry, Warsaw, Oradour, Marzabotto, and Hiroshima... Finally, in his address, Dr Barnett Stross declared the garden a symbol to the world of all who had suffered through war, remarking:

"**So, the Garden of Peace and Friendship is opening today. When we expressed this idea in the UK for the first time, we had a British rose garden in mind, with participation of other nations. Today, we witness our dream come true: there are rose plants growing in front of us, having come from many countries all over the world. There are good reasons for this garden to flower in Lidice. We know very well that the Nazis obliterated hundreds of villages and towns in Poland, France, and the Soviet Union during the war, and that their innocent inhabitants were slaughtered mercilessly. Lidice symbolises all of them and belongs to the world of all who suffered hardships of war.**"

"**It is not directed against the rearmament of this people or that people, but against all weapons of mass murder of all kinds everywhere,**" he said.

Professor Hromádka invited Dr Stross to open the rose garden, but instead Stross passed the ceremonial scissors over to one of the Lidice women, Helena Leflerová, whose husband, father, and other male relatives were lost to the atrocity, and who herself had survived a number of years in concentration camps. Helena, now chair of the Lidice MNV *(Místní Národní Výbor, literally "Local National Committee")* proceeded to cut the ribbon. The strip was held by two of the Lidice children intended by the Nazis for re-education in German families - Václav Zelenka and Veronika Hanfová, later married as Rýmonová. At the cutting of the ribbon, Dr Barnett Stross declared:

"A new Lidice has risen from the ashes. It is a symbol of the common need for all peoples of the world to live together in friendship and peace. If Lidice dies again, our civilization will also perish."

Numbers of Czechoslovak visitors and tourists from abroad to Lidice dramatically increased following the opening of the rose garden. Not only did the visitors admire the beauty of the rose varieties and the landscaping, but they also had a place to commemorate the victims of the Lidice tragedy. More contacts were made, networking expanded and more working relationships and friendships were founded, so that during 1956 the garden was extended to 34 hectares with additional donated roses from the UK, Europe, Asia, and America. Altogether a combined international effort had piled in and 30,000 roses were contributed to the project from across 35 different countries.

In 1956, the musical composition *"A Rose for Lidice"* was commissioned retrospectively by the Lidice Shall Live Committee to celebrate the opening of the rose garden. The choral piece was written as a soprano solo with SATB (soprano, alto, tenor, bass) backing. With words by poet Randall Swingler, brother of MP for Newcastle-under-Lyme, Stephen; and music by Alan Rawsthorne, the five-minute-long song was dedicated to Jack Putterill, Vicar of Thaxted, and campaigner for the garden. *"A Rose for Lidice"* was premiered on the 10th of June 1956 in Lidice's *Rose Garden of Peace and Friendship*, and simultaneously in Thaxted's 14th century medieval Church by the Purcell Singers under the skilful direction of Imogen Holst, daughter of the renowned composer, Gustav:

Lidice lay unknown
In the lap of a lying world.
Lidice worked alone in the core of stone
Lidice had grown from the blood of the earth;
Coal and steel were bone of Lidice's birth.

Fate chose it for Hate's gangrened fury.
Hate said: Wipe out the name!
History shall abjure it!

Ah, the brave dust blew round the world;
The air flooded with blood of roses.
Hate had ploughed up the soil, Love sowed it.
Where the murderer's heel stamped on the eyes of children
The gardener's fingers fashioned them into roses.
Love is a ring once broken proves all untrue.
But the shed petals are token of the bud's renewal.

While man's love grows and blossoms in time's ground
Lidice hangs, a garland round the cross of the world.

Developments continued when the new Mayor of Lidice, Libuše Prošková, accepted from Barnett Stross a newly cultivated variety of rose on a visit to London on the 28th of June 1961. The rose had been bred for a special purpose by Harry Wheatcroft, the now world-famous rosarian and friend of the Lidice community. Before a distinguished embassy gathering, the Ambassador for Czechoslovakia christened it, "The Rose of Lidice." Light poppy red in colour, with a clear lemon base, and finely pointed, bushes were sold for 10s 6d each for planting in the Lidice Garden. The variant became popular with tourists as a contributor towards the costs of supporting the garden, and throughout the 1960s and 1970s the rose was commercially successful. Profitable as it was, it had more impact as a potent symbol of peace.

DECLINE & RESTORATION

During the 1980s, the rose garden deteriorated in parallel with the declining potency of communism as a world force, and by the 1990s, the garden was on the verge of ruin, with the remaining roses growing wild. Lidice had been affected by the political transformation happening across Europe. For decades, the Communist regime misused the idea of Lidice for its own ends, treating the memorial and rose garden as an asset *in the fight against fascism*. The newly consolidating Czechoslovak society of the 1990s, put into place following the Velvet Revolution of December 1989, under President Václav Havel, lost interest in Lidice because of its past associations with Communism – which the youth of Czechoslovakia, in particular despised.

Václav Zelenka, became Mayor of Lidice during the late 1990s and it is thanks to his dedication, the positive response of the then Prime Minister Miloš Zeman, and the support shown by Minister of Culture Pavel Dostál, that a new Lidice Memorial institution was set up in December 2000. One of its primary purposes was the resurrection and long-term maintenance of the Garden of Peace and Friendship.

THE ROSE GARDEN
The Path to Lidice

In 2001, the Rose Garden and the Barnett Stross Avenue were restored. The restorations were led by chief architect, Pavel Bulír of the Silva Tarouca Research Institute for Landscape and Ornamental Gardening. The former community centre building was converted into the Lidice Gallery, which began hosting the permanent exhibition of the Lidice Collection and became the home for the ICEFA - International Children's Exhibition of Fine Art Lidice (one of the largest fine art exhibitions for young people in the world). Barnett Stross's legacy has been revived for the benefit of many generations to come.

Today, the rose garden contains more than 24,000 rose plants across 240 varieties. The garden's artistic and visually prominent features remain as significant as they did when the garden opened in 1955; its power to inspire has not been diminished by time. The Lidice Memorial Rose Garden received the WFRS Award of Garden Excellence in 2015.

Dr Stross visited Lidice in September 1954 to meet with Professor Hromádka and associates to discuss the feasibility of their plans for the creation of a rose garden. There he spoke with horticultural experts from the Průhonice Research Institute to verify the suitability of the soil for the purposes of growing roses, as well as meeting civic leaders, Lidice Mayor, Mrs Růžena Krásová; and the Chair of the Lidice National Local Committee, Helena Leflerová. Stross would fly back to Britain reassured and would press on with the campaign. Czechoslovak Life Magazine ran an article on his visit - the above photo is a promotional still from the piece - featuring Helena Leflerová to the left of Stross and Mrs Krásová to the right.

19th June 1955: Top - Harry Wheatcroft being presented with wild strawberries by young girls, dressed for the day in the blue berets and overalls of volunteer marshals. 7,000 British rosebushes were among the 10,000 planted at Lidice in memory of the destruction of the village. Bottom - Dr Barnett Stross and Professor Josef Hromádka at the cutting of the ribbon ceremony - with Madame Leflerová and two Lidice children holding the chord - Václav Zelenka and Veronika Hanfová.

THE ROSE GARDEN   The Path to Lidice

Clockwise: Dr Barnett Stross and Lidice residents discuss the concept of the rose garden; Dr Josef Hromádka: theologian, academic, social campaigner, and Chairman of the Czechoslovak Committee for the Establishment of the Rose Garden, who presided over its grand opening on the 19th June 1955, as well as other public events held at the village; Lou Kenton, anti-fascist campaigner and Secretary of the British-Czechoslovak Friendship League in the 1950s; the "Lidice" rose; the "Peace" rose; Harry Wheatcroft at the opening of the Rose Garden walking with Rev J, Putterill of Thaxted Essex, another member of the British delegation - with flags from the thirty-five contributing nations flying in the background.

Rose Garden - - Lidice Calixto Moraes - 2022

COLD WAR TIMES

The mid-1950s saw times of heightened global tension, a natural progression from the post-war political fallout and chaos. With the threat of destabilisation and nuclear conflict looming large, levels of security and surveillance of public figures rose. In such an atmosphere, it was necessary for Barnett Stross to provide reassurance to the public that his activities did not pose a danger to Britain. *Democratic Czech Exiles* continued in their attempts to undermine his work, making their views felt through Josef Josten's *Information Service of Free Czechoslovakia*; while anti-communist campaigners, such as Lord Vansittart, were asking why elected representatives should collaborate on projects with a *Warsaw Pact* nation. In a country inexorably drawn westwards, fellowship with, or conciliatory statements about, those perceived to be Britain's current adversaries were seen as suspect. Only Dr Stross's qualities of logic, probity and trustworthiness could convince many otherwise:

1957 DELEGATION TO LIDICE

"LIDICE LIVES AGAIN" was the headline in the Lancashire Evening News on January the 21st 1957 as it displayed an invitation from the British Lidice Committee for members of the public to visit Czechoslovakia in June for **"the 15th pilgrimage to Lidice, commemorating *the little Bohemian village* erased by the Nazis in 1942"**. The article emphasised the impact of **"the now world-famous Lidice Shall Live movement,"** as well as referring to the international subscriptions raised towards the post-war rebuilding of Lidice, and the donations of British rose trees contributed by local councils, churches, trade unions, and many individual citizens— **"making possible the inauguration of the great International Rose Garden of Peace which now stands on the site of the old village."** The invitation read:

"Lest we forget the horrors of war and ever-urgent need to bring the common people together in peaceful pursuits, we, the undersigned, appeal for a strong and representative pilgrimage from Britain to Lidice this year.

The British Lidice Committee, which is entirely non-political and non-sectarian in character, is chartering planes from London to Prague on June 15th, to take those who wish to participate in the international commemoration being arranged by the Czechs on June 16th. We believe that the dangers and disappointments of recent months make this pilgrimage more, not less, necessary, and desirable.

Will all those interested please write now to the Organising Secretary: Lidice Committee, 20 Pont St. London S.W.1 for particulars?

-Boy Orr Chorley. John Baird. A. D. D. Broughton, Harold Davies, W. J. Owen, G. A. Pargiter, W. Reid, Harriet Slater, S. Swingler. B. Stross and George Thomas. The House of Commons, London, S.W.1."

1960 DELEGATION TO BRITAIN

The Lidice Committee organised British-Czechoslovak cultural and educational bilateral exchanges with its Czechoslovak equivalent, the Society for the Restoration of Lidice, for well over a decade. One of the last took place in early June 1960, when the committee invited elected representatives and residents of the village to England. The delegation, which was headed by the Deputy Mayor, Mrs Marie Jarošová, was welcomed by several English cities, and the party completed a very demanding programme in three days, touring 16 exhibitions and attending many official lunches and dinners.

After visiting Oakhill Modern High School, Marie Jarošová and her party had lunch with the Lord Mayor, Alderman Harold Clowes, and his wife, Christine, at the *Potters Club* at Federation House. Following Marie's opening of a trade exhibition at the British Ceramic Research Association laboratories in Penkhull, the Czech party travelled to an industrial display in Hanley Park, before viewing several buildings in the city, and spending time at the Harold Clowes ballroom in Bucknall.

The next morning the delegation visited an exhibition of artworks at the City Museum in Hanley - where the idea for the Lidice Shall Live movement was first aired, before attending the annual meeting of the City Council, followed by an official lunch at the town hall in Stoke. In the afternoon they visited a show of ceramics, had tea with councillors from Burslem, and in the evening attended a formal dinner. On the day of their departure, Marie visited North Staffordshire University College, toured the city, and had lunch with the city's new Lord Mayor and the Lady Mayoress, Mr and Mrs Gordon Dale.

On Monday June the 6th 1960, speaking on Radio Prague, Mrs Jarošová thanked Stoke-on-Trent for her stay in England. The interviewer referred both to the forthcoming 18th anniversary of the destruction of Lidice and the founding of the Lidice Shall Live movement in the Potteries. Marie explained:

"I had the opportunity to talk to many people, and I was pleased to find out that everyone knew the fate of our village, Lidice. Most people who I met had visited Czechoslovakia, and everyone assured me that they had happy memories of their stay in our country and that they like to remember their visits. However, I was somewhat shocked to find that many others have a very distorted view of life in Czechoslovakia."

CHILDREN'S VISIT TO BRITAIN 1962

The Lidice Shall Live Committee organised for children from Lidice to visit Britain on a number of occasions. One such cultural encounter took place in the summer of 1962 when 15 children and 5 women arrived on Tuesday the 19th of June to be the honoured guests of communities such as Coventry, Stoke-on-Trent, London, and Deal in Kent. From June the 19th to July the 3rd, the party enjoyed a roller coaster ride of civic luncheons and receptions, exhibitions, as well as more informal leisure time, during a visit which served as part holiday, part ambassadorial experience.

A familiar welcome awaited the guests at the beginning of their stay. On landing at London Airport, they were met by the coach driver, Mr Jan Vavara, a Czechoslovak who lived in Stoke-on-Trent. With the permission of the accompanying officials, he greeted the visitors in their own language. Mr Vavara then proceeded to drive the party to Coventry for a special tea with the Lord Mayor Alderman Arthur Waugh. On Wednesday morning, the party paid commemoration to Coventry's air raid victims as Karel Lander and Mrs Marie Jarošová laid a wreath on their communal grave at London Road Cemetery. Later, the delegation visited Stratford-upon-Avon, the birthplace of William Shakespeare.

Thursday, they arrived in Stoke-on-Trent at the invitation of the Lord Mayor Cllr Thomas Beddow. While welcoming the guests, the Lord Mayor recalled his recent visit to the 20th Lidice Commemorative gathering. He said that he found the village a "charming place to live" and added:

"It is a monument to bravery and pride of the inhabitants of Lidice, who are the victors over the wild atrocities caused by the Nazis in the last big war. Stoke-on-Trent has launched a call for help in rebuilding the village, but in addition to these tragic beginnings, our two communities have formed friendships that will last for all time."

The women and children kicked off their stay in Stoke-on-Trent with a visit to WT Copeland and Sons in Stoke, there then followed a specially arranged lunch at the Jubilee Hall where Dr Stross gave a speech welcoming the youngsters, an opportunity to visit the Victoria Hall, in Hanley, where the Lidice Shall Live movement had held its inaugural meeting, before returning to Coventry for dinner.

A ceremonial reception took place on Friday at the Czech Embassy in London as well as a tour of London, and then it was away to Kent, as the women and children spent a week at the seaside in the town of Deal as guests of mining families.

Back in the capital, before leaving for home, on the 3rd of July, the Lidice women laid a wreath at the Whitehall Cenotaph and had lunch at the Houses of Commons with Dr Barnett Stross. The fortnight long trip was funded by Coventry City Council and Stoke-on-Trent City Council; the Transport and General Workers' Union; the National Society of Operative Printers and Assistants, Kingston upon Thames; as well as engineers and miners from Betteshanger Colliery in Kent.

The memories of Zdenka Kotková:

"I was 13 years old. We were very happy! Our friends, who couldn't go, were very sad. Our mothers started to buy everything for our journey. We learnt English words, songs. For all of us it was the first time on a plane. And it was the first time we saw the ocean! We flew from Prague by TU104 Soviet plane. From windows we saw the English Channel and soon landed at London's airport. A bus took us to Waverley Hotel in the town. We were at London about three days.

We saw old London, Buckingham palace, Tower bridge, some museums, London Zoo, double-deckers, with Dr Stross we visited Parliament. We had lunch there. We visited the Czechoslovakian embassy. There were diplomats about from other countries."

"After London we went to Stoke, there we sleep in miners building in big park. From Stoke we go to Coventry. We saw the Cathedral, monument, and the town. We have own show, and I danced as a Japanese girl, because I am going ballet. And boys play and all we sing English songs. At Stoke

we was at a ceramic factory where we got some presents. We stop at Stratford-upon-Avon. It is wonderful for us to see Shakespeare's theatre, his home. We all was happy full to at first time to see ocean. We wait was be a first. When we saw this, we call. We was two weeks in small town Deal. We sleep at own house with typical English women. We make friendship with boys and girls from Deal. Name of my girl was Penny Knight. She was nice and quiet. Give me very nice bangle and silver animals. I give her something, when I returned, I sent her typical Czech gift. Every day we go swimming at sea. We was happy, but ocean is not quite. We visited France and we go to see towns near Deal like Dover, Canterbury. We had lunch in the gardens. We was also at some amusement park. All the time was with us about three miners. In London and Stoke was with us Mr Barnett Stross. If I see Dover's cliff, English country, London buildings, Stoke's towers I remember our fantastic holiday."

I came back to Stoke in 2015. I was with Gerrards. I saw Lidice's monument in front of Victoria Hall, Lidice Way. l was at school and children know much about Lidice. Now, that our flags are on buildings of Stoke those children know why. I was at Stadium Stoke city with Cheryl. Lunch with player's, played Stoke with Leicester 2:2. I met with our friends in Fenton Hall. I was sleeping in hotel at Hanley. Yes, Mr. Stross was visionary! He said in year 1942 "Lidice shall live". And now Lidice is new, with big park of roses, with gallery, all thanks Mr. Stross. Next year is 80 years of tragedy in old Lidice. Many peoples, friends of Lidice will come - From England, Greece, Brazil, Cuba, USA, French, Mexico, Italy, and others. Women's named Lidice are about one thousand."

Zdenka Kotková – Honorary Member of Lidice Lives

1962 – "LONG LIVE PEACE!" - AS THE CURTAIN FALLS

The horror of that fateful day seemed far away as tens of thousands of pilgrims made their way to the 20th Lidice Commemorative Event on Sunday the 10th of June 1962. A US correspondent wrote,

"... it was a warm and sunny day and the atmosphere was almost that of a holiday. The stands selling frankfurters, ice cream, and soft drinks did a bonanza business. Whole families dressed in their Sunday best sat on the grass or strolled, enjoying the sun, and talking. The general attitude seemed to be one of gratitude for peace and for the relatively higher living standards seventeen years of peace had brought."

Yet, despite the sun, warmth, and the smiles, in terms of East—West relations, the coldness of the mood was about to freeze into a crystalline hiatus which would last decades:

From the podium on the grandstand, First Secretary of the Czech Communist party, and hard-line President of Czechoslovakia, Antonín Novotný proceeded to deliver a scathing attack on the Western powers. Novotný accused them of playing a **"false game"** ever since the end of the Second World War. He charged that they never intended to fulfil the settlements of the 1945 Potsdam Conference concerning the disarming and demilitarisation of Germany and had now put **"German imperialists and militarism"** in power in West Germany. He stated:

"The United States has not dared so far to give West Germany atomic arms because of the pressure of hostile public opinion" but he added that the recent meeting of the North Atlantic Treaty Organisation in Athens **"took dangerous steps toward the atomic armament"** of the West German Army.

Instead, the President stressed the country's allegiances, announcing that the people of Czechoslovakia had bound their fate proudly and indissolubly with that of the Soviet Union. He said that they had learned to distrust the word of their former allies, Britain, and France, whom he accused of having sacrificed Czechoslovakia to Hitler in 1938 in the interest of their anti-communist goals. The thousands gathered there, to mark the anniversary, received the address intently. They applauded only occasionally and showed the most animation when Novotný concluded by exalting, **"Long live peace!!"** This cry was acknowledged by many and chanted rhythmically. The speech was rapidly and broadly syndicated in the press and broadcast media on both sides of the political divide.

Because of this address, the incumbent positions stiffened. Within such a toxic atmosphere, only the predisposition of friends on either side of the *Iron Curtain* could have a chance of keeping relations alive in the most informal of senses. Even then, they would run the risk of investigation by members of their own Government's Secret Service.

Well into his middle age and not in the best of health, an internationalist with an agenda built around the advancement of culture and peace, to lift people out of mundanity, Barnett Stross was not interested in shirking the task. For the last five years of his life, he worked as hard as ever to maintain and develop British-Czechoslovak relations.

Dr Barnett Stross addresses the crowd at the 15th Lidice commemorative gathering in 1957. Later he would be awarded with the Freedom of the village.

Top: On June the 10th 1962, the 20th anniversary of the razing of Lidice, the First Secretary of the Central Committee of the Communist Party and President, Antonín Novotný inspected an exhibition of children's drawings and works of art at the House of Culture in Lidice. Five years later, the International Children's Exhibition of Fine Arts Lidice (ICEFA Lidice) would be established to commemorate all child victims of war. In 2022 it enters its 50th year. Bottom: The same day, 80,000 people attended a demonstration for peace and friendship between nations, organised by the Czechoslovak Committee for Friendship and Peace, the Czechoslovak National Front and the Lidice National Local Committee. Photo credits ČTK

DR BARNETT STROSS

EARLY LIFE

Barnet *(spelt with one "t" in his early years)* was born to a Jewish family in the Polish town of Pabianice, near the city of Łódź on the 25th of December 1898. Pabianice was second only to Łódź in terms of the production of cotton, wool, and mixed fabrics. The town had become an indispensable part of the region's *Promised Land* - where you could do good business and earn a decent income. Barnet's ancestors were French survivors from Napoleon's ill-fated invasion of Russia in 1812 and had settled in Pabianice on their retreat from Moscow. His parents - Samuel Strosberg and Celia Herzkowicz, daughter to a Rabbi, were married in 1880. Samuel owned a textile mill and was successful. Barnet, later called "Bob" by his family and friends, was one of the youngest of 12 siblings.

It is unknown whether the last decades of the 19th century in Pabianice had improved, maintained, or lessened financial security for the Strosbergs, nevertheless the family left Poland in 1902 to escape a repeat of the murderous anti-Semitic riots of 1881-1884 - something Samuel and Celia considered likely. In the event, their suspicions were confirmed when a series of violent and bloody attacks against Jews broke out across Eastern Europe between 1903 and 1908, including several in Poland - the Białystok pogrom the most shocking of all - *though decades later a tsunami of anti-Semitic hatred was to engulf Pabianice and communities like it from the west in the form of Adolf Hitler and the Third Reich.*

The Strosbergs changed their surname to Stross on emigration to England. Settling in Dewsbury, the family soon moved to Leeds—where Barnet's father founded a textile factory. By 1911 the family was living in the Chapeltown Road area of the city - at No. 6 Woodland Grove. Now altered, one can still make out the Victorian brickwork on the right of the street, but the space which occupied *No 6* is now a set of functional 1970s semis. Growing into Leeds, Samuel and Celia had enough capital for the children to be educated at a private school, and this was the balanced first decade that Barnet settled into.

However, losing his father at the age of twelve and his elder brother at eighteen brought significant changes to Barnet. As a young lad he was protected from serious emotional upset by the love of his mother, who was ably assisted in the task of bringing her youngest children up by her eldest daughters. But as a young man coming of age, news that his 24-year-old brother David, a Second Lieutenant in the Royal Flying Corps had lost his life in the Great War, on the 12th of March 1917, must have come as a hammer blow, leaving him disabused of any notion about the rights and wrongs of war.

Though, much of the development of Stross's character over his formative years is a matter of conjecture, he may certainly have felt his frustration at the carnage of the Somme campaign of July 1916 - *the oft repeated full-frontal assaults employing British manpower to secure insignificant breakthroughs on the Western Front*—compounded, as leaders planned for a similar attack against German forces in July 1917 at Passchendaele in Belgium. A politically astute young Stross may well have felt incentivised to protest about the issue.

It is likely that Bob Stross would have been in his 18th year and studying for his Higher School Certificate of Education at Leeds Grammar School when he met the woman who was to become a permanent fixture in his life for four decades. Born on the 7th of September 1898, Olive Marion Baker was effervescent, reflecting the in-vogue art deco fashions and designs of the 1920s perfectly. Little is known about her life prior to her meeting Bob other than she was local to Leeds, non-Jewish, a drama student, attractive, tall, and slender with dark Mikado hair, was good company, and drank and smoked quite heavily. But for some in Barnet's family Olive was a divisive character: to some she was brazenly eccentric and unconventional, what you might call "bohemian"—rumoured to be a life model for artists and often in the company of like-minded radical people from the world of music, art, literature, spiritualism, or politics. At first glance, she did not seem a good influence on a young man entering the serious world of medicine. Aileen Hyman, granddaughter of Rosa Kalinsky née Stross, one of Bob's eldest sisters and a mother figure, says of her grandmother's influence,

"I know that for some family members it meant his marriage to Olive was a big problem, and they unravelled with him, but my grandmother had support and Olive liked her. My mother, Marie Kalinsky, as a child, was with Bob and Olive during school holidays in the 1920s at their house in Stoke-on-Trent. He was a general practitioner there."

It did not matter. By the time Barnet was half way through his Sciences degree at Leeds University in January 1920, he and Olive had fallen in love and were married. By 1923 the couple were living at Clarendon Place, next to Leeds University's campus. This was convenient, as Barnet was now studying medicine at Leeds Medical School. It was during these days balancing young married life, socialising, studying, and entertaining that Stross discovered his love of art and culture - through the profound influence of Olive, who was a drama student. Aileen continues: *"It was she who introduced Bob to this bohemian society and through her to Bob he developed his lifelong interest in art and then his professional knowledge in the field of painting. Bob's interest in art contained an extensive personal collection from Sickert and Lowry. In later years some of the paintings were donated, I believe, to Keele University - a new university facility near Stoke, Bob helped establish."*

Although there is no definitive proof, merely a coming together of facts and happenings to corroborate a strong likelihood, it was around the early 1920s that the couple frequented the internationally renowned *Leeds Art Club*; the phenomenon had been making an international reputation for itself since the 1890s and by 1920, this had been expanded to encompass early psychoanalysis, experimental drama, post-impressionism, and abstract art. It was the perfect stimuli for a young medical student and his performing artist wife.

The club met at 8 Blenheim Place - just a few hundred metres away from the Stross's home, at a time bursting with talented British painters and writers, many of whom would become his friends, contacts and suppliers over the decades: Jacob Kramer - a native of Chapeltown like Stross, Jacob Epstein, L. S. Lowry, Raymond Coxon, Henry Moore, Barbara Hepworth and other artists whose works would come into Barnett Stross's hands, usually in exchange for free medical care in a world of private health care provision; many of which would later be donated to the plinths and walls of establishments across North Staffordshire and beyond. In 1923, as the club began to falter, Kramer tried to continue its work under the auspices of the *Yorkshire Luncheon Club*. It could be here that Olive and Barnet took a more active role. Indeed, there is a report of an experiment in hypnotism taking place at the Stross's home - 16 Clarendon Place - where Stross hypnotised a guest, then performed a feat of telepathy by *"influencing"* the guest to follow through the concealed instructions of a member of the audience.

STOKE-ON-TRENT

In 1925, Dr Barnett Stross attained his Bachelor in Surgery and Medicine degrees, specialising in respiratory illnesses.

When, in 1926, Dr Stross set up his practice in the district of Shelton, Stoke-on-Trent, he swapped the ailments and illnesses suffered by workers in the Yorkshire coalfields and textile factories for those associated with the mines and the smog belching *potbanks* of North Staffordshire. From now on, the world of respiratory illnesses and word *silicosis* would be constant companions. It was here that he and Olive would receive a baptism of fire - thrown into a unique, hellish industrial landscape of monstrous proportions.

Their choice of home was at the epicentre, with the furnaces of Shelton Bar, the *bottle ovens* of the Cauldon Potteries, the local slag heaps and shraff tips, and the Hanley Gas Works dominating the surrounding land. A distraction, of course, were the queues of mostly industrial workers facing ill health - with no financial support to help their families. It was within Shelton that the Strosses would make their mark within the community. And the doctor especially.

At Richmond House, he and Olive were supported by housekeepers, Amy Lynch (cook) and Elsie Shufflebotham (parlour maid). They had a time keeping up with the whirlwind of activity going on around them as, according to accounts, the Stross household was depicted as *chaotic* in 1939. It was also described as *eccentrically* furnished—reflecting the owners' unorthodox tastes. Most of the doctor's patients came from the poorest areas of Hanley and Shelton, and many of them became his friends, and later his loyalist supporters.

"Our family doctor, Barnett Stross, was a Polish Jew who worked amongst the poor of the district... I am told that shortly after my birth he circumcised me on the kitchen table; I never found out if this was for a medical reason, or if all the baby boys in Shelton were done!" Don Edwards

Barnett Stross's marriage to Olive was good, the evidence suggesting that they were very much in love. They would be seen at engagements, often appearing photographed together in the newspaper columns. Olive was visible within the community herself and played an active role defending art and culture in the city, as well as appearing as an actress in local productions for the Stoke Repertory Players. A glimpse into Olive's character can be gleaned by the letter content she sent to the local newspaper - the Sentinel, which appeared on Friday the 3rd of May 1935 concerning the prominent artist Stanley Spencer - who was protesting because the Royal Academy had rejected two of his paintings:

"It is a notorious fact that criticism is handicapped by its own lack of creative ability. It seems apparent that appreciation of a contemporary work of art is difficult, or almost impossible, for the 'man in the street' to understand.

A work of art, whether by poet, painter, sculptor, or musician, is an offering of an abstract idea clothed in symbols. The symbols differ with every age and every civilisation, and, whereas a cultured "man in the street" may comprehend symbolism of the bygone generation, he flounders in the presence of his own. This is why youth so often despises its elders, only to be despised in its turn.

It is utterly incomprehensible to me why St. Francis should be portrayed (or is expected to be portrayed) with the face of a Botticelli angel.

Mr Beech is right. Spencer and Epstein will live. - Yours truly,

OLIVE M. STROSS. Richmond House, Shelton, Stoke-on-Trent."

Ian Macilwain is a well-known photographer and his aunt was Gwendoline (Gwen), a close friend of Barnett and Olive, who later became Barnett's second wife. Ian provided many private memories to former Czech PhD student Gabriela Literová for her 2010 thesis and it is thanks to Ian and Gabriela that we have several rare selections, such as family photographs and transcripts of speeches included in this book.

Ian recalled his meeting with Bob and Olive in 1959 when he was visiting Aunt Gwen. He also described the differences between Olive and Gwen:

"**My first memories of Bob and Olive Stross are from a visit to see Aunt Gwen. I think it was in 1959. I remember as both were very interested in teaching us 'tongue twisters' - e.g.,** *"Peter piper picked a peck of pickled pepper"* **and a few others that were brand new to me. Gwen and Olive were very different. Gwen was serious, but she had a good sense of humour and was very kind. Olive was bohemian and artistic.**"

Olive Marion Stross, the free-spirited, often outspoken former art student became Barnett's companion for the majority of his life.

One suspects her influence on the philosophical architecture of Dr Stross far exceeds the quantity of material available to us concerning her background.

Correspondingly she remains a relatively mysterious character in the story of the Lidice Shall Live campaign and the life-script that was about to play out.

Olive Stross died in 1961.

Clockwise: Barnett Stross's mother and father: Celia (10th of Dec 1861 - 13th of Nov 1940) and Samuel (1st of Mar 1859 - 11th of Apr 1910); elder brother David who lost his life during the Great War (born 1895 - 12th of Mar 1917); Stross, aged around 25 - picture from Royal Aeronautical Club membership card (25th of Dec 1898 - 13th of May 1967)

Clockwise: The school where Barnet Stross received his basic education. Originally founded in 1552, a "new" boys-only Leeds Grammar School (pictured) was opened next to Woodhouse Moor in June 1859. Its alumni include Barry Cryer OBE, comedian, and writer; Ricky Wilson, musician, lead singer - Kaiser Chiefs; Colin Montgomerie OBE, professional golfer; Richard Price MBE, film, and theatre producer; Jeremy Dyson, writer, and author; Lucy Manning, special correspondent for the BBC; Thelma Ruby, actor; In January 1920, Barnet Stross married Olive Marion Baker. By 1923 the couple were living at 16 Clarendon Place, next to Leeds University's campus. Barnet was studying Medicine and Olive studied Arts. It was at this time that Stross discovered his love of art and culture - through the devoted influence of Olive; A politically astute young Stross may well have been affected by the large anti-war Socialist conference held at the Leeds Coliseum Theatre in June 2017, which was attended by many future senior Labour Party figures, e.g., Ramsay MacDonald, Ernest Bevin and the like.

Top: Dr and Olive Stross shared a friendship with the young Michael Ayrton and would invite the artist to their house in Shelton. Ayrton, the London based painter was always taken aback at the living conditions in the Potteries and was fascinated at the cheek by jowl nature of industrial and family life. This inspired him to paint and sketch prolifically during his stays. "The White Country," painted in 1946, shows a view to the back of Richmond House; it was eventually donated to the Lidice Collection, which was formally opened in 1964; *Bottom:* The White House was formerly one of the doctor's surgeries. When Charles Austin Brook was Lord Mayor of Stoke-on-Trent in 1942-43, he initiated a fund for the purpose of commemorating the life and work of the aeronautical engineer Reginald Mitchell. Part of the money was used to found engineering scholarships in Southampton; the rest was for a Youth Centre in the Potteries. After searching for a suitable central site for several years without success, the Reginald Mitchell Memorial Committee bought the White House, Broad-street, Hanley, from Dr Barnett Stross, MP for Hanley, for £8,000.

POTENTIAL INFLUENCES

EARLY SOCIALIST EXPERIENCES & THE GREAT WAR

Barnet Stross was in his 19th year when the *Socialist and Labour Convention on the First World War* was taking place at the Coliseum in Leeds on Sunday June the 3rd 1917. An array of future illustrious high ranking British politicians and activists attended the schedule of events, such as Sylvia Pankhurst, Ernest Bevin, Clement Attlee, and Ramsay MacDonald. They took inspiration from the February Revolution in Russia, which saw members of the Duma, a body resembling a house of representatives, assume full control of the country, and form the Russian Provisional Government led by Alexander Kerensky.

In the wake of the trauma associated with the Somme offensive the previous year, many people in Britain felt hostile towards plans for continuing the bloodshed on the Western Front and the convention offered a platform for them to have their say. With 1,100 delegates standing for several million members complemented by an audience from the Leeds general public, ***"The proceedings were somewhat lively at times..."*** reported the Lancashire Evening Telegraph.

Mr Robert Smillie of the Mineworkers' Federation of Great Britain was to have been the chief speaker at an open-air demonstration, planned for the evening in the city's Victoria Square, but, according to reports, due to civic concerns posters were distributed rapidly by the Lord Mayor and the Chief Constable prohibiting the holding of an open-air meeting of any sort, so that the public rally had to be held in the Coliseum instead - *though a small section of the delegates in the afternoon clamoured for the outdoor meeting to go ahead as planned* - in order to demonstrate that the Convention had the teeth **"to act as well as talk."**

Although criticised by some contemporary commentators as merely providing lip-service rhetoric for the consumption of those abroad, the meetings proved there was still appetite for mass rallies along Chartist lines. Living amongst it all, the young Barnet Stross, and his family, with their continental familiarity with the subject, may well have felt drawn to find out more. If Stross did, he would certainly take from these assemblies, lessons and apply them to his own future campaigning.

POLITICAL FIGURES IN STOKE-ON-TRENT

The early 1930s saw the nation gripped in economic crisis as Stoke-on-Trent City Council sought to build on the plans of the Federation of 1910 and Stoke-on-Trent's elevation to city status in 1925. The days when philanthropy determined the politics of local government administration were rapidly passing. Civic procedure was moving away from a non-political chair, directed by the Lord Mayor, and towards the leader of the largest party-political group instead. Charity was giving way to politics, and in Stoke-on-Trent politics was the politics of the working classes, and those they elected to represent them were from within their own ranks.

Young Dr Stross's first encounters with such characters no doubt stemmed from this time of national emergency as he grappled with the dual roles of medical advisor and as an elected representative from 1938. He dealt with leading figures at the council, within the local miners' federation and the pottery union, as well as the associated trade associations. He saw first-hand the leadership of men like George Herbert Barber, a man who strove for social improvement based on ground level motivation rather than top-down patronage. He witnessed the passion and achievements of Arthur Hollins, the General Secretary of the North Staffordshire Pottery Workers' Union, who was to become the Lord Mayor in 1933. He saw the moral fortitude of Hugh Leese, Arthur Baddeley, Fred Hancock, and the other leaders of the North Staffordshire Miners' Federation in fighting for and securing improved terms, conditions, and facilities for their members throughout the 1930s. He saw the bravery, creativity, and resourcefulness of those fleeing Nazi persecution - who had found a safe haven in Stoke-on-Trent, and who were now helping to improve their adopted local communities - people like Jan Strasser, Chair of the Czecho-Slovak - British Friendship Club, who was patenting the first semi-automatic pottery cup handling machine. He recognised, and identified with, those resisting fascism across the city. Barnett Stross encouraged and promoted them wherever they might be.

ECONOMIC VIEWS

During the Second World War, and until the 1970s the mainstream policy position held by governments was grounded in the achievement and maintenance of *full employment* through the use of *Keynesian Demand Management* policies as set out by the economist John Maynard Keynes in his thesis *The General Theory of Employment, Interest and Money*, published in 1936.

Barnett Stross's views on economics and a governmental structure for post-war Britain can be gleaned from a speech he gave as a prospective Labour candidate at Hanley Town Hall to representatives of the *Workers' Educational Association* and the *Fabian Society* on the 3rd of July 1942. Here, he suggested it was essential to formulate strategies for the future if the nation were to avoid the mass unemployment and disillusion that followed the Great War, and he outlined plans for social security:

"... the rebuilding of Britain must be worthy of its people. No interests in land or property should be allowed to interfere. Adequate social services must be available so as to secure positive health for all, optimum nutrition for all, and full and proper care for the old. There must also be the fullest educational, social and economic opportunities for the young."

Dr Stross believed that a scheme for social security should be comprehensive and be administered by a government department:

"It should serve all who needed security, whether in sickness or accident. It should apply to widows, orphans, and old people. Whatever the contingency, the payments should be in cash and adequate... family allowances for dependent children were long overdue, and the nation's health should be safeguarded by a comprehensive medical service."

In describing the steps that must be taken to obtain a comprehensive scheme of social security, Dr Stross said that **"... when the war is over, much of Europe will be ravaged and impoverished and there will be less credit and capital available than ever before."**

"If the standard of life of the British worker were to be maintained, certain steps were essential. There were some things that must be owned in common and others that might well be left to private enterprise. The country, as a whole, must control capital and credit,

the land, imports and exports, transport (included shipping) and fuel and power. There was no need and it would be most undesirable to bring into creation an enormous bureaucracy. We had in this country fully trained executives and fully experienced business ability which would serve the people as a whole at least as well as it served restrictive monopolies. We could well afford to encourage the business man and assist him on condition he ran his business well, but irresponsible capitalism must be controlled. It was possible in this way to enlist the help of every clear-thinking man and to retain in the time of reconstruction the unity that had been forged in battle."

In the language of the 21st century, Dr Stross is undoubtedly considered to be on the left of the political spectrum. But it is clear that he believed in markets where they functioned competitively for the sake of society. However, monopolies and those markets which were prone to price fixing and collusion for the profits of shareholders were another matter. Where there was a likelihood that the public could lose out, especially in staple markets such as Fuel, Transport, Housing, Utilities and Health, Stross believed in the need for nationalisation to ensure that those industries not only gain from the economies of scale that would accrue but also the re-investment of profit into infrastructure and technology - to achieve best prices and reliable and safe supplies across the nation, in order to ensure that consumers benefit well into the future.

THE MOSLEYS & FASCISM

Like other industrial cities across the nation, Stoke-on-Trent had provided a foothold for the British Fascist League since the party's inception in the early 1920s - in fact, each town of the Potteries had its own branch. In 1929, with the onset of a deep depression looming and levels of deprivation about to sky-rocket, the insidious problem of bigotry within society would begin to manifest. Dr Stross realised that the industrial workers of Stoke-on-Trent and North Staffordshire were at risk. A British Government which supported the economics of *laissez-faire*, and the appeasement of the nefarious forces of fascism and Nazism abroad throughout the 1930s, could see workers fall foul to influences which could strip away their morality and rights. For Barnett Stross, the psychological fight against people like the notorious Sir Oswald Mosley and other British fascists, and the campaign for the creation of a new Lidice and its rose garden were all part of the same ongoing effort to heal worldwide divisions.

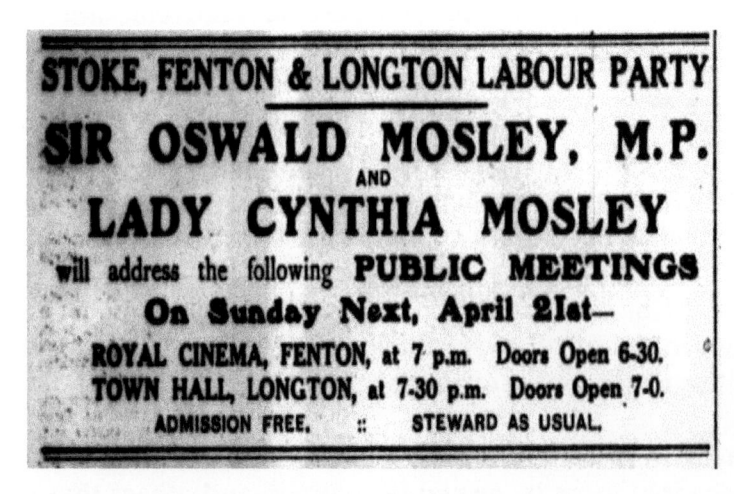

However, it is interesting to think for a moment that during the 1920s North Staffordshire was a familiar stamping ground for Sir Oswald Mosley MP—his grandparents had owned Apedale Hall, after all. Finding his feet as a GP and an advisor to the North Staffordshire Miners' Federation and the Pottery Workers' Union, the young Dr Stross and wife Olive would read about him every day in the papers.

Egotist he may have been, but there was little reason to consider Mosley and his spouse Cynthia as anything other than charismatic, albeit entitled figures of the left, with exciting ideas. Oswald was one of the first political advocates of John Maynard Keynes' macroeconomic theory of *aggregate demand management*, which argued that governments should intervene to prevent their economies from stalling or over-heating to protect their citizens' livelihoods. As the Labour MP for Smethwick, Mosley made speeches around the country, and several in Stoke-on-Trent, expounding the benefits of Keynesianism for the British economy—particularly following the *Wall Street Crash* of *Black Tuesday*—the 29th of October 1929.

Lady Cynthia Mosley was an inspirational MP for the Stoke Division, which included the towns of Stoke, Fenton and Longton, much respected by a significant majority of her constituents for the empathy, passion, and hours she committed to their cause.

As unemployment rose, Mosley felt compelled to produce solutions to the economic crisis which had plunged Britain and the world into the Great Depression. These were compiled in the affectionately titled *"Mosley's Memorandum."* This proposed three main things: control imports, set up a commonwealth partnership, and establish a national economic plan.

Hopeful that Ramsay MacDonald and the Cabinet would administer his prescriptions, Mosley, the Chancellor of the Duchy of Lancaster, was to grow frustrated when his solutions were rejected; and he resigned from the front bench of the Labour Party on May the 19th, 1930. In October, he was defeated again when he failed in his attempt to persuade the Labour Party Conference to accept his ideas.

Disillusioned, on the 28th of February 1931, Mosley left the Labour Party, launching the New Party the following day. From this point on, Oswald Mosley's political affiliations became increasingly extreme - gradual at first and behind a screen of respectability, then more obviously bigoted with the formation of the black-shirted British Union of Fascists from 1932.

But a question lingers about the influence the Mosleys had on Dr Stross and Olive. Certainly, as Mosley's ideology became more transparent with the launch of the British Union of Fascists, aligning itself closer to that of the antisemitic Hitler, it was clear that Mosley's policies represented the antithesis of everything Stross had ever stood for, and Stross would have felt repugnance about that, hardening his resolve to fight for the cause of democracy.

However, the case prior to 1930 is unclear, for it could have been that Mosley was a positive variable within the equation which inspired Stross to join the Labour Party. To know if that were the case, it would be helpful to know the exact date Dr Barnett Stross submitted his application.

Top: Dr Barnett Stross and Olive Stross celebrate with local people following his election on the 31st of October 1938 as councillor for Shelton, known as Ward 13, in the Stoke-on-Trent Municipal Elections. Due to his popularity in the area the Etruria section of the ward returned him unopposed leaving the doctor with a winning majority of 910 votes out of the 1,493 votes cast against his opposition, the independent Mr J. T. Bettany; *Bottom;* From his home near Denham in Buckinghamshire, Sir Oswald Mosley and the breakaway MPs involved in the "New Party" left to right - Mr. W.E.D. Allen MP, Dr Forgan MP, Lady Cynthia Mosley MP, Sir Oswald Mosley MP, Mr John Strachey MP. After dreadful showings in the 1931 General Elections on Tuesday the 27th of October, Mosley made plans to travel to Italy to meet with Mussolini.

THE POST-WAR YEARS

DOCTOR IN THE HOUSE

Following the war, Barnett Stross was elected MP for Hanley from 1945 to 1950, and then MP for Stoke Central until 1965. He was an authority on industrial diseases and appeared as an expert witness on behalf of pottery workers before a committee of inquiry into silicosis. Alleviating the disease's effects became a devoted cause for Dr Stross, and successive government schemes providing compensation for people suffering from pneumoconiosis and silicosis were introduced as a result of his campaigning. He devoted much of his life to improving conditions in the Potteries, and in 1950 was instrumental in securing *The Pottery (Health and Welfare) Special Regulations* which prescribed much improved conditions for workers - this included the control of chemicals, pottery dust *(a cause of silicosis)* and workshop conditions including maximum and minimum working temperatures. Latterly, he successfully launched a media drive to secure a financial settlement for miners who had suffered serious occupational lung disease prior to nationalisation. An advocate for the miners and potters in the courts and at tribunals, he spoke up for people as individuals, not as anonymous pieces of data; at the heart of his philosophy was an awareness that human beings are the foundation to all businesses, organisations, cities, and nations.

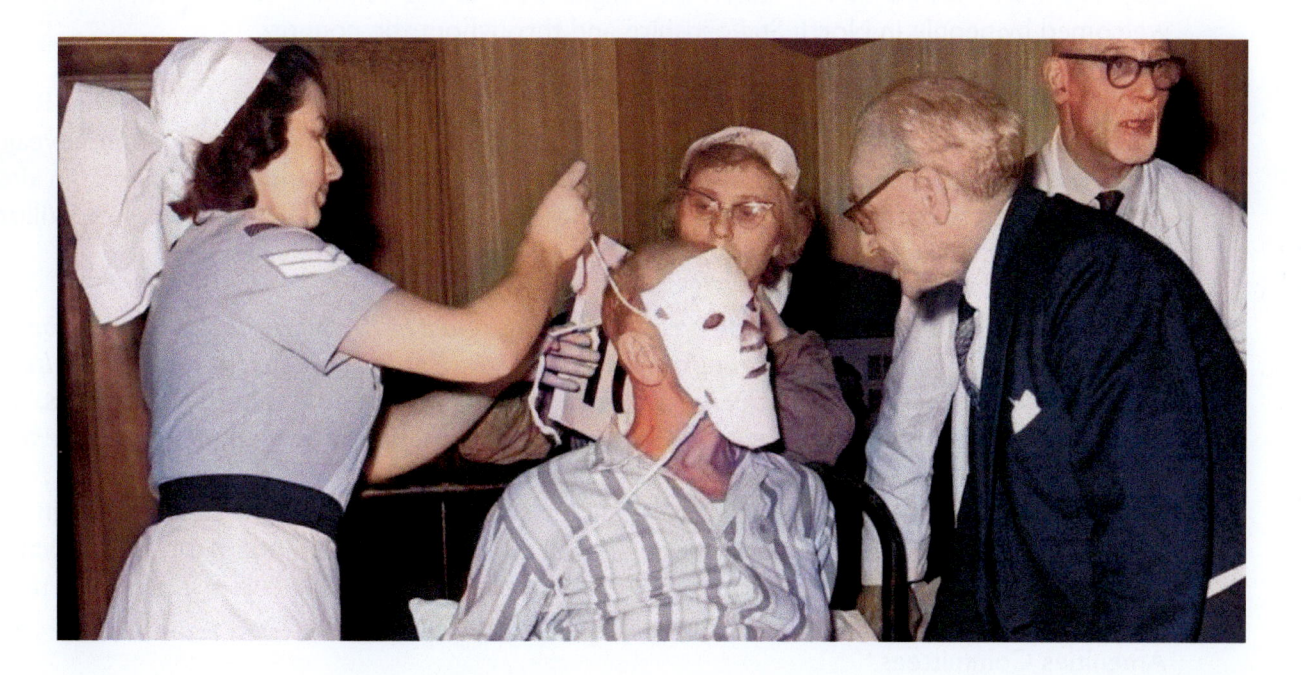

One of Barnett Stross's earliest ambitions was to see the establishment of a National Health Service. As a MP and a member of the Socialist Medical Association, Dr Stross became the nation's GP when he was immediately recruited onto the Parliamentary Standing Committee set up to ensure that the foundations of the National Health Service were implemented according to the guidelines set out by the Beveridge Report of 1942. He took on the role with gusto.

The Government launched the National Health Service on the 5th of July 1947. Dr Barnett Stross proved to be a quiet, no-nonsense, but crucial ingredient in creating its infrastructure and guiding principles. Scanning through the newspaper archive today it becomes clear just how critical a role Dr Stross played in Public Health, reassuring Britons during the severe austerity of the late 1940s as the NHS found traction amidst the backdrop of acute rationing and one of the coldest winters on record—1946-47. Stross seemed to be everywhere - giving advice on how to make the best of the situation: calorie intake, keeping warm, child welfare, as well as playing a very visible role in getting the NHS up and running in practical terms. He was, for many years, concerned with the problems of nutrition and the dangers of lung cancer through smoking and used the outlets available to him to reach out to the public in an attempt to effect change.

Newspaper articles and pamphlets spanning three decades reveal his determination in raising the level of public information on health and community issues and his resoluteness in exposing all that was potentially harmful for the benefit of society at large. *"Dr Stross and the effects of night work," "City MP and lung cancer," "Town Hall by Dr Stross," "Dr Stross and stage hypnotism," and "Public Health and Food Inspection"* are a random selection from the many such headlines over the years.

ARTS AND CULTURE

Stross was co-founder in 1945 of the Arts and Amenities Group of the Parliamentary Labour Party. He was first secretary of the group and then chairman. His support for the arts was non-political, and he was able to influence both Labour and Conservative colleagues. On Valentine's Day 1964, Dr Barnett Stross received a knighthood for his services to *The Arts,* which was welcomed by people in North Staffordshire and throughout the country.

Dr Stross was active at Westminster in attempts to secure support for the Royal Shakespeare Theatre. On December the 6th, 1960 he drew the matter of the Commonwealth Arts Festival of 1964 to the Chancellor of the Exchequer, Mr Selwyn and suggested that in view of the importance of this international occasion and to celebrate the 400th birthday of William Shakespeare, the nation could build on the South Bank of the River Thames…

"… an art gallery, a national theatre, and a conference hall, that the total cost to be borne will be less than £5 million, and that this would make the South Bank one of the great cultural centres of the world? If the Chancellor cares about such things, and we all hope he does, will he take action when he is approached to see that such plans may be brought to a fruitful end?"

Between 1955 and 1965, Art and Amenities overrode party political boundaries in the House of Commons thanks to his working partnership with Sir Hamilton Kerr, Conservative MP for Cambridge. Divided politically but united in their artistic interests, the pair won many hard-fought battles for the Arts, as chairmen of their respective parties, Arts and Amenities Committees.

In a 1965 interview with journalist Richard Seddon reproduced in the Birmingham Daily Post on Tuesday the 9th of November, Sir Barnett described his role in protecting and promoting the nation's art and culture. From his Kensington flat, he said,

"It was in 1945 that, with the support of Mrs Barbara Ayrton Gould MP, I persuaded the Prime Minister, with Party approval, to form the Arts and Amenities Committee. It was only a beginning and to get as many as 80 members to attend a meeting was really something."

> "One of our early concerns was when we saw the danger of London losing its position as the art market of the world because of the war. We went to various Ministers and said: *'Help us not to lose this.'*"

> "In 1947 and 1948 we asked George Tomlinson (then Minister of Education) to assist municipal and privately endowed galleries, museums, and libraries. We thought that £1/4million would help the most needy municipal and private collections. Unfortunately, the Association of Municipal Corporations feared that help of that kind might mean Government inspection and was unwilling to pay."

About 1953, the Conservative Government created an Arts and Amenities Committee like that of the Labour Party, with Sir Hamilton Kerr as chairman. In the House, he and Stross worked collaboratively and were known as the *"Heavenly Twins,"* because if a minister had to be approached, they usually went to see him together. This cross-party presence gave them twice the power and their proposal an increased chance of success;

> "Hamilton Kerr and I called our method the *'bi-partisan technique'* and with it we brought about our ideas in the House, and we gained great support. I recall Hugh Gaitskell saying: *'This is the way to do it!'*"

In his interview with Seddon, Sir Barnett told of the time when he and Sir John Barbirolli addressed a gathering in Manchester and staved off the withdrawal of the city's £18,000 grant to the Halle Orchestra; of how the *"Heavenly Twins"* pressed for and secured on both sides of the House agreement for more funds for the national collections; of how they tackled Mr Harold Macmillan on the iniquities of the Entertainment Tax; then there was the prevention of the export of the Goya portrait of the Duke of Wellington; the Civic Society's struggles to preserve and restore famous buildings and streets…

However, the campaign which evoked the most passion was the da Vinci drawing of *"The Virgin and Child with Saint Anne and Saint John the Baptist"* (right). The only extant larger-scale drawing by the artist Leonardo da Vinci, in 1962 the *"cartoon"* was put on sale for £800,000.

Stross, at the time the Chairman of the Arts and Amenities Committee, was horrified and immediately led the drive to keep the Leonardo drawing in Britain. On Friday the 9th of March, to the press Dr Stross made a pledge - in terms of emotion and conviction it was reminiscent of another promise he had made in Hanley 20 years before:

He declared that he would organise a deputation from both sides of the House to ask the Chancellor to authorise a special Treasury grant to buy the drawing. And seek the help of wealthy businessmen interested in art in the hope of persuading one to buy the Leonardo.

Said Dr Stross to the Daily Herald:

"It would be a tragedy, I would even say criminal, if Britain lost this Leonardo."

"If I was Chancellor of the Exchequer and allowed it to be taken away from Britain by a foreign buyer, I would die of a broken heart."

The following week, the Daily Mirror announced: "An All-Party group of MPs will act this week in an effort to stop the possible export of Leonardo da Vinci's charcoal drawing of the Virgin and Child worth about £1,000,000. In a move to put its finances on a steadier footing, the Royal Academy of Arts has announced that the masterpiece is for sale. The MPs, led by Dr Barnett Stross (Lab) and Sir Hamilton Kerr (Con) fear the drawing may go to an overseas buyer. They are likely to press for a Treasury assurance that no export licence would be issued."

Consequently, the drawing was exhibited in the National Gallery, where it was seen by over a quarter of a million people in a little over four months, many of whom made donations in order to keep it in the United Kingdom. The price was eventually met, thanks in part to contributions from the National Art Collections Fund and the help given by Robert Lindsay, 29th Earl of Crawford who, according to Stross, **"did a wonderful job"** in raising the public subscriptions.

Divided politically but united in their artistic interests, Sir Hamilton Kerr, Conservative MP for Cambridge (left) and Sir Barnett Stross won many hard-fought battles for the Arts, as Chairmen of their respective parties Arts and Amenities Committees. Between 1955 and 1965 Art and Amenities overrode party political boundaries in the House of Commons thanks to this working, "Heavenly Twins" partnership.

Top: A small ceremony took place in Lidice on the 21st of June 1957 which saw Dr Stross receive the freedom of the village of Lidice from the Mayor of the village, Libuše Prošková; Bottom: On the 10th of June 1962 Dr Stross spoke with President Novotný at the 20th commemoration of the Lidice atrocity. Stross led an extensive Midlands delegation with representatives from Stoke-on-Trent City Council, Coventry City Council and other cities. He accompanied the President around the Lidice Gallery to view an exhibition of children's artwork. The inaugural annual International Children's Exhibition of Fine Art would take place in 1967.

In June 1962, while visiting Lidice, the place that he had grown to cherish so much, Dr Barnett Stross found inspiration for his final and most culturally significant Peace project. With the growing realisation that his time on earth was coming to a close, Stross harnessed his love of artwork and friendship, making it the catalyst for an appeal to respected art contacts and other invited artists from around the world, as he requested their donations with the express intention of establishing a unique, specialist collection of paintings, sculptures, and other pieces of fine art - to warn future generations about the horrors of warfare. The Lidice Collection of Modern Art was collated in 1964 and is now housed in the Lidice Gallery of the Lidice Memorial.

LANGUAGE & DEBATE

In order to make his case effectual, use of pathos, word-play, metaphor, allegory, the nuances of language, combined with societal, historical, and cultural references emboldened Stross's speeches; for example, when alerting the British House of Commons to the potential consequences of insufficient aid to the Indian sub-continent, Stross turned to a knowledge of Indian culture to describe the tragic effects a lack of adequate foodstuffs would cause:

"I should like to crave the indulgence of the House in saying that many years ago, I came across an example of unnecessary suffering associated with poverty, which I have been unable to forget. In those areas of the world where drought is frequent, crops can fail and sometimes almost entirely fail. At such times, particularly in the Central Provinces of India, a particular vegetable, a sort of vetch, named lathyrus sativus, will grow when everything else fails. Everyone has known for a very long time that this is a poisonous plant when it becomes the staple diet of the people for many weeks. The earliest Hindu medical literature mentions it. Hippocrates described its poisoning effect. Attempts have been made by legislation, without success, to stop it being eaten, for when hunger is real, we cannot legislate to stop people from eating anything they can. In 1921, 8% of the people in the Central Provinces were afflicted with poisoning through eating this vetch, which they ate because they had nothing else to eat. In a bad year, 60,000 people had been known to die of it.

The disease is called lathyrism. It struck me as particularly horrible, because first paralysis of one or both lower limbs begins to take place and the man afflicted shuffles along, holding himself up with one tall stick. Later, one sees him with two sticks for support, and finally his legs will carry him no longer and he shuffles along the ground, pushing himself with his hands, which he protects with wooden shoes. He is fortunate when he dies. It is a horrible complaint because it chiefly afflicts males between the age of 15 and 35 years, in the very prime of life. The knowledge that such things happen should enable the House at least to accept that this is a serious Motion, and should offer it no opposition, but give it full support."

Dr Stross's passion for the diverse to elucidate his arguments delighted his colleagues in the House.' An interesting occasion was his anecdote about how the breakfast-table pot of marmalade got its name. Stross told the 'Commons that he understood oranges were originally worth £10 each, and that it was recorded that Mary Queen of Scots received a confection of orange and sugar to combat her migraine attacks. As a result, some people claim that the word "marmalade" came into existence as a corruption of "Marie et malade." Stross was using the example to move the annulment of the Welfare Foods (Great Britain) Amendment (No. 2)

Order, 1957, with particular reference to the supply of orange juice to children who had reached two years of age. He declared the Order meant that the Minister was to deny this important welfare food to children after their second birthday, while they had had this privilege until they were five. Orange juice was provided to young children to supply an ancillary food factor, Vitamin C, to protect them in their most tender years against scurvy and allied disorders.

LATER YEARS

The health of Dr Stross declined from 1960. He had asthma and bronchitis, was very thin and was constantly coughing. This was especially because of his lifelong smoking habit; he had spent so much time warning others of the consequences of the addiction he had neglected to do anything about it himself! Despite these issues, according to his young relatives, nieces, and nephews, he always stayed an educator, was very talkative and interesting company.

As his health failed in 1964, Sir Barnett Stross, the MP, found it difficult to cope with the extra responsibilities the post of Deputy Secretary of Health within Prime Minister Harold Wilson's Government demanded of him. Stross worked on the left wing of the Labour party and had become a friend of Wilson, thanks to the support of Aneurin Bevan, Minister of Health. But Wilson's majority in parliament was so slim that even sick people, including Bob, had to be brought in to Parliament to vote on crucial matters. But Bob was becoming too frail to fulfil these obligations, and he felt compelled to resign from political life.

Stross had married a family friend and long-term secretary Gwendoline Chesters in 1963. They lived together in a flat in London and would spend their free time in Ramsgate, Kent.

As both his marriages were childless, Stross enjoyed the company of his nieces, nurturing in them their interests in art, literature, and politics.

Olive had been kind but was eccentric. Gwen was considerate, tender, and very gentle to Barnett. She cared for him when he was already in poor health. Ian Macilwain states:

"I heard Bob describe how he proposed to Gwen. He did it in a coffee shop and bought some flowers. But the cafe was very crowded, and when Bob asked for her hand, another lady was sitting at the table with them. Bob asked her if she could move, but she refused. So, he decided to continue with the marriage proposal, anyway! The older lady listened and then said, 'That's nice!'"

Barnett Stross received another award from the Czechoslovakian Government on the 4th of September 1963. At a ceremony in Prague, Stross was appointed an Honorary Member of the Czechoslovak Society for International Relations for his work advancing Czechoslovak - British Friendship, alongside Mr Stephen Swingler, MP for Newcastle-under-Lyme.

During Barnett Stross's final years, he became very ill and aged quickly. Ian has a few memories of visiting the Stross couple's apartment in Palace Gate behind Albert Hall, London - and recalls his unusual appetites:

"We visited them several times in their apartment. I remember their apartment as very dark with atmosphere and quiet acoustics. On one side of the chaise lounge in the drawing room were the pedestals on which were placed many of Epstein's bronze statues - heads, which Bob had in his collection. These were accompanied by niches in which numerous were exhibited paintings by Lowry, Sickert and several others...

... I clearly remember Bob and Gwen's favourite snack—because we, as children, hated it! She served slices of tongue with chicory and chicory salad with monotonous regularity. At first it was a shock and then terribly bitter! Now, through the wisdom I have gained with the distance of time, I know that their food has been influenced by the Jewish tradition, but we did not perceive these details at that young age."

Sir Barnett Stross died from a heart attack at University College Hospital, London, on Saturday the 13th of May 1967. Tributes poured in from people in all walks of life, folk who knew him as a politician, doctor, reformer, internationalist, or patron of the arts. Sir Barnett, who was 67 years old, was a Stoke-on-Trent MP for 21 years and served as Parliamentary Secretary to the Ministry of Health in the Wilson Labour Government. He was knighted in 1964, was a member of Stoke-on-Trent City Council from November 1938 until May 1952, and during this time was an Alderman for 21 years.

The funeral of Sir Barnett Stross took place at Golders' Green Crematorium, London, on the afternoon of Wednesday the 20th of May 1967. It was preceded by a service in the Liberal Synagogue in the crematorium grounds—right up to the end, he saw past petty political affiliation. Family recollections of the service are that it was secular in nature, with one psalm being read - Psalm 23, which Bob chose himself.

MAN OF THE PEOPLE

Dr Barnett Stross wanted to help and enrich the lives of others by carrying through the work he did. That was why he trained as a doctor in his university days, eventually arriving in Stoke-on-Trent from Leeds to help ease the chronic industrial diseases of the potters and the miners, which were worsened by the poverty of the 1930s.

The years following the *Wall Street Crash* unleashed tremendous hardship on people in cities across the Midlands. It was this urgent need to find solutions, which more than anything drove Stross to join a political party in 1930 and become the councillor for the Shelton ward in 1938. He soon realised that in order to make a significant difference, it would be necessary to stand for Parliament. Even then, as a young man, he saw that his most telling contribution would be to bring about changes in national policy by Parliamentary means.

In 1926, when Dr Barnett Stross was appointed medical adviser to the North Staffordshire Miners' Federation and the National Society of Pottery Workers, it was a time prior to the existence of a Welfare State in Britain and many people were desperately poor. Stross supported the many thousand factory and colliery workers of the area, who, due to their work, often contracted occupational diseases and accidents. Often, if the worker was in no position to pay, he would do this for free. Not only did he care for their health, but he would extend the offer of help to the whole family. He launched a campaign in the media for financial compensation for former miners who suffered from severe lung disease problems; he campaigned to compensate employees who endured an accident at work, or other serious diseases with permanent consequences.

Sir Barnett Stross devoted the largest part of his life to his political career, playing a leading role in the preservation of relations between the UK and Czechoslovakia and in the renewal of the village of Lidice. As a member of the Foreign Affairs Committee, he kept in touch with Czechoslovakia until the end. On the 20th of June 1947, the Czechoslovak Government awarded him the highest state award, Commandership of the Order of the White Lion, for his effort to support the renewal of Lidice. Indeed, it was the establishment of the movement to support Lidice, which Stross considered his greatest personal success; he maintained that the real achievement of the campaign was the effect it had as a psychological weapon of warfare. He regarded it a great personal honour to be awarded the Freedom of Lidice on the 21st of June 1957.

Bob Stross was a stoic, someone who tirelessly worked, without exception for the welfare of others less able and less fortunate than himself. He loved being within the community of Hanley and Shelton at a sing-song, a dance, or some other event. Memorable social occasions were held regularly during the war at Tinkersclough Mission Hall, off Clough Street, in a room from which they were eventually bombed out. Here, with relish he would add his own compositions like "Lidice Shall Live Again" to the set, and play other North Staffordshire related songs such as "The Potters' Song"—he would inspire the audience to sing along too, as he played expertly on the piano and led the way with a smooth baritone voice:

"So, it's 'throw, throw, throw,' and it's 'turn, turn, turn,'

Then it's into the oven and it's 'burn, burn, burn,'

On and on from morn' till night, working hard and going strong,

While all the wheels around us sing "The Potters' Song."

Many North Staffordshire people felt indebted to Sir Barnett as the man who fought the impersonal machinery of the former Ministry of Pensions and National Insurance, and its predecessors in efforts to obtain or increase industrial injuries benefit for them. But in terms of the MP—constituent relationship, in terms of the residents of Hanley and Shelton their indebtedness was reciprocated. Of North Staffordshire people, he once said:

"I doubt if there is a more hospitable group of people in the world, or a group who are more kindly disposed to the stranger in their midst. I have found it very easy to serve them. It has always been a joy to do so."

Dr Stross was a reassuring type, a calming influence who put people at ease. When he first spoke to the Women's Council on *Comfort and Health versus the Danger of Bombs* on Wednesday September the 18th 1940, one of the first matters Stross brought up was sleep. Now the importance of people not getting enough sleep was, in all likelihood, not on the members' minds as they made their way to the presentation. Yet, they listened as Dr Stross explained how deprivation of sleep would cause a lowering of public morale - one of the Nazis' aims.

"As night-time beverages he advised them to drink cocoa, chocolate or---best of all---hot milk, as being inducive of sleep: as against tea or coffee, which stimulated the brain and had the reverse effect. If tea was drunk at all, it should be as weak as possible." the Sentinel reported.

During the Second World War, the Coalition Government's Ministry of Food sought Barnett Stross's expert knowledge, to which he contributed by giving healthy lifestyle lectures up and down the country to workers in factories and a variety of associations and community groups - gathered together in packed works canteens and village halls, where wives and mothers paid attention to his recipes for healthy living. During one of these lectures, a German bomb struck the auditorium, and he was extracted from the rubble bearing serious injuries. Somehow, through all this, he attended most of his City Council meetings where, in the months leading up to the war, he had been publicly warning others about the dangers of appeasing or making peace with Hitler.

Dr Barnett Stross and constituents stop for a photo outside St Marks Church, Shelton, Stoke-on-Trent before setting off for a tour of the Houses of Parliament in June 1948.

The mild speech and cultured manner of Bob Stross veiled great passions and causes. They were never far away from his thoughts and they would surface spontaneously in speeches when opening exhibitions or would show up as off-the-cuff quotes in newspaper articles. As we have seen, notwithstanding Lidice and the welfare of workers and the less well off, just some of Dr Stross's many other campaigns included raising funds for Manchuria, Spain and Russia; providing support and promotion to artists and ceramicists fleeing Nazi Germany; a universal superannuation scheme to enable everyone to retire with dignity; alongside Ellis Smith, MP for Stoke-on-Trent South; concerted efforts to raise the quality of life for people in Asian and African nations; work with UNRRA and the Save the Children Fund; a myriad of local and national public health drives; several international fundraising and preservation programmes; and, on a less serious plane, his regular rebukes to Stoke-on-Trent for not buying enough decent pictures.

By the end, Sir Barnett Stross had earned deserved recognition as a doctor, an authority on industrial disease, a community leader, a politician, a supporter of the arts, a promoter of peace, an internationalist, and a philanthropist with a streak of generosity a mile wide. And he certainly was a big-hearted man. North Staffordshire, in particular, was often showered with donations of artwork, either directly from Stross himself or indirectly, through his connections. When he left for London in 1952, works of art from his collection were also to be seen at Cartwright House, Hanley; the local WEA Headquarters; and at the Potteries Museum and Art Gallery. Latterly, he gave a choice of paintings to the Harold Clowes Community Association in Bentilee, near Hanley. Finally, let us not underestimate his personal dedication to the cause of higher education in North Staffordshire and of setting up its University College in 1949 *(today's Keele University)* and to making a full commitment towards its success through his donation of 60 paintings and an Epstein bronze.

Such was the extent of Dr Stross's global ambition that, unconventionally, he would use the word *"International"* as a proper noun. His desire for inclusiveness, fellowship and togetherness can be found in this simple habit—which certainly does frustrate Microsoft's spell checker! Throughout his political career, he did it—refusing to split East from West. We can see it as a fundamental flaw in character, that for all his cultural and linguistic strengths in the field of art, society, medicine, and politics, Stross was a naïve and dangerous figure, prone to place his colleagues in geo-politically fraught situations. Alternatively, we can see Stross as a visionary, ideologically timeless man, one of the world's great stoics who preferred to be a good man than waste time arguing about what one should be. One could argue that if only more could follow in Stross's footsteps, we would have more rose gardens and more children fed.

Dr Barnett Stross's sensibilities towards youth are best illustrated in a report published in the North Staffordshire regional paper, the Evening Sentinel. Stross, in declaring a *Children's Art Exhibition* open at the Burslem School of Art, a mere nine days before the Lidice tragedy, on Monday the 1st of June 1942, said the young people's artwork was,

"... most interesting and stimulating. Their drawings, representative of many countries, held a remarkable unity of thought in artistic expression. Their work represented a true brotherhood of life. As regards the post-war era, the problem of educational reorganisation must be placed to the fore - however war-weary or tired people might become, time must be found now to decide on the more simple things which should be done, such as raising the school-leaving age and providing a better system of education. An immediate duty after the war was to make effective arrangements for feeding the schoolchildren of Europe, and then, after steps had been taken to preserve world peace and order, to plan for the unification of the peoples of the world."

How amazing that those sentiments should still remain and be carried forward today by the Lidice Gallery's International Children's Exhibition of Fine Arts (ICEFA).

Dr. Barnett Stross, who opened an exhibition of international children's art at the School of Art, Burslem, yesterday, admiring one of the exhibits in company with Mr. Gordon M. Forsyth, Mr. J. F. Carr, Alderman J. A. Dale and Mr. E. J. Wheldon.

"Dr Barnett Stross" by Grete Marks - late 1930s. Marks was one of the first female students to be admitted to the famed Bauhaus school of art and design in Germany. Famed for her pottery, when she had to flee Nazi Germany for fear of persecution, Barnett Stross helped her to gain recognition and employment in the ceramic wonderland of Stoke-on-Trent, by organising exhibitions and championing her work;

Dr Barnett Stross opened an international children's art exhibition at the Burslem School of Art on Monday the 1st of June 1942. The fortnight long display was organised by the Refugee Children's Evacuation Fund movement, had already appeared in London and other cities and arrangements were being made for it to be presented in America. The exhibition featured artworks produced by refugee children ages 2 to 17 years old, from Germany, Austria, Czecho-Slovakia, Yugo-Slavia, Spain and China, as well as evacuees from several British cities. Their work included paintings, sketches, and line drawings of an excellent standard.

TRIBUTES TO SIR BARNETT STROSS

Among the many tributes received by the North Staffordshire based Evening Sentinel, were the following:

Mr Stephen Swingler, Joint Parliamentary Secretary, Ministry of Transport and MP for Newcastle-under-Lyme said:

"Bob Stross, as we all knew him, was an outstanding and lovable character. He will be long remembered as an ever-helpful general practitioner. A first-class spokesman for industrial medicine, a great patron of the arts and the man who took a unique initiative during the war in founding the international movement to rebuild the ruined Bohemian village of Lidice. In all these spheres, Bob made a special contribution to North Staffordshire and its community life, and it was a great blow when he had to give up office on account of ill health. His own fortitude, and his wife's devotion, sustained the long struggle against terrific odds, which was characteristic of the battle he had fought on behalf of industrial workers throughout his life. We shall miss him very much and our heartfelt sympathy goes out to his widow."

Sir Albert Bennett, Leader of Stoke-on-Trent City Council, and a former Lord Mayor:

"I knew Sir Barnett as a doctor - to my family, as medical adviser to my trade union, as a friend, and as an idealist with great persuasive powers. In his capacity as a medical expert in the industrial field, he performed great service to the industrial workers and impressed the many tribunals before whom he appeared on their behalf. He was the man who inspired the Lidice Shall Live movement. He was an aesthete, an idealist - but also a realist. He was a great man of the people, a man who lived an extraordinarily useful life."

Mr Harry Taylor, former Town Clerk of Stoke-on-Trent, who was associated with many aspects of Sir Barnett's work:

"Dr Barnett Stross was in every sense a great man whose many talents were readily made available by him for the benefit of his fellows and his name will be remembered in the City of Stoke-on-Trent not only in official records but by what may be called the rank and file - the many hundreds of men and women who had direct contact with him in his medical practice, and through that channel the pottery and mining industries, and his political work. I suppose the best thing I can say about him is that he was accepted as a Potteries man, and that is indeed a tribute in this city.

He specialised in industrial diseases which attacked the workers in our staple industries, and while dealing with the wider implications on a national scale, also brought personal comfort to his many patients. He found time to become a member of the City Council and a very active member, too, in connection with health and welfare work. His immense professional knowledge was always readily available to the members and officers of the corporation. I can only touch on his work for the Lidice movement. He was the inspiration behind the effort which arose to try to right in some small measure the evil results of war. He made many gifts of paintings and works of art to the City of Stoke-on-Trent, the University of Keele and, most recently, to the Harold Clowes Community Hall.

I think, however, that his work as a Member of Parliament must rank high in his achievements. The combination of his medical knowledge and Parliamentary know-how, together with the solid support of the Members of Parliament for North Staffordshire, was responsible for many health reforms connected with our local industries and together they did a wonderful job in helping the city in many other ways. He did remarkably well for his adopted country, and he will be missed in a very personal way."

Mr Jack Ashley, Labour MP for Stoke-on-Trent South said:

"I never had the pleasure of meeting Bob Stross because he retired before I entered the House of Commons, but he was frequently spoken about in the most glowing terms by many of his former colleagues. His death has caused great sadness among all those MPs who knew him and loved him in the House for so many years."

Warm tributes came from two retired Potteries MPs who, along with Sir Barnett, formed the trio known in the House of Commons as *"Stoke United."*

Mrs Harriet Slater, speaking from her home in Anglesey said:

"The death of Bob Stross has really upset me. He was such a great fellow. He always gave himself for other people. He did everything with such charm, but with much determination. The people of Stoke-on-Trent owe him a great debt, not only as a doctor, but as an MP who fought for improvement in their lives. In the last Parliament, when we depended on every body's vote, he never shirked his duty even when he was desperately ill."

Mr Ellis Smith, who has been ill for some time at his home at Eccles, commented,

"Sir Barnett Stross and I were always the best of friends. He was one of the most public-spirited men I have ever known. He was well-informed but satisfied to use his knowledge for the sake of others. I regret his passing very much and I am sorry to be unable to travel to London for the funeral. My sympathy too, goes to his wife, Gwen."

Mr Alfred Dulson, General Secretary of the National Society Pottery Workers said:

"Sir Barnett's work for this union is very well known. He was our adviser for a great many years on industrial diseases. He *(took?)* the union's case to authorities to obtain the 10 Pottery Health and Welfare Regulations, a great step forward in the industry and after he became an MP, he continued to help in an honorary capacity. If ever we were in doubt, we consulted him, and he always responded. Sir Barnett was a wonderful friend and adviser to all members of this union. He devoted his life to public service, and to this union especially, he gave a great part of his time."

Mr Jack Lalley, Midland Area President, N.U.M wrote:

"Sir Barnett's association with the miners of this area began in 1926, when he was appointed their medical adviser at the same time as a similar appointment to the pottery workers. He represented those two bodies in the House of Commons until his retirement. He assisted in introducing legislation in connection with industrial diseases, and he always held the miners and the potters in the highest regard. A year ago, he told me that he treasured a gift of silver, which the miners presented to him in recognition of his devotion. We are, of course, also very conscious of the fact that it was with Hugh Leese, a former Secretary of the North Staffs Miners' Federation, that he planned the campaign, which resulted in the Lidice movement. We shall deeply miss Sir Barnett, and we extend our sincere condolences to his widow."

Dr Barnett Stross c1934

CONCLUSION & OBSERVATIONS

Thanks for making it this far. There are just a few pressing thoughts I need to get down, including a few matters which gain in significance the closer you are to the project. To my friends in the Western Hemisphere, I apologise this section is mostly about Britain. Hopefully, at some point, I will complete a more in-depth look at the Lidice Lives campaign and its dissemination across Latin and South America.

SUMMING UP

During the harsh winter of 1947, following a war which necessitated Britain selling off the family silver to continue fighting the Nazis, it became clear that Britain was a former world power, economically brittle and reliant on the USA. Following years of openly supporting the Soviet Union and much that it stood for, stepping into line, changing sides, or keeping quiet in an increasingly Americanised Britain became the preferred options for campaigners formerly linked to pro-Soviet wartime causes. Adopting a colourful, nuanced position was not the fashionable course of action and could land you into trouble in this new, binary world. The case of the Lidice Shall Live movement and its leaders is a prime example. Britain's new bold propagandist approach, outlined so forthrightly by Ernest Bevin MP early in 1947, brought the need to reflect and reassess one's own stance within the hierarchy.

During the latter years of the 1940s, one by one key figures of the Lidice Shall Live campaign quietly left the friendship movement or openly spoke out against it. Will Lawther, Arthur Baddeley, Hugh Leese, Harold Lockett, and George Jones, all keen to see a nationalised coal industry succeed, promoted an Anglo-American Moral Re-Armament agenda to their members. Frank Hampl, Sudeten German Jew and Secretary of the Lidice Shall Live movement, was deported back to Czechoslovakia. With few members left, from around 1950, the movement effectively became a front for Dr Barnett Stross MP and his ideas and campaigns, working in tandem with Lou Kenton and the British-Czechoslovak Friendship League based in London. This partnership organised many projects: the campaign for the rose garden of 1955, the *Rose of Lidice* venture, the Lidice art collection of 1964, and the many bilateral exchanges being the most prominent.

In the USA, the Lidice atrocity impacted an American society still reeling from the bombing attack on Pearl Harbour. The sense of collective moral outrage provided the newly formed Writers' War Board with an opportunity to use Lidice as an effective propaganda tool to help bolster calls for America's full entry into the European War and the fight against both Nazi Germany and Japan. Britain was in a different situation: there, an affiliation comprising a mix of nationalities, occupations and classes had been actively working with a common purpose to survive the war for years. The majority of working people in Britain disapproved of Chamberlain's policy of appeasement towards Hitler from the very start and publicly declared their sense of shame at the signing of the Munich Agreement. Across the British trade unions from the time of the annexation of the Sudetenland in 1938, there was an agreement made to help victims of Nazi subjugation in Czecho-Slovakia. The Mineworkers' Federation of Great Britain led on this promise. This assured the North Staffordshire Miners' Federation's idea of Lidice Shall Live, put forward as a motion by George Jones of the Midland Miners' Federation on July the 20th 1942, would be carried unanimously. In Stoke-on-Trent, the launch pad and heart of the campaign, the miners would lend their support to Dr Barnett Stross - a Polish,

Jewish *immigrant.* Motivation was not an issue. Empathy and camaraderie for those experiencing the fullest savagery of Nazi tyranny led to a fundraising cause to build the village anew.

Looking back through the history of the Lidice Shall Live campaign, it is possible to make a case of it being a failure. When it launched, the target for the fund ranged from £100,000 to £1,000,000, the money was going to rebuild completely the village, the new Lidice would provide for the returning villagers everything they would need to live their later years in complete comfort and peace, and Lidice would be the site of a prestigious mining educational and research institute. Moreover, the initial spectrum of support the campaign received painted a rosy picture of what a new, post-war working relationship with a freshly installed, *socially democratic,* Czechoslovak Government would be like.

As we know, things did not turn out the way campaigners envisioned. In reality, the total reached was a fraction of the target set by the campaign leaders; the £32,375 raised could only ever be a significant contribution towards the total cost of constructing the new Lidice—which was principally paid for by the new Czechoslovak Government, able to commit £250,000 to the Lidice project since it was buoyed by the economic aid provided to it by the US led UNRRA programme. The mining institute that Barnett Stross and the North Staffordshire miners were so invested in was adopted but given instead to the Moravian mining city of Ostrava. And, it transpired that the new Czechoslovak Government, which overthrew democracy in February 1948, was in the pocket of Stalin and the USSR. Worse still, several members of its national assembly who had played a part in the Lidice Shall Live campaign would be persecuted for their links to the West.

Despite all the reservations, the fact remains that today the legacy of the *Lidice Lives* and the *Lidice Shall Live* campaigns is a brotherhood drawing together like-minded peoples thousands of miles apart—just like the original grassroots movements. It exists. It is there. It is a precious gift handed down to descendants by ancestors who decided to name their young baby daughters in honour of all child victims of persecution; fight to ensure this dreadful massacre would not win out in the end and that right would prevail; show camaraderie for a fellow mining community in need; and reverse the attempt to wipe out Czech heritage and culture.

As Dr Barnett Stross and others explained, the Lidice Shall Live movement's significance was more psychological than financial at heart. The campaign meant a lot to the war-torn people of Czecho-Slovakia, its émigrés and those left behind under Nazi, and later Communist rule; it helped restore their faith in the people of Britain and the West. The Lidice Shall Live movement sent out a clear signal to the British Government that kowtowing to Hitler over Czechoslovakia had always been objectionable to a majority of ordinary British people, applying the added pressure on Foreign Secretary Anthony Eden MP to secure the public annulment of the Munich Agreement a few weeks before the campaign's launch in Hanley on the 6th of September. The miners of North Staffordshire and Durham, who followed soon after, gave the same half-crown donation to Lidice as they had done for major international campaigns to help Spain, Russia, the Red Cross, China, as well as the national appeals for urgent supplies of weaponry, such as tanks and planes. This happened after both regions had suffered devastating pit disasters during some of the darkest days of the war - Sneyd and Murton Collieries. Instead of looking for differences, the cultural, social, and working relationship between Czechoslovaks and the British during and immediately after the Second World War was based on shared sensibilities, characteristics, and tastes. Finally, the reaction to the Lidice atrocity by the free world sent a clear signal to the Third Reich that they were steadfast and that justice for the Czechoslovak people was just a matter of time.

TWO OBSERVATIONS

POLITICAL EXPEDIENCY

I think that the chief lesson we can take from the Lidice Shall Live movement, when we consider its successes and failures, is that the propagation and development of *Peace and Friendship* between nations need not be arduous work but it requires regular observation and maintenance. It is no coincidence that the movement was most cohesive and effective when the outcome of the war was still undecided and all parties were pulling together in a common cause. From my experience over the last 11 years, to use a potted analogy, I would describe it as a very rewarding but fragile process, as priceless as the finest porcelain, but easily damaged over time if vulnerable to disturbance or not sensitively overseen; easily abused if not entered into in all sincerity through a long-term common vision, supported by a comprehensive, agreed strategy by parties who share cultural, political, economic, and human sensibilities. It is a sad reality that internationalist programmes are the first to be pushed to the side-lines when political expediency dictates - as was the case when the Attlee Government decided it was time to make an Alien of the Lidice Shall Live campaign from 1947; we could say the same about the UK's decision to leave the bilateral Erasmus+ educational scheme because UK - EU relations have become strained since the Brexit vote.

THE SPIRIT OF MAN

The most critical aspect to history's litany of wicked atrocities, of which the tragedies of Lidice, Putten, Oradour-sur-Glane, Telavåg, the Katyn massacre, Srebrenica, the Siege of Aleppo, the Mỹ Lai massacre, and Bloody Sunday make up just a tiny representative fraction on a timeline, concerns the contributions they can make to increasing empathy and co-operation in today's world. Each aberration of humankind has its own narrative distinct from the next and it is of critical importance that each *story* be told, uncovered in a world in which income disparities are widening, human displacement is escalating, and the abuse of power by many governments is a significant threat to human rights and life itself.

In keeping the memory of the Lidice Shall Live campaign alive, the element of human sensibility and the innate quality of *"spirit"* are relevant; how a *"spirit of man"* applies to the tragedy in the roles that fate has in store for the respective protagonists, regardless of whether looked upon as a religious construct or as a state of mind at some psychological snap-shot. There is a *"spirit of man"* that destroyed Lidice. Then there is the *"spirit of man"* that built Lidice anew. One walked over men, women, and children with a callousness, without a thought for humanity and with no sense of reason or empathy; its life giver is blind devotion to an ideology, its reward career advancement in exchange for stamping out life and opportunity.

The other *"spirit"* is a more holistic concept whose reward is more qualitative in the short term because it usually involves sacrifice and often only modest financial reward, but it involves mutual support for the greater good. Building a new Lidice attracted campaigners thousands of miles of apart, and the village's construction in the late 1940s and 1950s brought volunteers from around the world - it also spawned a legacy of positivity which continues to this day.

The dark and the light spirits live within us all, the issue is an undercurrent running through this book. In the narrative, several of the historical characters covered by this work turn up more than once. Seldom is there a consistency in their behaviour throughout years, as governments change and political allegiances realign. Most players in the script reveal their complexities, their idiosyncrasies. The simplest actor to critique is Dr (Sir) Barnett Stross. His political and human sensibilities remained consistent yet nuanced, though they might well have landed him in trouble had he not been Parliament's doctor, dishing out free healthcare to the other MPs. But Stross's greatest gift was his far-sightedness, manifested in his ability to turn savage atrocity into victory, with a worldwide legacy that has stood the test of time.

A FINAL ROUND-UP

In 2011, at our first meetings with Mrs Ivona Kasalická and Mr Červencl of the Lidice Memorial; the Mayor of Lidice, Mrs Veronika Kellerová; and staff at surrounding schools, there was a resounding consensus to combine efforts to restore the name of Sir Barnett Stross and his work in creating an international network which worked for peace. A classic example of this would be promotion of the tremendous Garden of Peace & Friendship, which he conceived, and inaugurated in 1955. Henceforth, we decided that projects running from Stoke-on-Trent would highlight the celebratory aspects of the Lidice Shall Live movement, as well as the commemorative aspects of the events which took place at Lidice; the village's relationship to Stoke-on-Trent; and the ongoing international legacy of Lidice's rebirth, in order to emphasise the victory of love over hate.

Today, the communities of San Jeronimo, Mexico; Phillips, Wisconsin, USA; Lidice, Rio Claro, Brazil; Stoke-on-Trent, UK; and many other fellow towns and neighbourhoods remember the events of the 10th of June 1942 with reverence. But now, several mark those dates associated with the building of the new village, putting on events linked to re-christening anniversaries or the launch of the Lidice Shall Live campaign - as in the case of Stoke-on-Trent. On social media gathers an entire community of thousands. There, members share photos of their town, events, discuss their background; and a community of ladies christened "Lidice" meet up from across North, Latin and South America to chat. To date, with help from partners in Stoke-on-Trent and the rest of the UK, Lidice and the rest of Czechia, South America and the United States, the non-profit making organisation Lidice Lives has directly completed and facilitated exhibitions, sculptures, commemorations, books, cultural exchanges, school exchanges, and dance pieces, plaques, and films; presentations in schools, resource packs, merchandise, and social media campaigns to share knowledge of this inspirational account. I cannot speak for the other trustees of Lidice Lives, but the objectives for me include securing full recognition of Sir Barnett Stross, expanding the gift of international fellowship, and creating a sculpture garden honouring the role the world's communities played defying Nazism and ensuring Lidice was built afresh, with a special place reserved for the many cities, towns and villages with direct experience of atrocity, such as Distomo in Greece, but also, those towns and cities in North, Latin and South America, Europe and elsewhere who share an *empathetic bond* in terms of their commemorative relationship with Lidice and communities like it.

"Liberty is strengthened by Freedom not by blood and iron"
Tomáš Masaryk

As a native of Stoke-on-Trent, I vaguely remember acting out parts in primary school plays which featured the "pits and the pots" in the mid-1970s. I cannot remember any mention of Lidice or Sir Barnett Stross, unfortunately. Looking back now, it would have been nice to have known about the Lidice Shall Live campaign as it is indeed a proud moment for the city - as it surely is for cities like Derby, Nottingham, Coventry, and Birmingham too. Finally, casting an eye over the Lidice Shall Live movement, perhaps it really does put a lid on an age-old argument about where Stoke-on-Trent spiritually belongs... It is a Midlands town, after all.

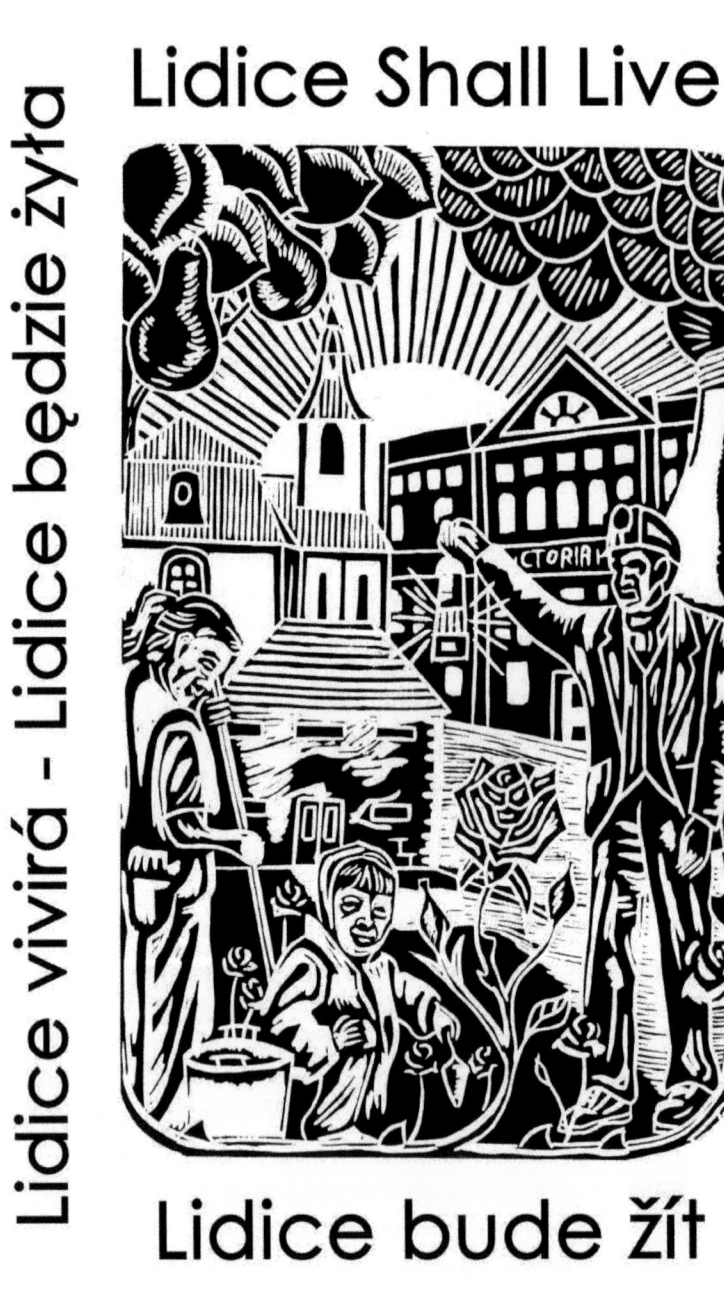

Lidice Shall Live

Lidice vivirá - Lidice będzie żyła

Lidice viverá - Лидице будет жить

Lidice bude žít

And in that sense the incongruousness of beauty in such an ostensibly dark place, allows a space for contemplation about the past, the present, the future; and the part we have to play in it. AG 2022

APPENDICES

LEADING BRITISH FIGURES WITHIN THE LIDICE SHALL LIVE CAMPAIGN

FRED HANCOCK

Fred Hancock was born in 1873 in Talke and attended Butt Lane National School, just outside Stoke-on-Trent. Hancock was connected for the greater part of his working life with the coal industry in North Staffordshire. As a coal miner, Hancock became active in the North Staffordshire Miners' Association.

In 1914, he was appointed to take charge of the National Health Section, and the following year he became Financial Secretary and Organiser of the District Federation. He was appointed President in 1925, and in 1930 became Secretary and Agent when he succeeded his predecessor, Samuel Finney. He was also a member of the Midland Miners' Federation for 20 years and President for 14 years. In the course of his official trade union activities, Hancock paid visits to many countries. In his younger years, he had spent time in America, where he studied at Allegheny College in Pennsylvania; and Russia, where he formed a close friendship with Solomon Lozovsky, Soviet Propaganda Chief, who was then Secretary of the Soviet trade union movement. He frequently attended the Trades Union Congress, and in 1937 was its delegate to the Trades and Labour Congress of Canada.

Fred Hancock was an official of the North Staffordshire Miners' Federation for 27 years. For his retirement, in October 1941, a reception was held at the Co-operative Guildhall in Burslem, where key representatives of the North Staffordshire Miners' Federation, Coal Industry employers and associates met to celebrate the part Mr Hancock had played in advancing industrial relations. Employers' spokesperson Isaac Cumberbatch, Chairman of the North Staffordshire Colliery Owners' Association, paid a fine tribute to Fred describing that whilst in America, he had been in charge of a church and that he had done such an outstanding job of it that he was pressed to enter the ministry of the United States, but that he instead remained loyal to mining in North Staffordshire. He described how in 1914, Mr Hancock became an official of the Staffordshire Federation and, from then on, his…

"… **wonderful record of faithful service to miners and the mining industry**" ensued, "**and he could be proud of having played an important part in the many changes, industrial and social, which had been effected in North Staffordshire. High ideals and integrity of purpose in championing the causes of the workers.**"

Like other executives on the Board of the North Staffs Miners' Federation, Fred Hancock was a Methodist lay preacher in his spare time.

ARTHUR BADDELEY

Arthur Baddeley, an employee of the Chatterley Whitfield Collieries, was appointed *"Organiser"* to the North Staffordshire Miners' Federation at the monthly meeting of the District Council held at the Miners' Hall, Moorland Road on the afternoon of Monday September the 29th 1930.

Members selected him from a list of fourteen nominees submitted from across the district. Arthur is closely linked to the Lidice Shall Live campaign, having been President of the Federation at the movement's inception.

In early March 1948 it was announced that Baddeley, as Secretary and Agent of the North Staffordshire Area of the National Union of Mineworkers since 1946, had been elected, by ballot, full-time President of the newly constituted Midland Area of the NUM, which embraced North and South Staffordshire, Shropshire, Warwickshire, Cannock, and Highbury, with an approximate membership of 49,000.

Arthur Baddeley became a magistrate on the 30th of September 1944 - Miners' Hall House, Park Road, Burslem - President and treasurer of the North Staffs Miners' Federation.

"Though it has been totally destroyed, and our brother miners have been murdered, and the women and children battered and brutally treated by the Nazis, we say this village shall be remodelled and rebuilt, and the people shall rise and live again in a new spirit of fellowship and brotherhood. The miners would say to the world at large that their comrades of Lidice would never be forgotten and that the widows and orphans would be rescued, and that the village would be rebuilt as a lasting monument that this crime against humanity should never succeed."

In 2012, Muriel Stoddard, daughter of Arthur Baddeley, shared some of her recollections about her dad's experiences with an amateur film crew:

"In January 1942, there was a massive disaster at the Sneyd Colliery. Dad was part of a delegation that had to go around telling people that they had lost loved ones. And in that same year, we heard of the disaster in Czecho-Slovakia, when the tiny village of Lidice was razed to the ground by the Nazis. A lot of the people from the village were miners, and so the miners of Stoke-on-Trent became aware of what had happened in Czecho-Slovakia. Dad was part of a delegation which went out from Britain to Lidice for the stone laying ceremony and when he came back, he told us of things that had happened, but he didn't dwell on it. And he didn't say 'Oh, I'm the proud owner of a medal.' He was very modest. He had the medal, and that was it. He was very grateful and very honoured, I think, to have received the award"

HUGH LEESE

Mr Leese, who had been brought up in a Methodist household, became one of the best-known miners' leaders in the Midlands in the first half of the 20th century. Leese had entered the mining industry as a boy of 12 and became full-time Registration Officer of the North Staffordshire Miners' Federation in 1918, and was subsequently Treasurer, Secretary and President.

All sections of the mining industry were represented at a function at the Co-operative Cafe, Stoke, on Saturday November the 30th 1946 to celebrate his work in the federation upon his retirement, including colliery owners, managers, trade unionists, elected representatives, and industrial advisers.

Mr Harold Lockett, President of the North Staffordshire Area section of the newly formed National Union of Mine Workers spoke of the ability of Mr Leese as a negotiator and said that he had laid the foundation of the spirit of good feeling which existed between the colliery owners, managers, and men of North Staffordshire. Mr Leese said that he had enjoyed every minute of his work with the Federation and the industry. He went on to speak appreciatively of the work of all his colleagues and said that had it not been for the goodwill of the owners' representatives, the managers, and the officials of this district they would not have been able to build up the Federation. In thanking the owners for their co-operation and goodwill in the past, he said he trusted that, under nationalisation, the same feelings would continue. It was up to all those engaged in the industry, he said, to see that nationalisation worked successfully because once it was launched it would be too big a job on which to turn back.

Others spoke of their long associations with Mr Leese and of the valuable service he had rendered, not only to the Federation, but to the district and industry in general:

Mr Isaac William Cumberbatch, General Manager for the Coal Board North Staffordshire Area, said Mr Leese had got more for the miners in this district than any other man, with the result that North Staffordshire was the envy of every district in the country because of the harmonious conditions that existed between the owners and the men. Alderman Webb said that in Mr Leese, the trade union movement was losing a great man. Mr Emmett also paid tribute to Mr Leese, whilst Mr Crofts said that he had always had great confidence in the judgement of Mr Leese.

The following tribute to Hugh Leese was published in the October 2005 edition of the Newchapel Church Magazine and was contributed by his granddaughter, the late Doreen Booth:

Hugh Leese was born in 1880 in a cottage which at that time had only two bedrooms on High Street, Rookery, at the bottom of Harriseahead Lane, North Staffordshire. Being a family of nine boys and two girls, it must have been rather over-crowded. The boys all worked in the local pits and after the shift ended, they would race home to try to be the first in the tin bath on the hearth;

"Grandad would often tell us the last one in the water came out dirtier than when he went in! He had a wonderful sense of humour, which he retained the whole of his life."

By the 1930s, Leese had moved to number 26 on High Street and was next-door neighbour to colleague Arthur Baddeley. He lived there until he moved to the Miners' Hall in Burslem.

"Through hard work, he became Chairman of Kidsgrove Urban District Council. Later, he was appointed the Miners' Secretary of the North Staffordshire Miners' Federation and went to live at the Miners' Hall, Burslem. This was situated on the corner of Park Road and Moorland Road."

"As children, my brother Bernard, sister Jean and I would go with our parents from Rookery to visit Gran and Grandad. No cars in those days, but oh! the excitement of getting off the bus in Burslem by the old Swan Bank Methodist Chapel. Bernard, Jean, and I would run up Moorland Road to the Miners' Hall. We always knew if there was no one in, we only had to go through the park gates to find Gran and Grandad sitting on the seat by the Band Stand. In his deep booming voice, Grandad would say, *"Well! look who's here, it's Bernard, Jean, and Doreen."* The joy of that greeting has always been a memory to treasure.

He had a black swivel chair in his office and in turn he would whirl each of us round, laughing as much as we did."

"Grandad was on the Board of Management of the former Burslem and District Industrial Co-Operative Society. He became a Justice of the Peace and was a staunch worker at the Hamil Road Methodist Church. He visited many countries, including the Soviet Union. Wherever he went, he was well respected and looked upon as a fair and just character. After his retirement, he and Gran came back to live on Lawton Street, Rookery. He lived and worked tirelessly for the chapel on the High Street and was devastated when it finally had to close due to lack of funding. By this time, we had children of our own and they always referred to Grandad as *'Well done Grandad.'* The reason for this being, at family gatherings, the children would sing or recite, and granddad would clap his hands and say, "Well done my Alison, Melanie, Andrew or Adrian."

He was a granddad who we all loved and were very proud of. What more can I say except, "Well done.""?

The character of Hugh Leese draws particular comparison to the sensibilities of the early Chartists and Primitive Methodists, and their methods and teachings. Like the 19th century reformer William Lovett, a man who fought for universal suffrage and equality through the powers of creativity and vision, Leese was a 1930s exponent of the use of *moral force* in raising the standard of living of the working man. Like the rest of the 'Federation's executive, Leese was interested in solutions to crises, not their exacerbation. The idea of transforming Lidice into a *"model mining village"* with accompanying mining research institute could have been Leese's concept: on evidence, he was the most enterprising of a dynamic and intelligent executive. He had been instrumental in securing better conditions for his members for well over a decade; and he had a reputation for instigating schemes which improved his members' housing, provided them with sports facilities and pit-head baths, and secured them paid holidays and better representation.

GEORGE JONES

George Jones, 1884—December 1958, was a British trade unionist and politician. Born in Hednesford, Jones began working as a pit-boy at an early age. He became active in the Cannock Chase Miners' Association and was elected as its president in 1912. In 1914, he became the full-time general secretary and agent for the North Warwickshire Miners' Association, being made general secretary and agent for the larger Warwickshire Miners' Association in 1919. George Jones was active in politics, serving on Tamworth Town Council, and eventually serving as the town's Mayor. However, at the 1931 and 1935 General Elections, he stood unsuccessfully in Lichfield.

Around 1930, whilst remaining leader of the Warwickshire Miners, Jones was elected as secretary of the Midland Miners' Federation. He served on the executive of the Mineworkers' Federation of Great Britain, seeing through the nationalisation of the coal industry as the unions federated into the National Union of Mineworkers, but left his trade union posts in 1947, to become Labour Director of the West Midlands Coal Board, before taking up the role of vice-chair in 1950. George Jones retired in 1952; he continued to serve as a part-time member of the board until his death in 1958.

WILL LAWTHER

William Lawther was born on the 20th of May 1889 in Choppington, Northumberland. From leaving the town's school, he became a collier and soon became actively involved in the Northumberland Miners' Association, which funded him to study at the Central Labour College. Although Lawther is known as a politician, he is best remembered as a trade unionist. He was elected to the General Council of the Trades Union Congress (TUC) in 1935, and as the President of the Mineworkers' Federation of Great Britain (MFGB) in 1939. Lawther saw the coal workers through the challenging war years and helped steer the industry through the rocky process of nationalisation. By the time the National Union of Mineworkers was inaugurated, Lawther remained President. In 1949, he was President of the TUC, and later that year, he was knighted. In 1954, Lawther retired from trade union work and died in 1976.

Lawther's role in the Lidice Shall Live campaign was pivotal. Without the enthusiastic support of the President of the Mineworkers' Federation of Great Britain, it was sure to remain a parochial, North Staffordshire based fund raising project. However, that was not to be the case. The emotion shown in Lawther's address at a conference at Blackpool on the 20th of July 1942, much of it repeated in Hanley later on the 6th of September, added a weight of personal human sentiment the whole of the British coalfield could not ignore. And neither could the Foreign Secretary - a fortnight later the Munich Agreement had finally been annulled.

Following his death, declassified archives have shown that Will Lawther had covertly been working with a secret Cold War propaganda department attached to the British Foreign Office called the *Information Research Department* and was paid by the British government to promote anti-communist material. This would devalue his denouncements of the British-Czechoslovak Friendship Club, that it was "merely a tool" for the Communist Information Bureau (better known as the Cominform).

HARRY WHEATCROFT

Harry Wheatcroft was a flamboyant, bewhiskered rosarian, a lifelong humanitarian and pacifist, much given to wearing loud suits. The wonderfully charismatic expert, who was to give so much to the project to install a Garden of Peace and Friendship at Lidice, came into the rose growing business in 1916 because he was **"chesty and needed the open-air life"**. Though he started with one acre of land by 1966, Harry was cultivating 1,350,000 roses on more than three hundred acres at his Nottinghamshire based nurseries, and his love of them he carried wherever he went with **"a rumbustious sincerity that gladdens the heart"**. The manifestation of this speciality as a grower was a prolific moustache, which mingled in rapaciously with a pair of undeniably impressive sideburns, which he defended stoutly:

> **"It is not showmanship. I grew it because I was working outside and just didn't need to face the world with a shining, clean cut exterior. I hope I am known because of roses; it would be a very disappointing life to think that fame depends on some peculiarity... Gardening needs patience and a real appreciation of the beauty that it can produce—because there is a terrific satisfaction in seeing life and colour coming to things in the garden after the bareness of winter... You can never tire of it because you are dealing with**

living things. What I like about roses is that you do not have to know an awful lot about them. They grow in spite of you. The reason is simple: they have been about this world for more than 30 million years. In that time, they have learned to understand all the peculiar things that the human species does to them."

US NAVY SECRETARY, FRANK KNOX'S SPEECH

The full transcript of US Navy Secretary Frank Knox's speech. Given at the United Nations Rally at Boston Garden on Sunday the 14th of June 1942:

I am glad to be here today. It was only yesterday that my boss and your boss -the President and Commander-in-Chief- suggested that I come to Boston for this magnificent meeting.

I was glad to come for several reasons: First, because this is United Nations' Day and there is something deeply symbolic to me about celebrating this stirring concept of a new world understanding in Boston where our own concept of political freedom took shape, and to which countless thousands of people have come from the old world in search of liberty and opportunity in the new. I was glad to come because you are instituting here in Boston an important project. I refer to the unification of all the relief campaigns of our brothers in arms. And, finally, I am glad to be here because I was born here in Boston! Out in Chicago, they say that's a confession - but I never miss a chance to confess that I was born in Boston!

I am a Republican - as some of you with long memories may remember, and so is my great colleague, Colonel Stimson, the Secretary of War. We are both serving you under one of history's inspired leaders, Franklin D. Roosevelt, Republicans, though we are. We are both serving a Democratic administration. But Republican or Democrat, Jew, or Gentile, Irish or English, in the government, in the factory, on the farm, in the Army and in the Navy, we are all Americans fighting like hell to obliterate these wolves who are tearing the world apart; those bloodthirsty jackals who know neither God nor principle, neither compassion nor pity: who know only the lash and the noose, only corruption and conquest!

They have had an awful time in heroic China, and they've died like flies on the long plains and in the deep forests of Russia at the hands of a mighty and outraged people fighting for their fields and firesides. And now they have tangled with another people who paid dearly for liberty and will lose it more dearly. We have hit 'em in the wastes of the Pacific - and we've just begun to fight!

In a few months, the wily Jap has snatched a vast and priceless empire in Asia, but, as my mother used to say about me at the dinner table, "his eyes are bigger than his tummy." The Jap will never eat his dinner; he'll wish he had never ordered it! You in Massachusetts know what "Lexington" means, and it means something the Navy will never forget. When the gallant Lexington went down, the Japs sowed a dragon's tooth in the Coral Sea - and they too will never forget what "Lexington" means to Americans!

The brutal Nazi has conquered an empire that would make Caesar jealous. The iron heel rests on Europe from cold North Cape to the olive groves of Crete. But the iron heel or the "heel," if you prefer an Americanism - is uneasy. Things seem to happen in France in spite of the daily blood bath; they seem to go right on in Belgium, in Holland, in Norway and there are still a lot of tough Yugoslavs in the hills who don't know when they are licked and never will!

If future generations ask us what we were fighting in this war, we will tell them the story of Lidice. Last week, Lidice was a simple mining village several miles outside of the Czecho-Slovakian capital of Prague, it stood a bit off the main highway. It had about 90 houses, a church, a blacksmith shop. Through it ran a Wilson St., named in honour of Woodrow Wilson. Like thousands of other villages and towns and cities from one end of Europe to another, it was filled with simple people, who don't care much for Nazi tyranny or Hitler's glamorous "New Order." Hitler said the villagers had harboured the assassins of his dear friend and personal hangman, Heydrich, what happened? How did Hitler spread the blessings of the "New Order" to the people of Lidice? How did he convert the doubters and enlighten them about the meaning of the "Greater Germany?" It was very simple, very quick, and very effective. He killed them. Last week, the Nazi savages swept down without warning. All male inhabitants were shot in cold blood. Every woman in the village was shipped to a Nazi concentration camp. Every child in the village was ordered into Nazi "educational institutions," which are nothing more nor less than reform schools of the "New Order" - where children are taught to love, respect and obey the masters who orphaned them. The Nazi madness did not stop there. Every building. every bit of brick and stone was levelled to the ground. Were the Nazis ashamed of this monstrous act? Having committed it, did they try to hide it from the world? Having outraged every tenet of civilized man, did they keep their tongues and try to forget the massacre? Not on your life! When they kill helpless hostages, they're proud of it. But when they wipe out a whole village, it's exhilarating. The Nazis boldly announced to the world that Lidice had been reduced to rubble and its name extinguished forever.

Here is our answer to the Nazis: You have not extinguished Lidice; you have given it life everlasting. You have made it a name which will live forever in the hearts and minds of free men everywhere. You have made it a symbol of the fight for freedom; you have made it a battle cry for millions who treasure their liberty more than their lives. You have reminded us once again exactly what it means to live under the "New Order."

We have villages too, thousands of them, and some of the most beautiful are in New England the stores, the common and the white houses and fields. We know what it would mean to us if the neighbours we love and respect were brutally murdered by a foreign invader. We know that a towering, righteous wrath would envelop us. We know that we would feel exactly as the Czechs feel today, exactly as the Norwegians and the Dutch and the Greeks and all the unconquered peoples feel.

We will not stop this fight until these butchers are swept from the face of the earth, even as the Nazis obliterated Lidice. There is this difference, though. Lidice lives on and will rise again. But the Nazi ideas of degradation and enslavement of the human soul will be crushed.

Lidice was no isolated instance of Nazi terror. But somehow it has touched the hearts of all men. We had become callous to the brutal Nazi policy of mass murder. We had become accustomed to reading in the morning paper that they had shot another batch of innocent hostages. We had almost lost the meaning of this dreadful system of mass murder of innocent people. The Nazi terror, like the Nazi lie, has been exercised on so wide a scale that our imaginations revolted, our senses were numbed... Lidice suddenly brought the whole horrible system into clear focus, and has restored our balance, our understanding, and our conscience.

And yet, even today, we who live in an America based upon justice and right can barely conceive of a nation which will permit its leaders to commit such crimes. How long will the German people permit their leaders to commit such crimes? Will they rise to denounce this terrorism? Will they permit such orgies to go unchecked? How long do they think a civilized world will continue to separate the German people from their leaders? The German people must sense that unless they make clear their own revulsion, unless they stop the sowing of the seeds of hate, they will reap the whirlwind after this war.

We often hear it said that the sober German people detest the Nazi regime - that the Nazis have them under such strict control that the slightest murmur of resistance would be instantly silenced. But from all parts of occupied Europe comes word of resistance to the Nazis. The Poles are being systematically murdered as an entire people and are being subjected to unspeakable brutalities. Still, they manage to get word of their resistance out to us. What about the German people? The Czechs are resisting Hitler with every source of strength. We have word of slowdowns in Czech factories, of industrial sabotage, of supply trains destroyed. We know that when a Czech patriot crawls out into the night to blow up a Nazi troop train, he takes into his hands not only his own life, but also the lives of his family and neighbours. But still the reports come out of Czecho-Slovakia: A troop train blown up here, a munitions dump there. If the Czechs manage to resist against such odds, what about the German people? Likewise, the Norwegians. Every act of repression that the "New Order" inflicts upon them is met with firm and stubborn resistance. The workers sullen and slow; production is unsatisfactory; Norwegian boys slip away under cover of night to England in small fishing boats. If the Norwegians manage to resist the Nazis with the cards stacked against them, what about the German people?

The United Nations will crush the Nazi system by force of arms, but for the sake of their consciences and their skins, the Germans owe it to themselves to repudiate the Nazis. It is up to them to convince the world that they know the Nazis leaders have led them astray. The burden of proof is on them. Before mankind takes them back into the family of nations, it is their job to convince the world that the whole populated system is abhorrent to them and will never rise again on their soil. Then, and only then, can peaceful peoples feel safe with them. Then, and only then, can the German people take their rightful place in the post-war world erected by nations united to defeat bandits, to assure freedom from fear and freedom from want.

For the confident determination of the United Nations is to win not only a victory but to win the war, and that means to build together a better world based on universal and simple principles of justice and common good. Even as this meeting illustrates the importance on the home front of concentration of effort among relief agencies, recent and historic events illustrate the importance of united concentration on the destruction of our enemies and then on the erection of a new international society.

We are making agreements with our allies under the Lend-Lease act, looking ahead to the problems of relief and reconstruction as well as combat. Britain and Russia have signed a treaty to police Europe pending joint action with ourselves and other like-minded people to preserve the peace. The conversations between the President and Foreign Minister Molotov indicate the growing solidarity. Already, the day of the enemy's choice of battlefields and the enemy's control of strategy is fading. And as the great pattern of solidarity among free peoples unfolds and expands, Hitler's prospects for mastery of the world of tomorrow begin to fade.

Every day, the United Nations become more closely knit in war and peace. Every day they become a mightier concert of determine Powers. Today we welcome our sister republic, Mexico, and the fighting Commonwealth of the Philippines into this grand alliance pledged to fight tyranny to the death today and to build a better world tomorrow.

It is well that we celebrate this day all over the country. It is an occasion for great jubilation. Its portent for the future is vast and majestic and very sobering. For all of us here, all of the peoples of the United Nations everywhere, stand on the threshold of another new era in man's slow progress toward the promised land of peace and security. Our success in attaining our goal of a peaceful international society will depend largely upon the wisdom and far-sighted vision of the American people to whom the world looks for leadership and upon whether, like our forefathers in Boston, we have the courage to give the last measure of effort to winning the war and then, although weary and sorely tired, whether we have the courage to step boldly out upon hard and obscure paths to peace, never trod yet by man. Our forefathers who made this America a land of realized dreams and visions were never ones to falter. Nor will we!

PEIXOTO SPEECH – 10TH JUNE 1944 – RE-CHRISTENING EVENT – VILLA DE PARADA TO LIDICE

In 1944, the Brazilian community of Villa de Parada, formerly Santo Antônio do Capivari, was re-named Lidice. The speech given by District Administrator Ernâni do Amaral Peixoto at the inauguration ceremony is presented in full:

"This place, quiet and beautiful, in the Rio de Janeiro mountains is the meeting point for men from all corners of the earth, speaking the most varied languages and enjoying the most diverse beliefs. What is the superior reason that brings us together? What do we have in common? We, the ones who gather here? Why the weariness of these roads and the pause in our usual activities? We come attracted by an ideal, ready for an affirmation, ready for a fight that we want to remain free and that we will fight for it. It is the same feeling that animates millions of men on all continents and determines the boldest military deeds, the greatest demonstrations of resistance by the populations of the occupied countries and which, we never had any doubts, will be the most positive factor of victory.

The evolution of warfare methods in the application of its principles. immutable chaos caused the peoples, already affected by the demands of total mobilisation, to be more deeply wounded. The military occupation of almost all of continental Europe by the Nazi hordes revived vandal scenes, already lost in the memory of times. And, among all of them, the one lived in Lidice exceeds the others in cruelty and stands as a symbol for the world. However, it is not this sacrifice that moves us, but the firmness of those brave Czechs who, we believe, honouring their memories effectively collaborated in the resistance to the hated invader.

Behold my patrician inhabitants of this village! Could they remain indifferent to the enemy who, occupying these surroundings, would nullify the freedom of the motherland, plunder their property, take away their tranquillity, invade their homes and disrespect their families? Great and beautiful example for humanity! Let all know for a while that there will always be people capable of dying for the good of the country and for the freedom of its people. This read magnificent dog of this holocaust and, to keep this feat always present, Lidice appears on Brazilian soil. Brazilian inhabitants of Lidice:

Meditate on responsibility of this name and remember that it is not only at the supreme moment of the fight that Patria has rights over us! All of our energy must be permanently at your disposal for the constructive work of greatness and love constantly to unite,' because only in this way will we be able to respond to the blessings that fill us.

Czechs: Your heroic conduct offers yet another great lesson: Had ALL your leaders been heard, the course of this war would have been another. The sacrifice of everything that was most dear to you—your freedom—was not used by other peoples for the preservation of peace. Let everyone understand for the future that the freedom of one is common to all and that the threats that weigh on a nation affect humanity.

"... the death of any man does not diminish me because I am part of the human race. And so do not ask for whom the bells toll; they toll for you."

We will only be worthy of so many lives lost by redoubling our efforts to conquer victory and assuming the firm commitment to work for a better world, based on an efficient international legal order, capable of ensuring harmony among men. The courts that emerge will be the great monuments to the dead of this conflagration and in their porticoes the great hecatombs we are witnessing today must remain inserted, so that those of then, knowing the joys of peace and the beauty of freedom, appreciate the horrors of war and of oppression."

WENDEL WILLKIE'S SPEECH AT STERN PARK GARDENS - JULY 12th, 1942

"Fellow citizens and all who love freedom everywhere:

Let me tell you a story. Ten miles west of Prague, in Czechoslovakia, there was a little village called Lidice, spelled LIDICE. It was a mining village, a mile off the main highway, with some lovely old inns, a blacksmith or two, a shoemaker, a wheelwright, a tailor. The village had been there for over six hundred years.

Above the ninety roofs of the town rose the spire of St. Margaret's Church (SIC), built in 1736, the home of the faith of the community. This town was remote, peaceful, almost like a village in a fairy tale. But it was not a village in a fairy tale, for its people had tasted the bread and wine of freedom. In this village one of the main streets was named Wilson Street, after an American who had a vision and wanted to share it with the world. And the people of Lidice dreamed the same dream, saw the same vision.

But the Nazis came and with them misery and hardship. The altar of St. Margaret's Church was no longer open to the people as it had been for over two hundred years. Men had to watch their words and in their actions they could no longer be free. But in their hearts, the hearts of the innkeeper and the tailor and the farmer and the miner and the priest, was the stubborn independence of their fathers.

Not far from Lidice ran a winding road. On this road on May 27, six weeks ago, at 10:30 in the morning, a motor car was passing, carrying Hitler's Governor of Czecho-Slovakia, Hangman Heydrich, for his cruelties the most hated man in all Europe. The car was held up by two unknown men. Bullets burrowed into the spine of Reinhard Heydrich. The two patriots disappeared, and one of them, it is said, is now safe in London.

I do not wish to speak of the reign of terror that thereupon swept over all Czecho-Slovakia. I wish to speak today only of Lidice, and I will give you only the facts. This is not my version of the facts. This is not a version of the facts issued by any of the United Nations as propaganda. These are the facts as officially attested by the German Government. They are facts of which the Nazis are proud. They are facts they wish the world to know. They are facts they believe will frighten you and me, and turn our hearts and our knees to water, and make us cry "Truce!"

For Heydrich, the Hangman died in agony, as he had caused thousands of innocent people to die. No proof from that day to this has ever been adduced to show that any of the inhabitants of Lidice had anything to do with the assassination. But the Nazis made their own proof. They were afraid not to, for Heydrich was one of their great men. "One of the best Nazis," Hitler called him, and that, no doubt, is true.

On June 10, an official German statement was issued, not for domestic consumption, but for the world to hear. I quote from it: "It is officially announced that in the course of the search for the murderers of General Heydrich it has been ascertained that the population of the village of Lidice supported and assisted the perpetrators who came into question. Because the inhabitants, by their support of the perpetrators, have flagrantly violated the law, all men of the village have been shot. The women have been deported to a concentration camp and the children sent to appropriate centers of education. All buildings of the village were leveled to the ground and the name of the village was immediately abolished."

That is the official Nazi report.

They came in the night, men in boots and brown shirts, and they took from their homes the bewildered miners and farmers, the tailor and the priest, the boy of 17 and the old man of 70, more than 200 in all, and they shot them, because they could think of no other way to avenge the death of Heydrich. Fifty-six women they took also and killed, and proudly listed their names. The rest of the women they drove into what they called concentration camps; and these women the world will never see again.

They herded the pale, terror-stricken children into trucks and carried them off to correction schools where they would be taught that they must honor the murderers of their fathers and the brutalizers of their mothers, The ninety homes they burned to the ground, the church of St. Margaret they stamped into the earth. And the name of the little town of Lidice, through which ran the street called after a President of the United States, they rubbed out, they thought, from history. Why did they do this deed, more terrible than anything that has happened since the Dark Ages, a deed not of passion, but of cold, premeditated, systematic murder and rapine? Why? They did it because they are afraid. They are afraid because the free spirit in men has refused to be conquered. Theirs is a system of force and terror and Lidice is the terrible symbol of that system.

But it is not the only one. Of the 500,000 men, women and children who have been shot in Europe by the Nazis, at least 25,000 have perished in mass massacres. Poland, Norway, Belgium, Yugoslavia, all have their Lidices. But this one-a symbol of all-we have sworn to remember, if only because the Nazis themselves demand that we forget it. Once more they have misjudged the human spirit. Because a hangman was killed, Lidice lives. Because a hangman was killed, Wilson Street must once again be part of a little Bohemian town. Because the lanterns of Lidice have been blacked out, a flame has been lit which can never be extinguished. Each of the wounds of those two hundred men and fifty-six women is a mouth that cries out that other free men and free women must not suffer a like fate."

AN EYE FOR AN EYE

Penned by Dorothy Thompson in New York on June the 11th, 1942 and released by the Bell Syndicate, Inc. Published on the 12th by the Quebec Gazette;

"It was years ago back in 1930 that one of the most gifted and sensitive of my German friends cried aloud: "Deutschland hat eine ansteckende geistestkrankeit." (Germany is the victim of an epidemic madness.) It was so. We read daily in our papers of events that reveal so morbid a sickness of the soul that they baffle the normal imagination.

Peter Viereck, the brilliant twenty-six-year-old son of George Sylvester Viereck, the German agent, has made the atonement of youth for the sins of his parents by revealing the sources of this illness in one of the most illuminating books about German psychology yet published "Meta politics from the Romantics to Hitler."

It should be much more widely read and much more thoroughly reviewed than has yet been the case. It belongs with Konrad Heiden's History of National Socialism, Rauschning's "The Revolution of Nihilism" and "The Voice of Destruction," as one of the few books read by a fairly large public that really tell what's up in Germany.

The German American Bund, an organisation which shared the principles of Nazi Germany, held a massive rally at New York's Madison Square Garden on February the 20th 1939, drawing 20,000 attendees. Thompson disrupted the meeting, heckling that Fritz Kuhn, the Bund leader was spewing "bunk"; she was escorted out of the arena by uniformed Bund supporters - for her own safety.

What is happening now cannot be judged by any normal standards. It is abnormal. It is sick - as the whole Nazi regime has been a sickness, from the first. In this sickness, as often in profound neurosis, there is and has been a great deal of cool intelligence. There is nothing wrong with the Nazi brain; there is everything wrong with the Nazi soul and psyche. The hysteric and psychotic can be very shrewd in achieving his purposes, as every victim of the hysteric knows. - Alfred A. Knopf, 1941.

The terror in Czecho-Slovakia is abnormal. It is the terror of men who are sick, who are afraid in their hearts, who are haunted by their former deeds, knowing that they are doomed - knowing it however, in their nerves, not acknowledging the fact in their brains - men who are suffering a claustrophobia in the immense space of their conquered territory: feeling hemmed in by their own conquests: leading and distrusting everybody: conquered peoples; their own soldiers; the rank and file of the party: even people at the top of the party. Snarling at each other and finding temporary releases only by murder; the typical behaviour of the paranoic whose case history moves from persecution mania to delusions of grandeur, to homicide, to suicide. We are seeing the third stage; the suicide is not yet here.

The paranoic never sees his real condition. But there have been cool observers in Germany who have recently reached here, and they do see it. The Germans are hungry. They do not even acknowledge this fact - they are undernourished; rickets have developed in their children; but they live in the illusion that they are eating enough. Strange as it may seem, people can starve without knowing it. The collapse of morale is apparent. But it does not manifest itself in rebellion, but merely in relapse in universal apathy and in hatred of themselves and of everybody. Revolt requires morale, too. There is none.

The utter failure of conquest is revealed by the fact that thousands of Russian workers have been imported into Germany because the fields on which they once worked in the Ukraine cannot be worked. There is no machinery, and the guerrillas are too dangerous, for there is morale there, in that seared hell. The compulsory agricultural economy has failed to overcome nature and human nature. The outlook for this year's crops 13 worse than last, and last years were bad.

There is an almost complete disappearance of decent manners. That is not normal in distress. Distress can have two consequences it can drive men to stick together and help one another, as it has done in England. But the paranoic does not act that way. He is an egotist, and it is always somebody else's fault; it is a plot, a conspiracy. It is a plot of the whole world, and it is a plot of one's next-door neighbour. And the nearer the enemy the better for the paranoic. He knows how to act. If he cannot conquer Russia or bomb Britain, he turns revengefully against the nearest and weakest - he murders Czechs.

And all this is accompanied by a rationalization, by which he "sublimates" civilization into an utterly unreal realm of words. Heydrich is praised as a great humanitarian by Himmler! Everything that Heydrich did, we are told, caused suffering to his soul. It really hurt his sensitive heart more than it did his victims. Every time he shot an old woman or a student, he felt the wounds in his own flesh. And all Prague is forced to drape itself in mourning for him. The offenders cannot be apprehended, so an entire village is destroyed, every man shot, every woman and child deported, and the name of the village erased. And the thing is organised in a masterly manner. In this absolutely senseless destruction, there is perfectly functioning bureaucracy. And Himmler, no doubt, weeps.

Thus Goering, too, described in his last speech the terrible spiritual sufferings of the Führer on the Eastern front, whose heart bled for his unfortunate troops - while, we find now, that whole units of German troops were shot for mutiny. The self-pity of the Nazis must be given real grounds, then perhaps we shall see a nation snap into a normal reaction. At present the Nazis feel self-pity is no path to repentance. It is escape from repentance. When every hostage killed brings swift reprisals upon themselves, upon their own villages, the German people, who share the neurosis but in lesser degree than their sicker overlords, will turn their aggression against the Nazis themselves. Until then, the sufferings of other peoples will make not the slightest impression on them." (Released by the Bell Syndicate, Inc.)

THE SILENT VILLAGE

Having received consent from the President of the Mineworkers' Federation of Great Britain, Will Lawther, in August 1942, the British Crown Film Unit began scanning the country's industrial coalfield looking for a filming location. Aspiring producer, Humphrey Jennings wanted a community with both a physical resemblance to Lidice, and a similar social and political history.

According to one of the film's actors, Jennings asked the advice of Welsh miners' leader and South Wales Miners' Federation president Arthur Horner as to a suitable location. Jennings had the co-operation of Arthur Horner, who felt that the proposed film should be symbolic of the unity and solidarity felt by all mining communities with the people of Lidice. Jennings arrived at the town of Ystradgynlais, nestling in the upper reaches of the Swansea Valley. Immediately, he took an interest in the nearby self-contained mining hamlet of Cwmgiedd.

Cwmgiedd was selected by the producers as the setting because of its striking similarity in scenes, industry, communal life, and typical characteristics to Lidice. Jennings discussed the project with the local mine workers and their families and found them to be receptive to his ideas. The small community was enthusiastic about the project. For the purposes of the production, Lidice was to become Cwmgiedd and Czecho-Slovakia became South Wales, and while the story is told mainly in English, the Welsh passages which intersperse give it a touch of realism. The manner in which the amateur actor-miners adapt themselves to their respective parts is truly remarkable, lending the film gravitas it would not necessarily have achieved with seasoned, professional actors.

The end result has a claustrophobic intensity about it, especially as it is produced entirely in the village. Given that not a single professional performer took part, how fitting it was that the residents of Cwmgiedd were the first to see the film. On Friday the 28th of May 1943, four hundred men, women and children of the village attended the premiere of the picture at the Astoria Cinema, Ystradgynlais. As they witnessed the result of their efforts on the screen, they were repeatedly moved to applause.

The picture opens with a service in the village chapel, with the congregation singing a favourite Welsh hymn, *"Pen Calfaria,"* with touching effect. We then see domestic scenes in the peaceful homes, in the village school, and the grocer's shop. The village inn, too, comes into the picture, with miners fresh from their toils in the pit discussing trade union affairs over a pint of beer. Then the real story begins with the appearance in the village streets of the German broadcasting van exhorting the people of Cwmgiedd to co-operate with the Reich in the rebirth of their country.

The people display no interest in the announcement and the underground movement develops, with members of the miners' lodge committee appealing secretly to the men to *"Go Slow"* in the pits. Threats issued from the loudspeaker van have no effect, and the attack on Heydrich follows. All villagers over 15 are compelled to register, and refusal to betray the attackers results in the order for the shooting of all adult males and the handing over of women and children to the authorities. There is a touching scene as the men march boldly to their doom, singing lustily *"Hen Wlad fy Nhadau."* The climax sees Cwmgiedd being razed to the ground.

"This tiny mining village is shown as suffering the same fate as the murdered Czech village of Lidice. Loud-speaker cars and radio blare forth the harsh edicts of the protecting."

"Nazi invaders, who shoot villagers in brutal reprisals and finally raze the place to ruins. Hollywood does this often enough. But the dynamic force of this 35-minute picture lies in the brilliant human intimacy by which director Humphrey Jennings has presented the tiny Welsh-speaking community - its miners, chapel, school, shops and humble homes." P. L. Mannock - Daily Herald 10th June 1943.

The key propaganda message of the picture is the solidarity of the working class and their faithfulness to the national cause. In that sense, it is a direct extrapolation from the Lidice Shall Live campaign, the film having been authorised by Will Lawther following the successful launch of the movement in Hanley only weeks before. As for the film itself, it was released to fit in with the first anniversary of the tragedy to befall Lidice, as a warning to the British people of what could happen if their emotional resolve were to slip. The film is a triumph of production as it was made possible only by the co-operation of the entire community. Jennings praised the services rendered by local miners' leaders, notably Mr D. B. Evans, miners' agent, and Mr Chris Evans, Vice-Chairman of the Seven Sisters Lodge.

The executive committee of the South Wales Miners' Federation had already seen the film prior to the reels being flown over to Dr Beneš and Jan Masaryk in America in time for release there. With its re-enactment of the horror set within a community, The Silent Village would bring home "the distant realities of the brutal fascist occupation of Europe" to many Americans. Both Masaryk and Beneš expressed their appreciation of the people of Cwmgiedd and their efforts in raising awareness of the plight of the Czech people.

The residents of Cwmgiedd were first to see The Silent Village when on Friday the 28th of May 1943, 400 men, women and children of the village attended the premiere of the picture at the Astoria Cinema, Ystradgynlais. According to reports, as they viewed the result of their efforts on the screen they were repeatedly moved to applause. The Silent Village officially opened on Friday the 11th June at the Empire, Regal and Leicester Square theatres in London, and then Monday the 14th at Olympia, Cardiff, and then in Bristol and Liverpool. Shortly thereafter the film went on general release.

NATIONALISATION & GETTING ALONG

On the 12th of July 1946, the National Coal Board (NCB) was formed and given sole responsibility for managing and running the industry.

It was just part of a sweeping package of reforms across all sectors of society the new Attlee Government had promised and one which movements such as Lidice Shall Live had illuminated; because Lidice had supplied a blank canvas to the creative forces within the Mineworkers' Federation of Great Britain to consider how model mining communities could look and function in a modern post-war industrial Britain.

Miners' leaders fought to see these ideas followed through. This was the culmination of many years of struggle for the public ownership of their industry.

They were loath to see the opportunity wasted.

But outcomes are rarely ideal or straightforward. Many miners found the new set-up irksome. British businessman, Lord Hyndley, was made the first chairman of the National Coal Board at its creation. Hyndley was a director of the Bank of England between 1931 and 1945 and was managing director of Powell Duffryn Ltd collieries from 1931 to 1946. His Deputy, Sir Arthur Street, came straight out of Whitehall with no mining experience. Controls over matters such as coal output and prices, investment in technology, wage negotiations and staffing levels were simply passed across from the former private owners to the new National Coal Board - which would still be run to make a profit.

On New Year's Day 1947 came the nationwide announcement across all coalfields, on the wireless, in the press and on the newsreels that all pit production was for *the people*:

A Message from the Prime Minister -

"To-day, January 1st, 1947, will be remembered as one of the great days in the industrial history of our country. The coal-mines now belong to the nation. This act offers great possibilities of social advance for the workers, and indeed for the whole nation.

If all alike - workers, National Coal Board and Government - shoulder their duties resolutely and use their rights wisely, these great advances will be assured.

I send my best wishes to all engaged in this vital work."

But it seemed that despite the Attlee Government's pronouncement, in reality the same type of people held influence over the operation of the mines, with new managerial positions often being taken up by men from the middle classes: former military or colonial men or former employees from the wartime civil service, for example.

Ebby Edwards, long-standing, respected by miners and former Secretary of the Mineworkers' Federation of Great Britain, had been co-opted onto the nine-man National Executive of the National Coal Board as Director for Labour Relations; but he soon felt unhappy with the direction the Government was looking to take the industry and he left after a year. Though a "socialist," the Government Minister of Fuel and Power, Manny Shinwell, was profoundly unpopular with the men, failing to keep the distribution of coal moving during the harsh winter of 1947, causing the whole nation to grind to a halt.

These issues meant that the latter half of 1947 was a critical time for Britain. It was not clear that the success of nationalisation of the coal industry was secured, or even in the nation's interests, for that matter. Many miners resented the way nationalisation had taken place, to all intents and purposes replacing like for like in their eyes. A covert psychological battle was planned to win over the hearts and minds and restore harmony between workers and their new employers - the British Government.

Once more, the North Staffordshire Miners' leaders, those who had led the Lidice Shall Live campaign, were at the forefront in the attempt to bring these protagonists together. The familiar faces of Arthur Baddeley, Hugh Leese and Harold Lockett in Stoke-on-Trent, and George Jones, former Secretary of the Midlands Miners' Federation in Tamworth, all championed the need to work together to ensure the nation had enough coal to survive.

A main vehicle in this campaign would become the play, *The Forgotten Factor*—an effective piece of propagandist theatre written by Alan Thornhill for the American Moral Re-Armament (MRA) organisation, conceived in 1938 by the *practical theologian* and businessman, Frank Buchman, that sought to preserve world peace through the dissemination of Christian values. Among the American cast of The Forgotten Factor, who disembarked the Queen Mary in Southampton on the 30th of April 1946, was Ray Purdy, who was thirteen at the time. In 2012, he recalled for Pamela Jenner, author of the book Changing Society through Drama:

"We came by train to London and then drove through the streets in buses to the MRA headquarters in Hays Mews. The evidence of the wartime blitz lay all around, and it made a deep impression on me. I was a young cast member of the play, which had toured America, and which Frank Buchman brought to Britain as a vehicle to help revitalise and arm the country for the coming ideological struggle for post-war Europe, which he foresaw."

"All through that winter of 1946-7 the play was performed, night after night, busloads would come from collieries, factories, schools, farms and towns all over the country. It was an amazing winter. I experienced pea soup, fogs and bitter cold, but I count myself so lucky to have been part of this initiative."

In 2013, David Hassell, part of the stage crew on The Forgotten Factor, described the play's popularity to Pamela:

"In the spring and summer of 1947, I was in the stage crew of The Forgotten Factor at the Westminster Theatre. People came in great numbers to the theatre and the cinema. We had a large team driving up audiences and organising coach parties. There was something in The Forgotten Factor that turned a key for a lot of people, particularly the miners. We had lots of miners coming in organised parties from South Wales and elsewhere. Ernest Bevin said at the time *'Give me coal and I'll give you a foreign policy.'* The Forgotten Factor worked in America, so we brought it across to Britain. The unions responded very well to it in the States and it had a bearing on the war effort. It also had an effect in factories. Bad industrial relationships had threatened production for the war effort. The Forgotten Factor was a major contribution of Moral Re-Armament to the allied war effort. This was publicly recognised by Truman. The same thing happened in Britain."

On Tuesday the 29th of April 1947, an audience of around 1,500 people - made up of representatives of the workers and officials of the North Staffordshire coalfield, the pottery and other local industries filled the Queen's Hall, Burslem for the first of five performances of the play, officially described as a *national drama for industrial teamwork*. The show, which had been running at the Westminster Theatre in London since October '46, had come to the Potteries at the request of the North Staffordshire miners and of local colliery officials, and was making its provincial premiere. As before, with the Lidice Shall Live movement, North Staffordshire's miners' leaders were playing a pioneering role in taking the play to other coalfields to create a sense of unity between management and workers within the recently nationalised coal industry.

Before the show began, from the stage, Hugh Leese, a principal visionary at the heart of the Lidice Shall Live campaign, welcomed the play to the district and pointed out to the audience the necessity to learn from the lessons it was bringing with it. Alongside him, Mr. George Sanders, the new Manager of Sneyd Colliery, stated that he was privileged to see the play in Switzerland, and mentioned that parties had travelled to London from local collieries to see the production. At a reception after the performance, the Lord Mayor of Stoke-on-Trent spoke in high appreciation of the production, saying that what had made such a great impression on him was that the players were **"acting from their hearts."**

Later, the newspaper had this to say in its review of the play:

"First-class entertainment, the play, written by Alan Thornhill, has sparkling dialogue, humorous, dramatic and pathetic incident, and is brilliantly acted by a cast representative of Great Britain, the Dominions and the United States, who have taken part in performances in these countries and in Switzerland. 'The forgotten factor' is God - Who is mentioned only once during the whole course of the play. The story revolves around the families of an American industrialist and a labour leader and agitator who come to realise the folly and danger of class suspicion, pride, misunderstanding and distrust, not only in their dealings with others but in their own domestic relations. Out of this simple theme, built up with great dramatic skill, comes the message, plain and simple, the need for the stimulation of the spirit of co-operation and team work in the fight for increasing production."

But the play was about more than that: people wanted change, they were sick and tired of austerity; they saw what seemed like the glitz and glamour of every day American life and they wanted a slice. Women wished to be "housewives" once more but dreamt of being the American kind, with the lifestyle to match. British working men aspired to be their US counterparts. It was about passing on a moral obligation for conciliation, via the conduit of God, for workers to do the right thing and agree, in this case, with their new managers on the National Coal Board, who were sometimes their old colleagues, like their leaders from the old mining federations - men like Alderman George Jones, former Secretary of the Midlands Miners' Federation and one of the leaders of the Lidice Shall Live committee, now Labour Director of the West Midlands Division of the National Coal Board.

The Forgotten Factor played to packed houses for a week in Stoke-on-Trent. All were welcomed, and miners and workers and their families from across the Midlands, Wales and the North West visited the Potteries to see the play; like the party of Welsh miners reported in the Rhos Herald on the 10th of May 1948:

"**Although the play had been given previously in some industrial centres in the provinces, this visit to the Potteries was its nearest approach to North Wales. The Moral Rearmament Movement has friends in Rhos and surrounding District, and we understand that quite a number of our people especially from the ranks of the miners and their officials, have taken a real interest in the play, and a number of them welcomed the opportunity of visiting Burslem last week.**"

On the 6th of May, it was reported how in parts of the Queen's Hall the night before, an audience of 2,300 had stood *"ten deep"* at the play's final performance. Again, there were speeches before the show as local representatives took their opportunity to press home the key messages contained within the narrative. Tom Collier, Area Labour Officer for North Staffordshire on the West Midlands Coal Board, spoke from the stage on the five-day week for miners. He emphasised the need for *all* the managers, trade union leaders and the men present to become accustomed to new ways: *"together with the spirit portrayed by The Forgotten Factor, North Staffordshire could give a lead to the country,"* he said.

Civic representation graced the last performance as it did the first, with the Deputy Lord Mayor and Lady Mayoress Alderman and Mrs. Percy Williams present. The Evening Sentinel's report continued: **Introducing the play with Mr. Collier were Mr. George Sanders, manager at Sneyd Colliery, and representatives from the National Union of Mineworkers: Mr. Hugh Leese (former Secretary and Agent, North Staffordshire Area); Mr. Arthur Baddeley (Secretary and Agent); and Mr. Harold Lockett (President). Before a reception which followed the play, bouquets were presented by Miss Marion Clayton Anderson (producer) to Mrs. Sanders, Mrs. Collier. Mrs. Baddeley and Mrs. Lockett.**

Following the success of the run, miners' leaders issued a *North Staffordshire Committee of Invitation*, inviting every colliery in the country to send representatives to see an exclusive performance on the 14th of June 1947 to support the coal industry, organised in conjunction with the Moral Re-Armament organisation, at the Westminster Theatre, in London. The coalfields responded magnificently: 200 came from the West Midlands, including the Biddulph Male Voice Choir, three bus-loads from Cannock Chase, and the whole Executive Council of the Warwickshire Miners. Parties were arranged from the coalfields in Scotland, North and South Wales, Yorkshire, Lancashire, Nottinghamshire, Durham, and Kent.

All this was being done when the Lidice Shall Live campaign was reaching its climax, as the campaign leaders were preparing themselves for the visit to Lidice to present the Beneš Government with the total funds raised by the movement at the inauguration of the new village on the 15th of June. Harold Lockett and Arthur Baddeley, both attending the dedication in Lidice, had this to say in their telegram home about the performance in London:

"We believe that the spirit of this play in every coalfield would ensure national recovery."

For the secular, the cruel element deep-rooted within a play like The Forgotten Factor is the suggestion that we are all equal when we are not, be it in financial, social, gender, genetic, or racial terms. Taking one of the most obvious examples: when in pay disputes, the pressures on bosses and managers do not amount to much compared to the life and death struggles often faced by workers and their families; especially relevant during the winter of 1947. And yet, the omnipotence of the Christian Church across British society in the 1940s meant that the starting position of workers, managers, and owners in industrial dispute resolution put forward by the drama is one of a level playing field. Stripping God away we can approach the play as an unfettered observer. It could be argued that Moral Re-Armament was and still is a right-wing phenomenon intended to bring workers along with management, in order that the needs of owners and shareholders are prioritised at the expense of employees, and their protections and rights. The net effect is an undermining of the employees' sense of self-worth through a dependence on an employer who, via his grip on the purse strings, becomes *the agent of God*.

In Britain, during the war, the psychology behind Frank Buchman's project never came under scrutiny. There was not time, there were more important things to think about, and investigation would not have been welcome under such a febrile atmosphere. And post-war, the way Britain had committed itself to the United States, plays like the Forgotten Factor were heavily promoted by the Attlee Government and the Coal Board exactly because they were the kind of material that could lead to the reduction of socialist yearning amongst the masses and the eradication of industrial disputes, both justified and unjustified. Interestingly, when Ted Heath tried to re-introduce the play in the early 1970s to resolve disputes between the unions and management it failed miserably and the nation slipped into a state of emergency, manifesting itself in the surrealness of the three-day week and the defeat of the Government in 1974. Because the fall in the popularity of religion meant that there was no longer a Divine, invisible, unchallengeable intervention to seal agreements between managers and workers; and the miners of the 1970s felt less of a personal stake in seeing the nationalised coal industry work—it felt less theirs.

The spirit of the Forgotten Factor lives on today - with workers prepared to accept less than they are worth, sacrificing the value of their labour to the owners of capital and those profiteering from their labour, the result being that the latter disproportionately benefit at the formers' expense. Good people like Hugh Leese, Arthur Baddeley, George Jones, and Harold Lockett promoted it because the play imperfectly drove the aspirations of the unions, and they wished to see nationalisation succeed, something for which they had always fought. Moreover, their roots in Methodism were flattered by the principal character in the play - mentioned once - God.

But what of Frank Buchman and the Moral Re-Armament movement? Well, Frank Buchman was a man of contradictions. A man of peace who openly praised the work of Hitler for the stand he took against the Soviet Union, in the New York World-Telegram of the 26th of August 1936 he was quoted, *'I thank heaven for a man like Adolf Hitler, who built a front line of defence against the anti-Christ of Communism'*. He is referred to as a huckster on the one hand and a right-wing fundamentalist zealot on the other. Buchman used *doublespeak* to indoctrinate his followers *(Buchmanites)* and confound observers. Words were given alternate meanings: *Sanity* was following a "God-controlled" life; anyone seeking support outside the Group became *Insane* and was condemned; *Surrender* "to God's will" meant joining the Group; *Confession* was a cool recruitment tool; *Guidance* was akin to a seance with God; *Unbelievers* were outsiders, regardless of their faith or practice. It was all cultist behaviour: brainwashing through the alternate use of severe reprimands and gushing praise of members, and obstructing real communication between members and the uninitiated, unindoctrinated masses. But it is also rumoured that Buchman had a strong influence on *The Family*; a secretive pro theocracy, militarist, and anti-labour policies group functioning in America and abroad.

*Frank Buchman (left) brought the play, The Forgotten Factor to Britain with the backing of President Truman to marginalise socialism - which they both openly despised. According to the testimonies of those involved in the delivery of the show, Buchman's visitation to Britain was more to do with politics than artistic considerations. His intention was to stamp out communism before it had a chance to infect Britain. But not every politician was happy with the Moral Re-Armament's entry into Britain. On Friday the 3rd of May, the Daily Mirror reported how the night before in the House of Commons Tom Driberg (right) MP (Maldon) questioned the rationale of allowing the American's entry into Britain with one hundred of his "Groupers", calling him a **"soapy racketeer"**, someone who had formerly expressed enthusiasm for Nazi leaders. Nonetheless, the presence of Buchman and his play suited the Attlee Government and in particular Ernest Bevin, who was promoting his aggressive anti-Soviet foreign policy with fervour. Before long 50 Labour MPs had signed and published a letter disassociating themselves from Mr Driberg's remarks.*

Top: The National Coal Board in its first session at Whitehall. Left to right: Professor Sir Charles Ellis, Thomas Eric Boswell Young, Ebby Edwards, Sir Arthur Street (Deputy Chairman), Lord Hyndley (Chairman), Sir Walter Citrine, Sir Charles Reid, L. H. H Lowe and John Crandon Gridley. Bottom: The presentation of The Forgotten Factor at Tamworth in the Warwickshire coalfield in 1948, left to right - Eric Bentley, who played the employer; G A Mawbey, Manager of Kingsbury Dexter Colliery; Frank Painter, President of the NUM Warwickshire; Paul Campbell, who played the union leader, and Alderman George Jones, former Midlands Leader of the Lidice Shall Live committee, and Labour Director of the West Midland Division of the National Coal Board.

LIDICE – THE NAME

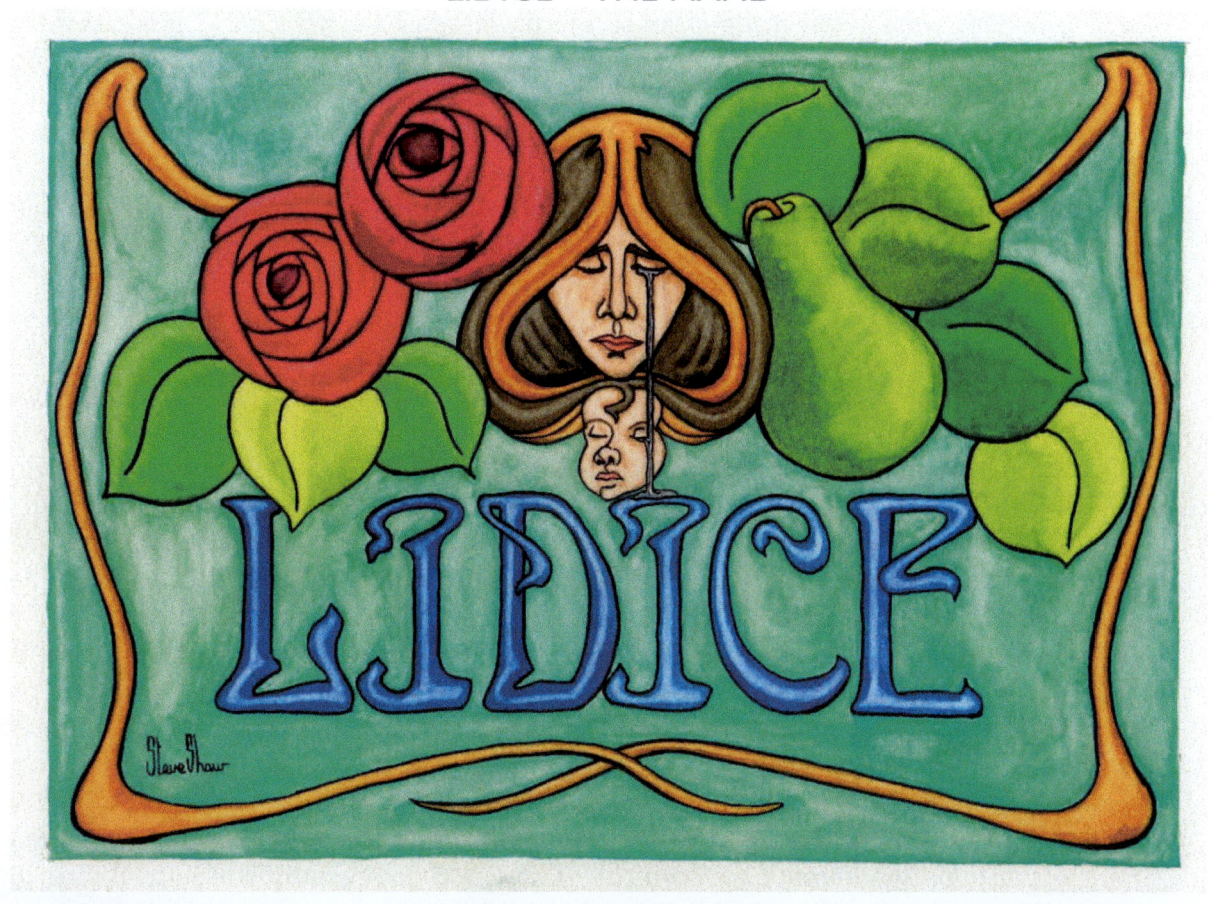

Lidice – Steve Shaw - 2015

If there is an instance of a catalyst for the trend of christening baby girls *"Lidice"* it would be José D'Elía (21 June 1916 - 29 January 2007). The high-profile Uruguayan labour leader, trade unionist and politician, worked as a shop employee at first before joining the trade union movement. By 1945, he was taking part in the establishment of the Worldwide Labour Union Federation. In 1942, he participated in the foundation of the General Union of Workers (UGT) and was its General Secretary. That same year, his wife gave birth to a baby girl on June the 10th. The following day came the dreadful news about the razing of Lidice. For Jose D'Elía, there seemed only one proper course of action. His daughter must receive the most honourable and best sounding name her parents could think of—*"Lidice."* When the Uruguayan trade-unionist later visited Czechoslovakia, he brought back to the girl a handful of Lidice soil and some flowers. While we cannot verify that the case of Jose D'Elía and his wife is the first of parents baptising their daughter with the name of the village, it certainly was not to be the last.

Throughout the summer of 1942, the reports from the East relayed increasingly alarming news about the whereabouts of the children of Lidice. Nazi statements about their so called *"re-education"* could not be independently verified and soon information about the children dried up entirely. The free world became gravely concerned about their welfare. Soon, across the Western Hemisphere and other nations of the world, while the young of Lidice were losing their names, lives and culture, people of goodwill began preserving those names. The baby girls christened Lidice stamped the village's name on humanity for generations to come, along with the inalienable and invincible power of life.

The plight of Lidice struck a particular chord in Cuba and here the intentions of parents and guardians were often made clear to the press and to legates, as in the case of Ignacio Madrigal, a resident of the Cuban town of Sagua la Grande in the Province of Santa Mara, who took the opportunity to send his family's views in the form of tributes to the Czecho-Slovak people via the Embassy in Havana. **"In view of many American nations, having named their communities after Lidice, thus spreading the news about the cruelty of fascism, committed against that village and its inhabitants, my wife and I have registered our youngest daughter under the name of Lidice Atenia Guerra Gonzales. We announce this to show that our family has paid tribute to this glorious name."**

Rafael Enrique Marrero, the Cuban writer, poet, actor, and radio and later television director of Havana, christened his daughter Patria Lidice Marrero. He stated he had done so **"in honour of the village destroyed in so cruel a manner, and in memory of those who had sacrificed their lives for the sake of a better world."** Lidice was the name given to a girl born in the Havana suburb of Quanabacoa, to another of the Province of Matanzas, and to yet another girl born in the town of San Severino. Here, the girl was christened Horacie Lidice Carmona Hernandez; and her father, Er Carmona of Matanzas, wrote: **"I have always been an admirer of Czechoslovakia and have therefore baptised my daughter, born on November 14, 1943, Lidice, in memory of the Lidice victims, their poor mothers and heroic fathers."**

An unrestrained spontaneous outpouring of fellowship stretched across all nations of South and Latin America. According to the Cigánek book *"Lidice,"* the godfather of another child, Lidice Alexandra Betancourt, Francisco Betancourt Gonzales, of Campaguera, said of the baptism: **"It was with great pride that we gave the child the name Lidice, the name borne so gloriously by the heroic Czechoslovak village, a cogent example of patriotic revolt and splendid sacrifice for the world freedom."** And they gave four more girls the name in quick succession: Lidice Megalhaes de Silveira of Rio de Janeiro, Lidice R. Moura of São Paulo, Lidice Marie Oomes de Silva of Aracaju, and Lidice Sascha de Pareira Lima of Recife.

Over the years, the number of ladies and girls christened Lidice has grown. The arrival of social media with its removal of barriers and wiping away of oceans has spread the *"message of Lidice"* and brought the positive news to a far larger audience. The hope is that the impactful fore-name is receiving a boost in popularity as I write and even finding a new market in nations hitherto unexplored. Today, thousands of people named Lidice celebrate the rebirth of the village and work for peace in a network of fellowship each day. It takes place on social media, mostly and although it has its hang-ups, the worldwide networking resulting from the reconstruction of Lidice has to be one of Facebook's finest achievements. Several friends have volunteered a paragraph or two, giving readers an insight into what it is to own the name Lidice. I am very appreciative of their contributions:

Lidixe Montoya

My story comes from my mom. She was told the story from a union member who had visited the place and she, who was workers' union leader and very oriented to social justice, decided to honour the victims of this atrocity by naming me Lidixe. I know now that is misspelled. I grew up during the civil war in El Salvador, and mentioning the whole story was dangerous because Czechoslovakia was part of a socialist country, which was "illegal" there, so we were very careful to not to say the real reason of my name.

I am very honoured to have this name. I cannot see myself with a different name. Although my whole life I had heard so many mispronunciations and misspelling of it. When I was young, I really got angry of people who cannot say it correctly, now I just try to understand. When I came to the US, I thought, "finally I won't have to repeat my name so many times and still not getting it in the right way", but I was so wrong! I am very happy and proud of my name and if I had the blessing of a daughter, she would be named Lidice too, but maybe that will be the next Lidice, to perpetuate the story.

Lidixe Montoya – USA

Lidice Holanda

My father was a historian and owned a collection of WWII books, one of which was Lidice. From then on, he decided to baptize me by that name, as a symbol of strength. For several years, I thought I was unique. After meeting other women of the same name, and a city here in Brazil, I felt happier and more honoured by the name and all that it represents in the history of the world. I was the creator of the first Lidice meeting in Brazil, an event broadcast on national television. I looked for how many Lidices there are in Brazil, and I created a blog which includes the history of Lidice, how we remember it here in Brazil and how the Lidice women come together to keep alive the name "Lidice"

Lidice Holanda - Brazil

Lidice Belen Fragoso Calderas

Allow me to narrate what my father Porfirio Fragoso wrote about my name... "It was the year 1973, when the representative of the Czechoslovak Embassy in Mexico, attended the Primary School Anniversary "Republic of Czechoslovakia" located in the Colony Ahead. During the ceremony, the authorities of the school presented a special present of a little book, that when the representative opened and leafed through it, he realized that it narrated the terrible tragedy of Lidice. Reading this little book caused my father a deep impression, which led him to propose to his girlfriend, today my mother, that his first daughter be called Lídice. Quoting verbatim, the words of my father:

"In 1977 we got married and on July 16, 1979, my wife gave birth and so I baptized and registered my first and precious daughter, with the name of that heroic Czech town, that she takes with great pride, LIDICE, FOREVER WILL LIVE!" -

Lidice Belen Fragoso Calderas

Lidice Rivas Cortes

My dad worked in San Jeronimo Lídice 58 years ago and there he met a secretary named Lídice, and liked the name very much, and then decided that when had another daughter would be called "Lídice". But oh surprise, 4 boys were born, so the desired one did not arrive! My mom told me that when I was born, my dad took me some earrings to the hospital and said, "Finally Lídice arrived!" They registered me as Maria Lídice Rivas Cortes because my grandparents did not agree very much, since they said that Lídice was not a name that existed in the calendar and then what was God going to call me day that I died? I knew the meaning of my name until the age of 18 years, when I was working in Texcoco, where I met an old man by trade shoemaker, who liked a lot of reading and he told me that my name was from the Republic Czech, and that it was a village that had been destroyed Hitler. When my youngest daughter was born, I asked my husband to also called Lídice, because I wanted this name not to be lost and continue to endure, and he agreed. I have been in contact for about 3 years on social media with women's groups called Lidice, but my daughter and I are surprised by the number of women that exist in the world, and we thought we were unique. Thank you very much.

Lidice Rivas Cortes

Lidice Cuadra Rivas

My name Lídice is something so significant for me, representative and beautiful. I love that people ask me what does your name mean? And I will tell you a little about the meaning of the village of Lídice. In my school when we talk about the history of Czechia, I love to deploy all knowledge from Lídice. It is a great honour to have the name that my mother also has, and it was thanks to her that I have this great name, since I cannot imagine myself with another name, something that identify so much, something so beautiful that is my name: Leader. Thank you so much

Lidice Cuadra Rivas

Zoe Lidice Luna Lopez

When my parents got married, they curiously observed how my mother's name was after married, and they realized there were 3 letters "L" in her new name: Lourdes López de Luna. So, they decided at that time that their children would also have the 3 "L" in their names. When my mother was pregnant with me, she already had the first name Zoe, but she was missing the name that starts with "L" and combines with the first name and that it had a special meaning. In their search they found the name of Lídice and knowing the importance that this name has in the history of the world, they decided to call me "Leader"...Thank you very much

Zoe Lidice Luna Lopez

Lidice Irene Ramirez Molina

Maybe it was 1989 when my parents became very serious and they explained to me that my name had a meaning in particular. They gave me a book that had on the cover my name engraved in gold letters. I received that white book that inside told a story in print handwritten and black and white drawings that I hardly understood. Both my mom and dad took on the task of explaining what that story meant. It was not a story or images precisely for infants, but they were sure that as I grew up, I would understand the importance of what is there counted. I can almost remember that my mom told me that my commitment was take care of it as it was a valuable item that my dad had bought especially for me. It had been an expensive acquisition. It became my little treasure because it reminds me of the weight and the significance of my name and moves me to a constant search to be a good person, to be congruent, to carry with honour my name. Sometimes I like to read it, see it again and remember with emotion the first time I had it in my hands, it's like I found something very mine and I smile: I think how lucky I am and I get happy. I sound romantic, and yes, I like to be like that, so "Leader" how can I be, because happiness is my way of honouring people from that small mining town that they did not have the opportunity to live a new day ...

Thank you very much

Lidice Irene Ramirez Molina

Lidice A Candelario Matos

I am a 67-year-old lady from Puerto Rico. I was born in Mayaguez, which is a town in the western side of our island. Since I was a little girl, I was upset by my name. Everybody was asking me about my name and how to spell it, because it was not so common. When I was 12 years old my doctor, who happens to be a soldier when he was younger, told me the story about my name. My mother then told me that when she was having me at the hospital Bella Vista in Mayaguez, there was this nurse-nun that was from "Czechoslovakia," that ask her to name me LIDICE. She did it and that is why I have my name."

Lidice A Candelario Matos

Clockwise: Lidice Ganchozo, Ecuador; Lidice A Candelario Matos from Puerto Rico; Lidixe Montoya (with Andrey) - Lidixe originally hails from El Salvador but now lives in the USA; Lidice Holanda lives in Brazil and organises Lidice conventions open to all ladies christened with the symbolic, inspirational name. Over the years the number of ladies and girls christened Lidice has steadily increased. The arrival of social media with its removal of barriers and wiping away of oceans has spread the "message of Lidice" and brought the positive news to a far larger audience.

Lidice Ganchozo

Hello. My name is Lidice Ganchozo - Ecuador. When I was at school, no one called me by my first name Lídice, everyone called me by my second name, until I got to school and it was there when I began to discover the meaning of my name. However, I was not very clear about everything that they enclosed these letters, then when I got to the University, I had Macroeconomics classes and the professor passed the list and named me forcefully and told me: "Lídice Ganchozo". I obviously answered present and this professor tells me The Lost City of Lidice and I was stunned and told him how and he began to tell all of the group the story of Lídice. I felt so sad and excited at the same time. Since that day I began to investigate my name, I felt proud and powerful from that day, although sometimes I think that so much tragedy of my name influences my life, because when I fall, I always get up again ... just like that. the Leader City.

Lidice Ganchozo, Ecuador

Lidice Torres Lairona

I was born on May 11, 1967, and here is my story. My mother had a teacher when she was in high school who she commented on the fact and, at the call for Lidice to live, she named her daughter. That's why my mom thought that if she had a daughter, she would give her that name. When he was born, it was decided and a notice from the Czech Culture House appeared in the press that day, summoning all the people by name who came forward. Apparently, my dad signed me up, then they sent me an invitation to the activity on June 10 of that year. My parents took me when I was only one month old to the Czechoslovak House of Culture, where there were more girls. They put a documentary on the massacre and gave me story books. Later, they sent me the doll with a traditional dress and a bronze coin with the name and a rose on one side and the year 1967 on the other. All the following years I continued to attend the commemoration in the same place until, after the fall of the socialist camp, the Czecho-Slovak House of Culture closed. I missed those encounters a lot, but the feeling of what happened in that village was already in me. I graduated as a doctor and worked as such in Cuba until 2013, when we decided, my family and I, to emigrate to Canada, where I began to surf the internet and meet other Lidices from all over the world.

In 2017 I went with my daughter to the commemoration of the 75th anniversary in the Republic and it was very exciting to realize a lifelong dream. There we met other Lidices from Brazil, Mexico, the Dominican Republic, and Cuba. After that meeting I decided to bring together all the Lidices of Cuba and I created a group on Facebook with that name. I contacted the Embassy in Havana to attend the commemoration in the park that bears the name and where there is a plaque explaining what happened. This is how we meet every year and share with the Embassy and diplomatic attachés in Havana. Due to the pandemic, it has been impossible for us to meet, but we did not ignore it, we will post videos in the group explaining why we were given the name and photos with pullovers with the group's logo. We aim to attend the 80th anniversary in Czechia. I know it will be difficult for those who live in Cuba due to the economic situation in the country, but they will try. Thank you for the opportunity to express ourselves and make ourselves known."

Lidice Torres Lairona

Lidice Brooks Raymond

I am a Cuban citizen, born in 1979 and an only child. The story of my name germinates in 1978 when my parents were still studying at the university. One day my father took an oral exam about history and one of the questions was to describe what happened in Czechia on the 10th of June... he passed his exam but couldn't remember exactly the name of that village destroyed by the Nazis. And he said to himself that when he had a descendant, he would put that name in remembrance... I was born and my parents inscribed me with that name, a name of which I carry immense pride... Since I was little, I knew about the history contained within its 6 letters, by my parents I was told about her, as an adult through magazine articles and the internet. In Cuba in the 1980s there was a Czech culture house that gathered every year on the eve of the commemoration of the date where girls and adolescents who had our name would meet, where activities were conducted and thus, they remembered what happened.

Since 2016 I have been associated with a group in social networks named Cuban leaders, where we gather women who bear that beautiful name who live or are outside the national territory. This group has given me the opportunity to know that there are at least 1,000 ladies named Lidice in the world, the Americas region being the one with the highest number of them. I am a veterinary profession. My biggest dream focuses on being able to visit Czechia and especially the city of Lidice to visit a monument to the child victims of such a heinous crime and thus pay tribute to those people who lost their lives. I live proud to call myself that, honouring the memory of the village and its horrible crime. A hug from the island of Cuba.

Lidice Brooks Raymond

WHAT I HAVE SEEN IN ENGLAND

Helena Leflerová - Published in Rudé Právo on the 16th of July 1952:

At the invitation of the British-Czechoslovak Friendship Union in London, I was invited to England to attend a memorial ceremony for the 10th anniversary of the Lidice tragedy.

Although a week-long stay does not provide an opportunity to get to know the life there in depth, what I have seen belongs in our republic, thanks to the USSR and our working people to the irreversible past. At every step, I appreciated the great happiness of being a citizen of a people's democratic country, filled with creative work and human happiness.

Although London is dressed in flashy advertisements of various companies, there are beggars on the streets, most of them war invalids. They have many medals, but they beg passers-by, or they sell various small items next to shops filled with goods.

Since I last visited London in 1947, the rationing of the most necessary daily necessities has expanded. Except for the white bread, everything is on the tickets. Some shops, such as textiles and fruit shops, are filled with goods like ours, but with the big difference that there are very few buyers. I saw a mother with two children in a fruit shop buying an apple, certainly not because the children wouldn't eat more, but because she couldn't afford more. There are very few meat shops throughout London, as there is a shortage.

England is, as I found out myself during a five-hour drive from London to Stoke upon Trent, a large meadow, where very few cattle graze. I didn't see a field of grain. Everything is to be supplied by the colonies, and today goods have to be bought expensively from the Americans. Therefore, it is not surprising that you would look in vain for dairy stores in London, such as ours.

I visited two parts of London, West Ham and Holborn, which were greatly destroyed by bombing during the war. They showed us plans and newly built houses. Barely a quarter of the demolished houses have been restored so far, and completion for example in West Ham is scheduled for 20 years. The City of London, which was heavily bombed is overgrown with grass. There are many empty houses everywhere in London that have been destroyed and have not yet been restored. There is a lack of steel and material that the state does not allow, of course, because it needs it for war purposes.

At the Coventry construction site, I spoke to a worker who I asked if he would also live in these houses, as is the case in our country. He answered in the negative, firstly, because primarily department stores are being built, and then because there is a high rent in new residential buildings, which accounts for up to one third of earnings.

In older apartments it is not much better, with rents accounting for a quarter of the salary. Rent is expensive because the owners of the land on which the buildings stand rent them only for very high amounts. Even with the fact that in a hundred years everything on them will fall back to the owner's heirs. This is how the capitalists provide their grandchildren with an idle, easy life.

The Wedgwood ceramics factory near Stoke upon Trent employs mostly women who work, as everywhere in England, for a lower wage than men. However, the workers understand the causes of their misery. They do not want to become an American colony; they do not want the capitalists to make weapons for a new war from the money they have exploited. This was said by the chairmen of the dock, the construction workers, the miners, and others I met, who told me about the struggles waged by the English people, which we are reading in the newspapers. Even the women in London I spoke to expressed their opposition to the politics of the government. Through protests and demonstrations, they are fighting for the rights to life not only for themselves, but also for the people in the colonial countries of the British Empire. Neither persecution nor prison can break this will, as it didn't Mrs Pat Sears, who protested against the screening of an American film celebrating Nazi General Rommel.

Progressive British art also shows the will of the British people. The exhibition of painters entitled Peace at the Royal Hotel, where I talked about our lives, is such proof of the struggle of progressive artists. At the beginning, a painter, who cannot devote himself fully to his art, also spoke, because to make a living he has to work as a gardener. Even his existential worries, however, cannot snatch from him the weapon of his art, which he put fully into the service of the fight against the war and its architects, who prevent him from living the full life of an artist.

When I was welcomed by the mayors of London's West Ham and Holborn districts, in the cities of Stoke on Trent and Coventry, at meetings and other occasions, I was met with sincere and cordial receptions. Everyone I met has the same goal as us in Czechoslovakia - to prevent war, to live in peace and friendship between nations. This friendship cannot be divided by borders or the ocean; it cannot be divided by the hatred of the capitalist monopolists. It is a friendship between the working class and all progressive peaceful people who have the same goal.

The concert of the London Philharmonic and our cellist M. Sádlo, which took place in the largest London hall - on the occasion of the 10th anniversary of the destruction of Lidice, was a massive manifestation of the friendship of the English people to our republic. M. Sádlo's performance evoked real enthusiasm and admiration for our musical art. Smetana's Blanik was heard with intense attention and rewarded with enthusiastic applause from 3,000 people present.

A film about the destruction of Lidice and a new film about Lidice, about our life today, which was screened on Sunday, June 8 in St. Pancras, left a deep impression on the audience. The storm of applause was caused by the image of J. Fučík, whom viewers know from the translation of his book 'Report Written on the Noose.' Trade Unionists, present at this meeting, who already visited the Czechoslovak Republic, described what they saw there and confirmed the joyful reality of our lives. "You are a role model for us," I often heard words, filled with fighting determination and a relentless faith in their realisation.

During my stay, I was often asked what I liked most about England and where I would get the best impressions. It is the simple, progressive, and peaceful English people that I liked most in England, who stand in the same line of peace with our working people. Their love and friendship for the working people of our Czechoslovak Republic, their militancy and unwavering faith in the better life of their country, these are the most beautiful impressions I have brought from England.

THE LIGHT DIES DOWN ON STERN PARK

On the 15th of June 1950, published in an article titled *"THE LIGHT IS OUT at Lidice"*, the Texas based *Alice Daily Echo* newspaper gave an update on the state of the Stern Park memorial in Illinois. Under a photograph of the damaged marble sculpture surrounded by long grass and weeds, which had been ceremoniously unveiled before thousands eight years before, it said:

"This is the monument, now just a place for children to play. It's chipped and muddy, too. Lidice, reborn, is dead again! Hitler killed it the first time. President Roosevelt called the martyrdom of Lidice Czechoslovakia the murder of a word. Wendell Willkie told the people, *'Because a hangman was killed, Lidice lives.'* He meant Lidice ILL, the community re-named so that Lidice should live forever. *'Living forever in the hearts of all who love freedom.,' 'the light that will burn forever in memory of the dead'.*"

Emotive phrases like these emanated from the lips of speech-makers and were blazed across the front pages of the newspapers on July 13, 1942, as a federal housing project, Stern Park Gardens, became a powerful rebuke to Hitler's actions

Prominent citizens who served on the committee for the establishment of the Stern Park monument and perpetual light admitted that they were drafted to serve because they represented one organisation or another. Where the funds for the light went, they don't know. Children swarm over the monument. It is chipped in places.

According to Adolf Kacer, President of the Czech American National Alliance, **"the light went out"** because the monument was moved. **"The mayor promised me he'd have the gas connected again, but he hasn't done it. I had to go out and wash the mud off the monument after it was moved."** Kacer was on the committee which planned the memorial. The monument was moved in 1943 to make way for housing, so at the time of the report it had been hidden away for seven years. Kacer felt that the neglect of the memorial was because the people did not like it: **"most of the Czechs have moved and there are only two or three Bohemian families left"** - it has become an Italian community.

Miss Mahoney, from Joliet's mayoral Office was more vehement about the whole affair. She named names and said that **"Lidice is not even a village. It never has been. It has never had a Post Office. It has never had any elected officials. Joliet's mail-carriers deliver the mail. Lidice was just a promotion scheme to sell lots. That's how it started. The houses built there are in poor condition and have changed hands many times. It may soon become incorporated as a part of Joliet. The Czech Embassy sent some dolls for the children of Lidice, addressing them to that community. No trace of them has ever been found."**

Neither has there been any trace of the light that will burn forever.

In one sense, the whole thing was a fraud and Hitler's wish was answered with a lie, as Lidice, Illinois never existed. There was never a post office, never a village or any other kind of organised municipality, according to Helen Mahoney, Secretary to the Mayor in neighbouring Joliet.

TRANSCRIPT OF SIR BARNETT STROSS'S SPEECH AT THE 1963 LIDICE COMMEMORATIVE EVENT

The speech is pasted as it was completed by Stross on his typewriter, including all the formatting errors.

"Mr President

Madame Mayor

Ladies and Gentlemen

And FRIENDS

115

When I first visited Lidice in July 1946 with the parliamentary delegation, there was only theNazi destruction of the village to see. I beheld only the mass grave and above it the toweringwooden cross with its circling halo of barbed wire. In the grave lay the remains of all theformer male inhabitants who were more than 15 years old. They had been shot on June 10th, 1942, following the slaying of Heydrich, the Nazi leader in Prague. The women were sent to concentration camps. The children perished in the gas chambers. Only seventeen survived. On June 13th, 1942, within a few days of this calamity, an exhibition was opened in the art gallery of Hanley, Stoke on Trent which commemorated the 'seven years of friendshipbetween Czecho-Slovakia and the USSR' The exhibition was organised by the Czecho-Slovak - British friendship club.

I had been requested to propose a vote of thanks to the speakers from the USSR and Czecho-Slovakia. Among other things which I mentioned, I said that the Nazis appeared tothink that this cold-blooded murder would serve two purposes. It would act as a deterrentupon rebellious Czechs and Slovaks, and it would appease Hitler for the assassination of Heydrich.

With my friends of the North Staffordshire Miners union I discussed what could be done. In a letter in July 1942 I asked for the support of the 20,000 miners of North Staffordshire andthrough them for the support of the miners of Great Britain. I wrote as follows 'it must never be forgotten that centres of resistance exist everywhere inEurope, and that men who struggle in the underground movement need all the help we cangive them.By their action, the miners declare their international solidarity with all their comrades andwith all men who are prepared to fight for freedom.

The miners' lamp dispels the shadows on the coal face. It can also send a ray of lightacross Europe to those who struggle in darkness.'

12. the rebuilding of Lidice

13. the rescue of the widows and children of those who were murdered. Our plans matured. We asked that Lidice be rebuilt as a modern village for miners and other workers, and that a research station be built in the village to collect all available data onsafety factors in coal mining and issue the findings to every mining centre. By this means themovement declared its intentions of protecting hundreds of miners' lives for every manmurdered in Lidice.

On September 6th, 1942, the inaugural meeting was held in the Victoria Hall Stoke on Trent. Three thousand men and women were packed in the hall and on the platform behind therostrum were massed the flags of the Allied nations. For the Soviet Union, the Minister Plenipotentiary, Mr Bogomolov spoke as follows:

"the humane idea of rebuilding Lidice demands that we put an end to the enemy as soon aspossible. So let us fight for the earliest defeat of Hitler, for final victory over the brutalenemy."

After the President of the British Miners, Dr Beneš, the president of Czecho-Slovakia spoke asfollows: -

"Only a hard lesson, not of revenge, but retributive justice will teach the Germans that it doesnot pay to attack other nations."

On the 9th September, the Yugoslav envoy broadcast his impressions of our meeting: -

"Every occupied territory in Europe has its Lidice. This Czech village, whose fate was publicly announced by the Nazis as a warning to the Czecho-Slovak people, has become asymbol and a challenge to all of us. It also exemplifies our determination to build a better and happier world."

In this way the "Lidice shall live" movement had its birth. The imagination of the people was stimulated and supported. The movement spread to other towns and cities, and demonstrations of the type that were held in Stoke on Trent were organised with great success in Birmingham, Derby, Leeds, and Coventry. "Lidice shall live" committees sprung up in many other towns such as Cardiff, Durham, Edinburgh, Aberdeen, and Leamington. In Britain, the name of the village that had been condemned to death became a household word.

In Coventry on Sunday 12th March 1944, Mr Beneš declared that there were three habitations of man that had been made deathless by suffering and persistence. These were Stalingrad, Coventry, and Lidice. "The moment is approaching where in my own country also a signal will be given, and the people will rise against their alien masters.

SYMBOLISM

From the very beginning we had in mind a movement which would play its part in giving inspiration and courage to all those who struggled under the Nazi heel. The Battle of Britain had been won by the courage of British pilots. The red army's defenceof Stalingrad dug the grave in which the hopes of Hitler were buried. Czecho-Slovak pilots joined the British air force in increasing numbers. In this way they gave open support to the resistance movement in Czecho-Slovakia. From the ashes of Lidice there would spring another village. Only free men should hew the stones and only free men should bind them together, for in this village as in so many others would dwell those whom the Nazis thought to enslave – the men, women, and children of a world free, secure and at PEACE.

The Rose Garden

In June 1955, the Rose Garden of peace and friendship was opened. In Britain we appealed to organisations, local authorities, and citizens. The warm response in Britain was shown by the gift of more than 10,000 rose trees. Quickly following our lead 35 other nations took part in the campaign.

117

Among our British rose trees several thousand were named "independence," "happiness" and "peace."

In 1955 we said that "Lidice belongs to the world and all who suffered the torments of war

Today mankind has one common enemy, and that enemy is WAR.

Only a realisation of our common humanity can save mankind in this age of the Hydrogen bomb."

For the 20th Anniversary the British Lidice Committee sent 2,300 trees of the "Rose of Lidice" This rose was newly developed to bloom in the soil of Lidice itself and help to remind the whole world of the need for an enduring PEACE.

Early this year in the Czecho-Slovak embassy in London, we presented to Madame Jarosova, the mayor of Lidice, paintings, and a piece of Sculpture. They are to be part of an international collection in Lidice.

We look at artists as poets and teachers and they bring a special message of beauty and peace. We offer you these gifts as one more link in the bond of friendship between our countries. Although we meet at the scene of one of the worst crimes in history, Lidice is indeed a symbol of LIFE. In our time there is no alternative to LIFE. In our atomic age LIFE and PEACE are indivisible.

"Lidice Lives

"Peace""

REMEMBERING VÁCLAV - 1938 – 2021

On Saturday the 13th of November 2021, the community of Lidice and all those who knew him the world over, raised a final glass to Václav Zelenka. Lidice had suffered yet another great loss with his passing but his impact on humanity remains indelibly imprinted on the very soul of Lidice for generations throughout the world for countless years to come. With former Mayor Hana Pokorná we look back on the life of the Lidice child who led the way in rejuvenating the village's rose garden and memorial following a sustained period of neglect:

"Václav Zelenka was born in Kladno. He was only 3¾ years old when the Nazis exterminated his village and the majority of its inhabitants. He was one of the first to be selected for Germanisation from the group of mothers and children held at the Kladno Grammar School Gymnasium; and was ultimately placed within a German family in April 1945 following a very hard Hitler Youth re-education process in Oberweis, Austria."

The Wagner family, who re-named Václav, Rolf, rarely had time to settle because of Allied bombing raids. After arriving in Bülhau (near to Dresden), the bombing of Dresden took place, necessitating a move to the Wagners' native home of Olbernhau; and in autumn of 1946, Rolf began attending German school. 1947 saw the whole family moved again to the town of Lohsa in Lusatia, 20 km from the Czech border, as Václav gradually transformed into a German boy, losing his 'mother tongue'. He had a very close relationship with his adopted father and although Václav lived in a German family near to the border of his homeland, the last child from Lidice did not return to Czechoslovakia until May 1947.

"Efforts had been ongoing since the end of the war to reunite the surviving Lidice women with those children who had been sent to German families. It was Václav's memories of old Lidice that helped to identify him. He remembered his old village, his house, and the clothes of his mother. In 1951 he moved with his Czech mother to the new Lidice."

Václav graduated at the Secondary School of Electrical Engineering in Prague, so after completing a national military service, he focused on technical professions. His last job was as a technician in today's Air Traffic Control at Prague airport. In 1962, he met Helena Šnáblová at a dance party in Lidice. They fell in love and later married. Václav's first son was born in 1962, the second in 1964 and the third in 1975. In the 1980s Václav became involved in politics and took a serious interest in the running of the town. In 1998, the future of the village looked in jeopardy and he became Lidice's Mayor. Under his administration the Lidice Memorial was established under the stewardship of the Ministry of Culture; the Rose Garden of Peace and Friendship was renovated; a communist peacekeeping memorial, still in the construction procedure was liquidated; and property issues in the village were resolved.

"Václav was an animal lover since childhood and particularly liked dogs. But he could be a paradox, for example he was also a passionate hunter. He loved the company of friends, colleagues and especially his own family. He never spoiled any fun. He did not like double-dealing, lies and dissemblance. In short, he had a genuine character."

Recent photo of Václav – © Martin Homola.

DAVE PROUDLOVE –

THE REBIRTH OF INTERNATIONALISM IN STOKE-ON-TRENT

If one was to define internationalism, it would probably be that it is a principle that promotes political or economic cooperation between states and nations, characterised by an opposition to isolationism and nationalism, and an outlook that celebrates and respects different customs and cultures. Internationalists tend to believe that humanity should unite across boundaries, be they national, political, cultural, racial or class. To be an internationalist is to be a decent human being.

Internationalism emerged in the Potteries through the success of Josiah Wedgwood and his ground-breaking industrialism and the circles in which he moved.

Wedgwood commercialised his creativity and went on to become one of the wealthiest entrepreneurs of the 1700s. He contributed to international trade missions – most notably to China – and with business partner Thomas Bentley, collaborated with engineer James Brindley to build the infrastructure with provided the means for the expanding Potteries to trade with America and Europe.

But it was during his later years that Wedgwood's internationalist principles truly shone through.

Through his friendship with abolitionist campaigner Thomas Clarkson, Wedgwood too became a high-profile figure in the movement, and his mass-produced cameos depicting the seal of the Society for Effecting the Abolition of the Slave Trade. The emblem was incorporated in bracelets and other similar items and went on to symbolise the campaign among the middle classes. Wedgwood's work became the most famous image of a black person in 18th Century art.

***

Although Wedgwood helped to establish strong international links and developed an internationalist outlook, it was almost 150-years until North Staffordshire truly adopted this mindset. And it was borne out of tragedy.

What happened in the Czech village of Lidice on 10th June 1942 was one of the worst atrocities in modern history and a demonstration of what evil looks like. But the response – the Lidice Shall Live campaign, spearheaded by Sir Barnett Stross – was the polar opposite. The Lidice Shall Live campaign was what good looks like, and it marked the rebirth of internationalism in North Staffordshire.

In hindsight it was perhaps inevitable and certainly fitting that it was Stross that led such a campaign. He understood internationalism and knew what it meant to be an internationalist. Stross was born to a Jewish family – a people already being persecuted by Hitler and the Nazis – in the Polish city Łódź on Christmas Day 1899. The Stross family moved to Dewsbury in Yorkshire when Barnett was three, and he went on to study at the University of Leeds. These experiences clearly shaped Stross's outlook, and on hearing of the Nazis' actions in Czechoslovakia, he was furious. But he turned that anger into a positive energy.

At the time, Stross ran a medical practice in Hanley, was a member of Stoke-on-Trent City Council – a Labour Party member – and was heavily involved with the North Staffordshire Miners' Federation. In a great show of empathy, Stross exploited his position in order to mobilise the North Staffordshire mining communities behind the Lidice Shall Live campaign which pledged to rebuild the vanquished village.

Both Stross and North Staffordshire stood strong in opposition to fascism and tyranny and raised £32,000 – the equivalent of around £1,000,000 today – towards the building of a new Lidice, which began in 1947. For his efforts, the Czechoslovak government awarded Stross the White Lion of Czechoslovakia, and he subsequently became the chair of the British-Czechoslovakia Society.

Stross considered the establishment of the Lidice Shall Live movement his greatest achievement, and he continued to develop and nurture the bond created until his passing, using art and the environment to build upon Lidice's rebirth. Stross recast the atrocity committed by Hitler and the Nazis as a message of peace and hope.

But it wasn't just a North Staffordshire/Lidice thing. Thanks to the work of Stross, other English cities such as Coventry and Derby supported the campaign, while it also took on a truly international aspect, flourishing in other parts of the world such as the Americas.

And the movement continued to flourish beyond these shores following the passing of Stross in 1967. Yet here in North Staffordshire, it began to wane. How and why did the Lidice movement become more or less an afterthought in the city of its birth? Was it due to a changing of the guard politically and the desire for Stross's Labour Party to look to the future? Was it due to the start of the decline of heavy industry in North Staffordshire and a weakening of the ties that bound our communities together? Was it a desire to leave the horrors of the Second World War in the past?

Beyond the naming of a couple of nondescript streets in Chell for him, Sir Barnett Stross was almost forgotten; he became our secret hero. But more pertinently we seemed to forget just why his intervention and the Lidice Shall Live movement and the messages that underpinned them were important.

While we quite rightly remember those that made the ultimate sacrifice in defence of our freedom, we don't often remember those that helped us rebuild.

∗∗∗

In more recent times, that has started to change. Thanks to the tireless efforts of Alan and Cheryl Gerrard, the links between North Staffordshire, Lidice and the Czech Republic have been re-established and the emotional bonds strengthened. But despite the obvious power of the story and the messages behind it, their efforts were initially resisted and stifled by the local Labour administration, a horrible irony given that the original campaign is such an important part of the party's heritage, particularly from a local perspective.

But they have continued their work and have strengthened the civic links in partnership with the present administration and have established Lidice Lives, which will be a long-term steward of those relationships that will endure regardless of any future political upheaval.

Through the development of Lidice Lives, Alan and Cheryl have anticipated the need for a new era of internationalism here in North Staffordshire. The Brexit Era leaves both the UK and North Staffordshire needing to construct a new identity on the world stage, and this has become all the more important with the tragic and mindless outbreak of war in eastern Europe. One of the lessons from the original Lidice campaign is that it drew on the horrors that war can bring and instead painted a different picture, one underpinned by peace; this is the golden thread than links Lidice Shall Live and Lidice Lives.

Right now, there is a void, and what's needed to fill that void is a new era of internationalism. Peace. Hope. Empathy. Friendship. Collaboration. Partnership. Shared goals. Solidarity. And most importantly, achieving things together. These are the principles that drove Sir Barnett Stross. They are also the principles that drive Alan and Cheryl Gerrard and underpin Lidice Lives and can prove to be the antidote to Brexit and the destructive forces of war.

They are ahead of the curve and will be at the forefront of a new internationalism in North Staffordshire. Policy makers and decision takers ought to take note.

DP

Stoke-on-Trent

13-Mar-2022

Dave Proudlove is an urbanist, writer, lover of great buildings, a born and bred Stokie, and an eloquent advocate for the Potteries.

A SELECTION OF PROJECTS

This last section of the book presents *a selection* of the projects that have taken place over the last decade between Lidice and Stoke-on-Trent to give you, the reader, a flavour of how the intention to improve *cultural awareness and understanding* looks put into practice. In most cases, these projects took place following the commitment to a reciprocal relationship between the two communities with the signing of a Memorandum of Understanding on the 7th of September 2012 at the Civic Centre in Stoke. See what you think. They are included here because we see the point of Sir Barnett Stross's work in encouraging camaraderie between international communities.

THE INTERNATIONAL CHILDREN'S EXHIBITION OF FINE ARTS (ICEFA) 2011 –

2022 was the 50th anniversary of the annual International Children's Exhibition of Fine Arts, organised by the Lidice Memorial. The event now attracts over 25,000 entries from young people across seventy countries, on average. The Lidice memorial selects the theme in cooperation with UNESCO and the standard and quality of entries is outstanding. Each entry is a statement by the child that they wish to see a future free of war and conflict, and with a greater degree of cultural understanding across borders. Paintings, drawings, lino and wood printing, photography, ceramics, glass, film and both individual and *whole school/class* entries are accepted, and the opportunity is open to all children.

Since our first visit to Lidice in 2010, Cheryl and I have encouraged children to take part in the ICEFA as part of our school presentations. The art exhibition is a positive way for children to celebrate the Lidice Shall Live movement. Teachers and their students are inspired by its spirit, they gain a sense of *place* and like the idea of taking part in a global peace project. So far, Theartbay Gallery, has shipped hundreds of entries over to Lidice. And many British children and schools have been recognised and awarded with *'Honourable Mentions'* and medals by the panel of professional judges appointed by the Lidice Memorial. We have also held prize giving events for the UK and international awards in theatres, art galleries, museums, and schools.

ANNUAL COMMEMORATIVE EVENTS - SAMPLES

LIDICE: Readers know that the tragedy which befell Lidice has been commemorated on site since 1945. But since 2011, once more, at the invitation of the Lidice Memorial and Lidice Mayoral office, the people of Stoke-on-Trent have been represented at the annual Lidice commemoration, held on the nearest Saturday to the 10th of June. During a most effecting, reverent part of the event, Czech soldiers escort delegates to lay their wreath at the site of the mass grave where the 173 Lidice men lay buried. It seems apt, for Stoke-on-Trent at least, that to help pay for the cost of this, funds are normally raised via *crowd funders* and donations, equivalently to the original Lidice Shall Live movement. FENTON: The first memorial service in modern history in Stoke-on-Trent was held in Fenton's Albert Square on the 10th of June 2011 and included children from local schools reciting the poetry they had written with poet and storyteller Alan Barrett, a trustee of Lidice Lives; school and Methodist Church Choirs; and dance performances. Stoke-on-Trent's Lord Mayor, Cllr Terry Follows, was also in attendance. HOLOCAUST MEMORIAL: On the 27th of January 2012, at the invitation of Staffordshire

University, we presented the history of Lidice and Lidice Shall Live Campaign. Included was a display of international children's artwork, together with a pop-up exhibition telling the story of Lidice. STOKE MINSTER: The 70th anniversary of the Lidice atrocity was marked on the 10th of June, with a full Civic Service at Stoke Minster. Organised by Stoke-on-Trent City Council, the service included a performance by the High Schools Community Choir, and Abbey Hill School and Performing Arts College. Nick Hancock, Stoke-on-Trent TV presenter, shared the story of the tragedy of Lidice. Stoke-on-Trent's Young Poet Laureate recited a Lidice poem. Ceramic roses were made at Gladstone Pottery Museum to represent Lidice's Rose Garden and distributed to guests at the service. FLAG RAISING: In October 2021, Stoke-on-Trent City Council raised the Czech flag from its public buildings three times a year, marking the anniversaries of the Lidice atrocity; the launch of the Lidice Shall Live campaign; and the birth of the Czech nation.

TALKS AND PRESENTATIONS (2010-)

Over the years, trustees, and friends of the Lidice Lives organisation, including Stephen Dyster, Alan Barrett, Cheryl, and I have visited many schools to tell the story of Lidice and how the people of Stoke-on-Trent helped others during those war years - it is an inspirational account, one which we should share. And as a former teacher myself, I can assure those in my profession that the topic of the Lidice Shall Live campaign is highly expressive, cross curricular subject matter, most conducive to poetry, art, role play and creative writing workshops. Illustrated talks and presentations have also been given to a substantial number of professional, business, social groups, and community organisations across Stoke-on-Trent and North Staffordshire, such as the Rotary Clubs, U3A, History Clubs, trade unions, and other groups. We have worked with the YMCA North Staffordshire and their young people on many activities to raise awareness of the Lidice and its links with Stoke-on-Trent: one of the National Citizen Service groups based at YMCA chose this as their project and created a social media campaign targeting younger people.

ARTWORKS - SAMPLES

Locally based artists have painted several original pieces of artwork. Three of these paintings have been accepted into official collections in Lidice. The late Sid Kirkham's watercolour 'Lidice' (2010) conveys the camaraderie shown by Stoke-on-Trent's mining community. Harry Davies (Aitch) produced a powerful watercolour piece "Document 379" (2012), whose title was derived from the document number given to the film showing the destruction of Lidice when used as evidence at the Nuremberg Trials of the Nazi German leaders in 1945. The artist, Steve Shaw, has painted a series of moving pieces in watercolour paint, pencil and lino cuts depicting various elements of the Lidice atrocity (2010 -). One of his pieces relating to the Pear Tree has been accepted into the Lidice Pear Tree Art Collection organised by Antonin Nešpor. The late Sue Law-Webb used oils to produce two canvasses, one painted 'live' during the Fenton service in 2011 and the other featuring St Martin's church (2012), reflecting the peaceful beauty of the village before the Nazi invasion. Angela Mason more recently produced a large mixed media piece showing the Pear Tree in bloom (2020). She was deeply moved following a visit to Lidice, which was the inspiration for her artwork.

70th ANNIVERSARY—2012

2012 brought with it the 70th anniversary of the launch of the Lidice Shall Live campaign and it was important that this was commemorated in a distinct way, to recognise our communities' friendship. We wanted to reciprocate the enthusiasm and warmth the city had received from the people of Lidice and so set up meetings with Stoke-on-Trent City Council representatives to put forward our suggestions and our willingness to act in partnership. Thanks to our persistence, many events and activities were organised during this year.

THE SCHOOL VISIT TO STOKE-ON-TRENT

At the end of May 2012, we facilitated a week-long visit to Stoke-on-Trent of some schoolchildren from Buštěhrad, the school which serves Lidice, and which we visited. They stayed at Copeland Cottage Brownie and Guide Camp site in Maer, owned by Guiding Divisions in Stoke, Longton and Newcastle. Working in partnership with Ormiston Sir Stanley Matthews Academy and Blurton Primary School, and Stoke-on-Trent City Council, we put together a varied programme and arranged for children of the same age to be *buddied up* together to encourage friendship.

Highlights of the week included a visit to Staffordshire University, working with media students to set up a virtual *meeting* with parents and teachers back in Lidice and Buštěhrad - we encouraged the Czech children to speak in English about their adventures; an evening musical performance by the Czech children held at Blurton Primary School—a packed hall saw the Lord Mayor of Stoke-on-Trent open the proceedings, which included dancing, songs and poetry; taking part in Stoke-on-Trent's Olympic Torch Rally. Other activities during the week included visits to the Wedgwood Visitor Centre, Gladstone Pottery Museum, the Potteries Museum and Art Gallery, wall climbing and football at YMCA. By the end of the week, the young people learned a significant amount about each other's culture and it was inspiring to see how children went from being shy and tongue tied at the beginning of the week to chatting like old friends by the end.

THE *CHILDREN OF LIDICE* VISIT STOKE-ON-TRENT

At the beginning of September, Stoke-on-Trent was honoured to receive the *children of Lidice* together with the Mayor of Lidice, Director of the ICEFA, and historians from the Lidice Memorial. Stoke-on-Trent City Council organised a number of civic functions. These included the unveiling of a plaque celebrating Sir Barnett Stross, donated by the Lidice community; a special evening concert at the Victoria Hall on the 6th of September 2012; an exhibition and documentary film presentation together with a question-and-answer session at the Potteries Museum and Art Gallery in Hanley; and heritage activities, such as visits to Wedgwood and the Gladstone Pottery Museum. The Potteries Museum and Art Gallery augmented the visit by putting up: the 2010 Barnett Stross exhibition; vibrant displays from the ICEFA; and educational panels describing the Lidice atrocity, Lidice Shall Live Campaign, the Rose Garden of Peace and Friendship, and Lidice today.

They Died for Our Freedom – Steve Shaw - 2022

Cheryl and I arranged for our friends to talk with children from the Stoke-on-Trent schools we had previously visited and told the story of Lidice. One of the most emotive parts of the visit was visiting OSSMA, Blurton Primary and Our Lady's Primary Schools. Here, small groups of children sat transfixed in circles and heard first-hand accounts of the savagery of the Nazis from the *children of Lidice*, who were, of course, then in their 70s and 80s. It was a triumph of inter-generational communication. The impact on the schoolchildren was palpable as they realised the elderly people sitting with them had experienced unspeakable horror at ages equal to themselves. It was a valuable, humbling experience for all.

MEMORANDUM OF UNDERSTANDING

Friday the 7th of September 2012, and the city's friends from Lidice attended Stoke-on-Trent's Civic Offices. As is tradition, we hosted the group in the Lord Mayor's parlour prior to being escorted through to the 'Chambers. It was here that a Memorandum of Understanding was then signed by the Lord Mayor of Stoke-on-Trent, Cllr Terry Crowe; the Mayor of Lidice, Veronika Kellerová; and representative from the Lidice Memorial, Ivona Kasalická. Though not the full twinning agreement that we had hoped for, this was a way forward, a recognition of how important the links were between Lidice and Stoke-on-Trent.

The document *created* an official partnership, with a commitment from all parties to continue developing cultural and friendship links for years to come.

The signing of the Memorandum of Understanding between Lidice and Stoke-on-Trent. Photo - left to right: Mayor of Lidice, Veronika Kellerová; Lord Mayor of Stoke-on-Trent, Cllr Terry Crowe; Director of the International Children's Exhibition of Fine Arts at the Lidice Memorial, Ivona Kasalická.

70th ANNIVERSARY SCULPTURE—UNEARTHED

Unearthed is a conceptual sculpture to be found outside Victoria Hall in Hanley and unveiled in 2013 by the Lord Mayor of Stoke-on-Trent, Cllr Sheila Pitt; and Luba Hédlová, curator of the Lidice Art Gallery. Stoke-on-Trent City Council commissioned it as part of its 70th anniversary commemorations. Besides celebrating and raising awareness of the Lidice Shall Live campaign, the work serves a practical purpose by cladding an electrical substation next to Hanley's Bus Station. Locally based artist collaboration, Dashyline won the commission to create the sculpture, which comprises 3,000 metallic discs, each representing a miner's tag and inscribed with the initials and date of birth of the person who took part in the project.

75th ANNIVERSARY - 2017

THE HOUSE 116 PROJECT

House 116 is a wonderful renovation of one of the original *new* Lidice houses built after the war and opened in 1949. Situated just below the Lidice Gallery, the house had fallen into disrepair over several years. The Lidice Memorial bought the property with plans to incorporate the house as part of the Museum experience, by re-fitting the space with fixtures, fittings, and furnishings in keeping with the original specifications for the building project, as created by the Society for the Restoration of Lidice. Original furniture was sourced and some rooms are now displayed to give the visitor a flavour of Czechoslovak contemporary tastes and fashions, the interior design of the original Lidice houses, and everyday life in mid-20th century Lidice.

Sliding panels form part of a permanent exhibition titled *'Building the new Lidice,'* which includes detailed information about the construction of the new village; background to Sir Barnett Stross and the Lidice Shall Live campaign; and highlights how the campaign contributed to the building of the new Lidice after the war. A significant contribution towards the set-up costs of House 116 was received from Stoke-on-Trent's Lidice Lives organisation; made up of grassroots donations and City Councillor ward budget contributions, and from a fund-raising concert that was staged by our organisation.

THE KEY TO LIDICE

In May 2017, Stoke-on-Trent was honoured to be awarded the *Key to Lidice*. At an official ceremony, the Mayor of Lidice, Veronika Kellerová, expressed sincere thanks and gratitude for contributions made by the Czechoslovak people; and by Britain, the United States and Russia. She presented symbolic keys to their nations' official representatives in recognition of friendship and for commitments to rebuild the village of Lidice.

Back in the Potteries, on the 2nd of December, the city of Stoke-on-Trent hosted a visit from the Czech Ambassador at the Bet365 stadium. There at pitch side, during the half-time break of Stoke City's match against Swansea City, in front of thousands of fans, Libor Sečka presented the key to the Lord Mayor of Stoke-on-Trent, Cllr Ross Irving. The *Key to Lidice* can now be seen at the Potteries Museum and Art Gallery.

THE MESSENGER OF HOPE—THE LIDICE PEAR TREE

When the village was invaded and razed to the ground by the Nazis, the only living thing remaining in Lidice was a small pear tree sapling. The Czech government gave that *"Mother tree,"* now 80 years old, protection.

For many years, this highly symbolic tree has been nurtured by Antonin Nešpor, a resident of Lidice, whose mother survived the tragedy. After securing permission from the Ministry of Culture to take grafts from its branches, Antonin began sending 2-year-old saplings to communities of special significance. It was during our visit to Lidice in June 2017 that Stoke-on-Trent was honoured to receive its pear tree sapling from Antonin Nešpor, on behalf of the Citizens Association of Lidice; a gift to the people of North Staffordshire in recognition of the international fundraising campaign Lidice Shall Live.

Gardening novices, Cheryl and I were astonished to see the sapling was in fact 5 feet tall! Though packaged well for the flight back, we still had a degree of explaining to do at Prague airport, as wrapped it looked like a heavy machine gun. At one point, we were not sure security would allow us to bring it through customs. However, the Lidice Shall Live account is compelling and before we knew it, the *Pear Tree* was on its way back to North Staffordshire!

On the 20th of February 2018, following eight months nurturing, with the help of an acquaintance of ours, Zdeněk Valkoun-Walker, a Czech national who was Head Gardener at Dorothy Clive Gardens, we arranged for the tree to be moved to its permanent, and most appropriate home - outside the Victoria Hall in Hanley. The then Lord Mayor of Stoke-on-Trent, Cllr Ross Irving helped with the planting, and it is hoped as it blooms and fruits—the Stoke-on-Trent *Pear Tree* will play a crucial role in raising aspirations in everyone who learns of its history, spreading a message of positivity and *'hope.'*

DAY OF INTERNATIONAL PEACE AND FRIENDSHIP

In August 2017, we worked alongside the organisers of the annual Jazz and Blues Festival held in Penkhull, Stoke-on-Trent. The first day was a celebration of the Lidice Shall Live Campaign. The Czech Cultural Attaché from the Embassy in London attended, together with the Lord Mayor of Stoke-on-Trent where a special *Flag of Peace and Friendship*, designed by school children, was raised, and a presentation of the *Key to Lidice* was made by a representative from the Czech embassy in London.

Activities and stalls on the day included a mix of relevant international dance & drama groups, ceramic & art workshops, musicians, choirs, poets, storytellers, artwork displays, exhibition, films, specialist food providers.

A Pear Tree Grows - Steve Shaw - 2015

CELEBRATING THE CZECH CENTENARY—2018

CZECH CENTENARY MOSAIC

The 28th of October 2018 marked the 100th Anniversary of the founding of Czech nation. At Lidice Lives, we wanted to make a statement of Anglo-Czech solidarity at this special time. Collaborating with renowned artist Philip Hardaker, we commissioned two large circular ceramic mosaics, one for installation in Lidice and the other in Stoke-on-Trent. These impressive, circular pieces were deftly created by Phil, who interpreted the story of Lidice with the help of the young people of Stoke-on-Trent, employing century old fragments of china and earthenware retrieved from the heyday of pottery manufacture in Stoke-on-Trent. The artworks show how lightness has emanated from the terribly dark days of Lidice, and how people from all over the world showed defiance against Hitler's order that *Lidice Shall Die Forever*.

Funding for the Lidice mosaic was received from individuals and organisations via crowdfunding, ward budget contributions from some city councillors, while Stoke-on-Trent City Council funded the shipping costs. The mosaic was installed in the new park area of Lidice and the unveiling ceremony was performed by the Mayor of Lidice, Veronika Kellerová; the Director of Lidice Memorial, Martina Lehmannová; Cheryl & I; and British Ambassador to Czechia, Nick Archer.

INTERNATIONAL LEGACY GARDEN

In 2018, the Lidice Lives organisation was gifted a plot of land in Hanley, Stoke-on-Trent, by Tesco. Its location is a prime spot in the City-Centre. An exciting, colourful garden with sculptures, artworks, plantings, and seating is proposed for the site. People and communities from Britain and around the world are invited to take part in the project, so that it will truly represent international fraternity. Places that have suffered similar atrocities to Lidice; communities that have contributed to movements like the Lidice Shall Live campaign; or communities who have showed camaraderie in other ways, by re-naming their towns Lidice; or people who named their baby girls *Lidice*; - all in defiance of Hitler's order that *Lidice Shall Die!* - all will be invited to contribute!

Talented Stoke-on-Trent fine art sculptor Carl Payne designed an impressive centrepiece for the garden. A magnificent bronze sculpture comprising four life-size figures combining to create a commanding presence in the space; the figures being Sir Barnett Stross, a miner, a woman, and a young child. Tragically, Carl lost his life in December 2021 while this book was being produced. It has not yet been decided how the sculpture centrepiece will be progressed. Perhaps you have ideas…

MISCELLANEOUS PROJECTS 2011 –

BBC INSIDE OUT: series produced by Hannah Smith was aired in March 2011, following our approach to them. The Inside Out Series were 10-minute programmes highlighting little known issues, projects, and campaigns within the West Midlands region. Through Theartbay gallery we had a contact with local TV presenter and celebrity, Nick Hancock. He was intrigued by the Lidice Shall Live campaign and the role Stoke-on-Trent played in it and agreed to narrate the short film to create more awareness. LIDICE LIVES: is a mini documentary film produced by journalist James Truswell, created during his visit to Lidice with us in October 2010. 'Lidice Lives' can be viewed on YouTube and has had almost 100,000 views. ROSES FROM ASHES: In 2012, Stoke-on-Trent City Council commissioned the well-known Stoke-on-Trent historian, Fred Hughes, to produce a booklet about Sir Barnett Stross for the 70th anniversary commemorations year. We were pleased to help Fred with his research, supplying photographs, background information and contact details in Lidice. A RAY OF LIGHT: Russell Phillips is an author specialising in military history. After becoming aware of the Lidice Shall Live campaign and how the people of Stoke-on-Trent helped to rebuild the village after the war, he was inspired to author a short book on the episode. We helped Russell with some of his research, and his book was published in 2016. THE EUROPEAN FOLKLORIC FESTIVAL: was held over two years at the Potteries Museum and Art Gallery in Hanley. It was an inclusive event for all communities to celebrate cultures and traditions across European countries. Lidice Lives put together an exhibition which included a mix of information panels about the Lidice atrocity and the Lidice Shall Live Campaign, children's artwork, photographs, and leaflets. FUSION PERFORMANCE ARTS: the youth group led by Artistic Director Justine Cope created a drama piece by considering actual testimonies, historical research sources, and poetry and creative writing output. Their emotional performance was staged at several youth events in 2012, including the All-England Festival. LIDICE SHALL LIVE FESTIVAL: in 2015, two locally based performance artists, Natalie Bangs and Laura Stacey, worked with the Youth Creative Drama Group based at Victoria Hall. They put together a 2-day event bringing together drama and dance groups who staged moving and powerful performances at the 'Hall, interpreting the Lidice atrocity and Lidice Shall Live campaign within the movement's home. A BIKE ACROSS THE SEA: Stephen Dyster is a trustee of the Lidice Lives (not for profit) organisation, teacher, writer, and editor. He is also a very keen cyclist and in 2016, cycled from Stoke-on-Trent to Lidice with a friend to raise awareness and celebrate international friendship. A Bike Across the Sea tells the story not only of Lidice but their amazing journey across Europe. A LIGHT ACROSS THE SEA: As part of the 70th anniversary year commemorations a local film company called Inspored Film and Video produced a budget documentary film about the Lidice Shall Live Campaign. At that time, the incumbent MP for Sir Barnett Stross's old constituency of Stoke-on-Trent Central was Tristram Hunt. The film-makers needed our help, and we gave them all the free assistance we could, supporting them throughout the planning and production process, particularly in enabling smooth contact with our colleagues in Lidice with details of the commemorative event in June, and introducing them to Hunt as an ideal narrator.

A SELECTION OF PROJECTS

Clockwise: Near the end of their stay in 2012, the schoolchildren of Lidice and Buštěhrad attended a summer festival at Stoke-on-Trent's Hanley Park; the first memorial event to Lidice in Stoke-on-Trent took place in Fenton on the 10th of June 2011, in the town's square just off Christchurch Street; Marie Šupíková, alongside a member of staff from the Lidice Memorial talks to children at Our Lady's Primary School, Fenton, about her memories of the events of June 10th 1942, her experiences, and about life living in the new Lidice.

A SELECTION OF PROJECTS — The Path to Lidice

Top: Stoke-on-Trent's Pear Tree sapling is kindly presented to Cheryl and Alan Gerrard by representatives of the Lidice community and keeper of the "Mother" Pear Tree, Antonin Nešpor. Photo, from left to right: Ton Da, Josef, Cheryl, Antonin, and yours truly. Bottom: Saturday, May the 27th, 2017, and Mayor of Lidice, Veronika Kellerová presents three keys in a special ceremony: one to Czech President Miloš Zeman, the second to Jan Thompson, British Ambassador to Czechia at the time, and a third to US Charge D'affaires, Kelly Adams-Smith. A Lidice rose was also awarded to the Russian Ambassador for building the first memorial on the mass grave of the men of Lidice. Thompson recalled the activities of Sir Barnett Stross, "the British doctor and politician who led the Lidice Shall Live campaign, Stross pushed through the idea of the Friendship and Peace Rose Garden in Lidice", Thompson said. Photo shows Jan Thompson left, Mayor Kellerová centre, with Deputy Mayor Tomáš Skála to the right.

A SELECTION OF PROJECTS   The Path to Lidice

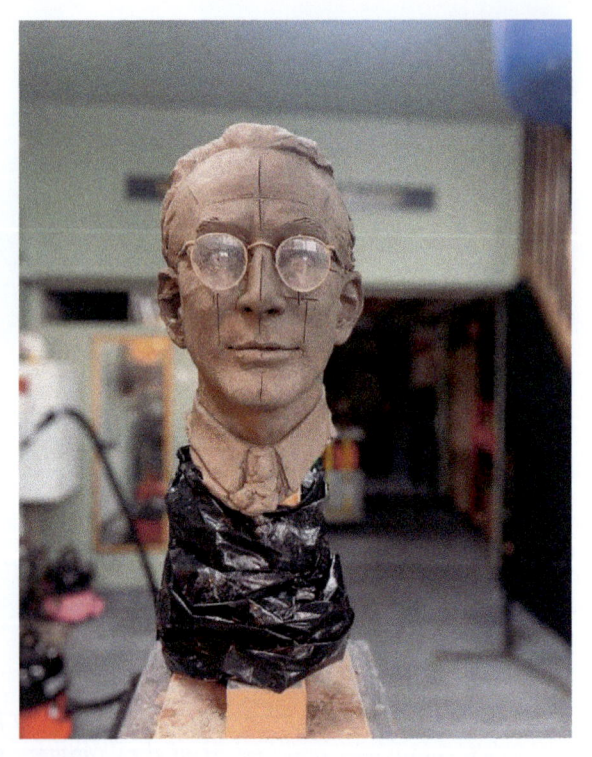

Clockwise: House 116 - this permanent exhibition, which opened in 2017 gives visitors the experience of an original Lidice house, built as part of the development, started in 1947; Cheryl Gerrard and Philip Hardaker look at the Centenary Mosaic in its formative stages; a work in progress bust of Sir Barnett Stross's head created by the late Carl Payne to promote the bronze sculpture, "LEGACY" proposed for the land at the bottom of Broad Street in Hanley, Stoke-on-Trent; on the 21st of October 2021, Stoke-on-Trent passed a motion to fly the Czech flag from its public buildings three times a year, on the following anniversaries: the Lidice atrocity, the launch of the Lidice Shall Live campaign, and the birth of the Czech nation.

THE MEMORIAL TO CHILD VICTIMS OF WAR

One cannot avoid being moved to tears at the sight of the magnificent yet emotionally crushing memorial to the child victims of the Lidice atrocity. The installation, which represents the 82 children murdered by the Nazis is the magnum opus of Czech academic sculptor Marie Uchytilová, who worked on the models of the children between 1970 until her death in 1989.

Marie Uchytilová planned to not only commemorate the Lidice children who died but symbolise the thirteen million child victims of the Second World War. Before starting on the castings, she met Lidice mothers and relatives to chat about their children and view them in photographs in order to form an impression of their physical characteristics and personalities. However, during the modelling process, she deliberately left their features vague to ensure the installation represented all child victims of war. Marie's dream would become a reality in bronze only after her death, when her husband, Jiří Hampl, took her sculptures and gained the support required to have them cast in bronze and sited on the memorial grounds between the years 1995 - 2000. The first thirty statues were installed in their positions in 1995. Some statues are so heavy that an A-frame had to be used in order to position them into their concrete foundations. Finally, on the 7th of June 2000, the last remaining bronze statues were inserted into the ground, and the installation has now stood for 22 years, complete on the memorial grounds overlooking the site of the old village. The children's representations are fixed at an oblique angle, so that they look forlornly towards the common grave of their fathers, grandfathers, and friends. The artwork is a haunting scene to come across, emotionally affecting all who experience it.

A SELECTION OF PROJECTS — The Path to Lidice

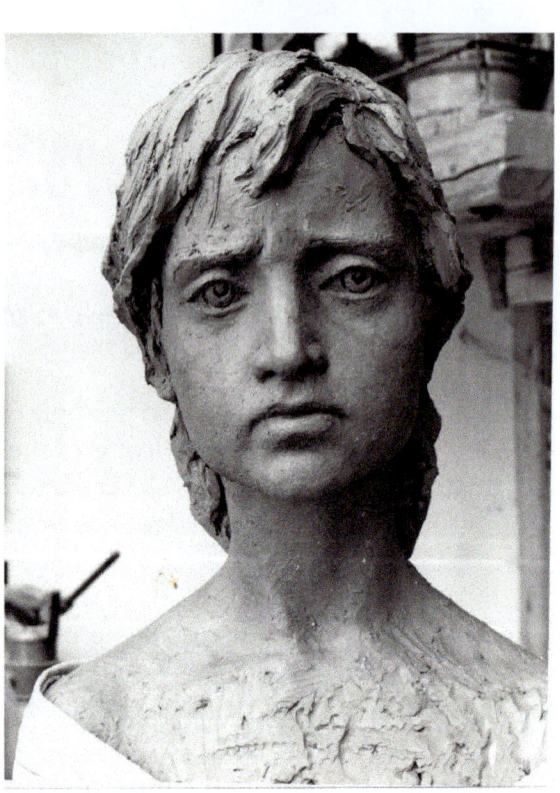

Models of the Lidice children created in plaster by Marie Uchytilová. Sadly, Marie lost her life in 1989, but her husband, Jiří Hampl was to take on the mantel to see the project realised. Financing came through donations from the Czech Government, but significantly individual and foreign donors such as the community of Albertslund in Denmark; the Lidice foundation, in Akita, Japan; Czech - German Fund of Future, Prague; Lidice 50th anniversary Committee, London; the German Federal Government; and many thousands of other donors from Czechia and other countries.

TIMELINE

1873 - Fred Hancock was born in Talke.

1880 - Hugh Leese was born on High Street, Rookery, at the bottom of Harriseahead Lane, North Staffordshire.

1889

20th May – Will Lawther born in Choppington, Northumberland.

1898

7th September – Olive Marion Baker born.

1899

25th December – Barnett Stross born in Pabianice, near Łódź, Poland.

1918

28th October – Czechoslovakia gains nation status.

1938

12th September – Adolf Hitler speech at Nuremberg castigates Czechoslovakia.
22nd September – Hitler demands independence for the Sudeten Germans.
29/30th September – Neville Chamberlain signs the Munich Agreement.
3rd – 5th October – House of Commons debate on Czechoslovakia.
5th October – Dr Edvard Beneš resigns as President of Czechoslovakia and leaves for America.
1st November – Inauguration of the North Staffordshire branch of the Czechoslovak - British Friendship Club.

1939

14th March – Slovakia secedes from Czecho-Slovakia and becomes a puppet state.
15th March – Wehrmacht troops enter Prague.
1st September – The Second World War begins with the German invasion of Poland.
17th November – 9 students executed in Prague on International Students' Day.

1940

22nd July – Churchill creates the Special Operations Unit task force.

14th - 15th November – The *Coventry Blitz* destroys more than 43,000 homes; just over half the city's housing stock, were damaged or destroyed in the raid.

1941

27th September – Reinhard Heydrich appointed Deputy Reich Protector of the Protectorate of Bohemia and Moravia.
28th December – Jan Kubiš and Jozef Gabčík flown out to execute *Operation Anthropoid*.

1942

1st January – The Sneyd Pit Disaster kills 57 men and boys in Stoke-on-Trent.
6th January – The Writers' War Board formed.
19th January – New Protectorate Government set up based on Heydrich's ideas.
21st January – Formal talks about the annulment of the Munich Agreement start.
22nd January – Barnett Stross speaks of the bond between Britain and Czecho-Slovakia.
15th March – Inauguration of the Leamington Spa Czecho-Slovak - British Friendship Club.
20th April – Czech President Emil Hácha presents a hospital train to Hitler as a birthday present.
20th May – Gestapo intercept coded message to London requesting *Anthropoid* be called off.
26th May – Mutual Assistance agreement signed between Britain and the Soviet Union.
27th May – Reinhard Heydrich is mortally wounded in Prague.
2nd June – A meeting arranged by the Gestapo in Prague Old Town Square in support of Heydrich attracts 60,000.
3rd June – Suspicious letter intercepted at Pala Factory, Slaný.
4th June – Lidice searched for the first time.
9th June – 7.45pm, the Nazis seal off Lidice and begin carrying out orders.
10th June – Men of Lidice executed; women and children driven off; village set ablaze.
11th June – Canadian Senate recommend the bombing of German villages in reprisal for Lidice
11th June – News of the Anglo-Soviet Mutual Assistance Agreement announced in Britain.
12th June – Jan Masaryk makes statement on the Lidice atrocity in Washington.
13th June - Dr Barnett Stross publicly announces the idea of raising funds to rebuild Lidice at the old Hanley Museum.
13th June – United Nations Day – New York Parade held down 5th Avenue.
13th June - Frank Knox makes speech in Boston.
14th June - United Nations Day – Chicago Parade.
15th June – Churchill holds meeting to discuss bombing 3 German villages in reprisal for Lidice.
17th June – Czechoslovak Government-in-exile vows retribution for Lidice in public statement.
19th – 21st June – Events across Britain celebrate the Anglo-Soviet Mutual Assistance Agreement.
26th June – Murton Colliery Disaster, Durham.
26th June – First meeting of the Lidice Lives committee.
29th June – Dr Beneš addresses the nation about Lidice via the BBC and on newsreel.
12th July – Service of Intercession for Czecho-Slovakia held at Newcastle Cathedral.
12th July – Re-naming of Stern Park Gardens (ILLINOIS) to Lidice.

13th July – At its meeting, the executive of the North Staffordshire Mineworkers' Federation announces its intention to fundraise to rebuild Lidice.
20th July – Lidice Shall Live project receives national approval on day one of the Mineworkers' Federation of Great Britain Blackpool Conference.
21st July – Announcement in press about the launch of the national campaign and the visit of President Beneš to Stoke-on-Trent.
5th August – Nullification of the Munich Agreement is announced.
8th August – President Beneš makes a statement on the BBC
10th August – Dr Barnett Stross addresses the North Staffordshire Mineworkers' Federation Executive.
22nd August – Stoke City fundraising match in aid of Lidice.
28th – 30th August – Three rallies in Stoke-on-Trent with Jim Griffiths, Albert Bennett and Dr Barnett Stross.
29th August – Tabor, South Dakota, dedicates its main street to Lidice.
30th August – Re-naming of San Jeronimo (MEXICO) to Lidice.
4th September – The North Staffs Miners' Federation agree £1,250 will be paid to the Lidice Shall Live fund.
6th September – Launch of the Lidice Shall Live Campaign at the Victoria Hall
21st September – Lidice Lives Committee formally announced.
Early October – Lidice Shall Live Committee formally constituted
6th October – Arthur Baddeley made President and Treasurer of the North Staffordshire Miners' Federation; Hugh Leese made its Secretary and Agent; Harold Lockett made its Financial Secretary and Organiser.
12th October – Premier of *We Refuse to Die*.
19th October – Broadcast of *The Murder of Lidice* by Edna St. Vincent Millay.
22nd October – *We Refuse to Die* released by Paramount Pictures.
1st November – Inauguration of the North Staffordshire Czecho-Slovak – British Friendship Club.
22nd November – Dr Beneš visits the Durham Miners Association.

1943

8th April – Meeting to agree on plans for Nottingham's *Lidice Week*.
1st May – Special Conference of the Durham Miners.
26th May – Bristol's *Four Nations Appeal* is born.
28th May – Premier of *The Silent Village* in Ystradgynlais.
30th May – Launch of the Lidice Shall Live Committee in Birmingham.
10th June – Christening of a public space in Havana, CUBA.
11th June – Service for Lidice at Bermondsey attended by Jan Masaryk.
20th June – Commemorative event and dedication takes in PERU.
4th – 11th July – GAL Limited organise Feltham's *Lidice Week*.
21st July 1943 – Derby elects Lidice Shall Live Committee.
5th – 12th September – Derby *Lidice Week*.
12th September – Rally at Darley Park.
12th September – The town of Regla, CUBA is re-named Lidice.
23rd October – *Four Nations Rally* takes place at Colston Hall, Bristol.

31st October – The village of Potrero in PANAMA is re-named Lidice.
24th December – Christening to Lidice of a residential area in Caracas, VENEZUELA.

1944

12th March – Coventry's *Lidice Week* is launched.
14th March – President Beneš presents a cheque for £1,000 to Coventry and Warwickshire Hospital.
10th June – Re-christening event – Villa de Parada to Lidice (BRAZIL).
27th August – Dedication of Phillips Memorial (WISCONSIN).
24th September – *The Last Stone* opens at the Phoenix Theatre, London.
25th September - K. H. Frank announces that the clearance of the Lidice site is complete.
9th – 14th October – Crewe's *Czecho-Slovak Week*.

1945

26th February – Czechoslovakia's funding from UNRRA is approved.
30th May – Civic and community leaders in Nottingham meet to discuss a *Lidice Week*.
6th June – Decision taken by Czechoslovak Government to build a new Lidice.
10th June – First Lidice Commemorative Service – the plan to build a new Lidice is announced to the public by Minister of the Interior, Václav Nosek.
10th June – *Prayer for Lidice* is held across several US STATES.
5th July – General Election in Britain elects Clement Attlee.
5th July – Barnett Stross elected the MP for Stoke-on-Trent, Hanley.
1st August – The Local National Committee begin to invite tenders for the reconstruction of Lidice.
13th September – Announcement of the establishment of a Lidice Memorial Committee in the US
30th September – Nottingham's *Lidice Week* launches.
5th December – British Cabinet agrees to US Loans of $3.75Billion.

1946

12th July – The National Coal Board was formed.
13th September – The Society for the Restoration of Lidice is formally established.

1947

1st January – The equivalent of $2.8billion worth of supplies has been shipped to Czechoslovakia *(2021 prices)*.
8th January – Ernest Bevin announces new British propaganda strategy.
30th April – Czechoslovak delegation visits Britain.
15th June – Foundation Stone Laying Ceremony takes place in Lidice.
20th June – Delegates presented with honours by Jan Masaryk at awards ceremony in Prague.
5th July – Launch of the NHS.

15th August – Whitehaven Pit Disaster in Cumberland, UK

1948

21st – 25th February – Communist coup d'état takes place across Czechoslovakia.
3rd April – Marshall Plan *(Economic Recovery Program)* launched by the US.
20th June – Miners' rally at the Victoria Hall, Hanley promoting *Moral Re-Armament*.
2nd August – Frank Hampl deported from Britain.

1953

12th August – Soviet Union detonates a 400 Kiloton Hydrogen Bomb.

1954

1st March – *Castle Bravo* Hydrogen Bomb test actioned on the Bikini Atoll by the USA.
5th April – Debate on Nuclear testing at the House of Commons.
15th July – Dr Barnett Stross makes a public appeal in London for the creation of a rose garden of peace to be created in Lidice.

1955

14th March – Construction of the Lidice Rose Garden begins.
21st April – Meeting in London to present roses to the Mayor of Lidice disrupted by the *Democratic Exiles*.
19th June – Inauguration ceremony of the *Garden of Peace and Friendship*.
25th June – Barnett Stross visits Mrs Šišpera in Prague.
16th July – Mrs Šišpera released and flies to Britain with her children.

1957

21st June – Dr Barnett Stross receives the *Freedom of Lidice*, from the Mayor of Lidice, Libuše Prošková.

1959

31st March – Society for the Restoration of Lidice dissolved.

1961

28th June – The *Rose of Lidice* presented to the Mayor of Lidice at the Czech Embassy by Harry Wheatcroft.

1962

19th June – 3rd July Children's visit to Stoke-on-Trent, Coventry, London, and Kent.

1963

4th September – Dr Barnett Stross is made an Honorary Member of the Czechoslovak Society for International Relations.

1964

14th February – Sir Barnett Stross receives a knighthood for his services to The Arts.

1967

13th May – Sir Barnett Stross dies of a heart attack at University College Hospital, London.

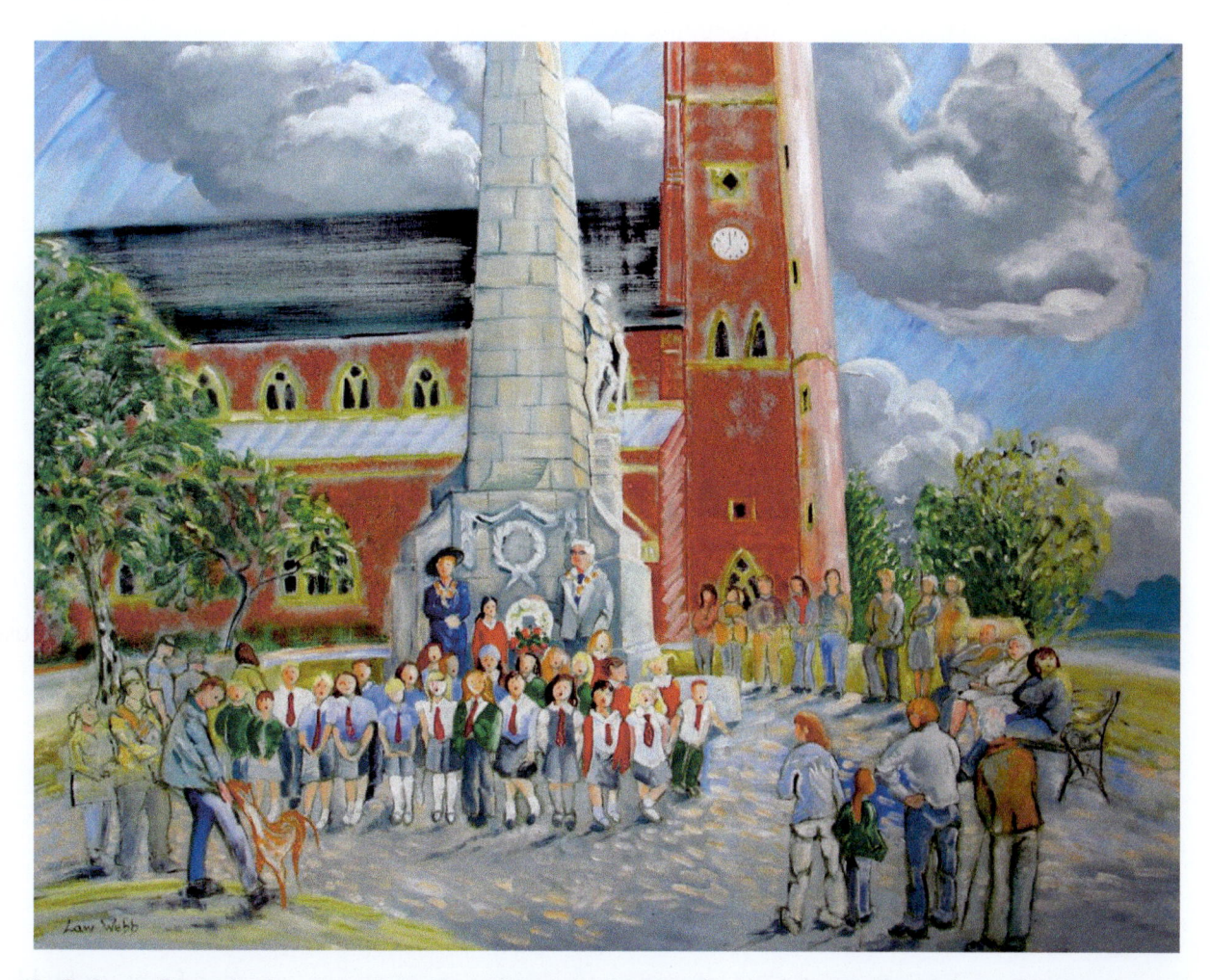

In Stoke-on-Trent, the first commemoration of the Lidice atrocity for decades took place in Fenton's Albert Square on June the 10th, 2011. The painting was completed in situ by the late artist and poet, Susan Law-Webb.

BIBLIOGRAPHY & SOURCES

PUBLICATIONS

Lidice - Ivan Cigánek – Orbis Press Agency 1982

An Illustrated History of The Gestapo – Rupert Butler - BCA 1992

From Refugee to OBE – Charles Strasser – Keller Publishing 2007

The Miners' Association / A Trade Union in the Age of The Chartists – Raymond Challinor and Brian Ripley – Lawrence & Wishart 1968

When I Was a Child – Charles Shaw – Guide mark Publishing

The Miners – One Union, One Industry – R. Page Arnot - George Allen & Unwin 1979

Who's Next? - The Lesson of Czechoslovakia - John Brown – Anchor Press 1951

Oh, My Country – Josef Josten – Latimer House 1949

Smear! Wilson and the Secret State – Stephen Dorril and Robin Ramsay – Grafton 1991

Bridge of Hope and Life – Lidice Memorial 2015

Methodism and the Struggle of the Working Classes – R. F. Wearmouth – Edgar Backus 1954

Methodism and the Working-Class Movements of England 1800–1850 – R. F. Wearmouth – The Epworth Press 1937

Fates of the Children of Lidice – Jolana Macková and Ivan Ulrych – VEGA-L for the Lidice Memorial

The Miners in Crisis and War – R. Page Arnot – George Allen & Unwin 1961

The Miners – Years of Struggle - R. Page Arnot – George Allen & Unwin 1952

Lidice Remembered Around the World – Toni Brendel - CreateSpace Independent Publishing Platform 2015

Building the New Lidice – Luba Hédlová, Pavla Bechnerová & Martina Lehmannová - Lidice Memorial 2017

The Frolik Defection – Josef Frolik – Leo Cooper 1975

A Short History of The British Working-Class Movement 1787–1947 – G. D. H. Cole – George Allen & Unwin 1948

Společnost pro obnovu Lidic (1945) 1946 – 1959 - Pavla Štěpánková 2006

Lidice Shall Live - Published by the Czecho-Slovak - British Friendship Club, 1942

Lidice Memories - Stehlík, Eduard - Praha 2007.

Gabriela Literová - WAR DEVELOPMENTS AND DAILY LIFE IN NEW PEOPLE (inhabitants of Lidice and their memories of reverential memories and life in the village) Prague 2010 Thesis

Alfred Orage and the Leeds Arts Club 1893 – 1923 – Tom Steele – The Orage Press 1990

The Masaryks – The Making of Czechoslovakia – Zbyněk Zeman

My Life with Roses – Harry Wheatcroft – Odhams 1959

In Praise of Roses – Harry Wheatcroft – Barrie & Jenkins 1970

Knight of the Burning Heart – Leslie F. Church – The Epworth Press 1938

NEW EVIDENCE ON THE SOVIET REJECTION OF THE MARSHALL PLAN, 1947: TWO REPORTS - SCOTT D. PARRISH University of Texas in Austin; MIKHAIL M. NARINSKY Institute of Universal History, Moscow Working Paper No. 9 1994

Changing Society through Drama – Pamela Jenner – Pinocchio Press – 2016

https://misandryangie.wordpress.com/2016/05/09/the-cults-of-frank-buchman-3/

NEWSPAPER SOURCES

The Daily Herald 10th June 1943
Daily Mirror - 6th April 1954
Daily Mirror - 17th September 1938
Daily Herald – 26th January 1948
Daily Herald - 30th June 1942
Daily Mirror - 16th December 1977
Daily Mirror - 4th October 1938
The Guardian - 12th June 1942
The Guardian - 19th June 1942
Daily Record - 16th June 1942

Belfast Telegraph - 19th December 1949
Belfast Newsletter - 26th July 1955
Belfast Newsletter 21st August 1942
The Northern Whig and Belfast Post - 2nd March 1949

Hull Daily Mail – 17th March 1947
Hull Daily Mail - 2nd August 1948
The Lincolnshire Citizen 16th June 1947
The Yorkshire Post & Leeds Mercury - 8th September 1942
Yorkshire Post and Leeds Mercury - 19th September 1949
Yorkshire Post and Leeds Mercury - 12th June 1942

Lancashire Daily Post - 27th September 1947
Lancashire Evening Post - 6th April 1956
Lancashire Evening Post - 21st January 1957
Lancashire Evening Post - 21st January 1957
Blackpool Evening Dispatch – 22nd July 1942
The Liverpool Echo - 26th June 1942
The Liverpool Echo - 13th July 1942
The Liverpool Echo – 5th August 1947
The Liverpool Post - 7th September 1942
Manchester Evening News - 12th June 1942

The Middlesex Chronicle - 11th July 1943
The Middlesex Chronicle - 24th July 1943
The Middlesex Chronicle - 25th September 1943
The Middlesex Chronicle - 3rd July 1943
The Middlesex Chronicle - 25th September 1943
Mid Sussex Times - 23rd June 1943
The West London Observer – 8th August 1947

The New York Times - 1st February 1945
The New York Times - 10th June 1945
The New York Times - 12th July 1942
The New York Times - 15th June 1942
The New York Times - 25th September 1945
The New York Times - 3rd June 1957
The New York Times - 13th October 1942
The New York Times - 28th November 1969
The New York Times - 16th June 1942
The New York Times - 11th June 1962
The New York Times - 16th June 1947
The New York Times - 19th June 1942
Alice Daily Echo – 15th June 1950
Bakersfield Californian - 29th April 1943
Bakersfield Californian – 1st June 1949
Boston Daily Globe - 15th June 1942
Boston Daily Globe - 13th June 1942

Western Mail and South Wales News - 6th August 1942
Western Mail and South Wales News - 4th June 1943
Birmingham Daily Gazette - 13th June 1947
Birmingham Daily Gazette - 13th July 1942
Birmingham Daily Gazette - 1st April 1955
Birmingham Evening Despatch - 28th May 1943
The Birmingham Mail - 2nd June 1943
The Birmingham Mail - 27th May 1943
The Birmingham Mail - 31st May 1943
The Birmingham Post - 20th June 1955
The Birmingham Post - 27th June 1954
The Birmingham Post - 27th June 1942
The Birmingham Post - 9th December 1954
Birmingham Evening Despatch - 10th September 1942
Birmingham Evening Despatch - 13th July 1942
The Evening News - 19th December 1957 (Marmalade)
Birmingham Post – 25th January 1974
The Birmingham Post - 14th December 1966

The Coventry Evening Telegraph - 10th October 1938
The Coventry Evening Telegraph - 13th March 1944
The Coventry Evening Telegraph - 11th March 1944
The Coventry Evening Telegraph - 16th March 1944
The Coventry Evening Telegraph - 28th February 1945
The Coventry Evening Telegraph - 2nd December 1943
The Coventry Evening Telegraph - 4th December 1943
The Coventry Evening Telegraph - 9th March 1944
The Coventry Evening Telegraph - 22nd November 1944
The Coventry Evening Telegraph - 23rd June 1947
The Coventry Evening Telegraph - 11th June 1955
The Coventry Standard - 13th May 1944

Crewe Chronicle - 14th October 1944
Crewe Chronicle 7th October 1944
Crewe Chronicle 20th May 1944
Derby Daily Telegraph – 23rd May 1947
Derby Daily Telegraph - 10th June 1948
Derby Daily Telegraph - 19th August 1943
Derby Daily Telegraph - 30th August 1943
Derby Daily Telegraph - 10th September 1943
Derby Daily Telegraph - 13th September 1943
Derby Daily Telegraph - 5th August 1942

The Nottingham Evening Post - 23rd June 1942
The Nottingham Evening Post - 7th December 1946
The Nottingham Evening Post - 9th December 1946
The Nottingham Evening Post - 1st April 1943
Nottingham Journal - 1st October 1945
Nottingham Journal - 4th June 1943
Nottingham Journal - 8th October 1945
Nottingham Journal - 8th September 1943
Nottingham Journal - 13th August 1943
Nottingham Journal - 11th June 1943
The Nottingham Journal - 13th June 1942

The Evening Sentinel - 26th September 1932
The Evening Sentinel - 25th May 1944
The Evening Sentinel - 26th February 1942

Brownsville Herald - 23rd September 1942
Birmingham Daily Gazette - 30th June 1942
Knoxville Sentinel - 12th June 1942
A Noite - 10th June 1944
Austin American Statesman - 1st July 1942
Cicero Life – 21st May 1943
Rapid City Journal - 31st August 1942
The Quebec Gazette - 12th June 1942
The Tennessean – 13th July 1942

Newcastle Journal - 26th June 1942
Newcastle Journal - 27th June 1949
Newcastle Journal - 31st January 1945
Newcastle Journal - 29th October 1942
The Shields Daily News - 21st January 1941
The Sunderland Echo - 14th October 1948

Illustrated London News - 28th June 1947
Illustrated London News - 1st April 1976
Illustrated London News - 25th August 1945
Illustrated London News - 23rd June 1962
Illustrated London News - 23rd August 1947

The Scotsman - 26th June 1942
The Scotsman - 18th February 1943
Stirling Observer - 6th August 1942
The Aberdeen Press and Journal - 13th June 1947
The Aberdeen Press and Journal - 24th June 1947
The Aberdeen Press and Journal - 12th April 1948
The Aberdeen Press and Journal - 27th May 1949
Dundee Evening Telegraph - 18th June 1947
The Falkirk Herald - 30th June 1943
The Falkirk Herald - 9th September 1942
Linlithgowshire Gazette - 11th September 1942
Motherwell Times – 29th October 1954
Northern Whig - 31st May 1949

The Sphere - 16th June 1945
The Sphere - 26th September 1942
The Sphere - 27th February 1943
The Sphere - 29th June 1957
The Tatler - 11th November 1942
The Tatler - 15th September 1943

Western Daily Press and Bristol Mirror - 22nd November 1949
The Courier and Advertiser - 31st July 1948
Bristol and Western Daily Press - 23rd October 1943
Western Mail and South Wales News - 31st May 1943
Gloucester Echo - 21st July 1948
Gloucester Echo - 2nd August 1948
Bristol Mirror - 11th November 1943
Bristol Mirror - 15th October 1943
Bristol Mirror - 21st October 1943
Bristol Mirror - 25th October 1943
Bristol Mirror - 27th September 1943
Bristol Mirror - 20th October 1943

The Evening Sentinel - 23rd September 1941
The Evening Sentinel - 6th September 1947
The Staffordshire Advertiser - 31st May 1947
The Staffordshire Advertiser - 12th December 1942
The Staffordshire Advertiser - 13th June 1952
The Staffordshire Advertiser - 3rd February 1940
The Staffordshire Advertiser - 8th August 1942
The Staffordshire Advertiser - 12th June 1948
The Staffordshire Advertiser - 12th September 1942
The Staffordshire Advertiser - 20th June 1942
The Staffordshire Advertiser - 22nd March 1930
The Staffordshire Advertiser - 24th April 1943
The Staffordshire Advertiser - 29th August 1942
The Staffordshire Advertiser - 31st May 1947
The Staffordshire Sentinel - 20th February 1939
The Staffordshire Advertiser - 24th August 1940
The Evening Sentinel - 17th September 1941
The Evening Sentinel - 21st June 1948
The Evening Sentinel - 22nd December 1943
The Evening Sentinel - 22nd February 1945
The Evening Sentinel - 11th April 1939
The Evening Sentinel - 1st May 1947
The Evening Sentinel - 13th June 1947
The Evening Sentinel - 30th April 1947
The Evening Sentinel - 10th September 1942
The Evening Sentinel - 15th March 1939
The Evening Sentinel - 2nd October 1942
The Evening Sentinel - 16th May 1944
The Evening Sentinel - 1st September 1942
The Evening Sentinel - 21st October 1942
The Evening Sentinel - 21st March 1949
The Evening Sentinel - 14th May 1992
The Staffordshire Advertiser - 12th September 1942
The Evening Sentinel - 19th April 1929
The Evening Sentinel - 2nd September 1942
The Evening Sentinel - 7th September 1942
The Evening Sentinel - 12th July 1944
The Evening Sentinel - 29th August 1942
The Evening Sentinel - 2nd December 1946
The Evening Sentinel - 19th January 1942
The Evening Sentinel - 5th February 1940
The Evening Sentinel – 7th June 1943
The Evening Sentinel – 17th November 1941

Leamington Spa Courier - 20th March 1942
Leamington Spa Courier - 21st August 1942
Leamington Spa Courier - 22nd May 1942
Leamington Spa Courier - 10th May 1946
Leamington Spa Courier - 6th November 1942
Leamington Spa Courier - 30th October 1942
Leamington Spa Courier - 31st October 1943
Northampton Mercury - 18th December 1953

Rudé Právo - 16th July 1952

Newchapel Community Paper - article about Hugh Leese

Picture and other Acknowledgements:

Thank you to everyone who has contributed images towards this not-for-profit project. These acknowledgements are in no particular order of significance: Lidice Lives, the Lidice Memorial, public domain, my personal collection; the Museum of Modern art - New York; thank you to Wikipedia and the tens of thousands of individuals who support it (including yours truly) - it means that this publication doesn't have to be a bland piece of continuous prose; the United Nations; Muriel Stoddard; Maureen Hayward; Melanie Key; Martin Homola, the British Newspaper Archive; the ladies christened Lidice who've volunteered their photographs; The Evening Sentinel; The Czech News Agency; Pavel Horešovský; and an extended thank you to relatives of Sir Barnett Stross who were able to share their photographs and memories with others. I am indebted to artists Steve Shaw, Harry Davies, Lídice Calixto Moraes, and Sid Kirkham. Thank you once more to friends and associates who have offered their creativity, expertise, and wisdom at no expense in order to make this book.

Translations: *Sascha Peacock Meier, Franceska Dante*

Painting index

This book features the following creations kindly donated by the following artists:
page 18 - Torture of Prague students - Géza Szóbel – from "Civilization" collection 1942
page 27 - Images from the Cigánek book – Lidice – courtesy of Orbis Press, Prague 1982
page 32 - Document 379 – Harry Davies 2012
page 35 - Waiting – Harry Davies - 2016
page 37 - Tears – Steve Shaw - 2015
page 48 - Kings of The Underworld - Steve Shaw - 2020
page 51 - White Damp - Harry Davies - 2009
page 54 - Drawn to the Light – Sid Kirkham - 2017
page 55 - Sneyd 57 - Steve Shaw - 2014
page 132 - Lidice Shall Live – Sid Kirkham - 2010
page 159 - Terror - Géza Szóbel – from "Civilization" collection 1942
page 237 - Roses - Lídice Calixto Moraes - 2022
page 258 - Rose Garden - - Lidice Calixto Moraes - 2022
page 271 - The White Country - Michael Ayrton - 1946
page 320 - Lidice – Steve Shaw - 2015
page 342 - They Died for Our Freedom – Steve Shaw - 2022
page 346 - A Pear Tree Grows - Steve Shaw - 2015
page 357 - Lidice Commemorative Service in Fenton 2011 - Susan Law Webb – 2011
Back Cover – Rose – Amy Johnson

CZECHOSLOVAKIA VS CZECHO-SLOVAKIA

I have tried to stay true to the spirit of the period by using the correct nomenclature wherever possible to describe the former Czechoslovakia and its derivatives. Put most simply, the unhyphenated form has been used to refer to Tomáš Masaryk's vision of a state, existent prior to the seceding of Slovakia from the Czech Lands, following the Second World War with the re-emergence of a coalescing nation. The murkier time of wartime occupation is prone to confusion, so my treatment of it is based on perceptions. I have used the unhyphenated version when referring to Czechoslovak exiles in Britain, the US and other nations, as their interests were almost exclusively to work or fight for Masaryk's nation, by definition. I use the term Czecho-Slovakia or Czecho-Slovak where I am quoting or describing a situation which involves a discussion of the wartime situation for Czecho-Slovaks in their dismembered homeland of the Protectorate of Bohemia and Moravia, Slovakia, and the annexed regions.

TERMINOLOGY

Often in the book, exact quotes are used to provide the reader with a lively, colourful and accurate picture of the goings-on at the time of the Lidice Shall Live campaign. One of the few downsides of this is that early to mid-20th century views on race and gender are sometimes detectable. We can argue whether they have changed these days, but certainly they are less openly expressed in the press.

THE AUTHOR:

Alan Gerrard is the Co-Director of Theartbay Gallery and Fine Art Publishing—a community focused exhibition space functioning in the heart of Stoke-on-Trent.

A trustee on today's Staffordshire based Lidice Lives organisation, Alan has co-operated on bilateral projects with friends and colleagues in Lidice and the wider Czechia for 12 years in the name of cultural awareness and understanding.

Alan began working in the pottery industry in the 1980s, before changing vocation in 1990.

He is fully experienced in teaching, economics, and governance.

THE ARTISTS:

Sid Kirkham

Admired for his affectionate depictions of life in industrial Stoke-on-Trent, atmospheric portrayals of football camaraderie and support for children's art and the region's links with the village of Lidice.

Sid's work adorns walls in all parts of the globe, earning him the title "The Potteries' Lowry".

Sadly, Sid passed away early in 2018, but he leaves a massive archive of joyous paintings, commemorating the lives that were led in mid-20th century industrialised North Staffordshire.

BIBLIOGRAPHY & SOURCES   *The Path to Lidice*

Steve Shaw is an accomplished visual artist who actively campaigns to restore links between Stoke-on-Trent and Lidice.

A multi-talented potter and a musician too, Steve has worked with the author on multiple heritage inspired projects, designed to bring hitherto disengaged folk into the fold of greater social and political awareness, starting with collaborations to commemorate the 25th anniversary of the UK Miners' Strike in 2010.

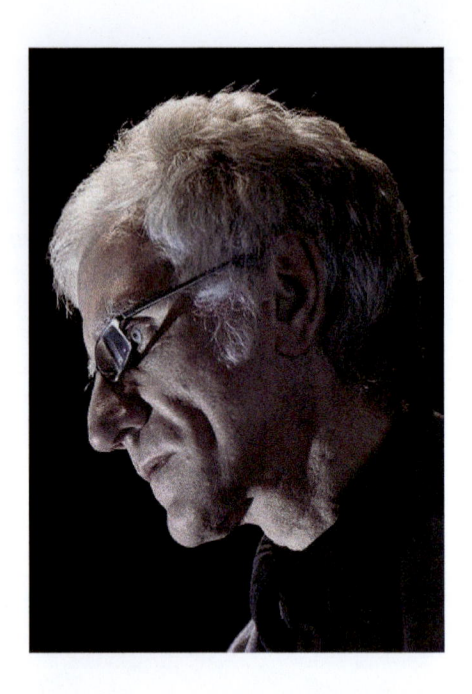

Harry Davies, known as Aitch, attended Portland House Art School in Burslem: "The course included life drawing classes which were taken by the legendary Arthur Berry, whose work still influences me today." Harry's paintings pay tribute to the people who have worked for and served industry in the past, and to those who are now breathing new life in to it.

In 2012, his painting Document 379 was presented to the Mayor of Lidice at the signing of the Memorandum of Understanding event in Stoke.

Born Rio de Janeiro and raised in the countryside of Brazil, educated in fashion design, and a former exchange student in Denmark, **Lídice Calixto Moraes** is determined to experience the world and explore all it has to offer.

Through her journey, she has discovered art as her calling, and education as her passion.

With each stroke of a paint brush, and each pass of a pen, Lídi seeks to visualize both life's identifiable and unanticipated marvels by sharing her unique perspective and wonder with others.

INDEX

A Noite 180, 361
A Prayer for Lidice 156
A. A. Wain 63
Acknowledgements 6
Adolf Hitler 6
Adolf Hoffmeister 148, 172
Adrian Knatchbull-Hugessen 39
Aid to Russia 47
Aktion Gitter 20
Alan and Cheryl Gerrard 1, 337, 338
Alan Barrett 5, 92, 339, 340
Alan Bush 202, 216
Albert Bennett 71
Albert Einstein 157, 158
Albertslund 353
Alderman Moore 98
Alec Turner 115, 116, 118
Alexander Bogomolov 74
Alice Daily Echo 361
Andrzej Miszak 36
Anežka Hodinová-Spurná 217
Anglo-Soviet Alliance 41
Ann Swingler 62
Anna Ambrose 216
Anna Hroníková 30
Anna Maruszáková 28
Anthony Eden 39, 40, 41, 66, 67, 69, 71, 73, 74
Antonín Novotný 264
Antonin Pelc 148, 172, 173
Arnold Bennett 82
Arthur Baddeley 47, 65, 79, 80, 83, 87, 211, 356
Arthur Hewitt 43, 78, 88
Arts and Amenities 279, 280
Bad Godesburg 8
Battle of Britain 65, 332
Bayswater 93
Ben Mason 115, 117
Benito Mussolini 8
Berchtesgaden 7
Birmingham Gazette 163
Birmingham Post 361
Bohumil Boček 196
Brendan Bracken 38
Brexit 294, 338
Bridget Boland 166
Bristol Mirror 361
British Union of Fascists 62
British-Soviet Friendship Societies 93
Buckingham Palace 10
Burslem Co-operative Society 46
Burslem School of Art 42
Buštěhrad 29, 30, 349
Buxton 63, 74

Čabárna 29
Captain Alan Graham, ... 38
Captain Peter McDonald 38
Central European Observer 83
Černín Palace 21
Changing Society through Drama 360
Charles Barratt 136
Charles de Gaulle 68
Charles G. Spragg 136
Charlie Chaplin 158
Chartism 4, 71
Chatterley Whitfield 87
Chell 337
Chełmno 34, 36, 64
Chicago Sun 150
Churchill's Secret Army 20
Clement Attlee 10, 13, 39, 40, 357
Clifton Fadiman 149
Cllr A. A. Wain 93
Cockpit 166, 167
Colonel Pankov 193
Conrad Henlein 6
Coventry Cathedral 17, 116, 119, 121
Coventry City Council 281
Coventry Evening Telegraph. 17, 116, 117, 119, 361
Cwmgiedd 312
Czech Army 15, 22, 84, 99, 115, 118
Czech Independence Day 62, 83
Czecho-Slovak - British Friendship Club. 43, 62, 63,
    64, 65, 70, 83, 84, 98, 99, 115, 124, 355, 360
Czecho-Slovak Army Choir 74, 75, 79
Czechoslovak Government-in-exile
    set up 10
Czechoslovakia
    under pressure 6
Daily Herald 63, 77, 361
Daily Mirror 361
Das Schwarze Korps 63
Dave Proudlove 5, 338
David Bourner 122, 123, 136, 212
David Lloyd George 12
Der Neue Tag 33
Dorothy Thompson 38, 39
Dr Barnett Stross 3, 43, 57, 62, 70, 71, 72, 74, 78,
    79, 80, 83, 84, 115, 117, 202, 211, 212, 213, 256,
    257, 271, 286, 288, 355, 356, 358, 359
    appeals for funds 42
    Hanley exhibition 43
Dr Drtina 74
Dr Franz Treml 36
Dr Goebbels 15
Dr Joseph Winternitz 83
Dr Lobkowicz 122

BIBLIOGRAPHY & SOURCES

Dr Mervyn Haigh 17
Dr Václav Vacek 214
Durham Miners' Association 14
Durham Miners' Association 95
Earl of Harrowby 73
Ebby Edwards 71, 84, 319
Edinburgh Lyceum 167
Edna St. Vincent Millay 157, 356
Édouard Daladier 6
Edvard Beneš 6
Edwin Dutton 47, 83
Einsatzgruppen 21
Emanuel Moravec 21, 24
Emil Hácha 14, 24, 355
Emil Synek 166
Enoch Edwards 47
Ernâni do Amaral Peixoto 180
Ernest Bevin 40, 270, 318, 357
Ernest Braddock 122
Ernest Thurtle 38
Eternal Prague 84
Evening Sentinel ... 42, 63, 65, 67, 70, 73, 78, 80, 82, 83, 84, 238, 361, 362, 363
Evžen Loebl 93, 94
Fenton 50, 71, 72, 86, 349
Final Solution 21
Fiorello La Guardia 138
First World War 6
Flag Days 84, 147
Four Nations Appeal 114, 356
Frank Buchman 318
Frank Carney 122, 123
Frank Hampl 62, 63, 66, 74, 79, 80, 83, 88, 93, 115, 123, 358
František Moravec 20
František Vybíral 29
Fred Hancock 47, 83, 87, 354
Frederick Leith-Ross 185
Fritz Kuhn 138
Garden of Peace and Friendship 251, 335, 358
George Briggs 136, 212
George Hodgkinson 136
George Jones 74, 83, 87, 95, 97
George. E. Hodgkinson 118
Gerald Kersh 164
Germanization 30, 34, 36, 194, 334
Gestapo 3, 20, 23, 26, 28, 29, 30, 31, 34, 36, 161, 355, 360
Géza Szóbel 18, 159, 171
Glebe Street 93
Gloucester Echo 361
Gordon Forsyth 42
Grete Marks 288
Haberspirk 7
Hana Pokorná 10, 5, 334
Hana Špotová 196

Hanley Town Hall 64
Harald Wiesmann 31
Harold Lockett 356
Harriseahead 81, 354
Harry Baker 136, 211
Harry Davies 1, 5, 363
Harry Leason 212
Harry McBrine 67, 78, 88
Harry Wheatcroft 256, 257, 358, 360
Harton Colliery Band 95
Havana 181, 326, 356
Hazel Lyth 3
Heinrich Himmler 21, 26, 63
Helena Leflerová 195, 196, 215, 255, 328
Henry Wallace 153
Herbert Morrison 39, 40
Hermann Göring 14
Heston Aerodrome 9
Hippodrome Theatre 117
Hitler's Madman 163
Horák farm 31
Horst Böhme 30
Hospital Train 24
Hradčany Castle 23
Hubert Ripka 66, 69, 79, 98
Hugh Bourne 47
Hugh Leese 47, 48, 49, 50, 65, 74, 78, 79, 83, 354, 356, 362
Humphrey Jennings 78
International Students' Day 18
Internationalism 336
Iron Curtain 3
Ivan Ciganek 5, 30
Ivona Kasalická 3, 5, 343
Jan Becko 10, 96
Jan Kubiš 22
Jan Masaryk 10, 14, 66, 67, 69, 71, 93, 117, 134, 136, 157, 185, 355, 356, 357
Jan Strasser 62, 64, 66, 83, 84, 85
Jan Thompson 350
Jan Zelenka 23
Jan Zelenka (Hajsky) 23
Japan 4, 98, 116
Jarmila and Marie Šťulík 36
Jaroslav Pála 28
Jas Gilliland 95, 96
Jim Griffiths 71
Jiří Hampl 352
Joe Jones 13
John Crandon Gridley 319
John Platts-Mills 93, 94
John Richards 47
John Swan 96
John Wesley 47
Josef David 93, 205
Josef Horák 211

Josef Josten 7, 360
Josef Kalla 105
Josef Valčík 24
Joseph Capper 47
Jozef Gabčík 22
Julius Firt 93, 188
Karl Frank 23
Karl Kreibich 42
Kde Domov Můj 75, 116
Kelly Adams-Smith 350
Kidsgrove and Talke 47
Kladno 28, 29, 30, 31, 33, 34, 36, 195, 204, 214, 334
Klement Gottwald 227
Kobylisy 24
Konstantin von Neurath 18
Košice Czechoslovak Government 194
Kurt Daluege 26
Ladislav Vaněk 23
Laurence Steinhardt 197
Leamington 98
Leamington Spa Courier 99, 362
Leeds flag day 133
Leonardo da Vinci 279
Lest We Forget 162
Ležáky 36, 71
Libuše Prošková 281, 358
Lidice Lives 2, 4, 5, 92, 123, 149, 158, 171, 333, 355, 356
Lidice Memorial 3, 335, 343, 349, 357, 360
Lidice Shall Live
    affect in Stoke-on-Trent 77
    committees 4
    discussions 66
    Durham miners 97
    inauguration of first committee 79
    launching the movement 70
    national campaign 93
    Nottingham campaign 123
    other committees 4
    overview 3
    the 6th of September 1942 72
Łódź 34, 36, 64, 187, 265, 336, 354
London Playhouse 167
Lord Hyndley 319
Lou Kenton 257
Ludvík Svoboda 196, 217
M.A.D 238
Madeleine Carroll 157, 158, 171
Madison Square Gardens 138
Manchester Evening News 38, 361
Marian Wilbraham 94
Marie Doležalová 194
Marie Jarošová 217
Marie Moravec 29
Marie Uchytilová 352
Marshall Field III 150

Marshall Plan 227, 358
Martina Lehmannová 5, 360
Maxim Litvinov 157
Memorandum of Understanding 343
message of Lidice 325
Methodist 49, 87, 95
Michael Ayrton 271
Middlesex Chronicle 361
Midland Counties Miners' Federation 46
Miguel Aleman 153
Miloš Zeman 350
Miners' Welfare Fund 49, 50
Mineworkers' Federation of Great Britain
    response to the Munich Agreement 13
model mining village 70, 91
Molotov Plan 227
moral force 47
Moral Re-Armament 318, 358
Moscow Radio 41
Mossfield Colliery 50
motivation 4
Mow Cop 47
Mr Alexej Shiborin 43
Mr Ellis Smith 74
Munich Agreement ..8, 10, 17, 22, 24, 62, 64, 66, 67, 68, 69, 73, 77, 354, 355, 356
    signing of 10
Murton Colliery 96, 355
National Assembly 195
National Coal Board 319, 357
National Council of Civil Liberties 94
National Front 264
National Health Service 71, 277
National Union of Mineworkers 134
Nazi Germany 4, 10, 15, 18, 21, 24, 44, 62, 68, 75, 76, 77, 98, 116, 171, 196, 288
Neville Chamberlain 6
    received at Buckingham Palace 10
New York City 138
New York Museum of Modern Art 173
New York Times 361
Newcastle Journal 97, 361
newsreel 40, 71, 355
North Staffordshire 1, 2, 3, 42, 43, 46, 47, 48, 49, 50, 62, 63, 65, 67, 70, 71, 73, 74, 78, 79, 81, 83, 85, 87, 90, 93, 95, 97, 122, 211, 331, 354, 356
North Staffordshire Miners' Federation 46
Norton Colliery 47
Nottingham City Council 122
Nottingham Journal 41, 123, 132, 361
Nottinghamshire Miners' Federated Union 122
Nuremberg Trials 1, 36
Oldřich Španěl 196
Olive Stross 84, 268, 271
Operation Anthropoid 3, 20, 355
Ostrava 204